Hispanic Technocracy

Hispanic Technocracy explores the emergence, zenith, and demise of a distinctive post-fascist school of thought that materialized as state ideology during the Cold War in three military regimes: Francisco Franco's Spain (1939–75), Juan Carlos Onganía's Argentina (1966–73), and Augusto Pinochet's Chile (1973–88). In this intellectual and cultural history, Daniel Gunnar Kressel examines how Francoist Spain replaced its fascist ideology with an early neoliberal economic model. With the Catholic society Opus Dei at its helm amid its "economic miracle" of the 1960s, it fostered a modernity that was "European in the means" and "Hispanic in the ends." Kressel illuminates how a transatlantic network of ideologues championed this model in Latin America as an authoritarian state model that was better suited to their modernization process. In turn, he illustrates how Argentine and Chilean ideologues adapted the Francoist ideological toolkit to their political circumstances, thereby transcending the original model.

Daniel Gunnar Kressel is a research fellow at the Koch History Centre at the University of Oxford, and specializes in the history of transnational right-wing ideologies and networks in Latin America, Spain, and Israel.

CAMBRIDGE LATIN AMERICAN STUDIES

Other Books in the Series

139 *Hispanic Technocracy: From Fascism to Catholic Authoritarianism in Spain, Argentina, and Chile, 1945–1991*, Daniel Gunnar Kressel
138 *The Power of Dissent: Urban Political Culture and the Fall of Spanish Rule in Charcas*, Sergio Serulnikov
137 *The Coming of the Kingdom: The Muisca, Catholic Reform, and Spanish Colonialism in the New Kingdom of Granada*, Juan F. Cobo Betancourt
136 *The Shamanism of Eco-Tourism: History and Ontology among the Makushi in Guyana*, James Andrew Whitaker
135 *Fallen From Heaven: The Enduring Tradition of Europeans as Gods in the Americas*, Nicholas Griffiths
134 *Global Servants of the Spanish King: Mobility and Cosmopolitanism in the Early Modern Spanish Empire*, Adolfo Polo y La Borda
133 *Plebeian Consumers: Global Connections, Local Trade, and Foreign Goods in Nineteenth-Century Colombia*, Ana María Otero-Cleves
132 *Peopling for Profit in Imperial Brazil: Directed Migrations and the Business of Nineteenth-Century Colonization*, José Juan Pérez Meléndez
131 *Being the Heart of the World: The Pacific and the Fashioning of the Self in New Spain, 1513–1641*, Nino Vallen
130 *A Tale of Two Granadas: Custom, Community, and Citizenship in the Spanish Empire, 1568–1668*, Max Deardorff
129 *A Colonial Book Market: Peruvian Print Culture in the Age of Enlightenment*, Agnes Gehbald
128 *Veracruz and the Caribbean in the Seventeenth Century*, Joseph M. H. Clark
127 *We, the King: Creating Royal Legislation in the Sixteenth-Century Spanish New World*, Adrian Masters
126 *A History of Chile 1808–2018, Second Edition*, William F. Sater and Simon Collier
125 *The Dread Plague and the Cow Killers: The Politics of Animal Disease in Mexico and the World*, Thomas Rath
124 *Islands in the Lake: Environment and Ethnohistory in Xochimilco, New Spain*, Richard M. Conway
123 *Journey to Indo-América: APRA and the Transnational Politics of Exile, Persecution, and Solidarity, 1918–1945*, Geneviève Dorais

Hispanic Technocracy

From Fascism to Catholic Authoritarianism in Spain, Argentina, and Chile, 1945–1991

DANIEL GUNNAR KRESSEL
The Koch History Centre, University of Oxford

CAMBRIDGE
UNIVERSITY PRESS

CAMBRIDGE
UNIVERSITY PRESS

Shaftesbury Road, Cambridge CB2 8EA, United Kingdom

One Liberty Plaza, 20th Floor, New York, NY 10006, USA

477 Williamstown Road, Port Melbourne, VIC 3207, Australia

314–321, 3rd Floor, Plot 3, Splendor Forum, Jasola District Centre, New Delhi – 110025, India

103 Penang Road, #05–06/07, Visioncrest Commercial, Singapore 238467

Cambridge University Press is part of Cambridge University Press & Assessment, a department of the University of Cambridge.

We share the University's mission to contribute to society through the pursuit of education, learning and research at the highest international levels of excellence.

www.cambridge.org
Information on this title: www.cambridge.org/9781009603041

DOI: 10.1017/9781009603072

When citing this work, please include a reference to the DOI 10.1017/9781009603072

First published 2025

A catalogue record for this publication is available from the British Library

Library of Congress Cataloging-in-Publication Data
NAMES: Kressel, Daniel Gunnar, author.
TITLE: Hispanic technocracy : from fascism to Catholic authoritarianism in Spain, Argentina, and Chile, 1945-1991 / Daniel Gunnar Kressel.
DESCRIPTION: Cambridge ; New York : Cambridge University Press, 2025. | Series: Cambridge Latin American studies | Includes bibliographical references and index.
IDENTIFIERS: LCCN 2025002739 (print) | LCCN 2025002740 (ebook) | ISBN 9781009603041 (hardback) | ISBN 9781009603027 (paperback) | ISBN 9781009603072 (epub)
SUBJECTS: LCSH: Technocracy–Spain–History–20th century. | Technocracy–Latin America–History–20th century. | Francoism. | Authoritarianism–Spain–History–20th century. | Authoritarianism–Latin America–History–20th century. | Christianity and politics–Catholic Church–History–20th century. | Spain–Politics and government–1939-1975. | Latin America–Politics and government–1948-1980. | Spain–Foreign relations–Latin America. | Latin America–Foreign relations–Spain.
CLASSIFICATION: LCC HB87 .K725 2025 (print) | LCC HB87 (ebook) | DDC 320.53089/68073–dc23/eng/20250402
LC record available at https://lccn.loc.gov/2025002739
LC record available at https://lccn.loc.gov/2025002740

ISBN 978-1-009-60304-1 Hardback

To my parents

Contents

Figures

Acknowledgments

I have accumulated many debts of gratitude throughout the making of this book, so much so that even the thought of writing this acknowledgments section makes me blush. Above all, I want to thank this book's conceptual forefathers, namely Pablo Picatto and Federico Finchelstein. Pablo was the ideal dissertation advisor whose intellect, patience, and profound humanism have inspired me to become not only a worthier academic but a better person. Federico was the "unmerciful" yet eternally supportive reader any historian would have dreamed of having as a co-advisor. His theoretical and historiographical input has left a mark not only on this book but on how I write history in general. I also want to thank the other members of my dissertation committee – Nara Milanich, José Moya, and Alberto Medina – as well as Caterina Pizzigoni, for their diverse and crucial contributions to this project.

Similarly, from The New School for Social Research, I would like to praise Oz Frenkel, Jeremy Varon, Julia Ott, Andrew Arato, and Carlos Forment for their helpfulness and kindness in backing my project in its earlier forms, at their outstanding institution. From Tel Aviv University, I am forever indebted to the support and inspiration of my former advisor, Raanan Rein, as well as to my exceptional teachers Rosalie Sitman, Jerardo Leibner, Igal Halfin, Iris Rahamimov, Ori Preuss, and the late Alon Confino. Last but not least, I want to highlight the wonderful staff of Columbia University's History Department – Sharee Nash, Patrick McMorrow, Patricia Morel, Patrice Turner, and Lawino Lurum – who have aided me in every way possible throughout this complicated transnational research.

This study is also indebted to the friends and colleagues who read my early texts and shredded them to pieces in various workshops. From Columbia University, I want to thank Rachel Grace Newman, Marianne González Le Saux, Alfonso Salgado, Paul Katz, Sara Daniela Hidalgo, Sarah Elizabeth Beckhart, Daniel Morales, Yesenia Barragan, Allison Powers, Elizabeth Schwall, Ariel Lambe, Fabiola Enríquez Flores, and Andrei Guadarrama. I want to send warm thanks to Luis Herrán Ávila, Javier Galeano, and Emmanuel Guerisoli from the New School – a very special cohort of Latin Americanists – as well as to visiting professor Norbert Frei of the Friedrich-Schiller University in Jena, Germany.

In the field, I have come across the generosity and companionship of several outstanding scholars and archivists. In Spain, I would like to thank Lorenzo Delgado, Ismael Saz Campos, Antonio Cazorla Sánchez, Fernando Camacho Padilla, and Alberto Moncada, for their conversations and advice. At the University of Navarra, Antonio Cañellas Mas, Pablo Pérez López, and archivists Inés Irurita Hernández and Marian Zabala made my work particularly pleasant and fruitful, and for that I am eternally grateful. Also, in Spain, I would like to express my gratitude to Gonzalo Fernández de la Mora (Jr.) for granting me access to his father's archive. In Argentina, my thanks go to Ernesto Bohoslavsky, Mariano Plotkin, Daniel Lvovich, Lila Caimari, José Zanca, Isabella Cosse, Gabriela Gomes, Laura Garciela Rodríguez, and Martín Albornoz, for much advice and ongoing assistance. Similarly, I would like to compliment the work of Alba Lombardi and the rest of the staff at Argentina's Foreign Ministry Archives. Thanks also to Roberto Bosca for the sincere dialogues and for putting me in touch with many of his close friends. One of them, Horacio Sánchez De Loria, was particularly generous with his time and sources, and I am grateful for that. In Chile, I acknowledge María Olivia Mönckeberg, Isabel Jara Hinojosa, Jorge Olguín, and Isabel Torres, as well as Jorge Soto, of the Jaime Guzmán Foundation, for their support. I also want to underline the assistance of the archivists of Chile's Foreign Ministry Archive.

As a postdoctoral fellow, in conferences, workshops, and talks, I have accumulated debts of gratitude worldwide. At the International History Department at the London School of Economics, I am indebted to Tanya Harmer for all her help during my exchange year in London, as well as to the organizers of the LSE history workshop, Alex Mayhew, Eline van Ommen, Grace Carrington, and Molly Avery, for their comments and friendship. Additionally, in London, I would like to express my gratitude to Paulo Drinot and Thomas Rath of University College London for their kind assistance, as well as to Tobias Rupprecht, James Mark, and José Manuel Castro Torres for their collaboration and commentaries on my work. In France, my thanks go to Raluca Grosescu, Laure Neumayer, and Sophie Baby for reading, revising, and publishing parts of my work. In the USA, I am grateful to James Sharder, Kirsten Weld, Ada Ferrer, Amy Chazkel, Ernesto Semán, Josh Savala, Federico Sor, María González Pendás, Rachel Nolan, Margaret Power, Andrea Davis, Benjamin Cowen, Mila Burns, Jennifer Lambe, Michelle Chase, Eric Zolov, Mary Roldán, Alejandro Velasco, Cos Tollerson, and Camila Vergara for their conversations, suggestions, and support. In Berlin, I want to thank Stefan Rinke for his support and co-work during my stay at the Freie Universität's Latin American Institute amid the challenging times of a global pandemic. Lastly, in Jerusalem, I want to thank Claudia Kedar, Aldina Quintana, and Jorge Gordin for supporting my research at the Hebrew University.

Several components of Chapters 1 and 3 were published as articles in *The Americas* and *Cahiers des Amériques Latines*. My gratitude goes to the editors of these journals, John Schwaller and Stéphane Boisard, respectively, for the extensive work they put into improving these early rough texts. In the same vein, I want to thank Cecelia Cancellaro, my editor at Cambridge University Press, and Kris Lane and Matthew Restall, the editors of Cambridge's Latin American Studies series, for their confidence in this book. I would also like to take this opportunity to thank the manuscript's outstanding anonymous readers for their vital commentaries.

Moreover, this book would not have come to life without the generous backing of several institutions and foundations, which include the Social Sciences Research Council, the Hoover Institution's Silas Palmer research funds, the Doris G. Quinn Foundation, the Minerva Stiftung (the German Federal Ministry for Education and Research), the Golda Meir and Lady Davis Fellowship Trusts, and the Koch History Centre at Oxford University.

To my friends Tehila Sasson, Dan Zahor, Yifat Gutman, Avigail Argov, Amir Friedman, Elik Elhanan, Miguel Patriota, Hammad Sheikh, Noa Gover, Eden Ladin, Neta Goder, Ricardo Max, Salar Rad, Diana del Olmo Campos, Chris Harris, Matan Cohen, Shimrit Piperberg, Claudia Horn, Ido Hoorvitch, Lena Michelsen, Khalia Williams, Eva Navon, Zohar Hazi, Rachel Feldman, Adaya Sasson, and Gray Hurlburt – thank you for being there for me at all times! Lastly, my most profoundly felt gratitude goes to my family. My sister and brother, Maya and Yohanan, and my parents, Lisbeth and Gideon, have supported me throughout this journey from miles away in countless Skype calls, and for this I am forever grateful.

Abbreviations

ACNP	Asociación Católica Nacional de Propagandistas (National Catholic Association of Propagandists)
AGA	Archivo General de la Administración (General Archive of the Administration)
AGMAE	Archivo General Histórico del Ministerio de Asuntos Exteriores (General Historical Archive of the Ministry of Foreign Affairs)
AGN	Archivo General de la Nación (General Archive of the Nation)
AGUN	Archivo General de la Universidad de Navarra (General Archive of the University of Navarra)
ALN	Alianza Libertadora Nacionalista (Nationalist Liberation Alliance)
AMREC	Archivo del Ministerio de Asuntos Exteriores y Culto (Archive of the Ministry of Foreign Affairs and Worship)
AN	Avanzada Nacional (National Advance)
ANEC	Asociación Nacional de Estudiantes Católicos (National Association of Catholic Students)
AP	Alianza Popular (Popular Alliance)
BNA	Biblioteca Nacional Argentina (National Library of Argentina)
CEDADE	Círculo Español de Amigos de Europa (Spanish Circle of Friends of Europe)

CEDINCI	Centro de Investigaciones de Izquierdas (Left-wing Research Center)
CEMA	Centro de Madres (Mothers' Center)
CENC	Comisión de Estudios de la Nueva Constitución (Commission for the Study of the New Constitution)
CGT	Confederación General del Trabajo (General Confederation of Labor of the Argentine Republic)
CODELCO	Corporación Nacional del Cobre de Chile (National Copper Corporation of Chile)
CONADE	Consejo Nacional de Desarrollo (National Development Council)
CONARA	Comisión Nacional de la Reforma Administrativa (National Commission for Administrative Reform)
CONASE	Consejo Nacional de Seguridad (National Security Council)
CONICET	Consejo Nacional de Investigaciones Científicas y Técnicas (National Council for Scientific and Technical Research)
CONSUDEC	Consejo Superior de Educación Católica (Superior Council of Catholic Education)
CORFO	Corporación de Fomento de la Producción (Corporation for the Promotion of Production)
CSIC	Consejo Superior de Investigaciones Científicas (Superior Council of Scientific Research)
DINA	Dirección de Inteligencia Nacional (National Intelligence Directorate)
ECLAC	Economic Commission for Latin America and the Caribbean
ERP	Ejército Revolucionario del Pueblo (The People's Revolutionary Army)
ETA	Euskadi Ta Askatasuna (Basque Homeland and Freedom)
FET	Falange Española Tradicionalista (Traditionalist Spanish Falange)
FNFF	Fundación Nacional Francisco Franco (National Francisco Franco Foundation)
FNPL	Frente Nacionalista Patria y Libertad (Homeland and Freedom Nationalist Front)

FNT	Frente Nacional del Trabajo (National Labor Front)
FRAP	Frente Revolucionario Antifascista y Patriota (Revolutionary Anti-fascist and Patriot Front)
FREJULI	Frente Justicialista de Liberación (Justicialist Liberation Front)
GOU	Grupo de Oficiales Unidos (United Officers' Group)
GRN	Guardia Restauradora Nacionalista (Nationalist Restoration Guard)
ICH	Instituto de Cultura Hispánica (Institute of Hispanic Culture)
ICI	Instituto de Cooperación Iberoamericana (Institute for Ibero-American Cooperation)
IDB	Inter-American Defense Board
IEP	Instituto de Estudios Políticos (Institute for Political Studies)
IHLADI	Instituto Hispano-Luso-Americano de Derecho Internacional (Hispano-Portuguese-American Institute of International Law)
IMF	International Monetary Fund
IPADE	Instituto Panamericano de Alta Dirección de Empresa (Pan American Institute of Senior Business Management)
ISI	import substitution industrialization
IWO	Instituto Científico Judío (Jewish Scientific Institute)
LNC	Legion Nacionalista Contrarrevolucionaria (Counterrevolutionary Nationalist Legion)
MAN	Movimiento de Acción Nacional (National Action Movement)
MCC	Movimiento de Cursillos de Cristiandad (Short courses in Christianity movement)
MIR	Movimiento de Izquierda Revolucionaria (Revolutionary Left Movement)
MNR	Movimiento Nacionalista de Restauración (Nationalist Restoration Movement)
MNSC	Movimiento Nacional-Socialista de Chile (National Socialist Movement of Chile)

MNT	Movimiento Nacionalista Tacuara (Tacuara Nationalist Movement)
MRNS	Movimiento Revolucionario Nacional Sindicalista (Revolutionary National Syndicalist Movement)
MUN	Movimiento de Unión Nacional (National Union Movement)
OAS	Organization of American States
ODEPLAN	Oficina de Planificación Nacional (National Planning Office)
OEI	Oficina de Educación Iberoamericana (Ibero-American Education Office)
OSE	Organización Sindical Española (Spanish Syndical Organization)
PCE	Partido Comunista de España (Communist Party of Spain)
PN	Partido Nacional (National Party)
PRN	Proceso de Reorganización Nacional (National Reorganization Process)
PSOE	Partido Socialista Obrero de España (Spanish Socialist Workers' Party)
RN	Renovación Nacional (National Renovation)
SEPAC	Secretaría de Estado de Promoción y Asistencia a la Comunidad (State Secretariat for Community Promotion and Assistance)
TFP	Tradição, Família e Propriedade (Tradition, Family, and Property)
TVE	Televisión Española (Spanish National Television)
UC	Universidad Católica de Chile (Catholic University of Chile)
UCD	Unión de Centro Democrático (Democratic Center Union)
UCRI	Unión Cívica Radical Intransigente (Intransigent Radical Civic Union)
UCRP	Unión Cívica Radical del Pueblo (The People's Radical Civic Union)

UDI	Unión Demócrata Independiente (Independent Democratic Union)
UNAFE	Unión Nacional Femenina (National Women's Union)
UNAV	Universidad de Navarra (University of Navarra)
UNES	Unión Nacionalista de Estudiantes Secundarios (Nationalist Union of Secondary School Students)
UNESCO	The United Nations Educational, Scientific and Cultural Organization
UP	Unidad Popular (Popular Unity)

Introduction

Turning Fascism into Authoritarian Technocracy

In 1967, Gonzalo Fernández de la Mora arrived in Santiago de Chile for a celebratory lecture series. He was the Director of Cultural Cooperation at Spain's Ministry of Foreign Affairs and the official representative of one of the most notorious dictatorships in modern history, namely Francisco Franco's Spain. His interlocutors were Chilean conservatives who, unlike him, were citizens of a country renowned for its democratic institutions. This did not deter Fernández de la Mora from bragging about his regime's supposed achievements. "In a short time, Spain has experienced the industrial revolution, economic democratization, and change of mentalities that took Great Britain a century to achieve," he told his audience. His country, he even alleged, consisted of people "whose only 'ideology' is economic development, that is, no longer an ideology proper, but a rational and realistic impulse." These were no ordinary times in Chile. Since 1964, when Eduardo Frei Montalva's Christian Democratic government took power, this Andean nation had witnessed a mobilization of its working classes – in what Frei called the "Revolution in Liberty" – and, subsequently, was in the thick of a steep political polarization. Frei's revolution, it seemed, irked the Spanish guest. Economic development cannot be born "either by paying attention to the street or from the street," he lectured his supportive spectators.[1] Chile was not Fernández de la Mora's first destination. Before arriving there, he had visited Argentina, which had recently witnessed its parliamentary democracy being overthrown by a peculiar new dictator: Juan Carlos Onganía.

That Fernández de la Mora gloried in Spain's "economic miracle" of the 1960s was hardly surprising. Somewhat unusual, however, was his perception of "ideologies" and how the Spaniards had ostensibly lost them. This person was a type of ideologue Latin America had not quite encountered hitherto. He was one of the most prominent theorists of a regime that had symbolized the rise of the fascist international in the 1930s but that was now in the midst of its so-called technocratic era. In fact, he arrived in Latin America to promote a book in which he proposed a unique authoritarian alternative to parliamentary democracy. Who he and his audiences were and how they perceived the world in which they lived is my book's *subject*. The book's main *object* is the ideology these people cultivated and how it impacted their respective countries. In short, this is a story of the emergence, apex, and demise of a distinctive post-fascist ideological school, which I have termed Hispanic technocracy. Despite not identifying themselves as such, Fernández de la Mora and his interlocutors were, for our purposes, Hispanic technocrats. At a particular moment in Cold War history, military dictators chose them to design their regimes' state ideology. Hispanic technocracy's transformation from being an abstract theory to informing the state apparatus first happened in Francisco Franco's Spain (1957–75); next, in Juan Carlos Onganía's Argentina (1966–73); and last, in Augusto Pinochet's Chile (1973–82). Undoubtedly, these dictatorships rose to power in entirely different historical contexts. Yet they exhibited strikingly similar public discourses, and their intellectuals conducted lively dialogues with one another. In short, this book is a comparative history and, simultaneously, a story of reciprocal influences, networking, local adaptations, and misinterpretations.

To say that Hispanic technocracy's emergence mirrored the early Cold War's political, economic, and cultural settings would be a simple way to start discussing its character. A more provocative way to put it would be that this is a book about the moment when fascism dovetailed with, or transformed into, neoliberalism, not within marginal right-wing circles but as the state ideology of countries that are nowadays proud members of the OECD. As Fernández de la Mora's words lay bare, by 1967, he believed his society to be as developed as that of Great Britain. Only that to his mind, and against the logic of the so-called modernization theory, his country's modernizing leap forward did not result in political moderation and democratization but in eliminating mass politics as such and the advent of an entirely new modernity. What this fantasy entailed and whether it ever became a reality is another topic this book explores.

It may come as a surprise, but promoting authoritarianism in 1960s Latin America was not as simple as it might appear. After all, the continent underwent a substantial democratization process in the aftermath of the Second World War. Indeed, Latin America's authoritarian turn of the 1960s and 1970s – when military dictatorships toppled democratically elected governments in the name of anti-communism – was hardly foreseeable in 1946. Back then, openly advocating tyranny stood in stark contrast to the USA's commitment to defend liberty and democracy. So why did Fernández de la Mora think he could do so twenty years later? To put it simply: Democracy did not deliver, at least not in the way Latin America's financial elites had hoped it would. In this telling, rather than ushering in an era of economic progress, in Latin America, democracy has only prompted a perverted and populist mobilization of the working classes, thereby causing the continent to lag behind in the modernization race with the Western metropole. The "frustration" of Latin American conservatives with democracy in the 1960s is another topic this book covers.

I.1 BETWEEN THE DOWNFALL OF FASCISM AND THE BIRTH OF NEOLIBERALISM

Scholars of multiple disciplines have made ample attempts to characterize the Cold War military dictatorships in Latin America, Southern Europe, and East Asia. Spanish sociologist Juan Linz has suggested, for instance, that these regimes were not "totalitarian" but "authoritarian," given that they did not foster "intellectually elaborated" utopian ideologies.[2] Political scientist Guillermo O'Donnell, for his part, has coined the term bureaucratic authoritarianism to characterize them. Using Onganía's regime as his case study, he has defined this dictator as an "apolitical" man, guided by a "Christian conception of politics" at best.[3] For O'Donnell, bureaucratic authoritarianism represents a bid to undo the "political activation of the popular sector," amid a process of "economic transnationalization."[4] For all their theoretical rigor, Linz and O'Donnell's analyses quite obviously restate their subject matter's apolitical self-labeling. Worse yet, they overlook the genealogy linking the rightists of the 1960s to their forerunners, namely the interwar fascists.

I am one of those who are committed to dispelling the belief that fascism was eradicated in May 1945. A cultural and intellectual history, this book focuses on semi-peripheral nations wherein fascism morphed into new anti-Enlightenment political projects. While it is true that the fascist international, if it ever truly existed, came to an end with the defeat of the Axis powers in May 1945, the ideology and networks of fascism continued to operate across Europe and Latin America throughout the

Cold War, evolving into neofascist and post-fascist schools. Why these hackneyed taxonomies? My answer is straightforward: This book's protagonists had once believed in fascism wholeheartedly. Many of them visited fascist Europe or had fought in the Spanish Civil War, and were immensely preoccupied with the legacies of European fascism and their position vis-à-vis this relic. In other words, the meanings of fascism were essential *to them*. While reluctantly accepting the Cold War's division, they never concealed their resolve to purge modernity of the Enlightenment's ideologies and rekindle a pre-modern societal and spiritual harmony. Some remained loyal to the fascist state model, sought to develop it further, and were thus, for all purposes, neofascists. For others, the traumas of European fascism were too colossal to gloss over, which led them to rescue fascism's moral absolutes within new state models. Indeed, Juan Perón's rule in Argentina illustrated just how quickly European fascism could be reformulated into a sui generis "third position" between communism and capitalism. And if Peronism was Latin America's first post-fascist moment, then this book's protagonists embodied the post-fascist project that set out to replace it. Indeed, the conflict between neofascists and post-fascists, and among post-fascists themselves, came to define right-wing politics in Cold War Latin America.

To understand what differentiated neofascism from post-fascism, one needs to agree on what the term fascism means – for contemporary scholars and our protagonists alike. I believe both sides would agree that, as an abstract ideology, fascism explained itself as a *revolutionary* modernity against the political myths of the French Revolution. Anti-liberal, anti-socialist, *and* anti-reactionary (as in historian Ernst Nolte's seminal "fascist minimum"), it showcased a theory of state, society, and human essence that was at the same time dogmatic in its moral absolutes but, according to Benito Mussolini – the unquestionable author of European fascism – flexible (or "in the making") in its configuration of the state apparatus.[5] Actually, not all fascists may have agreed with this last notion. As I will discuss in more detail, Mussolini's progenies – the Spanish fascist José Antonio Primo de Rivera, for one – touted intricate "programs" detailing every aspect of the state apparatus. Still, we can confidently say that, in theory, fascism was a totalitarian ideology (or "statist" at a minimum) that belied both the liberal and traditionalist ethos. With their leader as the chief conduit for the nation's common good, interwar fascists aspired to be omnipresent in their citizens' lives in a way that revoked any remnant of parliamentary representation, separation of powers, and a free public sphere.

As for the fascist state model's *raison d'être*, beyond immediate national salvation from communist collectivization or liberal decadence, fascism's militarization of society was aimed at imperial conquest and, in the case of Nazi Germany, the breeding of a master race. However, a closer look reveals that in places such as Fascist Italy, whose invasion of Ethiopia and Albania took place more than a decade after coming to power, empire was instrumental in a different undertaking, namely the founding of an entirely new society and human being. This "new order" was to simultaneously restore pre-modern social hierarchies and integrate the alienated proletariat into the national fabric through a new conception of the community (or *Volksgemeinschaft* in the notorious Nazi terminology). As such, the fascist "third path" promoted not a centric position between socialism and capitalism but an ethically superior form of existence. In this paradoxically modern-yet-atavistic society, bourgeois decadence was to be replaced with a totalizing, irrational, and sublime spiritual experience – a "community of experience," as historian David Ohana has recently framed it.[6] Violence, self-sacrifice, and a profound connection to the "depths of the unconscious," in the words of historian Zeev Sternhell, were the means to this mental condition.[7] Thus, violence was not only a means for taking over the state – what fascist theorist Carl Schmitt defined as a "state of exception" – but a moral absolute in and of itself.

While contemporary political scientists perceive interwar fascism primarily as a political "style" marked by messianic and utopian undertones, this was rarely how Cold War neofascists and post-fascists perceived it. For them, fascism represented an entirely programmatic state model that revolved around "corporatism" – a term that will appear repeatedly in what follows and that was hardly a fascist innovation. Since the mid nineteenth century, there has been hardly any European traditionalist – that is, a thinker belonging to the movement that sought to eradicate the Enlightenment's ideologies and restore the ancien régime's system of political legitimacy – who did not propose an alternative to parliamentarism, featuring an authoritarian ruler, preferably a king, handing over power to an altruistic aristocracy. This ostensible separation of powers, based on supposed natural social structures such as the "family, municipality, and guild," would be identified with thinkers such as Charles Maurras and Juan Vázquez de Mella, as well as with Pope Leo XIII's encyclical *Rerum Novarum* (1891) and Pius XI's *Quadragesimo Anno* (1931), and is what political scientist António Costa Pinto defines as *societal corporatism*.[8] Interwar fascism made corporatism into something somewhat different, though. In its effort to defang the communist revolution in Europe and pledge to solve the capitalist labor–capital divide, Fascist Italy co-opted corporatism into a scheme where a totalitarian state enforces a hermetic system of representation based on society's "organic" units, on the one hand, and harmonizes capital and labor through vertically controlled apparatus on the other. As I shall discuss shortly, Iberian fascism would have a distinctive role in promoting the concept of "national syndicalism" – the epitome of what Costa Pinto calls *political corporatism*.[9] It was this model that Cold War neofascists were so keen to revive.

Giving meaning to "corporatism" is, to my mind, an exercise in futility since this was a political myth par excellence (not to be confused with mythology). Similar to how philosopher Chiara Bottici has regarded Georges Sorel's "general strike" as a political myth – that is, as a fictional tale constructed in a "future dimension" – so should we understand corporatism.[10] It was put into practice, but only as political theater. Nobody seemed to understand this fact better than our protagonists, who gradually cleansed their rhetoric of this word, all the while pledging to enact original systems of representation. Sure enough, the Hispanic technocrats had a vexed relationship with many other components in the fascist universe of meaning. They perhaps perceived political violence as unavoidable but only as a precursor for social peace. They were anti-communist and anti-liberal but demanded a *restoration* rather than a *revolution*. Thus, were Fernández de la Mora and his like mere traditionalists of sorts? Not if we asked them. They believed they were neither traditionalists nor fascists. If the nineteenth-century traditionalist model was the first version and 1930s fascism the second, their model was a third, entirely novel, interpretation of what authoritarian corporatism ought to be, they thought.

More concretely, the Hispanic technocrats believed neither parliamentary democracy nor fascist totalitarianism could produce the dramatic modernizing phase the Hispanic domain needed to transcend from the "sub-developed" to the "developed" world. Either an authoritarian Leviathan with extrajudicial authority orchestrated this operation, they purported, or their nations would go down in thrall to the two Cold War Blocs. From this point of departure, they began breaking away from the fascist mindset. The pages that follow will illustrate just how tenaciously they insisted that their regime was *not* despotic and that their military leader had relinquished executive power to "intermediary" groups within society – a deregulatory process they defined, at times, as the "subsidiary state." It was here that we can begin to notice how fascism and neoliberalism overlapped. Still, it is paramount to clarify what our protagonists wanted *from* the market. To their mind, opting for a market-based development model merely meant placing a new value-creating engine inside an otherwise fascist vehicle. In concrete terms, the Hispanic technocrats' mission was twofold: In the short run, they sought to stabilize their countries' economy and modernize their production lines, thereby bringing them closer to Western standards. In the long run, they aimed to transform the working classes' mentality through consumption, and, in turn, create a new order and a new human.

As to why O'Donnell chose to define Onganía and Pinochet's regimes as bureaucratic authoritarianism in the mid 1970s rather than as neoliberalism was because the latter term only became popularized in the late 1980s. As economist Sebastian Edwards has cogently maintained, the term "neoliberalism" had rarely been used internationally before the late 1980s when, amid the rise of the Washington Consensus, it stabilized in its current semantic scope – namely, as a theory of deregulation and privatization of state-owned enterprises and public services.[11] When discussing the "entry of transnational corporations into domestic markets," O'Donnell's work centered on what most analysts today would conceptualize as neoliberalism.[12] If you thought "fascism" was a tough nut to crack, wait until you try satisfactorily defining neoliberalism or deciding when it truly began. There is little doubt that the birth of the neoliberal *infrastructure* occurred around 1944, with the Bretton Woods agreements and the establishment of the World Bank and the International Monetary Fund (IMF) – when the global financial order and currency regime was put in place, and statistical figures such as GDP were harmonized internationally, through the Marshall Plan among others.[13] As an ideology, neoliberalism was also famously synonymous with a "thought collective" of intellectuals such as Friedrich Hayek and Milton Friedman, who operated within institutions such as the Chicago School, the Heritage Foundation, and the Adam Smith Institute. For my part, I treat neoliberalism as a self-propelling microcosm of narratives, couched in watchwords such as "rationalization" and "economic miracles." Using France, West Germany, Italy, and Japan as their case studies, agents such as the World Bank pressured our protagonists in strikingly simplistic ways to commit to economic setups that prioritized currency stabilization, positive trade balance, and, of course, foreign investment. Thus, ironically, the term bureaucratic authoritarianism contravenes what these regimes aspired to become: a deregulatory, anti-statist, and anti-bureaucratic modernization phase.

While it is easy to see in hindsight how the Bretton Woods Agreement set in motion the USA's global financial hegemony as we know it, this was not entirely obvious in 1950s Latin America. Believing they were far from the USA's direct orbit, places such as Argentina, Brazil, and Chile, not to mention Spain, Portugal, and Greece, saw political movements that openly defied the USA's economic order. Unlike them, the Hispanic technocrats entertained no such illusions. As sub-peripheral and semi-industrial societies, their countries had little choice but to join the Western financial system, they knew. To their chagrin, and in the spirit of the time, this position immediately led others to label them "technocrats" – which was then, as it is now, an undeniably pejorative term. Interestingly, this had not always been the case. As a neologism, "technocracy" was minted in the USA in the 1920s, during a period of increasing awe at technological acceleration. For its inventor, Howard Scott, the word signified a state where specialists, rather than politicians, harmonize industrial society's contradictory elements. Only in the 1950s did "technocracy" become tantamount to an agent who operates beneath elected officials, thus fostering economic policies that go against the political consensus on wealth redistribution.[14] So, are democratic and authoritarian technocracies similar? The answer is a clear no. The ones at the center of our inquiry operated under dictators and were not accountable to either a judiciary or a legislative chamber. Additionally, unlike Western technocrats, more often than not, they were not economists. The purpose of their appointments had everything to do with the fact that they were *more* than just economic specialists.

I.2 BETWEEN IDEOLOGY AND MYTHOLOGY: PRODUCING SPIRITUAL SUBJECTS DURING THE "LONG 1960S"

Latin America, historian Tanya Harmer has famously said, was the epicenter of the "Inter-American Cold War," understood as a "unique and multisided contest between regional proponents of communism and capitalism."[15] From this, however, it does not follow that the USA simply instigated Latin America's authoritarian turn. Despite the fact that Latin American military personnel studied anti-communist doctrines in places such as the School of the Americas, to say the Latin American conservatives parroted US anti-communist trends is a gross overstatement.[16] As we shall see, my protagonists fretted over the USA's global cultural domination at least as intensely as over international communism. In other words, anti-Americanism was hardly the dominion of the left.[17] In fact, the greater their reliance on Western finance the more rightists felt obligated to showcase a cultural project that defied the ominous neighbor from the north. This is why Franco's Spain is vital to our story. That Francoism was an anomaly in Cold War politics is not only a commonplace historiographic assessment but was the regime's public teleology. A harbinger of the "crusade" against communism, and fascism's most salient residue after 1945, Franco perceived himself as a proud alternative to *both* the Cold War Blocs until the day he died.[18] True, the conventional wisdom is that, between 1957 and 1975, this regime experienced a significant ideological moderation.[19] Even so, the more temperate Franco's Spain became the *more exemplary* it was for Latin American spectators. The fact that Hispanic technocracy first appeared as a state ideology in Spain therefore bore a special significance to how it spread to Latin America. Things could not have gone the other way around.

By "exemplary," I do not mean to say that Latin Americans simply mimicked Francoism, not least since Argentine and Chilean theorists played an integral role in conceiving Hispanic technocracy from the very start. How Chileans and Argentines identified with the Spanish experience stemmed from the political polarity their countries had experienced since the turn of the century. The two nations had been among the first in the continent to enact universal suffrage (1912 in Argentina and 1925 in Chile). While large swaths of their conservative sectors never acknowledged the democratic order and sought to destabilize it, their efforts were only partially successful.[20] In fact, after 1945, Argentina and Chile saw not only a revitalization of their democratic institutions but the relentless mobilization of their working classes in demand of broader wealth redistribution. Their conservatives' nexus with Francoism cannot be divorced from this ongoing loss of economic and political power. In the case of Argentina, the men heading the anti-democratic movement belonged to a group generally known as the "Nacionalistas."[21] Having identified with European fascism since the 1920s, some of them saw the Francoist post-fascist state as a possible model for overcoming their theoretical cul-de-sac. On the Chilean side, Franco's allies came from Chile's unique traditionalist, neofascist, and overall "corporatist" cliques. I will delve into the peculiar stories of these groups shortly, but for now suffice it to say that the fact that members of a postcolonial society would want to reconstitute an alliance with the colonizing "Mother Nation" is unheard of in modern history. Yet this was precisely what these groups did by evoking a unique type of mythological thinking.

A way to commence a discussion on what mythology is would be to underscore that, when claiming to belong to a post-ideological society,

Fernández de la Mora did not once insinuate that it was a place devoid of moral absolutes. Quite the contrary. He and his audience understood perfectly well that this was a place where a *different* morality reigned. True, on the face of it, Fernández de la Mora tapped into a global intellectual trend according to which ideologies were likely to disappear in the face of capitalist consumerism. By 1967, anyone from philosopher Raymond Aron to sociologist Daniel Bell had lamented the "end of the ideological age,"[22] by which they meant the decline of a specific nineteenth-century "complex of ideas and passions."[23] Still, the unspoken truth about Spain was that, unlike in Western Europe, where technocrats operated under the veil of parliamentary politics, its technocrats functioned in a society that had been violently purged of mass politics three decades earlier. This did not inhibit Fernández de la Mora from peddling an entirely deterministic theory wherein "ideologies" plague only "underdeveloped" societies and give place to "realism" with the advent of mass consumption. Hence, unlike Bell – who perceived the technocratic "cult of efficiency" as an ideology too – he did not believe himself to have an ideology.

Obviously, Fernández de la Mora and his peers used the word "ideology" differently from how contemporary historians would. For them, "ideology" signified the theories (or "isms") that were born during the time of the French Revolution – namely, liberalism, socialism, and anarchism, as well as rationalism and empiricism, and so on. Devoid of any metaphysical substance, they were all akin to "materialism" and useless as such. How should we understand "ideology" as a heuristic tool? One can turn here to ideology's foremost theorists. For Hannah Arendt, it represented any knowledge "that pretends to have found the key explanation for all the mysteries of life and the world."[24] This is a good start, although this definition can readily include religion. Religions can be made into ideologies, but not every ideology is a religion. By this, I mean that any modern ideology makes assumptions about the human essence and, consequently, about the ethics underpinning society's organization and the nature of the state's function. Thus, ideology can rely on a religious sacred, but more often than not, it does not serve a metaphysical deity but an imagined community. For instance, if Judaism adheres to God's will, then Zionist ideology acts on behalf of the "Jewish People." Ideology is also rarely meticulously outlined, as in the Marxist case. It usually relies on illusive "empty signifiers" that direct our sense of self, forms of enjoyment, and fantasies of the future – as theorists such as Ernesto Laclau and Slavoj Žižek have been explaining to us in the past two decades.[25] Still, to simplify this discussion, let us agree that any comprehensive conception of humankind, society, and the state is an ideology.

Clearly, we must also define the term "mythology," though this, too, is no easy matter. My suggestion is that, in essence, a mythology is a totalizing narrative that, frequently through means of historical induction, grounds an ideology as a timeless truth. "The history of all hitherto existing society is the history of class struggles," wrote Karl Marx in 1847. His ideology could not exist devoid of this minuscule piece of mythology. The Hispanic technocrats' mythological edifice was much broader, though it could also be encapsulated in one word: Hispanidad. I will consider this neologism in some detail and delve further into the deep-seated connection between mythology and ideology shortly. For now, I will say that this word represented a state of harmony that had been developing since the Middle Ages in Spain and that reached its apex in the seventeenth century during the golden age of the Habsburgian empire. In this telling, Spain on the one side, and Argentina and Chile on the other, were two "pillars" in the "bridge" of Hispanidad. Indeed, these Southern Cone nations' rightists, who still consider themselves today to be closest to the "Mother Nation" culturally and racially, had developed not only a formidable anti-American sentiment throughout the twentieth century but a particular teleology: a conception of their role in world history, the Catholic world, and Latin America that dovetailed with those of the neo-imperial "restorationists" in Spain.

"In the enlightened world, mythology has permeated the sphere of the profane," thus, dialectically, giving birth to irrational totalitarianism, wrote Theodor Adorno and Max Horkheimer in 1944.[26] Our protagonists could not agree more. In the 1950s, they too would allege that totalitarianism was the outcome of secularism – an acute condition that therefore *could only be solved by* a return to pre-modern mysticism. Unlike interwar fascism, though, they fostered a more holistic and less violent spiritual "technique" to reach this spiritual condition, they believed. They were hardly the only ones around posing such a proposition. By claiming to amalgamate the rational and the irrational, the Hispanic technocrats merely conveyed a variety of what scholars nowadays define as conservative modernity. Whether it be historian Jeffrey Herf's influential theory of "reactionary modernism" or political scientist Corey Robin's analysis of the *Reactionary Mind*, many have attempted to explain this paradoxical identity.[27] Such analyses have shown us that, unlike religious fundamentalisms, reactionary modernists do not repudiate modernity but interpret it differently, hence promoting a hybrid of modern and pre-modern elements. Latin American conservatives, I add, have never been equivocal about their determination to fuse these seemingly unbridgeable domains. Since the scientific project had not convincingly answered the mysteries of existence, they claimed, an injection of spirituality into the heart of the modern project was not only tolerable but mandatory.

Besides being devout Catholics, another thing Latin America's rightists shared was their *elitism*. They welcomed authoritarianism to maintain their social privileges, we are often told in the literature.[28] This notwithstanding, conceptualizing the Inter-American Cold War in terms of a class war between the elites and the have-nots is reductive. In the 1960s, Latin American rightists truly felt that they were at the forefront of a new global cultural war. If the 1950s are considered the most culturally conservative era in Western history, then the "long 1960s" were their antithesis. The civil rights movement, anti-colonialism, women's liberation, the sexual revolution, rock 'n' roll, hippies, the drug culture – the list of phenomena identified with the decade's revolutionary zeitgeist is undoubtedly extensive.[29] While we may nowadays approach the 1960s "cultural revolution" with some befitting sarcasm, it would be erroneous to belittle the impact it had on those who watched it from the side, aghast. *Hispanic Technocracy* surveys a cohort of men and women who came of age between 1940 and 1960. For them, the cultural revolution symbolized the opposite of how modern civility should be: heroic, disciplined, reverent, hierarchic, and intensely spiritual. Though sharing the fascist penchant for a redemptive "crusade" against the "enemies" of civilization, these people were, I argue, also original in the subtle techniques they promoted for "bridging" between new Western cultural trends and their "Hispanic" spiritual domain. The effectiveness of their mobilization stemmed not only from the levels of their anxieties but also from the calculated formation of networks of ideologues and avid travelers who identified themselves with a movement that went beyond their national settings. From this perspective, my book contributes to several ongoing debates on how ideologies "travel" across borders. While these are not viruses we are dealing with here, one must also remember that ideas moved in fairly distinctive channels in the 1960s – when a telephone line in one's home was still considered a luxury. When Fernández de la Mora arrived in Chile in 1967, his narratives had already been disseminated internationally within original apparatuses. If the fascist "movement" typified the 1930s, the Cold War saw novel transnational societies controlling right-wing ideological production. In the pages that follow, the reader will become acquainted with names such as the Instituto de Cultura Hispánica (Institute of Hispanic Culture, or ICH), Opus Dei ("the work of God") and Movimiento de Cursillos de Cristiandad ("Short courses in Christianity movement" or MCC). Originating in Franco's Spain, these movements formed branches in Latin America and were the sites where Spanish, Argentine, and Chilean ideologues collaborated. That is to say, the dialogue between the Hispanic technocrats relied not only on official diplomacy but on societies operating primarily through *soft power*. Joseph Nye's trope, which stands for the "ability to shape preferences of others" thanks to the faculty to "entice and attract," is entirely applicable to the organization at hand.[30] These post-fascist ideological apparatuses aimed to convince Catholics worldwide to replace their fascist pipe dreams with a sophisticated immanent "crusade." Their aptitude to persuade members of the armed forces of their prestige and ideological rigor granted them their place at the government table.

Before moving forward, a word is perhaps due on the methodology deployed in this book, which relies on two types of textuality. Primarily, I inspect ideological texts devised to impact the conservative public, including published texts and speeches. This profound corpus is then complemented with an exclusive collection of personal correspondence. To paraphrase sociologist Erving Goffman's now classic framework, if publications are the "frontstage" of intellectual production, then personal letters reveal its "backstage" – an arena where genuine motives and sentiments are expressed candidly, far from the public eye.[31] Bilateral protocols and internal government reports are also included in this category, as well as interviews and oral history databases.

The five chapters of this study present a narrative arc that could succinctly be encapsulated in the following themes and key questions. Chapter 1 explores the intellectual origins of the right-wing intellectuals who, in May 1945, sought to advance the anti-Enlightenment revolution further. It glances back to Latin America's reactionary *longue durée*, so to speak, when Spanish, Argentine, and Chilean intellectuals underwent similar trajectories when faced with the rise of liberal democracy since the early twentieth century. Notably, with the rise of Italian fascism, each in their own way aimed to "Christianize fascism," thereby amalgamating fascism and traditionalism into one doctrine. While interwar rightists in Argentina and Chile did not wait until the Spanish Civil War to collaborate, only from the late 1940s did they appear in Spain to partake in

Franco's new modernity. The chapter submits that the Instituto de Cultura Hispánica was where Francoism and Latin America's conservatives first truly cooperated in the open. In due course, they even postulated establishing a Cold War "Hispanic Bloc." A failed intellectual project, this was, I show, the harbinger of Hispanic technocracy on at least three counts: For one, this was the first effort to establish a post-fascist international that avowedly rejected the post-1945 democratic order. For another, it was there that Hispanic technocracy's networks were born. Lastly, as is often the case with abortive projects, the ICH disclosed the global political and discursive power setting. As such, it was instrumental in how the 1960s technocrats defined themselves internationally and to themselves.

Chapter 2 moves us entirely to Franco's Spain and offers an insight into this regime's transition from a semi-autarchic fascist dictatorship to an authoritarian technocracy. Indeed, the ICH could not encompass the fierce ideological struggle between Spain's fascist and post-fascist schools that touched not on mythology but on the state's role in society and its relationship with the Western financial order. In 1957, once the fascists had lost their hegemonic positions to the so-called Opus Dei technocrats, the so-called second Francoist era began. The chapter touches on Opus Dei's ideology, operational methods, and symbiotic relationship with Franco and, last but not least, on how it sought to replace the ICH in Latin America. The chapter then addresses how, once in power, the Opus Dei ideologues not only redefined the country's economic model but sought to replace the fascist corporatist political myths with new modes of representation and a unique spiritual and cultural project. I thus make the case that the Opus Dei technocrats arrived in Latin America propagating not only Spain's "economic miracle" but a roadmap for what they believed was an entirely original "post-ideological" society. Worse yet, they sought to secure their ideology's continuation after Franco's death as Spain's finite state model, the chapter clarifies.

Chapter 3 is concerned with 1950s Argentina and the acute political crisis its democratic system withstood in the wake of Perón's ousting and exile and the inability to conduct the integration of the country's economy into the global financial system with his control of Argentine politics from afar. It lends fuller attention to the widening chasm within the Argentine right-wing camp, between political corporatism-oriented Nacionalistas and a group of intellectuals who broke away from this habitat to establish an association named the Ateneo de la República (the Athenaeum of the Republic). Supported by local ICH and Opus Dei members, this was where Argentina's Hispanic technocracy was first conceived. Next, the chapter recovers the somewhat forgotten story of General Onganía, the nexus he established with the Ateneo, how he designed his dictatorship from 1962, and how he came into dialogue with members of the Francoist regime already in 1965. Overall, the chapter seeks to answer the question of what authoritarian model Onganía truly sought to enact in Argentina and how it differed from the Francoist precedent. In doing so, I ultimately seek to explain this regime's downfall in 1970.

Chapter 4 shifts our focus across the Andean mountains to Chile and accounts for the ways in which the country's conservatives mobilized in opposition to their own powerful left-wing mobilization of the 1960s. As we shall see, their ideological divisions were not unlike those of the Argentines and saw a rivalry emerging between revolutionary neofascists and original pro-market authoritarian groups, such as the "Gremialistas" – the chapter's main protagonists. Buoyed by the ICH and Opus Dei apparatuses, this group was responsible for devising an ideology akin to that of technocratic Spain and, subsequently, stood at the forefront of the opposition to Salvador Allende's government. Once again, we will delve into how a military strongman – in this case, Pinochet – chose this Hispanic technocratic group over Chile's neofascists and aging traditionalists to design his dictatorship's ideology. The chapter likewise surveys how Pinochet's regime sought to constitute a firm dialogue with the Francoist regime, on the one hand, and how it displayed a far more brutal and neoliberal version of Hispanic technocracy – one that transcended both Franco and Onganía's exemplars – on the other.

Chapter 5 brings *Hispanic Technocracy* full circle with a nuanced account of this ideological school's decline during the 1970s. Besides inspecting the root causes for this trajectory – many of which had to do with the unsustainability of the Hispanic technocratic economic model – the chapter addresses how the Hispanic technocrats sought to foil their country's democratization process (Spain); preside over it, thereby producing a democracy in all but name (Chile); or influence a new military regime to reuse their ideological formulas (Argentina). As such, I dispel any existing historiography crediting these men with intentionally or accidentally advancing their respective country's democratization. In turn, the book's epilogue provides a succinct theorization of the Hispanic technocratic ideology interwoven in a discussion of the technocrats' predominance in contemporary right-wing memory and their impact on the political pathologies that are nowadays compromising democratic life in Latin America.

1

In Defense of "Hispanidad"

Confirming the Mythological Foundations for Hispanic Technocracy (1945–1959)

In March 1947, Alfredo Sánchez Bella embarked on a special mission. In two months, he visited almost all Latin American nations, where he inaugurated chapters of a new Spanish-based organization, namely the Instituto de Cultura Hispánica (Institute of Hispanic Culture, or ICH). Writing to his superior, Spain's Foreign Minister Alberto Martín-Artajo, Sánchez Bella was candid about his objectives. Upon arrival, he would contact the most "prominent Hispanistas" in each country and bring them to Spain so they could see the Francoist regime's achievements firsthand, he vowed.[1] At first blush, it appears that his initiative was successful. In a matter of months, a network of ICH branches crystallized, and Spain began witnessing anyone from elderly intellectuals to impressionable teenagers paying homage to Francoism. "Spain still resonates in my soul, and I hope it will continue to do so my entire life," stated Arturo Fontaine Aldunate – a Chilean youngster whose "audacious trip," he remarked years later, had taught him about Spain and Chile's upcoming "surge in universal history."[2] Writing from Spain to his mother, another Chilean youngster named Jaime Guzmán testified that he was "bursting with Hispanismo" and is now an "arch-Francoist." This mental condition he attributed to witnessing how the Spaniards' "liberty" is oriented towards the "common good" rather than "to satisfy the absurd principle of the French Revolution – *Liberté* that ends up in debauchery."[3] In the 1960s, Fontaine would become the editor of Chile's foremost conservative daily *El Mercurio*. Guzmán ended up becoming Augusto Pinochet's most prominent intellectual. Indeed, the impact of these visitors on Chilean history cannot be overstated.

To gain as complete an understanding as possible of the peculiarity of this pilgrimage, one should first bear in mind how much the world had changed in the aftermath of the Second World War. The Nuremberg Trials (1945), the Truman Doctrine (1947), and the Universal Declaration of Human Rights (1948) attested that the Western Bloc was taking proactive measures to prevent the horrors of European totalitarianism from reoccurring. The region most impacted by this sea change was, in fact, Latin America, which witnessed its most extensive democratization wave to date. Indeed, our pilgrims' countries of origin were parliamentary democracies again, often after having been controlled by protofascist military dictatorships for nearly two decades. By contrast, Spain remained firmly a dictatorship. Still heavily impacted by the Spanish Civil War, it was therefore excluded from the Marshall Plan and even came under a brief period of international embargo. To link oneself with this half-starved fascist residue, let alone propagate its ideology elsewhere, was thus an unusual undertaking. Yet these travelers did precisely that. For them, years before Spain's "economic miracle," Francoism had already become exemplary. Who were these people, and what were their worldviews? What did they seek to achieve by associating themselves with Francoism? This chapter offers insights into these questions. I make the case that the "Hispanistas" with whom Sánchez Bella made contact were neither tourists nor passive spectators but confidants and forerunners of what they believed was a new international.

First, however, this chapter examines the historical contexts that shaped these people's lives and motivated them to join forces. After all, places such as Spain, Argentina, and Chile have showcased dissimilar national histories since the turn of the twentieth century. Nevertheless, at the crux of the Hispanistas' mythological thinking lay the notion that there was no fundamental difference between their nations' pasts. To their mind, the haphazard timing of their specific political crises was irrelevant insofar as these were the result of one root cause: the European Enlightenment and its political outgrowths. Indeed, the chapter excavates how the Spanish, Argentine, and Chilean anti-modern schools emerged and how they contextualized their local experiences within a shared metanarrative. Amid the rise of fascist Europe, they already operated as an international network – a process that reached its acme with the event that, for Latin American spectators, was no less traumatic than the Second World War: the Spanish Civil War.

Were these men fascist? At times, yes. Some had been fascist militants in the 1930s, while others rubbed shoulders with members of the Nazi Germany and Fascist Italy regimes or, in the case of Spain, were members of the Spanish fascist party, the Falange. Most of them betrayed sympathies with Mussolini but also referred to many other anti-modern European emblems such as Charles Maurras's Action Française. By the late 1940s, many of them preferred the title "traditionalists," while a few still wore their fascist identity as a badge of honor. Avowed fascists or not, none of them could ignore the monumentality of fascism's downfall and its impact on the global anti-Enlightenment movement. Subsequently, they were initially cautious not to propose replacing democracy with authoritarianism. Instead, they defined the moral absolutes that should guide those who would do so in the future. Their activity centered on disengaging themselves from European fascism and reaffirming the need to restore a pre-modern spiritual condition at the crux of the Occidental domain. Eventually, they even posited enacting a Hispanic Community of Nations against the Enlightenment's ideologies. Here, then, one begins to trace the trajectory of an intellectual network that would generate a definitive brand of authoritarianism for Hispanic dominion in the 1960s.

1.1 "AMERICA BEGINS AT THE PYRENEES": FRANCO'S SPAIN LINKS WITH LATIN AMERICA

Franco's Spain was a regime that evaded simple ideological taxonomies. Even the term "Francoism" is not without its problems. Unlike Nazism or Italian fascism, it was used mainly by the dictatorship's opponents. For Franco and his followers, their regime was simply the "New Spanish State." Sure enough, they prided themselves on being "a different country."[4] To their mind, Franco's "confessional state" was the definite climax of the opposition to the Enlightenment dating back to the liberal Constitution of Cádiz in 1812. Aside from its short-lived First Republic (1873–74), Spain never succumbed to the Enlightenment until 1931, when King Alfonso XIII left Spain voluntarily, paving the way for the Second Republic, according to their narrative. Only then, in self-defense, did Spain's conservatives link with the Axis powers to remove the most catastrophic embodiment of the Enlightenment, as they saw it: a parliamentary democracy turning into a bastion of Bolshevism. Thus, the regime's spokespeople flatly rejected any equation between Francoism and European fascism after May 1945 and presented their society as a final condition of spiritual restoration.[5] Cleansed from liberalism and communism, Spain was now infinitely "Unified, Great, and Free."[6]

Irrespective of this narrative, whether Francoism was coterminous with fascism is a subject that has preoccupied countless scholarly analyses ever since Franco declared victory in the Spanish Civil War on April 1, 1939. This question also stood at the core of the Hispanic technocratic project and, therefore, is worth delving into briefly. Certainly, Francoism's Catholic dogmatism did not correspond to Italian fascism's anticlerical image. A straightforward way to address this question has been to argue that Francoism was a personalist dictatorship that "fascistized" itself briefly by adopting fascist insignia.[7] This hypothesis is valid insofar as one accepts the so-called fascist minimum definition of fascism as an anti-liberal, anti-communist, and anti-conservative totalitarian regime built around a leadership principle and a revolutionary party. Otherwise, it should be borne in mind that while Francoism presented itself as an amalgam of right-wing schools, it did not merely put on a veneer of uniforms and salutes but aspired to outdo the Italian precedent and lead the anti-Enlightenment international.

A closer look reveals that Spain had, in fact, been a forerunner of corporatist thought since the late nineteenth century. In a country beset by economic crises and civil wars between liberals and traditionalists (the Carlist Wars) and frustrated by the loss of its last colonies in 1898, traditionalists such as Marcelino Menéndez Pelayo and Juan Vázquez de Mella had preceded Maurras in conceptualizing social corporatism since the 1880s. But more importantly, Spain was not only receptive to Italian fascism but became a laboratory where Europe's fascist project developed and matured. To begin with, Spain featured Europe's first protofascist regime, namely Miguel Primo de Rivera's dictatorship that preceded the Second Republic. As in most European nations, Spain also saw the rise of a local fascist party, namely the Falange Española y de JONS. Its founder, Primo de Rivera's son José Antonio, had met Mussolini and was in thrall to his political corporatism but also claimed to transcend it. The Falange's program thus included the traditionalists' system of organic representation through family, municipality, and unions, and a vertical harmonization of capital and labor, or "national syndicalism," which, inspired by Georges Sorel's theories, sought to outshine the Spanish anarcho-syndicalist movement. Even if they acknowledged the veracity of the Catholic ontology of the spirit, like the Italian precedent, the Falangists did not promote a restoration of a pre-modern order but a revolutionary "style" that would replace ideologies as such, based on a "militia" mentality, which was enveloped in an aura of "masculine domination that glorified heroism, daring, bravery, and austerity," in historian Joan Maria Thomàs's words.[8] While it is beyond the scope of my analysis to elucidate the Falange's "style," the point not to be missed is that, whether they liked it or not, the Hispanic technocrats of the 1960s had little choice but to present a clear alternative to this revolutionary ethos.

The Falange was hardly a popular movement in the 1930s. It paled in comparison to Spain's traditionalist sector that, as the Carlist movement in Navarra illustrated, could also mobilize combat militias in a way the Falange never quite did.[9] Arguably, it was not the most fanatical far-right association in Madrid. In the 1930s, Ramiro de Maeztu, the editor of the journal *Acción Española,* and Ángel Herrera Oria, leader of the Asociación Católica Nacional de Propagandistas group (ACNP), showcased a rhetoric that was far more violent, anti-communist, and anti-Semitic than the Falange "poetic" revolution. Being a devoted *Acción Española* reader, Franco, some historians have stressed, borrowed from these groups' doctrine when constituting his own discourse.[10] Nevertheless, the Falange was the first to benefit from Franco's rise to power. As the leader of the revolt against the Republic, in April 1937, he ordered the merger of the Falange and the traditionalists into a single "movement." Outwardly dividing power evenly between them, this arrangement ultimately meant that the Falange – which was then led by Franco's brother-in-law, Ramón Serrano Suñer – became the regime's principal designer in its early years. Coupled with the fact that the Falange's programmatic social agenda appealed to Franco and his officers more than the traditionalists' vague anti-modernism, the regime's first Fundamental Laws – the 1936 Fuero del Trabajo, which regulated workers' rights, thus imitating Mussolini's Carta del Lavoro – were the Falange's brainchild. Hereafter, and until the mid 1950s, Spain would be a testing ground for an autarchic "national syndicalist" economy.[11]

In due course, Francoism acquired other more distinctively fascist traits. For example, with Primo de Rivera and Maetzu executed by the Republic, Franco was uninhibited from constructing a leadership principle in his own image ("Caudillaje Nacional"), accommodated by a one-party system ("Movimiento") and a corporatist chamber ("Cortes") analogous to that operating in Italy. His claim to rule by the "grace of God" also echoed the Nazi *Führerprinzip* and was hardly rooted in Catholic theology or taken seriously by the Church hierarchy.[12] Still, the most fundamental aspect of Franco's fascist inclination was how he chose to slay his countrymen. As a murderous political movement, fascism was perhaps born in Italy, but only crossed this conceptual Rubicon in July 1936, when Franco's armies in Africa and General Emilio Mola's Carlists in Navarra rebelled against the Republic. For even though Franco did not foresee his coup d'état resulting in prolonged civil war, he immediately framed his acts as an eschatological "crusade."[13] In other words, while Mussolini's armies were massacring foreigners in Ethiopia, Franco orchestrated a ruthless extermination campaign against his *fellow citizens*. Deemed by some historians the "Spanish Holocaust," and though resting on the fascist conception of the internal enemy as a death-deserving abject, Franco's murderousness was unimaginable even in 1936 Nazi Germany.[14] As such, Spain was the undisputed vanguard in what historian Federico Finchelstein calls the "global ideological civil war against antifascism."[15]

Like the Axis powers, Franco's Spain betrayed imperial aspirations, save for one difference: Still traumatized by their botched Rif War in Morocco, Spanish rightists rarely promoted imperial conquests in Europe or Africa, but were all for renewing Spain's imperial role in Latin America. For the Falange, the "will for empire" meant Spain ought to serve Latin America as a "spiritual axis" in its process of "cultural, economic, and political" unification.[16] Still, the Falange's nationalistic mythological writing – as appearing in Ernesto Giménez Caballero's *Genio de España*, for example – paled in comparison with "Hispanidad." Supposedly coined in Argentina in 1926 by the Spanish-born Zacarías de Vizcarra, the expression was adopted by Maeztu – then, Spain's ambassador in Argentina – who, upon returning to Madrid, made the "defense of Hispanidad" the traditionalists' ultimate rallying cry. Strikingly, Hispanidad quickly became a maxim for any Latin American who identified with Franco's armies. From now on, adhering to Hispanidad made one a "Hispanista."

What then *is* Hispanidad? For Maeztu, it principally signified the "spiritual equilibrium" of the 1600s – the Habsburg dynasty's golden age.[17] A condition of optimal societal harmony, it came to an abrupt end in 1700 once the unwelcome Bourbon dynasty adopted the Enlightenment's "false dogmas."[18] Yet Hispanidad went beyond this reactionary point of departure and came to signify the Spaniards' evangelizing *mission* acquired during millennia of colonization and "fight against Moors and Jews."[19] The theologue Manuel García Morente thus advocated Hispanidad as a mentality of a "Christian gentleman" (or "Paladín") whose characteristics include "stoically" accepting his civilizing mission.[20] On the one hand, unlike the Nazi theory of race, Hispanidad was universally inclusive and "never prided itself on skin color," in Maeztu's words.[21] On the other hand, it presumed one's affinity with Catholic and Spanish moral absolutes. Conscious of this dualism, many advised not to overthink the word's precise meaning, thus turning it into something of an empty signifier. García Morente, for example, stated that "Hispanidad" is "neither a thing nor being, but a mode, a way of being" that should be experienced "intuitively."[22] By the same token, Uruguayan Hispanista Carlos Lacalle claimed that "one lives Hispanidad, not thinks it."[23]

Whatever it was, Franco's Spain began using Hispanidad indiscriminately following May 1945, amid the regime's de-fascistization process and efforts to link with Latin America. In truth, Franco and his ever-powerful new deputy, Admiral Luis Carrero Blanco, had been ridding the regime of its fascist traits since May 1941, mainly by curbing Serrano Suñer's authority. By closing punishment facilities and removing Falange leaders from positions of ideological influence, from 1944, the dictatorship did its utmost to present itself as the protector of civil liberties.[24] Additionally, Franco initiated a constitutional phase, consisting of a political rights "charter" (Fuero de los Españoles) and, to the Falange's dismay, the 1947 Law of Succession, which declared Spain a monarchy and appointed Franco as its "regent" for life.[25] Ratified in a bogus national referendum, the law was supposed to secure the dictatorship's international legitimacy. That is not to say that the Falange disappeared from Spain's political landscape, but that traditionalism became the regime's more prominent facade. All in all, by the time Sánchez Bella set foot in Latin America, Spain was "fascist" no more.[26]

The appointment of Martín-Artajo, an ACNP member and avid Hispanista, as foreign minister illustrated how vital Latin America was to become in Spain's post-1945 diplomacy. The fact that Falangist intellectuals Pedro Laín Entralgo and Raimundo Fernández-Cuesta joined the efforts to define Hispanidad – a term they would never have uttered before 1944 – was likewise demonstrative of this sea change. Naturally, Franco's men expressed no scruples when justifying their intervention in Latin American affairs. After all, claimed Sánchez Bella, Spain had created the Latin American "family of nations" and, therefore, "Hispano-America begins at the Pyrenees."[27] Franco, for his part, alleged that empire had given Spain "an American character."[28] Thus, leading Latin America's spiritual crusade appeared in their texts not merely as the regime's "diplomacy" but as its reason for being.[29] Hence, Franco founded several institutions wherein the Spanish–Latin American intellectual linkage was to take place and which he allocated between the regime's ideological "families" in his typical divide-and-rule fashion: The Instituto de Estudios Políticos (IEP) became the Falange's intellectual hub, while the Consejo Superior de Investigaciones Científicas (CSIC) came under the influence of the then unknown Opus Dei.[30] Still, of the institutions operating in 1950s Spain, none was as decisive in its relationship with Latin America as the ICH. Replacing a failed body named the Consejo de la Hispanidad, from 1945, this was where Spain accosted Latin America's rightists – an operation skillfully led by Sánchez Bella.[31] Born in Valencia in 1916, this man began his political career in the Falange's radio services but was also affiliated with the ACNP and was, briefly, an Opus Dei member.[32] As the ICH's director between 1949 and 1959, he now embodied the quintessential Hispanista whose zeal and dynamism would prove crucial for Spain's linkage with Latin America.

The ICH was anything but a hub of cultural regeneration, as its name might imply. Rather, the institute prompted Latin American rightists to overtake conservative politics in their respective countries. The first step in Sánchez Bella's strategy was to establish the ICH's network, which, by 1951, totaled twenty-three chapters (Figure 1.1).[33] Designed to appear as autonomous "national entities," they adhered to the center in Madrid and were financed by Spain's embassies.[34] Why Sánchez Bella believed these centers could openly tutor conservatives towards "a new state of consciousness," thereby turning them into ideological actors who would "conquer the best universities in each country," is unclear.[35] Educating these men in Spain was much simpler. Sure enough, Sánchez Bella planned to host no fewer than 15,000 Latin American students in Spain by 1952.[36] There, the Francoist "moral and intellectual reality" would "permeate deeply" into the minds of these "companions for the road." Living in Spain, even if for a short while, would protect them from becoming "vulgarized," thereby building them to be "tougher" and "more of a man," he asserted.[37] Last, Sánchez Bella orchestrated the establishment of the ICH's sizable publishing apparatus, which included a lavish international magazine named *Mundo Hispánico*. This brazenly Francoist propaganda outlet, he fantasized, could one day be as popular "as *Reader's Digest* and *Paris Match*."[38]

The second phase in Sánchez Bella's program included the arrival of Latin America's intellectual elite in Spain, thereby transforming it into Francoism's "spontaneous and persuaded defender."[39] A system of annual massive congresses systematized this pilgrimage. Opening on October 1,

Institutes for Hispanic Culture 1952

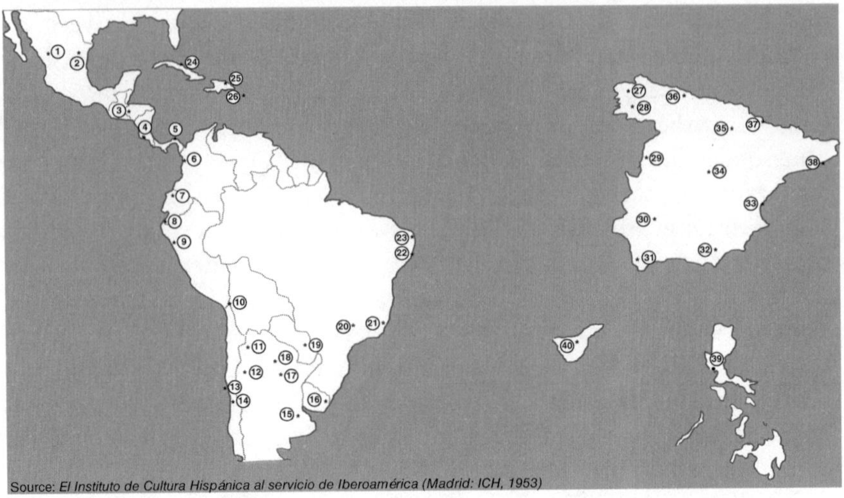

(1) Instituto Jalisciense de CH Guadalajara
(2) Instituto Regional de CH, Monterey
(3) Instituto Hondureño de CH Tegucigalpa
(4) Instituto Costarrigense de CH San José
(5) Instituto Panameño de CH De Colon
(6) Instituto Colombiano de CH Bogota
(7) Instituto Ecuatoriano de CH Quito
(8) Instituto de CH de Guayaquil
(9) Instituto Peruano de CH, Lima
(10) Instituto Boliviano de CH, La Paz
(11) Instituto Panargentino de CH de Tucumán
(12) Instituto Cuyano de CH de Mendoza
(13) Instituto Chileno Hispano de Cultura de Valparaíso
(14) Instituto Chileno de CH, Santiago
(15) Instituto Argentino de CH de Rosario
(16) Instituto Uruguayo de CH, Montevideo
(17) Instituto de CH de Córdoba
(18) Instituto de CH de Santiago de Estero
(19) Instituto Paraguayano de CH, Asunción
(20) Casa de Cervantes de São Paulo
(21) Instituto Brasileño de CH, Rio de Janeiro
(22) Instituto Cultural Hispanobrasileiro de Recife
(23) Instituto Cultural Hispanobrasileiro de Natal
(24) Instituto Cultural Cubano Español, La Habana
(25) Instituto Dominicano de CH, Ciudad Trujillo
(26) Instituto Portorriqueño de CH, Puerto Rico
(27) Asociación Cultural Iberoam ericana La Coruña
(28) Asociación Cultural Iberoamericana Santiago de Compostela
(29) Asociación Cultural Iberoamericana Salamanca
(30) Asociación Cultural Iberoamericana Sevilla
(31) Real Academia Hispanoamericana Cádiz
(32) Casa de América Granada
(33) Instituto Iberoamericano, Valencia
(34) Instituto de CH, Madrid
(35) Asociación Cultural Iberoam ericana Burgos
(36) Asociación Cultural Iberoamericana Oviedo
(37) Instituto Vizcayano de CH,Bilbao
(38) Instituto de Estudios Hispánicos Barcelona
(39) Instituto de Cultura Hispano Filipina
(40) Instituto de Estudios Hispánicos Puerto de la Cruz, Tenerife

FIGURE 1.1 The Institute of Hispanic Culture world map, 1952.
Data source: *El Instituto de Cultura Hispánica al servicio de Iberoamérica* (Madrid: ICH, 1953)

1949, and titled the "First Ibero-American Congress of History," the first of them had a somewhat odd objective: to constitute a "general theory" of Latin America's independence saga. Tellingly, any cooperation between the Mother Nation and its former colonies relied on setting the record straight on what had happened between the two in the early 1800s. Latin America's Wars of Independence did not stem from a concrete political context, the congress determined, but "from a complex spiritual process, linked to a universal history."[40] In other words, neither party was responsible for these wars. From history, the ICH congresses then shifted their attention to more contemporary themes. While the Intellectual Cooperation Congress (1950) revolved around Latin America's "autochthonic races" and how they should undergo "castellanization," the Feminine Congress (1951) sought to define women's role in society.[41] Interestingly, while deciding little on this matter, it saw Fernández-Cuesta positing that, as the "savior of mankind," Hispanidad should emerge as "a geographical and political framework."[42]

Indeed, up until this point, the Hispanistas had been reluctant to propose concrete political outlines to confront the Cold War power dynamic. So far, they had settled for suggestive remarks – for instance, that Spain was the only place on earth "deeply imbued with spirituality,"[43] or that it constituted the only "oasis of peace" in a secular world of nuclear arms.[44] By 1953, the time of Spain's concordat with the Vatican, they became more comfortable with advancing a scheme of political unification, however. Ultimately known as the Hispanic Community of Nations, it was cunningly couched in postcolonial terminologies. As "the proletarians of the world," who had arrived late to the "development of technology and industrialization," the Hispanic nations had no alternative but to unite in the act of anti-imperialist self-defense, Sánchez Bella stated.[45] Martín-Artajo, a pragmatist, foresaw a "supranationality" that would be "incorporated into the norms of government" in each country.[46] Baffled by Spain's absence from the UN's new Economic Commission for Latin America and the Caribbean (ECLAC), they even proposed founding an alternative "Iberoamerican economic community."[47] In time, they would come to refer to the Hispanic Community of Nations simply as a "Hispanic Bloc," wherein Spain, while perhaps being the "elder sister possessing the old family documents," was to serve as an equal member.[48]

While the Hispanic Community of Nations initiative never publicly suggested meddling in its prospective members' internal affairs, not to mention making them adhere to a regime model akin to Francoism, the ICH's internal memoranda shed light on a shadier side of the ICH's tactics. In 1953, Sánchez Bella embarked on another tour in preparation for the ICH's "third phase" of operations, in which its chapters were to move from "being mere private institutions to having a parastatal character," thereby influencing their "respective governments." More than anything, his classified report reveals how the Francoist regime perceived Latin America's new democratic era as a threat to the continent's well-being. By "making a pact with the Yankee" and allowing a free public sphere to flourish, Latin America's oligarchies had enabled not only communists but "Jews, Protestants, and Christian Democrats" to take over, Sánchez Bella lambasted his audience. For him, the ICH's mission was thus to encourage the replacement of Latin America's democracies with "authoritarian systems with popular support." These would be regimes that, unlike European fascism, would embrace the private sector and belie "autarchic industrialization." On this occasion, he also opined that the majority of Latin Americans wished for a regime "like Spain" but shied away from this option for fear of being labeled "Falangist or fascist." Therefore, Spain should assist them tacitly by teaching Latin America's "ruling classes" the Spanish "formula" to its "most intimate" components. Infiltrating "state apparatuses" and disseminating Francoism's "ideological bases" were valid tactics, too, said the ICH director.[49] Paternalistic at best and conspiratorial at worst, his suggestions uncover the paradoxes facing Latin American Hispanistas in the 1950s: how to inaugurate an anti-modern authoritarian regime while attaining popular support and without being marred by a fascist or Francoist image.

1.2 ARGENTINE FASCISM: BETWEEN AUTOCHTHONIC NATIONALISM AND HISPANIC TRADITIONALISM

As in Europe, the reaction against the Enlightenment in Latin America dates back to the French Revolution and its repercussions, the more prominent of which were Latin America's Wars of Independence. Ever since its liberation from Spanish rule in 1816, Argentina had been embroiled in a perennial civil war between liberal centralists and reactionary federalists, which had ended in the formers' victory and the establishment of the Constitution of 1853. From then on, the country's anti-modern movement would doggedly resurface as the twentieth century unfolded. First, during a period characterized by economic growth, European immigration, and social turmoil, in the early 1900s, the Argentine aristocracy rekindled its quest to restore the country to its anti-modern origins through movements such as the Liga Patriótica Argentina. Next, in the 1920s, Argentina saw the rise of a far more influential movement, somewhat insipidly named "Nacionalismo." Its association with Italian fascism would be a matter of dispute among historians and its members alike. In 1967, in a magazine report dedicated to their history, one Nacionalista alleged that Nacionalismo had consisted of Buenos Aires elitist Catholics who had sought to solve Argentina's crises with "a kind of fascism" while another stated that "we were not fascists" but "traditionalist and classic." [50] So, which one was it?

To fully understand this puzzlement, it should be borne in mind that, unlike in Spain, the Nacionalistas consciously sought to merge fascism and traditionalism – the "violent pens of French Action and Mussolini."[51] A more nuanced explanation would be that, unlike Falangism, the Nacionalistas' ideology fluctuated considerably between the late 1920s and the 1960s. The movement's first generation was preoccupied with purification and restoration, not a totalitarian revolution or political corporatism. Besides rejecting the liberal order in place since 1853 and seeking the purging of the racial elements that had allegedly infiltrated the nation in the early 1900s, Nacionalismo's primary objective was to abolish Argentina's parliamentary democracy, which had been in place since the 1912 Saenz Peña Law. Indeed, by the 1920s, Argentina was not only a multicultural society but a democracy that enabled the political mobilization of its working classes – a feat achieved by Hipólito Yrigoyen, the leader of the anti-oligarchic Radical Party and Argentina's president from 1916 to 1922 and from 1928 to 1930. As to what state model should replace Yrigoyen's populist "caesarianism," some Nacionalistas spoke in favor of a robust "presidential" regime,[52] while others envisioned a nondemocratic, elite-held regime based on "financial tribunals."[53] The Nacionalistas' programs – for example, the "action program" of Roberto de Laferrére's paramilitary group La Liga Republicana – did little to shed light on what this state model entailed. Only in 1931 did Rodolfo Irazusta propose a convoluted version of societal corporatism based on an authoritarian leadership backed by a handful of advisory civil bodies.[54] This was a far cry from Mussolini or José Antonio Primo de Rivera's totalitarian revolutions.

Deciphering the meaning of corporatism would consume the Nacionalistas only in later years. In the 1920s, their inner quarrels centered around defining the movement's moral absolutes. The first cause for contestation was defining the role of Catholicism in modern society. Leopoldo Lugones, the movement's most prominent forefather, was anti-clerical and obsessed with conceptualizing revolutionary violence (in 1926, he coined the movement's motto, "The hour of the sword"). Fathers Gustavo Franceschi, Julio Meinvielle, Virgilio Filippo, and

Leonardo Castellani, on the other hand, promoted a return to a society guided by scholastic law and were thus traditionalists, or "clerico-fascist" at best.[55] The Nacionalistas also disagreed on mythology and, more specifically, on the question of which moment in the nation's history represented the apex of its spiritual and societal harmony. On the one hand, people such as Laferrére, Carlos Ibarguren, Juan E. Carulla, and Julio and Rodolfo Irazusta adhered to "Rosismo." Synonymous with "Argentine historical revisionism," this mythology glorified the period between 1810 and the 1830s, when Argentina was ruled by the Argentine Caudillo Juan Manuel de Rosas, as the moment when the nation's ethical and spiritual essence was forged "autochthonously."[56] On the other hand, men such as Atilio Dell'Oro Maini, César Pico, Alberto Ezcurra Medrano, and Ernesto Palacios – who operated the influential elite circle Cursos de Cultura Católica and collaborated with Maeztu – considered Argentina's colonial era as the Viceroyalty of the Río de la Plata as the nation's spiritual acme.[57]

While these mythologies did not entirely coalesce, they were not antithetical either. At first, the two schools even joined forces in *La Nueva Republica* – a newspaper that buoyed the rise of military dictator José Félix Uriburu (1930–32) and served as his semi-official ideological mouthpiece. Still, rarely did a Nacionalista espouse both mythologies. Uriburu's downfall and untimely death in exile in 1932 and the onset of the Spanish Civil War made this division even more apparent as a younger generation of Nacionalistas shifted their foci more decidedly to Hispanidad and the nexus with Francoism. By so doing, they broke further away not only from the Argentine political establishment – which, under Presidents Agustín Pedro Justo (1932–38) and Roberto María Ortiz (1938–42), did not officially recognize Franco's Spain – but also from Lugones's secular Nacionalismo and Rosismo.[58] A cohort of Cursos de Cultura Católica apprentices was particularly responsible for the link between the two Catholic fascisms. Mario Amadeo (born 1911), Juan Carlos Goyeneche (born 1913), and Marcelo Sánchez Sorondo (born 1913) were in their mid-twenties when they arrived in Europe. After visiting Nazi Germany and Fascist Italy, they linked with Franco's intellectuals at his headquarters in Burgos. In turn, in 1938, they launched *Sol y Luna* – a journal devoid of Rosista mythology that championed a neo-imperial vision for "Hispanic America." Tellingly, its first issue featured Eugenio Montes, Franco's ambassador to Argentina, praising the two countries' "simultaneous discovery of a system of values."[59] Presenting his guest, Goyeneche declared that Spain's war was tantamount to the "world's rebirth,"[60] upheld that

Spain and Hispanic America were "one spiritual power, one unified culture, and a sole historical progression," and even admitted he suffered from "hispanofilliation."[61] Unquestionably, the link between *Sol y Luna* and Francoism, as indicated by the Spanish figures it hosted in Buenos Aires, such as Dr. Gregorio Maranón, Archbishop of Toledo Isidro Goma y Tomas, Laín Entralgo, and *Acción Española* traditionalist José María Pemán, was a highly unusual occurrence for a Nacionalista, or any Latin American right-wing, publication.[62]

The onset of the Second World War signaled the Nacionalistas' motion from reactionary to more "corporatist" terrain. Juan Queraltó's Unión Nacionalista de Estudiantes Secundarios (UNES) was a case in point. With its anti-oligarchic and anti-American tone, and "national syndicalist" jargon, this supposed student movement catered not only to elites but to the urban masses. Just when they began to be "revolutionary," the Nacionalistas' fortunes changed in the shape of Argentina's 1943 Officer Revolution (GOU) – a pro-Axis dictatorship that, under General Pedro Pablo Ramírez, was sympathetic to their ideology. With Nacionalista journals such as the pro-Nazi *El Pampero* "circulating in the barracks" and the regime employing people such as Amadeo, Goyeneche, and writer Hugo Wast as functionaries, this would be the closest the Nacionalistas would come to power until 1955.[63] But this heyday was also brief. In the wake of the Axis powers' defeat, by early 1944, the GOU began splitting into a Catholic-authoritarian faction, headed by Ramírez, and a faction seeking to institutionalize the regime by mobilizing the working class, led by Perón. Having served as military attaché in Fascist Italy and Nazi Germany, the latter was one of the few Argentines who could claim to have studied fascist Europe closely. Still, Perón was neither a fascist nor a Nacionalista. The story of his ascent to power is well-known, but is worth a quick recap: Relying on a political pact with the labor unions and after a host of pro-labor reforms, his faction declared war on Nazi Germany in March 1945, and was let back into the new Pan-American community (the Chapultepec Act). Following a hesitant process of return to democracy, and after demonstrating workers saved him from being ousted in October 1945, Perón won the February 1946 elections by a narrow margin, paving the way for the era of a populist movement never before seen in Latin America.

The Nacionalistas, who were not a part of Perón's coalition, initially treated him reverentially. After all, it was his anti-American rhetoric that had seemingly brought him the presidency. Additionally, his pledge to integrate the positive aspects of European fascism – as he understood them – into his anti-liberal and anti-communist "third position" meant that he ostensibly embodied their "flags, themes, and plans," remembered Sánchez Sorondo.[64] Then came Perón's dramatic decision to aid Franco's Spain economically in 1946 – in what came to be known as the Franco–Perón Protocols. Unsurprisingly, this brought Hispanistas on both sides of the Atlantic to believe Perón was about to align with Franco's Hispanic crusade. Sure enough, while hardly a devout Catholic, Perón constantly spoke of the supremacy of the spirit and identified with Hispanidad when it suited him. For instance, on October 12, 1947 – Franco's "Día de la Hispanidad" – he addressed the Spaniards on national radio, stating that Argentina was "the co-heir of Hispanic spirituality."[65] Prompted by the message of this new Argentine "Paladín," Martín-Artajo arrived in Buenos Aires in 1948, evoking earnest discussions in Spain over the latest "Hispanic parallelism" whereby Argentina had joined Spain as the second pillar of Hispanidad.[66] Still, by 1947, this exuberance could not conceal what had become patently clear: The two regimes presented Latin America with different post-fascist models. On the one hand, Peronism devised a revolutionary "third position" based on the democratically mobilized working classes. On the other hand, Franco sought to exclude the Falange's plebian tendencies, thereby moving from fascism towards an elite-oriented, and markedly pro-USA, dictatorship. Eva Perón's animated visit to Spain in June 1947 exposed this yawning gap. In a sarcasm-ridden speech, she declared that the Spanish workers applauded her because they knew her husband had won the "fairest elections in Argentine history" without resorting to communism.[67] Thus, she more than hinted that Peronism had discovered an ethically superior formula for bringing about Argentina's spiritual revolution, likened to which Francoism appeared as a fascist anachronism. Hereafter, Peronism and Francoism drifted apart. By 1950, Perón had even backed away from the Franco–Perón Protocols and, revealingly, refrained from using the term Hispanidad again.[68] The regimes' respective news outlets even traded insults – a public feud that ended only when Franco sent Perón a letter demanding he order his news agencies to halt their "slander and defamation" against the "leader of a friendly nation whom you have distinguished with your friendship."[69]

Some Nacionalistas chose to overlook Perón's ideological idiosyncrasy. Sure enough, people like Palacios and Queraltó – now heading a movement called Alianza Libertadora Nacionalista (ALN) – joined his movement and, in the case of the latter, would remain Peronists for the rest of their lives. For the most part, however, the Nacionalistas were straightaway irritated by Perón's "workerist demagoguery."[70] In fact, the *Sol y Luna* Hispanistas were the first to plot against him in a conspiracy that engulfed Amadeo, Goyeneche, Sánchez Sorondo, and Mario Díaz Colodrero.[71] It is against this background that we can begin to understand why Amadeo, Goyeneche, Pico, Ibarguren, and Juan Ramón Sepich arrived in Madrid in the late 1940s to partake in the ICH activity.[72] Better put, they arrived with the intention of leading and defining Hispanidad, this time as an "American reality,"[73] born not in Castile, but amid the "anxiety of a Spanish heart, dazed in the American landscape."[74] The amity between Amadeo, Goyeneche, and Sánchez Bella was the key to this network's longevity. It meant that, during Sánchez Bella's 1946 visit to Buenos Aires, he met every prominent Nacionalista intellectual in town.[75] Then, he appointed Goyeneche as vice president of the Board of Directors of the ICH's Institute of Iberoamerican Culture and Amadeo as the co-editor of the ICH journal *Cuadernos Hispanoamericanos*.[76] There was hardly anything hidden about their relationship.

The Argentine's influence on the ICH's mythology was considerable. It began in the mid 1940s when Pico published "Hacía la hispanidad" and "Nuestro Tiempo y la misión de las Españas" in Francoist journals. Pico was not only a Hispanista but a particularly sycophantic admirer of Franco. In 1947, he thus fulfilled the "desire of a lifetime" and traveled to Spain to meet Franco in person.[77] In his texts, he reinforced the truism according to which, prior to the French Revolution, Europe had been a place of uninterrupted spiritual harmony. Sounding more like a sociologist than the scholastic priest that he was, he explained that the reason this "mystical" Europe had caved into the "ahistorical" age of rationalism was the ancien régime's failure to cope with the continent's social "condensation" and the "atomization" of Europe's "social body."[78] By now, the Nacionalistas had denounced both the Enlightenment and secular European nationalism. José María de Estrada stated, in this respect, that nationalism could lead to "overdefensive" myopia and the "sin of excess." Arguing that Latin America suffered from "tenuous nationalities," he thus proposed Hispanidad as a remedy against communism *and* destructive chauvinism.[79] In brief, by underscoring that nations are ethically meaningless unless they discover a "vocation" within a supranational order, the Nacionalistas pointed to what they believed was the crux of the fascist fiasco: the inability to produce a politically sustainable international.

From their private correspondence, it is clear that the Nacionalistas were profoundly shaken by the fall of the Axis powers. That the last "formally ideological political possibility" had so grotesquely evaporated meant that the upsurge of the USA's global cultural hegemony was unavoidable, they noted.[80] Returning from a visit to Spain and Italy, in 1947, the Hispanista Máximo Etchecopar wrote to Amadeo that, by "naively posing its civilization in terms of aircraft, Frigidaire, and cinema," the USA might "volatilize" Europe's "rich humanity" in a generation.[81] How should one collaborate with this monstrosity without raising "polemical attitudes" against it?[82] As one of the forefathers of Hispanic technocracy, Etchecopar would present his solution to this question in the 1960s as head of the Ateneo de la República. In the 1950s, however, he and his colleagues had more questions than answers. Attacking the USA in the name of Hispanidad was, by then, a key feature of their strategy to destabilize Perón, who had begun to rely financially on US banks. On January 29, 1951, they led the Hispanista movement out of Franco's orbit to the city of Salta, Argentina, where, with representatives from Chile, Paraguay, and Uruguay, they drafted the "twenty-five points" of their "Hispanista ideals."[83] Their "Declaration of Salta" flatly rejected the US-led Organization of American States (OAS) as their representative body. While Goyeneche mocked the USA's "civilization of abundance and metaphysical misery,"[84] Amadeo declared that if Latin America was to be "loyal to its essence," it could never reach a "profound intimacy with the USA."[85] As the director of the ICH's Instituto Hispano-Luso-Americano de Derecho Internacional (IHLADI), he would continue to define the "Hispanic Bloc" as a zone where a different legality reigned – one that viewed Western human rights as "interventionism" and readily justified the "use of force as a political factor."[86]

By 1954, Amadeo and Goyeneche had become the undisputed architects of the Hispanic Community of Nations initiative.[87] Amadeo's speech at Franco's 1954 Fiesta de la Hispanidad in Zaragoza – which Perón overtly boycotted – served as a new roadmap for this enterprise.[88] In this performance, Amadeo took aim at Pan-Americanism and, more broadly, at the Western Bloc's hypocrisy concerning the post-fascist world: "Yesterday, they deemed us Nazis. Today, perhaps, we represent the archaic rebuilders of the viceroyalties. Tomorrow, without a doubt, we will be deemed communists. That is why we must ignore them," he declared.[89] Yet, ignore them, one could not. For all of Amadeo's bravado, this was a watershed moment for the Hispanic Bloc campaign, but not in the way he had hoped. Following Spain's concordat with the Vatican, and shortly before being accepted as a UN member in 1955, Amadeo's bellicose speech belied Spain's efforts to rejoin the international community. Failing to sense this sea change, he would never appear on official Francoist platforms again.

As it happened, by 1955, overthrowing Perón had sidetracked the Nacionalistas from the Hispanic Bloc initiative. But more importantly, the late 1950s saw them reconsidering their belligerent tone towards the USA and advancing, like Spain, towards what would later become Argentina's Hispanic technocracy. This occurred in journals such as *Quincena* and *Dinámica Social*. Presided over by the former Italian fascist Carlo Scorza, the latter in particular featured Amadeo and Goyeneche railing against Perón's "totalitarianism" and demanding the substitution of democracy with an authoritarian "new order" – one the world had not yet seen, and that would surpass the "moral, political, economic, and social" order born in the French Revolution.[90] This fantasy involved the masses relinquishing their democratic powers in return for a benign regime of specialists that would prompt "private initiative," all the while being corporatist in its social organization and adhering to the "primacy of the spiritual."[91] While promoting an economically liberal setup, these publications resonated with the fascist worldview by defining Argentina's "authentic revolution" as a spiritual alternative to the Enlightenment.[92] These embryonic formulas of Hispanic technocracy were to undergo more revisions until 1966.

1.3 CHILE'S HISPANISTAS: TRADITIONALISTS VERSUS NEOFASCISTS

While hardly as tempestuous as their Argentine peers, Chile's Hispanistas played a significant role in the ICH and operated one of its most dynamic chapters in Latin America. This is noteworthy because, unlike Argentina, Chile did not undergo significant political or social turmoil in the 1950s, thus appearing as one of Latin America's true bastions of democracy. Therefore, the fact that Chilean intellectuals made their way to Francoist Spain, not merely to study the Francoist formulas but to define Hispanidad, might seem even more outstanding. Yet the Chileans' enthusiastic embrace of Hispanic traditionalism was neither novel nor surprising. Like the Argentines and Spaniards, they had also resisted the liberal order established in Chile in the late nineteenth century. Liberalism, which initially benefited Chile's elites, became anathema to them with the advent of Chile's Constitution of 1925 – the moment that ushered in the country's complete parliamentary era.

In a nation ill-famed for inequalities between landed elites and the working classes, the latter's sudden entrance into politics correlated with the emergence of far-right societies named "patriotic leagues" that opposed the democratic order.[93] By the 1930s, Chilean conservatives had divided into more ideologically defined forces. On the one hand was Chile's Conservative Party. Alongside the influential journal *Estudios*, this was the political home of the influential Hispanistas Osvaldo Lira, Jaime Eyzaguirre, Julio Philippi, and Roque Esteban Scarpa. These men, also active in groups like La Asociación Nacional de Estudiantes Católicos (ANEC) and La Liga Social, were at the forefront of the effort to establish an authoritarian model to replace Chile's parliamentary system. As such, *Estudios* supported Franco's armies and published his ideologues' texts.[94] Still, it was not so much that the journal proposed a programmatic corporatist theory of the state, but that its writers, through recourse to mythology, sought to establish the moral absolutes that ought to guide Chile's social organization to begin with. The modern world's crisis, they posited, emanated not only from the "age of machination" but from parliamentary politics, the eradication of the ancien régime's social hierarchies, and consequent collective "infantilism" and "male impotence."[95] While advocating an "efficient pacifying action" to eradicate parliamentarism, Philippi clarified that he objected to this procedure being followed by the installment of fascist "totalitarianism." The way he saw it, a subtle spiritual "essence" should, then, oblige Chile's "inferior" communities to consent to a guilds-based premodern hierarchy.[96]

On the other hand, Chile flaunted an assortment of protofascist movements, the most prominent of which was the Falange Nacional. The history of this peculiar party dates back to 1935, when Eduardo Frei, Radomiro Tomic, and Alejandro Silva Bascuñán, among others, split from the Conservative Party, which they perceived as ideologically ossified. Inspired by José Antonio Primo de Rivera's ideology – not to mention his party's name –[97] they aimed to mobilize the working classes – for instance, by pledging to harmonize "labor and capital" in special "corporations," and maintaining private initiatives "subordinated to the community."[98] A far more fascist specimen was the Chilean Nazi Party (MNSC) – a group so ominous that, in 1938, President Arturo Alessandri executed its members in what became known as the "Seguro Obrero" massacre. This event, coupled with the Axis powers' defeats, pressured the Falange Nacional members to rescind their fascist image, identify with the progressive theories of Catholic thinker Jacques

Maritain, and, in the 1950s, rebrand themselves as the Christian Democratic Party. We will encounter these people further down the road. For now, suffice it to say that, by 1945, little remained of Chile's local fascist movements.

Thus, it remained up to the *Estudios* traditionalists to link with Francoism in the 1950s. Born in 1904 to an aristocratic Santiago family, Osvaldo Lira was the first to move to Madrid. There, he resided for many years, met Franco (and "admired and esteemed" him ever since), and, overall, felt "more Spanish than Chilean."[99] He also became a distinguished ICH member and one of Hispanidad's most prominent theorizers. His texts "Visión de España" (1948) and "Hispanidad y mestizaje" (1952), which were published in Spain, were conceived through his collaboration with Sánchez Bella.[100] Their main contribution to the Hispanidad corpus was their negation of Europe's modern political experience. Like the Nacionalistas, Lira was troubled by the meaning of the Second World War. By juxtaposing fascism with his Hispanic "revolution," he surmised that there was nothing that Latin America could learn from Europe's "pseudo-civilization."[101] In effect, he suggested that Latin America be purged of such ideological influences – be they the Reformation, nineteenth-century "isms," or nationalism – while preserving whatever it deemed valuable from Europe's "techno-industrial and experimental sciences."[102]

The second prominent Chilean to be associated with Franco was Jaime Eyzaguirre. Born in 1908, he was a leading member of the Conservative Party and the editor of *Estudios* for many years. Eyzaguirre was also a respected historian in his own right and the ICH History Congress's coordinator. As such, his input was manifested in historical narrative, especially that pertaining to Latin America's endemic virtuous aristocracy. Thus, he was responsible for the teleological placement of Chile within the Hispanidad cosmology. Whereas Argentina's economic might and cultural effervescence made it Spain's equal as the leader of Hispanidad, Chile's contribution was in the exceptional elites. Cultivated in cultural isolation since the conquistador Pedro de Valdivia set foot on Mapuche land, this "firm and sober class," Eyzaguirre wrote, had been educated in "austerity and effort, as the old nobility of Castile" and was, therefore, able to conduct a "vigorous structuring of society and save it from anarchy."[103] As importantly, he had a knack for narrating Latin American history as a tale of collective victimhood. Two decades before Uruguayan writer Eduardo Galeano published *Open Veins of Latin America*, which described the continent as a victim of centuries of colonial pillage, Eyzaguirre's *Hispanoamérica del dolor* brought to the fore a different viewpoint. Published in Spain in 1945, this booklet depicted the Habsburg Empire as a period of "perfect theological order," in which the "entire social body" had a "clear purpose." Alas, the arrival of "Yankee federalism, French Jacobinism, and British parliamentarism" extinguished this "ascensional, mystical, transcendent movement," he lamented.[104]

If Rosas was the Nacionalistas' mythological icon, then the Chileans' equivalent was Diego Portales – the author of the conservative Constitution of 1833. Unlike the unsettled relations between Hispanidad and Rosismo, "Portalianismo" and Hispanidad appeared more complementary. Better put, the former emanated directly from the latter. As one Conservative Party member, Bernardo Larraín, put it: "Our economic solutions must be rooted in the Spanish tradition, which is our own, and in the Portalian stimulus – the architect of our national structure."[105] In his 1948 book *Fisonomía histórica de Chile*, Eyzaguirre elaborated more on this foundational era in Chilean history. Rather than the late nineteenth-century liberal era, it was under Portales that Chile discovered its moral equilibrium, which entailed a rejection of the Spanish caste system and the introduction of a more authentic hierarchy system founded upon an elite loyal to its Hispanic spirituality, he alleged. The combination of Hispanidad and the so-called Portalian conception of Chilean society was henceforth to be a prominent feature in Chilean right-wing mythological thinking and, in turn, a primary feature of the 1973 military dictatorship's public discourse.[106]

While Eyzaguirre's work loomed large in the minds of Chile's Hispanistas in years to come, his collaboration with the ICH was ultimately halfhearted. As his correspondence implies, he believed that the institute's noticeable links with Francoism made it a dubious medium for promoting Hispanidad.[107] Others had fewer scruples when identifying as Franco's sympathizers, though. For example, the ICH's Congress of Intellectual Cooperation saw the presence of José Luis López Ureta and Ricardo Krebs. Members of the Círculo de Profesionales Hispánicos – yet another association promoting Hispanidad in Chile – the two likewise convened with Franco.[108] The Spanish-born Chilean poet José María Souvirón was another case in point. The director of the Chilean conservative publishing house Zig-Zag, he moved to Madrid in the early 1950s and dedicated himself to working at the ICH.[109] The case of Sergio Fernández Larraín was the most striking, however. This Hispanista did not merely "fight in Spain's defense, from the first day of the National

Uprising," in his own words, but was Franco's close friend.[110] The two went "hunting partridges in Toledo," he purported.[111] As a Conservative Party member and founder of Chile's ICH chapter, Fernández Larraín was also the first Chilean to receive Franco's Grand Cross of the Order of Isabel. In Chile, he was infamous primarily for his staunch anti-communism – for instance, when claiming that this ideology is "appropriating Chile's intellectual world, directed from Moscow and aided by waves of Cuban tourism."[112] In Spain, he was recognized for being Chile's ambassador in Madrid in the early 1960s. Sure enough, Fernández Larraín witnessed technocratic Spain's achievements closely and was deeply impressed with what he saw.[113] In turn, he would be responsible for bringing Fernández de la Mora, his friend, to Chile in 1967.

Moreover, the early 1950s saw Lira and Eyzaguirre's disciples providing their updated interpretation of Hispanidad. Notably, Jorge Iván Hübner Gallo (born 1923), an ICH fellow, completed his PhD in Madrid in 1950 and returned to Chile as the definitive authority on the "New Spanish State," his books featuring forays into progressive Catholicism and flattering portrayals of Francoism. "To write about Spain, after having visited it and studied its customs, institutions, and laws, is to fulfill the duty of every Christian to give a testimony of truth," he wrote in 1952.[114] Arturo Fontaine also belonged to this group. A leading member of the Chilean ICH, he had been Sánchez Bella's student. His letter quoted earlier (see p.16) was addressed to his former teacher. In addition to remarks on Spain's spiritual resonance, Fontaine's letter included comments on the ICH's mission as he saw it. "We must set up the Institute so that it becomes an intellectual basis for a burgeoning movement; the point of convergence and camaraderie for all the Catholic and pure people who today mobilize on this basis," he wrote. Then, Fontaine asked Sánchez Bella for "political news" so that he could publish them in his journal *Estanquero*.[115]

To be sure, *Estanquero*'s first leitmotif was not Hispanidad but anti-communism. Established in 1947, during the presidency of Gabriel González Videla – whose cabinet included Communist Party members – its writers immersed themselves in a paranoid campaign against the so-called Soviet virus.[116] Still, with Jorge Prat, a Hispanista and future leader of Chile's Partido Nacional, and Raul Bazán, future director of Chile's ICH, at its helm, *Estanquero* openly spoke in the name of an "authentic, Hispanic, sovereign, and proud Chile."[117] It also readily mocked Chile's "merely formal" democracy and the "partisan oligarchies" controlling it, though fell short of elucidating the nature of the regime that ought to replace it.[118] Not appearing as either oligarchic or authoritarian was a calculated strategy – at least according to Sánchez Bella, the journal's official correspondent in Spain. "The right is losing ground throughout America and especially in Chile since it continues to consist of the landed oligarchy of rich virtues and Spanish tradition, but is unskilled in adapting to the needs of our times," he first explained. However, the cunning of *Estanquero*'s "nacionalista group" – which comprised men "who have always been great friends of [Francoism]" – might lessen the conservatives' unpopularity, he reassured his readers.[119] Concretely, this approach meant that, on the one hand, *Estanquero* announced that it was "neither fascist, nor Nazi" while, on the other hand, it suggestively pledged to "impose honesty, discipline, and hierarchy in all public and private spheres."[120] In a way, *Estanquero* also thus displayed an embryonic version of Hispanic technocracy. Mindful of the global illegitimacy of fascist ideology, its theorists settled for defining moral absolutes but mostly kept their authoritarian fantasies to themselves.

In due course, though, Chile's conservatives began to betray sympathies with Francoism, not just openly but celebratedly. First, President Ibáñez del Campo renewed Chile's ties with Spain and signed a "dual citizenship" treaty with Franco in 1955.[121] Next, Jorge Alessandri (Arturo's son), upon being elected president in 1958, appointed Fernández Larraín as his ambassador in Madrid and Philippi as his minister of Justice and of Lands and Colonization – an outstanding achievement for the Hispanic movement, according to Sánchez Bella.[122] Subsequently, Franco presented Alessandri with the Grand Collar of the Order of Isabel – a gesture that had become a regular occurrence in his efforts to empower dictators like Getulio Vargas (1951), Rafael Trujillo (1954), and Marcos Pérez Jiménez (1956) and the Shah of Iran (1957). In response, Alessandri published a public letter. "My esteemed and respected friend," it read: "I am deeply grateful for this remarkable honor."[123] In summary, for Chilean conservatives, the declaration of Franco as their ally and friend had become a common and respectable practice.

The Francoist regime did not fail to recognize this sentiment. Being genuinely worried about "communist influences" in Chile, it expended significant efforts to influence Chile's conservatives during the 1950s. Like nowhere else, under the leadership of a Hispanista named José María Doussinague, the Spanish embassy sought to impact public opinion – even to the point of seeking to purchase a local radio station to broadcast Francoist propaganda.[124] Somewhat more successfully, it maintained intimate ties with the Chilean Foreign Ministry, conservative media, the armed forces, and local ideological groups such as the Círculo de Profesionales Hispánicos.[125] A memorandum sent to Franco from the Foreign Ministry during the late 1950s illustrates that, besides financing the Chilean ICH, Spain supported Chile's conservatives in various undisclosed ways.[126] In fact, it displayed a plan to "reconquer Chilean public opinion," for starters, by manning the Spanish embassy with Civil War veterans who "feel deeply involved in the spiritual climate breathed in Spain." Another aspect of the plan was to finance *Estudios* and "penetrate" the daily *El Mercurio* and the Catholic University of Chile. Another memorandum proposed Spain grant "discreet aid" to the conservative newspaper *El Diario Ilustrado*.[127] These documents reveal that the Spaniards were as concerned with communism as they were with the "Maritainian" influence on Chilean Catholics. The Christian Democrats' theorist could not be confronted with "an effective presence of Spanish Catholicism," one report lamented, due to the USA's classification of Hispanic culture as a "cunning sign of fascism." Thus, the link between Spain's "Hispanic action" and the Chilean rightists must never be revealed, for that would result in "fatal consequences."[128] Evidently, fearful of the USA's reaction, Spain's operations amounted to covert financing of news outlets. Still, Spain's "Hispanic action" went far beyond simple cultural cooperation.

1.4 THE COLD WAR'S POWER STRUCTURE OVERRIDES HISPANIDAD

On December 21, 1959, Dwight Eisenhower convened with Franco in Madrid, officially accepting Spain into the Cold War's anti-communist alliance. In truth, Spain had already signed secret treaties with the USA in September 1953 and allowed its naval bases to operate on Spanish soil, which did not augur well for the Hispanic Bloc initiative.[129] Worse yet, by the mid 1950s, it had become evident that the ICH was not achieving its projected goals. Of the institution's twenty-nine chapters, "only three have any content," bemoaned Sánchez Bella in 1954.[130] With Franco recalibrating his international image, it was up to the Nacionalistas to lead the Hispanic initiative. The ICH's 1958 congress in Bogotá was thus mainly Goyeneche's brainchild. Ever committed to the Hispanic Community of Nations vision, he now pledged to resist the "international monopolies" threatening Latin America.[131] In the late 1950s, Amadeo likewise continued to peddle the Hispanic Bloc pipe dream, even among Hispanics in New York City.[132]

All the same, the Hispanic Community of Nations initiative was defunct after 1954. As a result, the late 1950s witnessed the ICH undertaking more concrete, if discreet, methods to impact the minds and souls of Latin American elites. For example, by penetrating international organizations such as UNESCO, Sánchez Bella sought to legitimize Hispanic ideals as cultural heritage.[133] Franco's diplomacy of bilateral dual citizenship agreements, which facilitated bilateral movement and residency, was another case in point. Following Chile, between 1956 and 1963, Spain signed nine more of these treaties with Latin American nations – events that Colombian Hispanista Jesús María Yepes exaggeratingly deemed the onset of a "Hispanic supranationality."[134] The ICH's sub-agencies also began operating more systematically at this point. Adhering to the ICH but still not identified with Francoism, the aforementioned IHLADI, for instance, continued to define the unique legality upon which Latin American authoritarianism was to be established, against the "pseudo-values" of global international law.[135] An even more successful body was the Oficina de Educación Iberoamericana (OEI). Sánchez Bella's brainchild, it proclaimed itself to be an intergovernmental body promoting "educational unity in the Hispanic world."[136] The OEI had "no philosophy or political agenda," announced its first director, Carlos Lacalle. This did not prevent the OEI's internal communications from pledging to inspire "Catholic and Hispanista ideals" in Latin American youth, based on "the ideology that emerged from the pro-Hispanic Community of Nations."[137] All the same, by signing a treaty with UNESCO in 1957, the OEI was acknowledged as a legitimate international pedagogical body – a respectability Francoist institutions seldom enjoyed at the time.[138] As such, it was free to circulate pedagogical theories that combined "professionalism" and "spiritual education."[139] In the words of Nacionalista and OEI member Ramón Sepich, this educational method relied on scholastic and natural "sciences" but eliminated "speculative values."[140]

The OEI's strategies are essential for our story as they reveal how anti-Enlightenment sentiments were engrained in seemingly benign educational platforms. Lacalle went to great lengths to spell out the intricacies of this process. His following statement to the Falange newspaper *Arriba* even betrayed a somewhat apologetic tone:

> The men who in 1946 promoted cooperation among the Hispanic nations have reached 1958 truly satisfied ... However, Hispanidad is reborn as a controversial eruption ... With an anachronistic packaging, it is coated in a vague form and rigid sentimentality. Fortunately, we managed to fluidize its conception, link it to the [modern] historical process, and consider it as a continuation of a vital process born four centuries ago. This allowed us to avoid ... controversial situations, to disregard ideologies, and to rapidly constitute a group of organizations destined to orient and stimulate the cooperation between the members of our family of nations.[141]

In these elegant formulations lay a striking paradox: The OEI aimed to combine rational and irrational sciences. This, and the OEI's linkage to Madrid, did not go unnoticed in Latin America. By 1964, only seven countries had joined the OEI, excluding Mexico, Argentina, Venezuela, Chile, and Brazil. A minor achievement, it nonetheless illustrated that most Latin American governments did not fall prey to the ICH's operational tactics.[142]

Thus, in 1959, just before being transferred to the Dominican Republic to serve as Spain's ambassador, Sánchez Bella took stock of a decade of activity in frustration. "In all these countries, we are perceived as too conservative, too right-wing, excessively traditionalist," he admitted. The fact that Hispanidad appears "irrelevant to our times," he further confessed, meant that the leftists are winning the battle over public opinion aided by a "novel, more attractive, and stimulating political agenda."[143] Evidently, a month after Fidel Castro's Revolution sent tremors across Latin America, it had dawned on Sánchez Bella (Figure 1.2) that the defense of Hispanidad had reached the limits of its effectiveness as a mobilizing call among Latin American conservatives. Following his departure, the ICH perhaps remained a hotbed of international collaborations but never regained the aura of grandeur it enjoyed during the 1950s.

Sánchez Bella's disappointment is understandable but also reveals his hyperbolic initial expectations. Sure enough, the ICH yielded no concrete right-wing political action in Latin America, nor did the Hispanic Community of Nations materialize as the multilateral body as he had hoped for. A transitional stage between 1940s fascism and 1960s technocracy, Hispanidad was bound to fail as a political project for one obvious reason: It was at odds with its members' efforts to benefit from the Western Bloc's financial bonanza. Still, as an ideological project, the ICH was important for several reasons. For one, it represented a profound reckoning with the meanings of the failure of European fascism. The Hispanistas aimed not only to renounce their fascist lineage but to

FIGURE 1.2 Alfredo Sánchez Bella, 1960.
Bob Gomel / Getty Images

redefine their crusade and avoid a repetition of the fascist cataclysm. In doing so, they established a consensus on the mythological and ethical grounds that ought to be the bedrock of any future conservative modernity. As such, their work is crucial for understanding why and how Hispanic technocracy emerged in the 1960s. In fact, Sánchez Bella's lamentations were to prove erroneous. By the mid 1960s, hundreds of self-labeled Hispanistas were operating in Latin America and seeing themselves as members of a transnational crusade. Recognized as ideological powerhouses in their respective countries, they would reach positions of political power precisely due to their "Hispanic" and spiritual credentials. Indeed, the "technocrats" we will encounter in the pages that follow embodied a novel interpretation of Hispanidad's mythological thinking – not a break from it.

2

Technocratic Spain

Opus Dei and the Making of the "Second Francoist Era" (1957–1969)

In 1957, Spain was in a dismal economic state. While its infamous hunger years were perhaps in the past, unlike Salazar's Portugal, Greece, and even Turkey, Franco's Spain and Tito's Yugoslavia were excluded from the Marshall Plan. Thus, with its peculiar economic model – which entailed semi-autarchic production and protectionist markets – the regime suffered from an acute trade deficit, chronic inflation, and, more generally, seemed to be left behind in Europe's technological race. Then, instead of going under, Spain enjoyed a decade of astonishing economic growth rates that dwarfed even those of Germany and Japan. Following this "economic miracle," Spain – an allegedly underdeveloped agricultural nation – thus "changed its skin" socially, economically, culturally, and even psychologically, to take Fernández de la Mora's words at face value.

It is clear that the perception of this period of GDP growth as a "miracle" is a matter of perspective, shaped by one's expectations of the Spanish economy. In this chapter, I will indirectly address this question, focusing on the narrative of the so-called miracle. The Spanish economy, in many respects, was simply making up for years of stagnation. It is also more than fair to say that the regime exaggerated its economic accomplishments and used them as a tool to reinforce its authority. However, the economic upturn was an undeniable reality. It propelled the dictatorship to adopt a completely new narrative of its global role as an alternative modernity within the confines of the Western world. That is not to say that Francoism abandoned the legacies of the Civil War but that it found new justifications for its outbreak. Now, its anti-communist rhetoric gave place to a proudly technocratic theory of authoritarian development in which Franco appeared as a father figure who protected the country aloofly rather than directing it. More generally, for this chapter's characters, Spain came to represent how Hispanics could be both archaic and modern; to be technologically advanced consumers, while remaining as spiritually irrational as their pre-modern ancestors.

Opus Dei was the ideological powerhouse behind this transformation. Established in Madrid in 1928, this Catholic society developed a reciprocal relationship with Franco, thereby achieving a status of autonomy that civil society seldom enjoys in centralized military regimes. This chapter will first explore how Opus Dei initially functioned as an international ideological apparatus that promoted a holistic theory of humankind, society, and state. Next, we will inspect how this theory was put into practice and by whom when, in 1957, Franco appointed several Opus Dei members to lead his regime's economic overhaul. Opus Dei readily seized this opportunity to reshape the Francoist regime, thus replacing both the Falangist ideology of the 1940s and the traditionalist Hispanidad project of the 1950s with a regime model not previously seen in European history. Nicknamed "the technocrats," Opus Dei members thereby became synonymous with the "Spanish miracle." In sum, I will inspect Opus Dei as an abstract ideology, as an intellectual movement, and as a political actor that fashioned a palpable state ideology and concrete social realities.

One should be cautious about making sweeping generalizations about Opus Dei. It should be borne in mind that, contrary to its image in popular culture as a shadowy sect, this society has inspired generations of Catholics worldwide for nearly a century and has been an official organization of the Roman Catholic Church since 1947. This chapter focuses less on Opus Dei's practices and financial dealings and more on its ideological production at a particular point in time. As I will clarify in what follows, there was hardly anything secretive about Opus Dei's ideology. In truth, in the 1960s, it consciously and proudly sought to deconstruct fascist ideology and reorganize its elements in a new state model. As such, Opus Dei established itself in Latin America in ways that the ICH, as a semi-official Francoist institution, never quite could.

2.1 UNDERSTANDING OPUS DEI'S IDEOLOGY AND MODUS OPERANDI

While Franco distributed executive power among Spain's right-wing ideological "families," the Falangists were those who overall decided the regime's economic structure in its first two decades. Under the leadership of Fernández-Cuesta, in the 1950s, the Falange even underwent a political revival, thus promulgating an ever more confident ideology of state and society. As for the rest of the "families," these were traditionalists of various kinds who, as the 1950s progressed, were associated with one of two monarchist restoration groups: the "Juanistas" (who supported Juan de Borbón's claim to the throne) and the Carlists (who supported either Javier de Borbón-Parma or Carlos Pío de Habsburgo-Borbón). More often than not, these people participated in the 1950s Hispanidad movement, but their ideological orientation was less well-defined than the Falange's. Opus Dei was to arise from this habitat and give it a new ideological identity.

Opus Dei's link with the traditionalist camp dates back to 1928 when Josemaría Escrivá de Balaguer founded the society in Madrid. Only twenty-six years old, the priest was hardly a publicly renowned figure but nonetheless befriended several ACNP members, such as José Ibáñez Martín, Franco's future minister of education (1939–51). With the onslaught of the Spanish Civil War, Escrivá and his companions escaped Madrid and spent the war years in Burgos, where Escrivá befriended Franco and Carrero Blanco and even provided them with spiritual services.[1] "I have had and still have a good friendship with the Caudillo, who calls me frequently and speaks to me with great confidence," Escrivá said in 1969.[2] Even so, Opus Dei was hardly publicly renowned until 1946, when Escrivá and his inner circle relocated to the Vatican and persuaded Pope Pius XI to declare Opus Dei a secular institution. On this, the Madrid daily *ABC* reported laconically that Opus Dei members were "dedicated to the practice of Christian perfection ... through the sanctification of ordinary work and developing their apostolate within the intellectual sphere." Indeed, this would be the society's self-definition over the next decades.[3] Amid Spain's international isolation, Escrivá's acceptance into the heart of the Roman Catholic Church was an outstanding achievement.

Unlike previous traditionalist intellectual circles, Opus Dei operated as a community of believers who lived, and still live, according to the following basic format: Its "numerary" members, who take a vow of celibacy, reside in special abodes (or "casas") and work in ordinary jobs, whereas its "supernumerary" members marry and lead regular lives while partaking in the community's religious routines.[4] In the early days, all members pledged obedience to the society's semi-secretive "constitutions," which has made commentators question the true scale of their intellectual freedom.[5] All the same, while we know that Escrivá guided his followers on spiritual issues from Rome, it is also clear that Opus Dei never entirely operated as a hierarchical sect but rather as an ideological movement of like-minded disciples. Escrivá bestowed on them not political directives but two decisive instruments: a spiritual technique and an original ideological modus operandi.

Escrivá's spirituality is ostensibly simpler to approach, as it was canonized in one book: *Camino* ("The Way"). Written during the Civil War, and containing 999 stanzas, it is, however, an ideologically baffling text. Escrivá was unquestionably influenced by fascism when advocating a "crusade" against "the enemies of God," orchestrated by "militias" and "caudillos."[6] Still, the crux of his intellectual work was his technique of spiritual "perfection" within the modern world. Rather than negating modernity, he sought a format by which men and women could experience modern "everyday life" via a mystical sublime. Like the Jesuits before him, Escrivá proposed "spiritual exercises," a community built on the principles of "poverty, chastity, and obedience," and – perhaps Opus Dei's main contribution – a "sanctification" through everyday work as the channels for achieving this condition.[7] By performing their vocation to the best of their ability, thus becoming selfless servants "for the other," Catholic laypeople could "become saints" and experience the "supernatural" firsthand, was the theory. "No ideal can be materialized without sacrifice. Deny yourself! – It is so beautiful to be a victim!" was one of *Camino*'s most famous stanzas. This notion of self-sacrifice appeared in conjunction with a demand for outright infantilization. "As a child, when you truly are one, you are omnipotent," Escrivá wrote.[8]

All the same, how Opus Dei attained political power had little to do with this cryptic spirituality – or its public performance, which was hardly unusual in the Francoist liturgical landscape – but with Escrivá's cunning "infiltration" tactics into the "ecclesiastical, financial, political, and intellectual" spheres.[9] Having established itself in the Vatican, Opus Dei turned to mustering the financial resources to support its global operations. By the early 1960s, it controlled several Spanish banks and was discussed in public mostly as a financial corporation.[10] Regardless of whether it owned these enterprises, Opus Dei obviously could not have established its intellectual apparatus without considerably benefiting from them. Then again, given that Opus Dei's holdings were far from reaching the proportions of Spain's four big banking groups, its economic power should not be overstated.[11] Ultimately, Opus Dei's political power emanated from Escrivá's amity with the regime's leaders and his knack for persuading them of his movement's loyalty and dynamism.[12] How Opus Dei was pitched to Franco can be inferred from a letter sent to him from Álvaro del Portillo in 1952. Soliciting money for a new center in Great Britain, Escrivá's deputy flaunted his organization's global operations in the following manner:

> Our members' external activity has been directed primarily to the intellectual field, wherein the most urgent undertaking has been to collaborate and put ideas in order. In this field, we seek to work ... always through discreet and quiet personal intervention, which we consider the most effective. However, to better attend to the education of students it is necessary to establish some corporate institutions, and today we have ten colleges in Spain ... The influence of dark sects and subversive doctrines [might hinder] the achievements of the New State under the supreme direction of Your Excellency. [In Spain] there has been a complete restoration of a more Christian and just social order. We must devote ourselves to this difficult endeavor at all costs.[13]

Evidently, his letter promoted a symbiotic setup in which Franco would assist Opus Dei financially and allow it to flourish in Spain as a private institution, while the latter would direct its "corporation" against the regime's ideological foes internationally. Even more illuminating were the soft power strategies the letter proposed – namely, to "discreetly" mobilize Catholic elites worldwide by attraction. These words were in keeping with Opus Dei's constitutions, which instructed its members to make sure that their activities could "never be attributed to Opus Dei" while at the same time urging them to "hold official positions."[14] Sure enough, Opus Dei would always insist that its members attained power accidentally with no direction from above, thereby making them appear less an ideologically driven network than a sphere of impartial actors.

Still, Opus Dei's penetration into the Spanish intellectual sphere was anything but secret. A case in point was the CSIC, whose first director, José María Albareda, was one of Escrivá's first followers. An agronomist by training, this man strove, as a part of the "spiritual energies of Hispanidad," to restore the "Christian unity of the sciences, destroyed in the 18th century,"[15] which, for him, meant uncovering "God's footprints," so that one can "elevate oneself towards him."[16] Through CSIC, Albareda controlled the Spanish academy in an increasingly hegemonic fashion.[17] It was also here that Opus Dei's ideologues first became publicly visible, mostly in the CSIC's journal, *Arbor*. Led by Florentino Pérez-Embid (supernumerary) and Rafael Calvo Serer (numerary), the *Arbor* group – which included Ángel López-Amo (numerary), Vicente Rodríguez Casado (numerary), Álvaro d'Ors (supernumerary), and Víctor García Hoz (supernumerary) – first came to notoriety amid a heated philosophical debate with the Falange. Indeed, *Arbor*'s appearance coincided with a theoretical upheaval within the Falange. While intellectuals such as Francisco Javier Conde and Luis Legaz Lacambra focused on reviving José Antonio Primo de Rivera's national syndicalist doctrine, people such as Dionisio Ridruejo and Pedro Laín Entralgo began to promote the regime's political liberalization.[18] Strikingly, in his book *España como problema* from 1949, Laín Entralgo even dared to cast doubt on the Hispanidad mythology by stressing that the pre-modern "Hispanic" and modern "European" civilizations were not incongruous and could amalgamate.[19] The *Arbor* intellectuals seized this opportunity to prove to Franco their worth. In what became known as the "Spanish essence" debate ("ser de España"), Pérez-Embid confronted Laín Entralgo and confirmed the Francoist restoration of "spiritual unity."[20] Calvo Serer followed suit with a book titled *España sin problema*, where he restated that Hispanidad was "discordant to modernity."[21] Yet the *Arbor* ideologues went further than this and criticized the Falange's erroneous "revolution," suggesting instead their "theory of restoration." Sure enough, by the mid 1950s, Calvo Serer was musing over a "middle-of-the-road" state model between "fascist totalitarianism and a lame democracy."[22] He also founded an association named Tercera Fuerza ("Third Force") with Fernández de la Mora, in order to give this new "Hispanic Europeanness" a concrete meaning.[23]

Calvo Serer was a charismatic and prolific thinker but suffered from a temper that did not sit well with Opus Dei's discreet ways. Once he had done the unthinkable and criticized the Falange in a French far-right journal named *Ecrits de Paris*, in 1953, Franco excommunicated him.[24] Hereafter, it was the more astute Pérez-Embid who was to lay the foundations for Spain's Hispanic technocracy. This he began to do in 1953 with a book titled *Ambiciones españolas*, where he presented the decisive aphorism "Spanishization in the ends and Europeanization in the means."[25] It meant the Hispanic nations were to cherry-pick techniques to "scientifically" improve their material condition, thereby facilitating the formation of an insulated cultural and ethical domain. Next, in *Nosotros, los cristianos* (1956), he transformed *Camino* into a lucid ideology. The state should guide its subjects towards "Christian perfection, a supernatural life of surrender, and a life of holiness," it stressed.[26] Devoid of coercion, this society would be neither totalitarian nor liberal, it also clarified. In Pérez-Embid's words:

> In the liberal century, when we talked about freedom, we spoke of freedom of association, of expression ... of choosing political programs and ideals, of choosing parliamentary deputies ... today, we clearly see that the world is not a massive juxtaposition of independent, autonomous, unconnected microworlds, but an organic architecture of interdependent men, dependent on each other ... From this recognition, stems the idea of the Christian personal freedom of man.[27]

Patently, Pérez-Embid thought the Enlightenment had given man a phony liberty to choose between secular ideologies that ultimately led to atomization and ruin. The time was ripe, he thus thought, for a slight recalibration; for acknowledging man's "inner limitation" as a political subject, thereby granting him the "external liberty that he desires."[28]

Opus Dei's theory of anti-totalitarian "liberty" belied its unapologetic militarism and support of political violence. Notably, Álvaro d'Ors, a prominent Opus Dei thinker, had little scruples when railing against the Western "obsessive idea of peace," in a text instructively titled "*Silent leges inter arma*" (in times of war, the law falls silent).[29] This anti-pacific stance, which was indicative of how Opus Dei catered to the armed forces, became even more overt in Pérez-Embid's new project: the reformation of a nineteenth-century elitist forum named El Ateneo de Madrid. A lecture given there by General Jorge Vigon saw Pérez-Embid introducing his infamously ruthless guest speaker by praising the "spirit of July 18" and the Spanish armed forces liquidating the Republic.[30] Between 1951 and 1956, the Ateneo hosted prominent European guests, ranging from lightweight conservatives such as Christopher Dawson and Gustave Thibon to heavyweight fascists such as Carl Schmitt.[31] Sure enough, in the mid 1950s, Opus Dei not only echoed the Nazi theorist's theories of authoritarian action but competed with the Falange over publishing his texts – an effort that would wane considerably in the 1960s.[32]

Still, elitist intellectual circles were hardly where Opus Dei's ideological production truly played out. This took its complete form at Opus Dei's network of private colleges, the most significant of which were the Colegio Mayor Moncloa (Madrid) and the Estudio General de Navarra (Pamplona). Directed by Ismael Sánchez Bella (numerary) – Alfredo Sánchez Bella's brother – and renamed the University of Navarra (UNAV) in 1960, the latter was the only private university in Spain at the time and the only institution officially belonging to Opus Dei.[33] These centers operated in tandem with a substantial publishing apparatus (SARPE), which, financed by a special financial corporation (ESFINA), was primarily guided by Pérez-Embid and Antonio Fontán, the UNAV

Institute of Journalism's director. While the former directed the Opus Dei book publisher Rialp and the Biblioteca del Pensamiento Actual book series,[34] the latter edited the magazine *Actualidad Española* where he too argued that, between Americanization and Europeanization, Spain should devise a "third path," comprising "fundamental religious unity" and the modernization of its industrial production.[35] Fontán also edited UNAV's intellectual journal *Nuestro Tiempo*, which was to be the template for similar journals in Latin America, and was a theorist of the concept of the private "Catholic press" that should replace the Falange's state-sponsored propaganda.[36]

With the passage of time, it became evident that Opus Dei, too, was engrossed with Latin America. True, its first casas outside Spain were established in France, Italy, the USA, and West Germany, and it was absent from the ICH's activity. Even so, its ideologues readily joined the rest of the regime in depicting Latin America as an urgent ideological battlefield. Spanish-America must be fused into a "third great bloc," wrote Calvo Serer.[37] Pérez-Embid agreed. The "projection towards America," he said, is a "constant effort born of the very roots of our selfhood."[38] Yet Opus Dei's operational methods differed markedly from those of the ICH, as one of Pérez-Embid's strategy papers laid bare. To his mind, the thing that endangered Latin America most was not communism but Western cultural institutions that, "organized in a clear freemasonic fashion," operated independently from their mother nations. Spain's "cultural action," on the other hand, left much to be desired. Being heavy-handedly directed by "controversial institutions" supervised by the "embassies and legations," it discouraged Latin America's conservatives – who would otherwise "collaborate in the task of integrating Hispanic culture within a broad Catholic system of life" – from collaborating with Spain, Pérez-Embid lamented. Thus, he recommended a new strategy: First, Spanish numeraries would "settle in America permanently," thereby "spreading and integrating our common Hispanic culture" effectively. Second, Latin American recruits would be brought to study in Spain, and, thus, "in a relatively short time" Opus Dei would "have at its disposal" a "homogeneous group of intellectuals who would occupy vital positions in those countries."[39]

This was indeed the order in which things ultimately transpired. In 1949 and 1950, supported by local elites and a Francoist-sympathetic episcopal hierarchy, Opus Dei established casas in Mexico, Argentina, and Chile. In the case of Argentina, it was Cardinal Antonio Caggiano, archbishop of Rosario, who, having encountered Escrivá in Rome, readily assisted Opus Dei.[40] In turn, Ismael Sánchez Bella arrived in Buenos Aires in March 1950, with a diplomatic passport and sponsored by the ICH, to set the foundations for the Opus Dei operations there.[41] His conferences were replete with "Hispanistas, doctors, engineers, and young professionals," he recalled.[42] A similar dynamic occurred in Chile, where Adolfo Rodríguez Vidal (numerary) received Archbishop José María Caro Rodríguez's blessing, paving the way for Opus Dei's arrival.[43] Like Caggiano, Caro Rodríguez had befriended Escrivá in Rome and endorsed Opus Dei in advance.[44]

And sure enough, in the late 1950s, Opus Dei began bringing its Latin American recruits to UNAV, where they became acquainted with its methods of ideological production. A prime example was Carlos Llano Cifuentes. Born in 1932, this Mexican finished his doctoral studies at UNAV, returned to Mexico, and started the intellectual journal *Istmo* in 1959. Later, he became one of the founding members of the Pan American Institute of Senior Business Management (IPADE). Colombians David Mejía Velilla and Javier Abad Gómez underwent a similar trajectory. Upon returning to Colombia, they founded the journal *Arco*.[45] Perhaps the most salient example was that of José Miguel Ibáñez Langlois and Ernesto García Alesanco. Only nineteen years old when meeting Escrivá, these two priests would become Opus Dei's spiritual guides in Argentina and Chile respectively. As Ibáñez Langlois wrote to his teacher, the Hispanista Esteban Scarpa, he joined Escrivá to experience "the immense joy of living the spirit of Opus Dei fully."[46] Escrivá, García Alesanco later recalled, "wanted many of the first [Latin American] recruits at his side."[47] Thus, the two dwelled in Rome for a period, after which they relocated to UNAV, where they studied journalism and practiced publishing anti-democratic editorials in *Nuestro Tiempo*. "Democracy," García Alesanco wrote there, "is only a myth wherein different groups interfere with the government's freedom of action. It produces a profound economic, political, and military crisis."[48] In Navarra, they also "formulated the project, which later crystallized in the journal *Cuadernos del Sur*."[49] True to form, *Istmo*, *Arco*, and *Cuadernos del Sur* resembled *Nuestro Tiempo* stylistically and showcased many of Spain's Opus Dei intellectuals, along with articles on Escrivá's spirituality.[50] That Opus Dei priests such as José Orlandis stated that Opus Dei members "are in open opposition to the Franco regime" only rendered more manifest yet another of Opus Dei's soft power tactics: to promote authoritarianism unanimously while claiming to be a pluralistic spiritual society.[51] And promote authoritarianism they did, once again, to audiences still living under parliamentary democracies. To them, suggestively, Álvaro d'Ors now spoke of authority "regaining its privileges."[52] Political parties were detrimental to liberty, he also stressed, since they breed irrational "pressure and conquest" groups. Only Catholicism, he thus surmised, offers "a pluralistic structuring where freedom is constituted as a discharge of natural powers, instead of a concentration of power by a necessarily totalitarian state."[53]

Gradually, Opus Dei began promoting a more distinctive state model. Against the Falange's conception of national syndicalism, and siding with Juan III's political camp, its intellectuals led the theorization of Spain's authoritarian monarchy.[54] Ángel López-Amo was Don Juan's private council member, together with Pérez-Embid. His influential book *La Monarquía de la reforma social* had less to do with monarchism and more with the crisis of the modern state.[55] A "dead abstraction on a dead society," with a "fraudulent and corrupt" self-serving administration, parliamentary democracy will always lead to civil war in the Catholic world, he argued.[56] Mussolini's fascism, he added, likewise relied on a revolutionary elite that, true to form, was incapable of "working within society."[57] As an alternative to both, López-Amo proposed a new authoritarian template where the monarch serves as an empty symbol of authority, "stripped from what is not his to hold."[58] In the same vein, and being the tutor of Prince Juan Carlos – Juan III's elder son and heir to the throne – López-Amo wrote his royal apprentice a series of "academic letters" where he underscored another critical point: This king's mandate does not necessarily derive from the grace of God but from his constructive influence on "men of government, administrators and technicians" and overall "popular authority."[59] To back this theory, he and other Opus Dei intellectuals overhauled their mythological underpinnings. Rather than focusing on the Habsburgian era – the Hispanistas' undisputed "golden age" – they touted the Bourbon dynasty (1700–1810) as the epitome of a "homogeneous" administration skillfully integrating empirical sciences and Catholic spirituality.[60] For Vicente Rodríguez Casado, King Carlos III's reign, in particular, exemplified how a "modernizing traditionalist" had succeeded in salvaging an empire beset by modern sociological dynamics (the "growth of the middle classes") by applying both rational and irrational forms of knowledge.[61]

But if the monarch is a powerless authority, who will administer this non-statist regime? Or, in Pérez-Embid's words, how does one guarantee that the state becomes "neither the dictatorship of the proletariat, nor the dictatorship of the aristocracy, nor the dictatorship of the capitalist bourgeoisie"? His answer: The modern state should be administered by "directing minorities."[62] Certainly, one should *render unto Caesar* where the restoration of peace is concerned, posited Andrés Vázquez de Prada (numerary). Still, he wrote, from this point of departure, it is incumbent upon society to unearth its authentic "*élite politique*" – that is, a group of "disinterested"[63] men who would act for the common good while the rest of the citizenry "grazes as a flock of sheep."[64] In López-Amo's view, this also meant that the masses should appreciatively "decide to stop being masses" and allow these exceptional men to rule them.[65] Still, this new elite's political talent, Vázquez de Prada also highlighted, relied not on its aristocratic lineage but on a unique spiritual condition:

> The political effort must be born within the individual, as a family man, as a professional . . . If men and women perform their duties well, quietly, we will see a miracle: a nation rising to its feet . . . external change must be the product of inner renewal. There will be no advances through revolutionary bursts if the transformation does not occur "from within" . . . Monarchy or republic, authoritarianism or liberalism – these are all empty shells once the fruit goes inside.[66]

Unquestionably, these words disparaged the Falange's revolutionary ethos and questioned the conception of the state as an agent of social development. On the one hand, they betrayed a technocratic theory of an aloof state empowering autonomous specialists to do its bidding. On the other hand, Vázquez de Prada turned Escrivá's spirituality into a holistic theory wherein the anti-Enlightenment crusade shifts from the battlefield into the specialist's home and body. In short, Opus Dei reiterated the traditionalists' notion of aristocratic rule but also revised and broadened it. Sooner rather than later, it would set an example for how "directing minorities" operated as a spiritual modernizer in practice.

2.2 THE "TECHNOCRATS" IN POWER: REDEFINING THE FRANCOIST MODERNITY (1956–1967)

By the mid 1950s, Opus Dei was perhaps an ideological powerhouse but, despite its fidelity to the regime's principles, it had almost no executive power.[67] It was a crisis within the ranks of its ideological rivals, the Falange, that was to change this state of affairs. In February 1956, students from Madrid University – mainly followers of the Falange's liberal intellectuals – protested in a demand for academic freedom and were brutally dispersed. This rare incident led Franco to sack Ridjuerjo and Laín Entralgo from their academic positions, followed by Education

Minister Joaquín Ruiz-Giménez.[68] It also led to the replacement of Raimundo Fernández-Cuetsa with José Luis de Arrese as the Falange's Secretary General. A member of José Antonio's original circle, Arrese was a true national syndicalist who openly rejected the 1947 Law of Succession. In February 1957, he revealed his plan to promulgate the "Fundamental Laws of the Movimiento," which would instigate the Falange's long-awaited "pending" national syndicalist revolution and institutionalize the regime based on a one-party system. In 1956, the Falange, though it controlled the Movimiento, was witnessing a decline in its authority in economic matters compared to the Ministries of Labor and the Economy. Arrese's plan to centralize all economic activity under the Syndical Organization's control was a potential game-changer. It could have made the Falange the sole intermediary between the state and its citizens, if not a state within a state, significantly altering the existing power dynamics.[69]

Arrese's ambitious neofascist project galvanized an anti-Falange coalition around Luis Carrero Blanco. Also referred to as Franco's *éminence grise*, the admiral was a devout Catholic who believed in the "divine will" guiding Francoism.[70] He was also, to his mind, a military historian and specialized in the Battle of Lepanto – the Habsburg Empire's glorious victory over the Ottoman Empire in 1571.[71] In November 1956, Carrero Blanco approached an Opus Dei numerary named Laureano López Rodó (Figure 2.1) – a Catalonian, CSIC member, and an expert in public administration.[72] Thus began the "intimate collaboration" between him and "that great figure that was Luis Carrero Blanco," López Rodó later reminisced.[73] López Rodó was a sophisticated ideologue and the one responsible for Hispanic technocracy's motion from abstract theory to state ideology. In January 1957, his "Report on the Reorganization of the Central State Administration" was pitched to Franco by Carrero Blanco as an alternative to de Aresse's project and a roadmap for Spain's economic and ideological restructuring. In an unusually honest tenor, López Rodó stated that Spain lacks "corporations, municipal life, and organic life of any kind," not to mention a functional single party. Thus, he recommended that Franco neither resurrect any fascist model nor constitute a "useless" parliamentary democracy but establish an "effective, fair, and strong central power" supported by a system of representation – two entities that shall not "interfere or distort each other." This control center would prevent a "class-based" government from emerging and "decentralize the administration," a process that would also consist of replacing the Movimiento with civil councils within each ministry. As such, his plan

FIGURE 2.1 Laureano López Rodó, 1976.
Gianni Ferrari / Getty Images

reflected the Spaniards' "unmistakable physiognomy" better than the Falange's anachronisms, López Rodó assured his leader.[74]

More concretely, the plan envisaged a dictatorship wherein a supreme commander is assisted by a nonelected council and a "prime minister," who is chosen from and by the council and acts as a chief executive. Below them, a senate (Junta Suprema de Consejos) consisting of the ministries' councils functions as a legislative power. Last, beneath them, a national assembly provides society members with a conduit to express their opinions unabated to the "secretary of state" and, through him, to the government. Naturally, López Rodó's assembly would be devoid of political parties or "disruptive" general elections, and its members would be selected from their "organic" social units according to fixed quotas. Tellingly, the plan also undermined the representational weight of industrial unions (72 seats) – the Falange's assumed stronghold – in comparison with the municipalities (120), the universities (70), and the "agricultural sector" (90). On top of this, this entirely advisory system would be strictly limited to those holding "moral and religious values."[75] Despite all of this, given that the head of state was to react, if necessary, to his ministers' initiatives rather than administer the state, this model was, to López Rodó's mind, a perfectly fitting alternative to the Western democracies' modes of checks and balances and separation of powers, and would later be propagated internationally as such.

Irrespective of whether Franco fully understood López Rodó's convoluted scheme, there is no denying that, by 1956, he perceived the Falange as the anachronism that it was and identified Carrero Blanco as his "most loyal and intimate advisor," in López Rodó's words.[76] Thus, in December 1956, Franco heeded his deputy's advice and appointed López Rodó as general technical secretary of the Presidency of the Government under Carrero Blanco – a secretariat that was to be the engine behind the reform. A few months later, he reshuffled his government completely, replacing the Falange economic ministers with Opus Dei supernumeraries Alberto Ullastres (minister of commerce) and Mariano Navarro Rubio (minister of finance). On this occasion, Falange diehards such as José Antonio Girón and Hispanistas such as Alberto Martín-Artajo were likewise shown the door, while Arrese was relegated to an unimportant ministry and soon retired from politics. In brief, this was not an ordinary reshuffle; it was a regime forsaking its two ideological pillars – fascism and traditionalism – for an entirely unknown economic, cultural, and ideological future.

To be sure, López Rodó, Navarro Rubio, and Ullastres did not enjoy unlimited power. As always, Franco divided power between them and a handful of Falange ministers. The Movimiento, too, remained intact. All the same, the Opus Dei ministers had a brief opportunity to restructure the regime's economic and juridical basis as they saw fit. They seized it with both hands with two pieces of legislation. First, the 1957 Law of the Juridical System of the Administration granted supreme executive power to the Presidency of the Government to "channel and coordinate" all ministries according to the "common government program," as well as to establish its independent Office of Economic Coordination and Programming.[77] Second, the May 1958 Ley de Principios del Movimiento Nacional (Principles of the National Movement Law) showcased the foundation for a final Francoist constitution. The brainchild of López Rodó and Fernández de la Mora, this law abolished Arrese's constitutional project entirely by declaring Spain a "traditionally Catholic, social, and representative Monarchy" based on a system of representation through the "family, municipality, and unions."[78] These laws, López Rodó would state triumphantly, relieved Spain of the Falange's slogans, which "after almost a quarter of a century, were obsolete."[79] The stage was now set for Spain's economic remodeling.

When did the Spanish miracle begin, really? For many, it dates back to June 1957, with the advent of the SEAT auto company's "600" model, which came to symbolize Spain's new industrial era. To my mind, more fundamental dates would be May and July 1958, when Spain was incorporated into the IMF and the World Bank, respectively. Spain's 1959 Stabilization Plan, which was designed with the aid of Gabriel Ferrás, director of the IMF's European department, was announced two weeks later.[80] Its objectives were twofold: reducing inflation and decreasing foreign debt by creating "extremely favorable conditions for rapid growth."[81] Thus, its first measures included liberalizing foreign trade, reducing tariffs, and eliminating price controls. This was followed by the admission of international currency into the country and up to 50 percent foreign participation in Spanish companies. A second phase of measures included a 40 percent devaluation of the peseta against the US dollar, cutting Spain's foreign debt dramatically overnight.

For incorporating itself into the Western financial system in this way, Spain received an aid package of nearly $540,000,000 predominantly from the IMF, the US government, and US banks.[82] Retrospectively, López Rodó explained this intricate procedure in entirely simplistic, almost childlike, terms:

> No economy can cook in its own sauce. I believe that the integration into the supranational economic sphere is a decisive factor for economic development ... this intensification of growth rates carries no detriment to any of the countries that are integrated into a supranational zone ... According to the well-known phrase "the big fish eats the little one," one would think that Germany would eat Italy. However, the Italian economy has not suffered from integration into the Common Market.[83]

Yet Spain was not Italy. Devoid of the right to either strike or vote, its workforce was far cheaper and more docile than its Western European counterparts. Spain's consumer market, too, was entirely captive, and its citizens' capital was restricted (to prevent money from being sent overseas, the technocrats enacted harsh penalties on capital flight). Coupled with low tax rates and geographic proximity to Western Europe's industrial centers, it is hardly surprising that Spain quickly became a haven for foreign investors.

It did not take the international press long to notice the enigmatic group transforming Spain. No sooner had the Opus Dei ministers been assigned than *The New York Times* reported on the group's influence over the "government agencies that control public opinion."[84] Truly, from being a hitherto unknown society, Opus Dei quickly captivated the imagination of spectators worldwide. Escrivá was both surprised and delighted at his society's new political power. Detached from Opus Dei's activity in Spain, in his Rome residence, he might not have fully comprehended the consequences of these ideological shifts. Either that, or he applied Opus Dei's soft power language to Franco, too. Nothing else could explain the letter he sent Franco in 1958, expressing his satisfaction with the Principles of the National Movement Law. After underlining that he had been "removed from all political activity," he congratulated Franco for identifying the "divine blessing of the men now in positions of authority" and assured him that they would be the "best guarantee of the government's success."[85] Whatever the letter's ad hoc objectives were, it should be read primarily as Escrivá's pledge of allegiance to the regime.

Still, the reciprocal relationship with Franco jeopardized Escrivá's aspirations as an international spiritual icon. This fact meant that Opus Dei had little choice but to deploy various public relations strategies, the most prominent of which was stressing – demonstrably falsely – that the movement "is not involved in the public life of any country."[86] As Opus Dei's head spokesman, Pérez-Embid even went so far as to approach Western journalists to complain about their "political" coverage of the society.[87] Opus Dei has "no secrets," no "infiltrations," no "ownership of newspapers," and its members are "free to follow any ideological path they so choose," he asserted.[88] In elaborate interviews, Escrivá, for his part, conveyed a simple – and, to his judgment, apolitical – message of personal liberty and the love of work.[89] And when *Time* magazine's reporter Peter Forbath asked him whether Francoism had ever "contributed to Opus Dei's growth," he retorted that the opposite was true. "In Spain, we have had the greatest difficulties in making the Work take root," he complained.[90]

This statement, too, was patently false. Opus Dei ministers and intellectuals operated in coordination towards concrete political goals, often openly and celebratedly. And when they chose more discreet settings, Franco's agents were there to spy on them and report to their superiors on their activities. According to one such report: "There was a large number of Opus leaders with current political influence, including Fernández de la Mora, Pérez-Embid, Rodríguez Casado, López Rodó, and others. They addressed the next meeting of [Juan III's] Private Council in Estoril and the current internal political situation. As we know, Hotel Richmond is controlled by [Opus Dei]."[91] Indeed, from 1959, when speaking of the "technocrats," the Spanish press was referring to this group of men. While López Rodó, Navarro Rubio, and Ullastares oversaw Spain's economic reform, Pérez-Embid, Fernández de la Mora, and Rodríguez Casado narrated the country's ideological makeover in public. How the Spanish miracle was explained to the public was, actually, as paramount as the de facto economic shift taking place in 1960s Spain.

Why the Opus Dei ideologues operated in unison also stemmed from the Stabilization Plan's unpopular effects and how Opus Dei's adversaries weaponized them. By 1960, it had become clear who was paying the price for Spain's economic reforms: the Spanish working class. After all, the 1959 plan also comprised a wage freeze and the termination of unprofitable government-held industries, resulting in the laying off of thousands of workers. Additionally, with cheap foreign goods inundating the Spanish market, local products became unprofitable, leading to the closure of small businesses and further unemployment. Hence, while the plan did succeed in curbing inflation down to 2.4 percent in 1959 (from 12 percent in 1958), it left Spanish workers to their fate. Impoverished and unemployed, some three million of them would leave the country during the early 1960s to seek work in Western Europe, in what Franco's opposition called "exporting the poor and importing the rich."[92] The hard currency these men sent home (or "emigrant remittances") rose from $48,000,000 in 1960 to $238,000,000 in 1964, and made for some 17 percent of the state's revenue, which, together with a growing touristic economy, was a crucial unexpected factor propelling the Spanish miracle.[93]

The Stabilization Plan's cruelty also marked the first denunciations of the technocrats' state model, notably from Falangist quarters. In January 1962, Blas Piñar, who had succeeded Sánchez Bella as the ICH's director in 1959, published a text titled "Hipócritas," in which he attacked the USA for "yoking underdeveloped nations under total economic dependency."[94] He was one of several Civil War-generation Falangists who, by then, had become dismayed by Spain's submission to the USA's economic and cultural order and were demanding a return to José Antonio's "pending" revolution. While Piñar's conduct left Franco no choice but to dismiss him, he and his group, *Fuerza Nueva*, would become the technocrats' fiercest critiques from the right in the 1960s, as will be considered in Chapter 5.[95] The reforms faced further challenges in the spring of 1962 as Spain witnessed a series of massive workers' strikes, most notably at the Asturias mines ("La huelgona") – an event that ushered in an era of strikes and was solved after José Solís Ruiz, the general secretary of the Movimiento, caved into some of the strikers' demands. Against this backdrop, on June 5, 1962, Franco's democratic opposition came out into the open and, at the Munich Congress of Europeanists, demanded Spain's transition to democracy.[96] The fact that the conference was led by monarchists – most famously Ruiz-Giménez, but, as rumors had it, also by Juan III's representatives – led Franco to penalize the Count of Barcelona by empowering the Falange once more. First, he picked General Agustin Muñoz Grandes, a neofascist and Falange symbol, as his first vice president of government. Second, he appointed Manuel Fraga minister of tourism and information. A Falange intellectual and the founder of journals such as *Alférez*, Fraga was a power-craving ideological chameleon who seized the opportunity to take credit for Spain's touristic boom and brand himself the regime's reformer. In a parallel vein, Solís became yet another obstacle in the technocrats' quest for power. By expanding the Organización Sindical Española (OSE) – thus seeking to make the labor unions independent from the state – and promoting the industrial workers' welfare through organizations such as Educación y Descanso (Education and Recreation), he harnessed their support, thereby enhancing the Falange's political power.

As Fraga orchestrated Spain's "spectacle of tourism," the technocrats coordinated a marvel of a somewhat different nature.[97] At their request, in 1961, the World Bank sent a commission to study "all aspects of Spain's economy." Headed by Sir Hugh Ellis-Rees, its report was the basis for what soon became known as the first Development Plan (1964–67).[98] In López Rodó's view, the plan's primary objective was to utilize foreign investments to modernize Spain's "underdeveloped" rural areas and diversify their production.[99] By receiving a status of "poles of industrial development" and "polygons of economic promotion," these areas were to receive incentives for industrialists willing to build assembly lines there.[100] Consequently, from 1962, the Spanish public sphere was submerged in a wave of statistics about job making and the projected elevation in the nation's GDP. In this spectacle of social engineering, the Spaniards were expected to acquire a "development mentality," which meant being fully employed but not overconsuming ("save and export"), not for any Opus Dei Weberian "ethics" – as sociologists have claimed – but to maintain trade low deficits vis-à-vis the industrialized West.[101]

With three consecutive years of double-digit GDP rates under its belt, the regime turned to narrate its miracle in the most ostentatious of ways. In 1964, a book titled *España cambia de piel: (Nuevo viaje por la "España del Milagro")* presented this narrative's two quintessential tropes: the "Spanish miracle" and the Spanish "change of skin."

Written by the Mexican-born author Waldo de Mier, this was an extravaganza of statistics and exclamation marks ("Pamplona is already in the year 2000!"),[102] and the first in an avalanche of publications commemorating the regime's "twenty-five years of peace."[103] Devoid of Hispanidad sentimentality, these publications presented Spain's economic development as the fundamental justification for the war. At times, "peace" appeared as an accolade to the Spanish people for laying ideologies to rest and enduring a period of economic hardship for a better future.[104] At other times, "peace" appeared as the indisputable achievement of authoritarianism. López Rodó readily introduced Walt Whitman Rostow's theories into the Francoist context to clarify this point. The American economist, he argued, conditioned any "economic take-off" on the presence of "an exceptional man" who could "catalyze" the nation's "latent energies." Needless to say, for López Rodó, Franco was that man.[105] The peace his leader had granted his people *from* mass politics had transformed a country "in decay" into a "new resurrected nation," he told his Argentine audience in 1966.[106] Why the workers chose peace over ideologies was answered by crediting them with a nuanced understanding of both their inferior geopolitical status and the new necessities born with technological acceleration, or "vertigo." Modern life, López Rodó surmised, in its "dizzying pace of new collective needs," demands an "aerodynamic" administration that would throw away "as scrap, outdated and useless mechanisms."[107]

Still, as the 1960s continued, the technocrats depicted the masses less as conscious collaborators and more as passive consumers amid a deterministic motion from ideological to "realist" thinking. Fernández de la Mora had been writing on this topic from the early 1960s, in an effort that reached its apex in his 1965 book *El crepúsculo de las ideologías*. Published and promoted intensely by Opus Dei, it took issue with the myth of Spain's Quixotic irrationality, announcing that Cervantes's book was "ironic and absurd." Then, it portrayed the Enlightenment's ideologies as "products of mass consumption" that plague only underdeveloped societies.[108] This was hardly a unique theory in the 1960s. The exhaustive intellectual debate on the "end of ideology" – conducted since the late 1930s by Karl Mannheim, Raymond Aron, Daniel Bell, and Seymour Martin Lipset – had already become something of a cliché with the rise of the New Left. Fernández de la Mora merely sought to usurp it by using the Spanish miracle as his case study. He posited that, with the advent of consumption, humankind had undergone a "transformation of mentality" and a "leisure depoliticization."[109] Hence, he "no longer demands ideologists, but experts."[110] These assertions led Fernández de la Mora to demand that the masses be given what they wanted – namely, freedom from the malaise of politics. Strikingly, he did not reference Schmitt, or any theorists of authoritarian power for that matter, but relied entirely on the Spanish miracle and technocratic reasoning. As we shall soon observe, while understandably ignored by Western scholars, the text was enthusiastically debated in Latin American right-wing quarters.

By this time, the Spanish press had begun calling the Opus Dei ministers "the technocrats." Fernández de la Mora flatly rejected this label by stating that, unlike the amoral "passive" technocracy taking hold in the West, Spain's "active" technocracy recognized what growth "is good for."[111] López Rodó elaborated on this point by underlying that economic growth was the new motor behind the creation of a Hispanic "new man" at best or the "elevation of the stature of the Spanish man" at a minimum.[112] He also coined other catchphrases such as the "return to man" ahead of his second and third Development Plans, by which he meant that GDP growth aimed to produce "free men" living in solidarity and order, not through "coercion" but because of their material welfare.[113] "Our conception of the economy is genuinely humanist," he exclaimed.[114] And besides, he said, modern alienation – be it on the manufacturing line or due to the "vacuum" of being liberated from poverty – can only be answered through spiritual work and "sacrifice."[115] This "welfare" rhetoric responded not only to the Falange's criticism but to John XXIII's 1961 encyclical *Mater et Magistra*. As devout Catholics, the Opus Dei ministers could not ignore the pope's directive to social justice.

Not all Opus Dei intellectuals aligned with these ideas of depoliticization. In effect, theorizing a system for civil representation to replace the Falange's national syndicalism was an essential aspect of Opus Dei's intellectual work in the 1960s. Their point of departure was Vázquez de Mella's concept of "intermediary corporations." The French Revolution, claimed the Spanish traditionalist in 1908, had destroyed the "network of intermediary corporations operating between the individual and the state."[116] Their second theoretical pillar was Pius XI's 1931 encyclical *Quadragesimo Anno*, which canonized the "subsidiary state." Originally in quotation marks, this trope represented an authoritarian alternative to fascism that returned power to society – not to the workers, to be sure ("Strikes and lockouts are forbidden," the pope clarified), but to the elites. The terms "intermediary societies" and "subsidiary state" were most effectively merged in the works of Luis Sánchez Agesta. This Ateneo de

Madrid member's book, *Los principios cristianos del orden politico* from 1962, depicted a political order based on the "separation of powers" between society's "natural groups" and the state. His interpretation of subsidiarity boiled down to the following: Only natural groups – the family, professional associations, and the municipality – may have "natural rights" and thus acquire political power, with a peacekeeper benignly protecting, guiding, and only if needed, abetting them.[117] In 1964, Álvaro d'Ors joined Sánchez Agesta. In a text titled "Autoridad y potestad," he rejected Montesquieu's "artificial" separation of powers by conjoining the "subsidiary state" and "intermediary societies" into a supposedly superior power-division principle, based on an authoritarian ruler "renouncing power" voluntarily.[118] By 1966, Sánchez Agesta declared that Europe exhibited three regime models: the "liberal" (democracy), the "totalitarian" (communism), and the "pluralist-corporate" (Francoism), the latter being the only one to foster the "natural character of the intermediary associations." On this occasion, he also boasted that Spain's model is the most successful of the three, as it situates man in a "concrete world" of preexisting "channels for his activity" – rather than in a world of alienating abstractions – and, as such, has "a great future ahead of it."[119]

For all these contentions that Francoism had become a democracy of a different ilk, Spain remained an outcast in Western European politics. That its request to join the European Community in February 1962 was outright rejected by France, Italy, and Germany, confirmed this in the most humiliating way.[120] Even so, Spain was not only opening itself to the world but proactively seeking to establish itself as an international economic player. In the spirit of détente, it assumed amicable relationships with socialist regimes across Eastern Europe, and promoted acquisition deals for Spanish auto companies with Latin American regimes such as Castro's Cuba and Salvador Allende's Chile. True to form, these acts were presented as a natural continuation of Hispanidad and the struggle against US imperialism.[121] How did the Latin American conservatives view this change? Mariano Fontecilla, one of Pinochet's advisors, reflected on this issue retrospectively: "Spain wanted to show Europe, which until now had not treated it with much confidence, that it had ceased to be a country full of dated dogmas and was progressively opening up to the contemporary moment. Hence its relations with Cuba, the opening to Eastern Europe, and generous attitude towards … Allende."[122] Indeed, to its more perceptive admirers, Francoism exhibited how one could appear moderate in Western eyes, and even do business with communists while concurrently persecuting them within one's national borders.

2.3 PRODUCING "SPIRITUAL" CONSUMERS: OPUS DEI AND MORALISM IN 1960S SPAIN

Between 1960 and 1972, Spain saw foreign investments, mainly from the USA, West Germany, France, and Switzerland, swelling from $100,000,000 to $1,000,000,000 and its GDP more than tripling (from $408 to $1,708 in current US dollars).[123] As early as 1966, the Spanish miracle was considered internationally as a solid fact. For Rodney Mills, of the USA's Federal Reserve System Board of Governors, the word "miracle" seemed "particularly apt" in the Spain of 1965.[124] "One speaks of a Spanish miracle the same as of the German miracle," agreed a year later César Urien, Argentina's ambassador to Madrid.[125] Regardless of what we think of GDP as an index, there is no doubt that most Spaniards – Franco's opposition included – accepted by then that they were in the thick of a sociocultural sea change. Urbanization, international migration, tourism, and consumerism had led to a collective sensation that, for better or for worse, the Spanish psyche was undergoing a metamorphosis.[126] The technocrats keenly espoused this narrative but also sought to tame it. For even if people like Fernández de la Mora promoted Spain as a country where a new modernity reigned, they nonetheless insisted that their country's austere traditionalism was giving place to a novel, urbane concoction of modernity and spirituality. Thus, while Hispanidad faded from public discourse, the technocrats still vowed to protect Spain's "physiognomy and character."[127] To be sure, they were not the only ones to show this type of ambivalence. Fraga, for example, launched his "Spain is 'Different': Visit Spain" campaign, which betrayed an even more cynical approach. Consciously appearing in quotation marks, Spain's exoticism was now commodified to attract Western tourism, not Hispanista crusaders.

The restrained affirmations of difference notwithstanding, the technocrats were genuinely concerned by the swiftness of Spain's cultural change. Even more, they sensed that the Civil War generation's mindset was increasingly at variance with those that followed them. Spaniards of "twenty, forty, and sixty years" appeared to have a different "collective conscience," Pérez-Embid noted in alarm.[128] Ultimately, their anxieties focused on three major ills: youthful rebellion, women's liberation, and changes in sexual norms and public morality. All three could be, and indeed were, associated with one root cause: secularization. It is difficult to gauge the Spaniards' religiosity in the 1960s, as reliable public opinion polls or sociological analyses were scarce or biased. Still, the Spanish public sphere was rife with spiritual agencies that sought to halt the middle class's supposed loss of faith. A case in point was the MCC. Established in 1944, it offered a method for "evangelization and conversion" of Catholic laymen, much like Opus Dei.[129] Its leader, Bishop Juan Hervás, was admittedly inspired by Escrivá when conceiving a spiritual method consisting of three days of "joyful, fraternal, and intimate Christian coexistence," followed by "spiritual exercises" aimed to induce deference and humility. While his movement had seemingly minor political content, Hervás idolized Franco and, in the 1960s, held his movement's national congregations at the Valle de los Caídos – Francoism's sacred shrine. Impressively, in a short matter of time it too spread throughout Latin America.[130]

Still, amid the diminishing influence of the Catholic Church's more official organ, Catholic Action, Opus Dei was the most conspicuous spiritual group in 1960s Spain. By now, it controlled intellectual journals (*Arbor*, *Atlántida*, *Nuestro Tiempo*), dailies (*Madrid*, *Diario Nuevo*), magazines (*Actualidad Española*, *Actualidad Económica*, *Mundo*), religious journals (*Mundo Cristiano*, *Palabra*), women's magazines (*Telva*, *Ama*, *La Casa*), and student bulletins (*Moncloa*, *Gazeta Universitaria*). Additionally, it owned publishing houses (Rialp, Pomaire, and Cid) and media corporations (Sociedad Española de Radiodifusión, Distribuidora Hispano-Argentina, Rotopress, and Filmófono). Combined with its influence on Spanish National Television (TVE), this ubiquitous presence allowed Opus Dei to orchestrate pervasive indoctrination and cultural censorship. As Pérez-Embid explained it, Spanish history had been dominated by two cultural forces: Catholic "truth" and Western modernity. Fraught with "flashes, instrumental values, but also of successes and nuances," one cannot simply reject the latter. Thus, he opined, a system of spiritual "bridge keepers" would decide which parts of Western culture should be integrated into the Hispanic domain, as had been done in the past in relation "to the great reality of paganism."[131]

The "youth," particularly university students, were Opus Dei's greatest cause for concern. Following the 1956 uprising, Opus Dei intellectuals demanded students avoid questioning authority and choose, in "liberty," a vocation that would meet the country's development needs. On this occasion, they also attacked the Falangist youth cult. "Fascism gave vent to a strange political mythology of Youth ... the revolutionary thaumaturgy of dark impulses and prerational intuitions . . . this must end," Pérez-Embid noted.[132] Instead, youth would experience the battlefield against the Enlightenment more holistically through self-denial and altruism. García Hoz – a pedagogue and the CSIC's director in the 1960s – guided this theoretical approach. In keeping with Escrivá's gospel, his early pedagogy centered on "ascetic struggle."[133] In the 1960s, somewhat more serenely, he bid the youth to "become a child," for the child is "simply the new man." Willing subordination "serves man's freedom best," he further clarified.[134] As a prominent UNESCO member, García Hoz would ultimately be recognized for his theories of "personalized education," designed to nurture children's particular talents.[135] Born in the age of totalitarianism, he believed obedience and sacrifice should be a personal choice youngsters should make, once confronted with the unquestionable evangelical truth. Naturally, allowing their exposure to secular untruths was counterproductive. Be it Darwinism, Western philosophy, or environmentalism, these would be outlawed, mocked, or glossed over in Opus Dei's pedagogical world.[136] As early as 1960, the Opus Dei theorists also appeared alarmed by the global youth culture of irreverence and rebelliousness. In the words of Leandro Benavides (numerary), the West was possessed by a "rebellion without a cause," marked by neologisms such as "Teddy boys" and "blousons noir."[137] Juan José López Ibor was a psychiatrist and *Arbor* collaborator who, like Calvo Serer, wrote on the Spaniards' "inferiority complex" and entitlement to cultural autonomy. His solution to young people's rebellion and "irony" was to persuade them to become Catholicism's "restless" crusaders.[138] A student named Julián Aznar was receptive to this message. In the bulletin *Moncloa*, he expounded that, whereas an academic discussion on what "God has left to man's free deliberation" is welcome, questioning evangelical truth is harmful and forbidden. "Be restless, not rebellious," he advised his readers.[139]

Western feminism was a menace that Opus Dei intellectuals likewise sought to defang and rehabilitate. Despite the support for women's inclusion in the workforce, often under the guise of national productivity, Franco's Spain continued to view women through a rigidly patriarchal lens, with the Falange's Feminine Section being the one meager avenue for their social agency. Directed by Pilar Primo de Rivera, this organ's publications *Revista para la mujer* and *Medina*, advocated women's influence within the household and in the education system.[140] Opus Dei sought to go beyond this threshold. Besides operating its private women's section, it upheld a notable public discourse on modern womanhood – for example, in *Telva*, a vibrant lifestyle magazine, directed by numeraries Covadonga O'Shea and Pilar Salcedo and Opus Dei's most popular publication to date. Unlike the Falange's propaganda, *Telva* promoted itself as a platform where women could speak to one another on topics that mattered to them. In its opening editorial, Salcedo stated that "'Women's rights' might sound good, but we must be the tough ones, the mature ones. We need to be well informed so that when we earn our rights we will see in them the duty to work – at a European level – with greater seriousness."[141] In other words, she demanded that women be "serious" – unlike the Western feminists who demanded rights without meriting them. Thus, on the one hand, Opus Dei promoted women's professionalism and asserted that they should not wait for a "mythical Prince Charming" to achieve economic security.[142] On the other hand, it expected women to willingly prefer their homes as a vocation, as "men and women have equal civic rights, but different missions." Rather than trying to "be men" in a "race to establish their place at the center of the family and society," women should strive to be effective housewives, was the gist of the argument.[143] Accordingly, Opus Dei operated academic centers for the "professionalization of housework,"[144] and guided women on how to find joy in daily chores through a "spirit of service."[145] This womanhood often hinged on pseudoscientific arguments surrounding women's intrinsic melancholic condition – to the extent of questioning their ability to drive automobiles.[146]

By the mid 1960s, Opus Dei's publications were decidedly turning their attention to changes in sexual norms. At first, they focused less on sexuality proper and more on the causal link between the erosion of gender norms and social dysfunctionality. When the Beatles emerged as a global cultural phenomenon, this anxiety was the first to appear in their diatribes. In 1964, *Telva* mocked the Liverpool pop group for being as ugly "as bugs" and the result of "good PR."[147] Next, it published a "report" about "Michael and Patricia" – a dysfunctional unmarried couple dwelling in a deserted beach club in Catalonia. Michael, who was seven years younger than his lover, was a "Beatle mimic" who "neglected the basic rules of hygiene." This led *Telva* to conclude that the Beatles' influence "is spreading alarmingly among the strong sex" – a phenomenon that called for further "psychological study."[148] A mere six months later, after the Beatles had performed in Spain, the Opus Dei platforms eased their attacks and portrayed the band members as respectable self-made men who had now honored Spain with their presence.[149] This anecdote is indicative of two things: Firstly, Opus Dei's moralism addressed cultural phenomena – the feminization of men in this case – primarily through the lenses of economic productivity and social dysfunctionality. Secondly, Opus Dei chose its battles wisely. For *Telva*, to mock the Beatles in 1965 meant opting for an overprotective stance that might have damaged the image of Franco's Spain and Opus Dei alike. Spain was perhaps "different," but still modern enough to tolerate the Beatles, not to mention their Spanish emulations – Los Pekenikes.[150] In stark contrast, Opus Dei's neofascist opponent, Piñar, with his staunch anti-Americanism, could hardly bear to listen to jazz.[151]

Thus, it was the advent of hormonal contraception, not pop music, that drove Opus Dei into an unapologetic crusade against evolving sexual norms. During the 1960s, the concept of a "sex life" emerged in the Western world as a normative condition, detached from procreation, and, thus, justly facilitated by innovative birth control technologies. Opus Dei's perception of this development as catastrophic was not rooted merely in religious underpinnings – such as Pope Paul VI's 1968 encyclical *Humanae Vitae* – but also in economic, sociological, and geopolitical considerations.[152] To start with, its theorists depicted family planning as a financial hazard to developing nations, for stalling growth rates and creating labor shortages.[153] Next, they portrayed Western sexual culture as a cause for social dysfunctionality or, worse still, as the West's "sexual-economic colonization." *Playboy* was their bête noire, in this sense. Banned but regularly smuggled into Spain, the magazine infuriated the editors of the bulletin *Gazeta Universitaria*. In the USA, *Playboy* was responsible for "a million Americans being infected with venereal diseases each year," they alleged.[154]

Eventually, the campaign against birth control betrayed a more nuanced concern about the Hispanic spiritual economy. Sexual excess, even within wedlock, could impact the Hispanics in unforeseen ways, maintained Jesús Urteaga. The founder of the journal *Mundo Cristiano*, he was perhaps the most influential of Escrivá's disciples, primarily due to his cunning use of television. So popular was his program *Sólo para menores de 16 años: Siempre alegres para hacer felices a los* demás, which aired between 1961 and 1966, that it won him the TVE's 1965 National Award. Sure enough, unlike the Falange, Opus Dei did not shy away from this new medium, making it a platform for a public "dialogue" on morality. Expectedly, Urteaga promoted Escrivá's gospel: Once living "for the others," you will "glow with joy," he promised his audience.[155] More surreptitiously, he presented the public with a vision of celibacy that went beyond adolescent sexuality. Being a "soldier of Christ," for Urteaga, meant making one's body a "battlefield" wherein abstinence "is not subjection, but liberation." This meant that even married couples should avoid sexual activity detached from procreation. By "enjoying marriage while avoiding the burdens it carries," such couples are transforming a sacred ritual into a "poor, vulgar, and creeping flesh trade," he ranted.[156] Sure enough, his ideas were not extraordinary coming from a Catholic priest. What *was* different was his privileged position on national television. Urteaga was, in every respect, the regime's official spiritual guide and moral compass.

In summary, Pérez-Embid, García Hoz, López Ibor, Salcedo, O'Shea, and Urteaga were hardly private intellectuals speaking their mind in a pluralist public sphere. Instead, they were the vanguard of a coordinated network that, while the "technocrats" were busy engineering Spain's economic "miracle," prepared the Spaniards for life under an alternative modernity. Even if their rhetoric was devoid of Hispanista references, their mythological thinking was not dissimilar to that of their 1950s predecessors. Alfredo Sánchez Bella was one of the first to apprehend this fact. Being the brother of two distinguished Opus Dei members, he joined the technocrats' political camp in the mid 1960s. Still, Opus Dei's project went beyond rejecting the Enlightenment's political structures and sought to devise spiritualized alternatives to almost all walks of modern life. By consciously substituting fascism's ethos of violence and virility with a holistic "internal" crusade of joy, subordination, and purity, Opus Dei intellectuals believed they held a technique to successfully accommodate Western consumerism.

2.4 "FRANCOISM WITHOUT FRANCO": THE DESIGN OF SPAIN'S AUTHORITARIAN FUTURE

Whether Spain underwent a "change of skin" or not, there is little doubt that its leader was changing. Seventy years old in 1962, by the mid 1960s, Franco was famously "fishing and hunting" rather than running the state. Sotto voce, his followers thus contemplated who would be his successor, what state model would replace Francoism, and what mechanism would guarantee a peaceful transition from one model to another. The plot was thickening as early as October 1963, when Fraga delivered Franco a proposal for a final constitution. Once more, the Falange suggested replacing Francoism with a presidential one-party regime characterized by participation through the syndicates, wealth redistribution, and a pluralist public sphere. Opus Dei, alternatively, envisioned institutionalizing the model in the making since 1957. An authoritarian monarchy, it was to be characterized by a "liberal" economy, a restricted public sphere, and an administration maintained by spiritual "intermediary societies." The ideological struggle between the Falange and Opus Dei hence entered a new phase.

One of the concerns propelling this struggle was the identity of Franco's successor, should he suddenly die. By 1960, Opus Dei stood firmly behind the Bourbon monarchy. Their contender to the throne was Prince Juan Carlos, but he was certainly not the only candidate out there.[157] Javier de Borbón-Parma and his son Prince Carlos Hugo were the Carlists and the neofascists' contenders. For people like Sánchez Bella, Alfonso de Borbón y Dampierre (another of King Alfonso XIII's grandchildren) and Otto von Habsburg were also valid options. Naturally, the suitability of any challenger relied on their pledge to continue Francoism after Franco. Juan Carlos, Opus Dei thought, could be educated to be a Francoist ruler. Following a two-year military service in Spain, in 1960, he began his studies supervised by a committee consisting of men such as Federico Suárez Verdeguer, López Rodó, Pérez-Embid, and López-Amo.[158] The prince's candidacy became public in 1964, once he stood alongside Franco at the annual April 1 victory parade. That he openly expressed his admiration for López Rodó was a matter of deep concern for the Falange.[159] Luckily for its leadership, the impossibility of nominating the prince as Franco's successor, due to his age, presented it with a brief opportunity for yet another bid for power. This began with Fraga's 1965 Associations of Heads of Households Bill – a botched law proposal that aimed to integrate the Spanish family into the Falange apparatus in a "totalitarian fashion," according to Pérez-Embid.[160] More successful was Fraga's March 1966 Press Law. Elevating state censorship slightly, the law perhaps contrasted Opus Dei's ideas of a "Catholic press" but was applauded internationally.[161]

In the face of Fraga's actions, the technocrats accentuated their unique expertise in development. López Rodó's promotional tour of Spain's Second Development Plan – which included Peru, Chile, Brazil, Colombia, Argentina, Paraguay, and Uruguay – was as extensive as it was unusual for a minister with no diplomatic role. Officially traveling to reduce Spain's trade deficit in Latin America, his speeches conveyed an almost fairytale-like narrative of national redemption through economic modernization. To his Chilean audience, he said the following:

> Spain is no longer Europe's Cinderella ... Factories, new irrigation systems, splendid universities, magnificent highways, high-speed trains, and the best hotels in the world have appeared on its rough skin. We have achieved all this ... because, for the first time in many years, we have been able to work in order and peace. Your help and our efforts have made it possible for America's nations to look to us today as an example to follow.[162]

Fernández de la Mora followed suit and, in 1967, toured Latin America to promote his abovementioned book. As we have seen, his narrative was identical to that of López Rodó and captivated Latin Americans' imagination far more than Fraga's laws.

Ultimately, Fraga's initiatives left Carrero Blanco and Opus Dei with no choice but to "institutionalize" Francoism to their liking. In their boldest political move to date, in 1966, Fernández de la Mora and López Rodó drafted Spain's Organic Law of the State (Ley Orgánica del Estado), which, based on López Rodó's formulas from 1956, was to be the nation's "actual constitution."[163] Francoism without Franco would thus consist of a nonelected head of state (a king or regent), his selected deputy (prime minister), and a selected government. Instead of a senate, the Council of the Kingdom (Consejo del Reino) was to "assist the head of state" in drafting new laws. Of its seventeen members, ten would be elected by the parliament, which, in turn, would be partially elected by Spain's organic bodies (some 108 representatives were to be elected by heads of families and married women). Having no actual legislative power, the parliament would be where public opinion is "channeled" to the executive branch. Despite claiming to guarantee an autonomous judiciary, there was no inkling that the head of state, prime minister, or ministers would be overseen by it. Unsurprisingly, the laws considerably limited the syndicates' representation but, interestingly, paved the way for a full-fledged electoral system for mayors and provincial councils.[164]

It is questionable whether López Rodó believed these laws would ever materialize beyond political theater. What is beyond doubt is that, in 1966, Franco decided to subdue the neofascist pipe dreams still brewing inside his regime's state apparatus. In December 1966, he called upon his citizens to ratify the Organic Law in yet another sham referendum. The Falange's call to vote against it was in vain: The law was approved by an overwhelming 95.9 percent of the voters. It is worthwhile noting that neither Opus Dei nor Franco suggested that this democratic spectacle meant the onset of a more democratic era. On the contrary: They insisted that the executive branch should stay in the hands of a selected few. As Franco's speech writer, López Rodó's words resonated in his leader's speech at the city of Tarragona, a few months after the referendum. "For Spain to stay a living organism," said Franco, one must discover a "minority of individuals" with "faith and enthusiasm for the job" who can serve as "the channel where the nation's ideals and aspirations overlap with the duties of the state."[165]

With Spain's authoritarian future looming, the democratic opposition saw the unexpected inclusion of two new members: Rafael Calvo Serer and Antonio Fontán. Having mingled with Western intellectuals in the early 1960s, Calvo Serer, in particular, now believed Francoism should become a springboard for Spain's democratization.[166] In a new daily named *Madrid*, the two thus broke away from Opus Dei's technocratic circles.[167] In 1968, Calvo Serer published a diatribe against Charles de Gaulle, in which he declared the incompatibility of authoritarianism with "the structures of industrial society and with the democratic mentality of our time."[168] Fraga seized this opportunity to shut *Madrid* down, indicating just how limited his conception of a "free press" actually was.[169] Soon to be exiled, Calvo Serer became, from this moment on, a bona fide opposition member. Still, it must be stressed that these men showed no remorse over serving the regime in the past, but merely suggested that Francoism evolve "without rupture" into a democracy inclusive of socialism but "without Marxism."[170] While straddling the border between democratic reformers and authoritarian thinkers, they dreaded the prospects of Carrero Blanco becoming Spain's new dictator by making the Bourbon prince "his prisoner" – as Calvo Serer wrote to Franco.[171]

These concerns were not groundless. When Muñoz Grandes retired as vice president in 1967, Carrero Blanco took his place and immediately initiated a ministerial reshuffle on the premise that the tensions between the Falange and the technocrats could not be contained any longer. Now, he took advantage of an unforeseen phenomenon: the Basque national liberation movement Euskadi Ta Askatasuna (ETA). This urban guerilla underground, which attacked primarily military personnel, committed its first assassination of a Spanish serviceman in June 1968. In parallel, the Spanish workers' mobilization continued to broaden. Having endured yet another salary freeze, the Spanish workers made the summer of 1968 a spectacle of massive strikes and demonstrations. Resourcefully, Carrero Blanco weaponized these events, depicting them as a "public morality" crisis for which Fraga's reforms were to blame.[172] In January 1969, amid another welter of strikes and ETA attacks, he even declared a state of emergency, for the first time in decades.[173]

Compounding matters further, Pope Paul VI antagonized Franco's dictatorship and Opus Dei in an ever more confrontational manner. In a "very confidential letter" to Franco, Spain's ambassador to the Vatican reported that Opus Dei "has been the object of a warning by the Holy See" that consisted of an explicit order to "refrain from holding political or influential positions" and cease from "all control, propaganda, or ostentation."[174] As we shall see in Chapter 5, these threats would have a profound impact on Escrivá in the late 1960s. With the Second Vatican Council well underway, and to minimize this conflict, Franco co-opted Alfredo Sánchez Bella as his ambassador in Rome. Plotting inside Carrero Blanco's axis, his conspiratorial letters shed light on how he sought to persuade his peers that the regime could "give an impression" of setting about a democratic opening while, in reality, "further tightening the knots."[175] To Carrero Blanco, he was entirely candid about what should be done: "If we act now and carry out what we have agreed on; if [Franco] ... designates his successor himself; if we establish a crowned presidential state – which is what our era demands and what national and international public opinion is willing to accept – then the enemy's action could cause inconvenience but will not substantially affect Spain's historical evolution."[176] In essence, Sánchez Bella portrayed Spain's Hispanic technocracy taking the form of an authoritarian monarchy with a powerless monarch. Carrero Blanco needed no convincing. In what became known as the "Prince operation," he banished the Borbón-Parma contenders from Spain. Then, he pressured Franco to nominate Prince Juan Carlos as his official heir, which he did, on July 22, 1969, in a special Cortes assembly.

It was a bizarre moment in the dictatorship's history as hardly anybody in the audience knew for certain what the prince's ideological leanings were. In a sense, it mattered little. As we have seen, Carrero Blanco and Opus Dei expected him to be a powerless symbol at the center of a technocratic dictatorship firmly in the hands of the "prime minister" and his "directing minorities." Not only was Juan Carlos forced to take an oath to protect the "Principles of the Movement" and Organic Law, but he was ominously reminded by Franco that his future had been born "from that decisive act of July 18."[177] The succession announcement occurred at the exact moment when a scandal of colossal public money embezzlement exploded. Known as the "MATESA affair," it involved several Opus Dei institutions and instantly made it to the Falange newspapers' headlines.[178] The fact that the Falange used the scandal to disparage Opus Dei publicly led Carrero Blanco to force Franco to discharge

Fraga and Solís in October 1969.[179] Henceforth, for the first time, an ideologically cohesive Hispanic technocratic government would control Spain. Aptly nicknamed the "mono-color" government, it comprised Sánchez Bella (minister of information and tourism), Fernández de la Mora (minister of public works), Gregorio López Bravo (supernumerary, and foreign minister), and López Rodó (development plans minister). In short, "the technocrats' coup d'état" – as one Argentine newspaper called it – entailed three steps: the 1967 Organic Law, the 1969 Prince Plan, and the constitution of a mono-color government with Carrero Blanco as vice president. With Franco's looming death, nothing seemed to stand in the way of Hispanic technocracy becoming Spain's final state model.[180]

3

Juan Carlos Onganía's "Argentine Revolution"

Hispanic Technocracy to Surpass Post-fascist Populism (1956–1970)

Juan Perón's second presidency was synonymous with political turmoil. Eva Perón's untimely death in July 1952, a steep economic crisis, and, more famously, a conflict with the Catholic Church thus led the armed forces to overthrow Perón on September 16, 1955.[1] In what became known as the "Liberating Revolution," Generals Eduardo Lonardi and Pedro Aramburu – the men who displaced him – agreed on the need to free Argentina from Peronism but differed on almost everything else, including on whether or how Argentina should return to democracy. The armed forces eventually restored democracy in 1958, not before outlawing and violently purging the Peronist movement. Still, Argentina remained ensnared in an unprecedented condition. Exiled rather than dead, Perón continued to shape the identity of elected officials, using his loyal labor unions and guided constituency to maintain his grip on the economy and the political process. Consequently, the non-Peronist political camp faced a universal conundrum: Can one protect democracy from an anti-liberal leader by inhibiting a significant part of the population from partaking in the political game?

Exacerbating this crisis was the fact that Argentina was in the throes of a profound economic transition. For over two decades, its economy had mostly followed the guidelines of protectionist theories generally known as import substitution industrialization (ISI). Despite substantially elevating the working class's living standards, it ultimately resulted in a debt crisis, chronic inflation, and overall economic volatility. Hence, even those who had supported ISI – economist Raul Prebisch, to name one – rendered this model outdated by 1956.[2] In other words, not unlike Spain, Argentina faced an agonizing process of incorporation into global markets. Yet replacing protectionism with a free-market economy is not a simple undertaking in a democratic society, and even less so under a populist government. As Guillermo O'Donnell described it, having been politically "activated," the popular sector ("pueblo") now had "demands," which the "dominant classes" perceived as "increasingly dangerous."[3] In other words, in the absence of Perón, Argentina's financial elites expected the working class to politically "deactivate" itself by voting for candidates who would act against its interest. Once the workers refused to cut the Gordian knot between popular representation and economic redistribution, the ruling classes did it for them and abolished parliament.

While O'Donnell's depiction is not incorrect, it is also devoid of ideological nuance and, as such, is entirely reductive. For, as anyone who lived in 1950s Argentina would attest, Peronism was anything but a grassroots workers' movement of the "pueblo." It was a post-fascist revolution of national revival steeped in messianic undertones. This historical context is what led many of its opponents to believe that only a spiritual project of equal caliber could break Perón's spell. After all, Juan Carlos Onganía (Figure 3.1) named his regime the Argentine Revolution for a reason. As we shall see, he sought to change not only Argentina's

FIGURE 3.1 Juan Carlos Onganía, 1964.
Bettmann / Getty Images

economic structure but the pueblo itself. In other words, unlike many historians, in this chapter, we will for once take Onganía and his "revolutionary" rhetoric seriously. In essence, the chapter chronicles the story of a post-fascist regime that was determined to quell yet another post-fascist revolution – and the Enlightenment ideologies with it – in order to guide Argentina towards a modernization path analogous to that of Spain. Onganía, a firm believer in the Hispanic technocratic model, was resolute in his belief that these goals could be achieved without the need for Argentine bloodshed.

3.1 LIFE AFTER PERÓN: ARGENTINA'S RESTRICTED DEMOCRACY IN THE 1960S

In September 1955, there was hardly any certainty that Argentina would become a democracy again. Having conspired against Perón since 1950, the Nacionalistas' "union" group was an important factor in persuading General Lonardi to overthrow the government, hoping that a new dictatorial order would replace Argentina's democracy indefinitely. Lonardi, a general from a traditional Catholic family, was seen as a figure who could potentially sway even the Peronists to join the Nacionalista cause. By appointing Amadeo as his Foreign Minister, Dell'Oro Maini as Minister of Education, and Goyeneche as his press secretary, Lonardi implied that these were indeed his intentions. Unfortunately for him, these men's historical affinity with European fascism and his conciliatory attitude towards Peronism prompted a powerful anti-Peronist and economically liberal faction in the armed forces to take over the Liberating Revolution on November 13, 1955. One of the first things their leader, Aramburu, did was to assert that "Argentina is neither that of 1943 nor 1930."[4] Then, he executed some thirty Peronist military men and civilians, thereby sending an unequivocal message to the public that the armed forces would back the democratic order but would have no mercy for those seeking to mobilize the popular sectors as Perón had done in the past decade.[5] The mainstream press, which did not want to see a neofascist regime replacing Peronism, was relieved by this turn of events and even gleefully ridiculed Amadeo's "Francoist" leanings. "Gladly," they confirmed, he was "Argentina's Foreign Minister no more."[6] In ten years, its attitude towards him would change considerably.

Indeed, for Amadeo, Lonardi's humiliation was a watershed moment. According to one of his confidants, there and then he disowned Nacionalismo for a new "synthesis."[7] That may be an overstatement.

A more precise way to put it is that having seen three military dictatorships fail to enact a Nacionalista new order, Amadeo had concluded that any future authoritarian order could only be a civil one and the outcome of a collective decision.[8] Máximo Etchecopar, Amadeo's Hispasnista companion, reached similar conclusions. His 1956 book *Esquema de la Argentina* was cleansed of neofascist slogans and focused instead on how Argentina's "latently social aristocracy" should retake its leadership role within a new post-ideological order. Given modern society's "technological and functional organization," the elevation of living standards and buying power, Etchecopar confirmed, were a far more "democratic" standard than universal suffrage.[9] But how should this new order emerge? For the moment, the two men had no concrete answer to this question.

While Amadeo disengaged from his Nacionalista roots, others sought to incorporate its symbols into their political discourse. This was the case of Arturo Frondizi of the party Unión Cívica Radical Intransigente (UCRI), who rose to political prominence thanks to his program of "developmentalism." Envisaging an economy of private industries buoyed up by the state's investments in infrastructure and protectionism, his plan sounded to many like a "third path" of sorts. While it is true that Frondizi pledged to uphold Argentina's secular education, his anti-imperialist and anti-communist rhetoric targeted Peronists and Nacionalistas alike.[10] Certainly, he ultimately won Argentina's 1958 general elections not due to his propaganda, but due to Perón's public endorsement.[11] Still, for Amadeo, this was good enough. In what raised many eyebrows, in 1959, he joined Frondizi's administration and was co-opted as Argentina's ambassador to the UN. Justifying this decision to Sánchez Bella, he argued that he and his followers had not abandoned their cause but needed an "increase of prestige" as statesmen with a proven record.[12] Amadeo's treatment of the USA had also changed by then. "Our old ideal of friendlier relations with the USA, while committed to mutual respect, now does not seem to be a utopia," he told his Francoist ally.[13] Sánchez Bella was hardly impressed. Argentina's "false democratic scruples lead nowhere," he wrote to his friend.[14] "If our nations aspire to live," he further lectured, "they must accept authoritarianism as a lesser evil and as the only means to preserve their true liberties."[15] In return, Amadeo replied that he had not abandoned his Nacionalista values – only the coup d'état "tactics." He and his followers, he vowed, would henceforth pursue legal paths to political power.[16]

Amadeo's intuitions contradicted those of most of the Nacionalistas, who now regrouped in new affiliations, each in its way demanding to replace Argentina's crippled democracy with one version or another of political corporatism. The first of them emerged around Sánchez Sorondo's new newspaper – and, briefly, political party – *Azul y Blanco*, which pledged to replace Perón's "aberration" with a proper revolution – "clear, nationalist, and popular, above all parties."[17] Jordán Bruno Genta's Legion Nacionalista C ontrarrevolucionaria (LNC) was another case in point. Unlike Sánchez Sorondo, Genta promoted a "counterrevolution" rather than revolution. As such, the LNC's tabloid *Combate* showcased a peculiar ideological concoction of traditionalism and exaltation of José Antonio Primo de Rivera, laced with anti-Semitism.[18] Interestingly, Genta's Hispanic message was far more pronounced. In fact, he sought to effectively merge the Nacionalistas' myths of national origin by underscoring that Rosas was a "hidalgo" who sought to reconstitute Argentina's sacred "Catholic and Hispanic past."[19] Still, rather than corporatist state models, Genta was ultimately engrossed with producing his distinctive theory of "subversion," which first appeared in his 1962 *Guerra contrarevolucionaria* and that entailed a Manichean division of the world into "positive" and "negative" knowledge.[20] Hence, the two groups to explicitly advocate political corporatism were Meinvielle's Guardia Restauradora Nacionalista (GRN) and the Movimiento Nacionalista Tacuara (MNT). The former's "programmatic points" promoted representation through the "Family, Corporations, Municipality, and Province" and ending "class struggle" by organizing the nation's economic activity "corporately."[21] The latter went further than this and simply promoted Primo de Rivera's "national syndicalism" as its own. Led by a new generation of youngsters, such as Alberto Ezcurra, Juan Mario Collins, and Joe Baxter, the MNT was also the only group to merit the definition of a "paramilitary band" as it ultimately came to notoriety for its attacks on Jewish Argentines rather than for its economic platform.[22]

In no time, Amadeo's "group" came into a bitter public feud with the neofascist Nacionalistas, and in particular with Sánchez Sorondo, who weaponized the 1959 Cuban Revolution to depict Frondizi as a covert communist.[23] In reality, despite refusing to sever ties with Cuba, Frondizi only cultivated his anti-communist image further. On July 7, 1960, he traveled to meet none other than Franco. In what was the first official visit of an Argentine President to Spain in history, Frondizi paid tribute to the Alcázar in Toledo and the Valle de los Caídos.[24] In return, he received the Grand Collar of the Order of Isabel.[25] Reflecting on this celebratory rite, Sánchez Bella wrote to Amadeo that it was "the only way to maintain

[Frondizi] spiritually with us."[26] At first, his words seemed prophetic. Having earned his Francoist anti-communist seal of approval, Frondizi returned to Argentina reverberating Lugones's "unalterable union of the Cross and the Sword"[27] and spewing pledges to defend Argentina from "communist penetrations."[28] Notably, he also passed an anti-communist Law of National Defense.[29] And while he did meet with Ernesto "Che" Guevara in Buenos Aires in August 1961, this was by no means a sign of leftist leanings but a residue of his anti-imperialist posture that had, by now, all but faded away.[30]

It is neither necessary nor possible to survey Frondizi's turbulent tenure here, but suffice it to say that his public gestures took place amid countless military conspiracies that had little to do with anti-communist anxieties but more with Peronism. By and large, developmentalism remained illusory as, under the pressure of the armed forces, Frondizi co-opted liberal economists such as Álvaro Alsogaray and Roberto Alemann to cope with the mammoth economic problems bequeathed to him by Perón. Any ideas of state-sponsored industrialization thus gave place to the IMF-designed 1959–60 Stabilization Plan, based on foreign-investment-based development – even opening Argentina's oil industry to foreign companies – and harsh austerity measures. Of course, any effort to dramatically liberalize the Argentine economy could not have transpired without handing the Peronist unions political gains in return for their cooperation. Thus, it was not an economic crisis but Frondizi's agreement to allow Peronist candidates to run for office in the 1962 municipal elections that cut short his political career. On March 29, 1962, the armed forces ousted him, installing instead an interim government designed to lead the country through a new electoral process.

3.2 THE ATENEO DE LA REPÚBLICA: HOW THE HISPANISTAS AND OPUS DEI DESIGNED ARGENTINA'S AUTHORITARIAN FUTURE

Frondizi was an accomplished and astute politician. It was precisely for this reason that his fiasco became synonymous with the futility of either reasoning with Peronism or overtaking its constituency with a new "development" fantasy. Worse yet, in 1962, while the Argentine economy and political system were haplessly bogged down, Spain's economy was booming beyond recognition. This contrast was not lost on either Amadeo's group or, more importantly, on a particular clique of generals. Shortly after Frondizi stepped down, the public became privy to two epithets that represented rival sides of an ideological struggle within the armed forces: the Colorados ("reds") and the Azules ("blues"). Whereas the former sought to purge Argentina from Peronism through an extensive operation of a "revolutionary" military dictatorship, the latter was a self-proclaimed "legalist" faction and, as such, pursued more sophisticated ways to do away with Perón's influence.[31] Onganía, the emergent leader of the Azules, contended that the armed forces should intervene in politics only when necessary to defend the nation from Perón's "criminal regime."[32] Born in 1914 and having served as a soldier during the 1930s, he also recognized that generals did not have the skills to govern and should let experts manage the executive branch.[33] Following two deadly showdowns, in September 1962 and April 1963, the Azules overpowered the Colorados, thereby paving the way for Onganía's control over the future democratic process.[34]

Unemployed again and embittered by his foray into legitimate politics, Amadeo returned to his conspiratorial ways by founding an elitist forum named the Ateneo de la República. Led by eminent ICH Hispanistas, and joined by disenchanted "Frondizistas," it undertook a straightforward mission: coordinating Argentina's authoritarian turn, or in Amadeo's words, promoting the "right to be ruled by a dictatorship" with a "civil government."[35] He also clarified that this new authoritarian order must be both market-oriented and spiritual – quite the opposite of the neofascist Nacionalistas' totalitarian pipe dreams. In his words: "The struggle is not between those who are for 'representative democracy' and those who are against it, but between those who understand that what is necessary is a profound renovation of collective consciousness under an essentially Christian insignia and those who want to maintain, violently, the old socio-economic structures."[36] The Ateneo showcased a generation of young theorists, many of whom were Amadeo's protégés and intimately associated with Franco's Spain. Mario Díaz Colodrero, Mariano Montemayor, and Enrique Peltzer, for instance, studied together in Madrid under Sánchez Bella.[37] Other examples were Nicanor Costa Méndez, Jorge Mazzinghi, and Samuel Medrano, who studied at the ICH and reached high-ranking positions in Onganía's regime.[38] Likewise, Díaz Colodrero, Mazzinghi, and Medrano joined Opus Dei in the 1960s and 1970s. Thus, there was a recurring pattern in these men's biographies, starting with a Francoist ideological education and ending with a distinctive ideological production in the 1960s.

In a sense, the Ateneo functioned as Argentina's unofficial nexus with Spain, a fact that became apparent with the inauguration of the Buenos Aires ICH chapter in November 1965, in the presence of the ICH director in Madrid, Gregorio Marañón Moya. With Mazzinghi serving as its general secretary, and Amadeo, Díaz Colodrero, and José Mariano Astigueta as its board members, this chapter was indeed the Ateneo's domain.[39] Tellingly, in 1965, these men were the guests of the ICH in Madrid, where they experienced "conferences, night walks, and a climate of joy and friendship."[40] The Madrid dailies, for their part, characterized Mazzinghi as "Spain's great friend," hailed his "fervent pilgrimage," and spoke highly of his quest to "reinvigorate traditional relations with the Mother Nation."[41] As in the case of Chile, the Argentine ICH also acknowledged its "closest of ties with the Spanish embassy." Sure enough, Spain's ambassador, the Falangist José María Alfaro, was an ICH board member as well.[42]

These Francoist credentials may explain how the Ateneo acquired a prestige rarely enjoyed by Nacionalista associations at the time. It may have begun as a "ghost" association but quickly displayed "a remarkable cultural and social activity," Amadeo even boasted to Sánchez Bella.[43] The accuracy of this statement aside, the Ateneo indeed attracted the attention of the Azul generals. Better put, Amadeo aggressively promoted the Ateneo to them as the most significant elite society in Argentina.[44] In truth, the Ateneo was one of several associations the Azules sought to fraternize with, in order to get the Argentine elites on board with their political project. International religious societies such as Ciudad Católica (Cité Catholique) had arrived in Argentina by then, and quickly became known as nuclei for elite mobilization.[45] Founded in France in 1946 by Jean Ousset, its journal *Verbo* was one of the most prominent anti-Enlightenment voices in 1960s Argentina, vowing to eradicate the "Renaissance, Reformation, French Revolution, and Communism."[46] Another case in point was the traditionalist movement Tradição, Família e Propriedade (TFP). Founded in Brazil by Dr. Plinio Corrêa de Oliveira in 1960, its arrival in Argentina was the initiative of Hispanistas Cosme Beccar Varela (Jr.) and Federico J. Ezcurra.[47] Since 1956, they have been editing the journal *Cruzada* where they did not mince words about *Azul y Blanco*'s statist ideology.[48] In the Dominican Republic, Sánchez Bella observed their activities attentively. In a letter to Beccar Varela, he said:

> I just received last May's *Cruzada* ... You cannot imagine how much we appreciate this orientation and the clear defense of our principles ... The Yankee takeoff and the USSR's decline have begun, but [Latin] America cannot become either. The revolution of the middle class, which seems inevitable, must be based on firm respect for the Catholic religion and Hispanic traditions.[49]

Evidently, Sánchez Bella urged his confidants to proclaim a new order that would acknowledge the USA's economic hegemony while defending the essence of Hispanidad.[50] In any event, having identified TFP as a society that fostered an ideological concoction similar to theirs, Beccar Varela and Ezcurra coordinated the founding of its Argentine chapter, which soon became a hub for military–civil cooperation.[51]

As far as spirituality was concerned, though, the Azules were ultimately predominantly drawn to the MCC and Opus Dei. With its "spiritual exercises," the former functioned as a habitat where men such as Onganía underwent a mystical awakening and networked. True to form, the latter served as an intellectual powerhouse that articulated every aspect of Argentina's future post-ideological society for the generals – for instance, in Ibáñez Langlois and García Alesanco's *Cuadernos del Sur*, an ambitious intellectual journal that aimed to mobilize the Southern Cone's conservatives. In 1964, Ibáñez Langlois informed Pérez-Embid of his new platform, pledging to "shock the bourgeois" throughout Argentina, Chile, and Uruguay – or "South American Europe."[52] While it did not identify as such, it was Opus Dei's most conspicuous publication in Latin America to date. After all, its director, the supernumerary Eugenio Antonio Brusa, was one of Ismael Sánchez Bella's first recruits in Argentina,[53] and it published the work of almost all the Opus Dei intellectuals, including Urteaga and Escrivá de Balaguer.[54] As notably, its board of directors included Díaz Colodrero and Carlos Mendioroz – Ateneo members and the link between the two circles.[55] Costa Méndez, who published there too and directed Opus Dei's publishing house Pomaire, can also be included in this network.[56]

Cuadernos del Sur championed authoritarianism in a fashion that, by now, may sound familiar to us from the previous chapter. To start with, its authors posited that Latin America's dire need for swift economic growth demanded a "centralized power the likes of which European absolutism would envy."[57] Yet they also distanced themselves from the Western technocratic "dehumanization." *Their* regime, they underlined, would not comprise "hollow specialists," given its spiritual project. As Ibáñez Langlois explained: "The future of freedom depends on the spiritual force capable of teaching us to use the tools of power and technology without self-destruction … But who will inject into the souls of the masses who drive the machines … that inner space of freedom, warning, deliberation, of intimacy that redeems humanity from the immense machinery? The problem is, ultimately, religious."[58] Next, these ideologues presented democracy as an entity that was, by nature, incapable of such enterprise. "In Latin America, we pay a high price for an ideological political life ... a theoretical fabrication that seeks visions of infallibility often without connection to reality ... a dictatorship of abstractions," García Alesanco blustered.[59] To Ibáñez Langlois's mind, this condition could mean only one thing: the imperative to replace democracy with an "undoubtedly authoritarian" regime that is still "not despotic" but only renounces democracy's "formal values" while preserving its "essential content"; a regime that purifies the socialist state "from aphorisms" while assimilating its "technical efficiency and planning dynamism."[60] Simply put, he envisioned a society administered to its finest details by specialists in the economic and spiritual domains. While guaranteeing its citizens' liberties, it would abide by technical and Catholic truths, not ideological abstractions.[61]

Life under liberal democracies had made Latin American societies exceptionally prone to changes in public morality, they also warned.[62] More so than in Spain, *Cuadernos del Sur*'s writers were primarily bothered by the sexual revolution, which they treated as a phenomenon that was already heavily plaguing their societies.[63] Sure enough, they also knew who was to blame for it. Family planning was a Western "classist, monopolistic, colonialist, and paternalistic" enterprise that "neither liberates women nor promotes happier motherhood," Ibáñez Langlois clarified.[64] In fact, he went so far as to depict Western sexuality as a form of enslavement. Once "sexual energy is liberated from responsibility," he said, it "revolves around itself in a closed circle of delight" and therefore causes "immense confusion and, subsequently, homosexuality."[65] Based on such pseudoscientific notions of sexual economy, *Cuadernos del Sur* debated normative "sex life" within wedlock as a public health issue that necessitated state intervention. Banning contraceptives and replacing sex education with education for chastity were, for Opus Dei, the elementary prerequisites in a "total war" against these destructive forces of "nihilistic" science.[66] Slowly but surely, *Cuadernos del Sur* touched on almost all aspects of public morality besides sexuality. On the one hand, it acquainted its audiences with García Hoz, who railed against "statist pedagogy" while promoting a "subsidiarity principle" in education by which the state transfers its authority to societies that accept the "natural, divine, and international" law.[67] On the other hand, it boasted a distinctive cohort of women intellectuals – María Elena Aguirre (supernumerary), Elena Vial Correa (numerary), Lilian Calm (supernumerary), for example – who were Ibáñez Langlois's recruits and who took it upon themselves to conceptualize Opus Dei's alternative feminism.[68] Echoing

Telva's style, they too advised women to "raise their head from their pots, and stick their nose out of the house."[69] By this, they did not mean women should pursue professional careers. After all, women had, "against their nature," tried to appropriate men's professions and "lost the battle," Aguirre confirmed, mocking Margaret Sanger's supposed principles.[70] Women must instead "reclaim the work of the housewife" while remaining socially active, lest they end up being like a "beautiful Cadillac without gasoline," she stated authoritatively.[71] In short, *Cuadernos del Sur* exhibited the most up-to-date version of Opus Dei's holistic modernity. In 1966, when its contributors began serving as Onganía's ministers and functionaries, the journal would become something approaching his regime's ideological mouthpiece.

Still, in 1964, the Argentine Revolution was not yet foreseeable. From April 1963, José María Guido, Frondizi's former deputy and the pragmatic interim prime minister, led a delicate transitional phase under the eagle eye of the Azules generals, Onganía, Julio Alsogaray, and Alejandro Lanusse. A reluctant president, Guido appeased them with several gestures. A personal letter to Franco, sprinkled with flattery, was one of them.[72] More concretely, he appointed a handful of Ateneo members to ministerial positions. Thus, José Mariano Astigueta now became Argentina's Education Minister while Bonifacio del Carril – an ICH collaborator and a "passionate Hispanista" – became Foreign Minister.[73] In Astigueta's case, his anti-democratic rhetoric actually led to his dismissal.[74] In other words, this was hardly the authoritarian new order the Ateneo had hoped for.

With the October 1963 election set, the question arose as to whether Onganía should run as a presidential candidate.[75] However, once Perón had endorsed the candidate Vicente Solano López as the head of his front, in April 1963, this initiative fell. Instead, the Azules forbade Solano López's candidacy, which led the Peronist voters to cast blank votes, thereby paving the way for the UCRP's candidate, Arturo Umberto Illia, to win the election with only 25 percent of the popular vote. A physician from Córdoba province, the "good doctor Illia" was neither unfit politically nor did he lead Argentina into a colossal economic crisis.[76] Unlike Frondizi, he owed nothing to Perón, respected the Azules by preserving Onganía as his chief of staff, and rolled back some of Frondizi's legislation in the oil industry, hence acquiring a more "nationalist" image in the public eye.[77] Despite this, caught between the power-craving Peronists on one side and ever more authoritarian conservatives on the other, Illia's efforts to run a stable administration were to no avail.[78]

In later years, Onganía and his followers would allege that their regime answered the popular demand to replace the passive Illia with a "strong leader."[79] In this telling, Argentina could have been "one of the most important" nations in America but became "a farce" after 1945 because of Perón's economic policies,[80] and even bordered on becoming an irrelevant geopolitical "satellite."[81] As a result, considerable frustration developed among "all sectors of Argentine society," so much so that, when democracy vanished, "no one shed a tear."[82] But was this frustration real? While it is difficult to assess how the Argentine public felt at the time, there is no question that Illia's lack of a majority in parliament provided the perfect backdrop for anti-Peronist publicists to openly champion a dictatorship in the name of this so-called silent majority. Notable within this panoply of voices were people connected to the Ateneo, such as Mariano Grondona. An avid "Frondizista," he had studied at the IEP in Madrid and was close to Amadeo. Now, as the topmost column writer of the popular magazine *Primera Plana*, he argued that a "refined Roman-style dictatorship" was not only legitimate but mandatory.[83] "Everyone, myself included, contributed to creating a kind of myth about Onganía," he would admit in later years.[84] Another case in point was Montemayor. This Hispanista was given a platform in the prominent magazine *Confirmado*, where he now readily declared that Argentina was ready to "cross the Rubicon, leaving behind its fictitious legitimacies and incompetent management."[85] These men were hardly the only ones questioning democracy, however. Even Bernardo Neustadt, Argentina's most famous television host at the time, frequently juxtaposed the efficiency of the armed forces with Argentina's incompetent political system, in his magazine *Todo*.[86]

These declarations ran parallel to an effort to construct Onganía's image as an "austere Basque" who had refrained from taking over the country thus far (although he should have).[87] The more Illia's popularity withered in the face of unimpressive economic performances, the more his chief of staff appeared in the press as Argentina's de facto president.[88] Not only did Onganía not bother to deny this, he also refused to pledge allegiance to his president, when on August 6, 1964, in a speech at West Point, he vowed to defend Argentina from "political parties circumstantially in power" and from "exotic ideologies."[89] Seeking to attain international recognition, in 1965, Onganía also toured Europe and Brazil. Tellingly, he opened this trip with a week-long visit to Spain, where he encountered several high-ranking figures, most importantly Muñoz Grandes. Apparently, Onganía was deeply impressed by his host and told him that "Spain is the essence of Argentina's interior and exterior politics."[90] To the local press, Onganía boasted his Basque ancestry and demanded that the Argentine, Spanish, and newborn Brazilian military dictatorship form an anticommunist alliance – a testament to whom he saw as his closest ideological allies.[91]

In concrete terms, the dictatorship's planning began only after November 22, 1965, when Illia forced Onganía into retirement by appointing a senior general above him.[92] In late 1965, Onganía's home thus became a center for recurrent meetings where he probed the most programmatic right-wing actors in Argentina. These were not "conspiratorial meetings" but gatherings of people who understood that "the situation was unsustainable," Díaz Colodrero maintained.[93] In turn, in January 1966, Onganía met with Amadeo and his circle – a fateful encounter where the dictatorship's configuration took place. Amadeo was the "person who spoke," promoting the idea "that a coup was necessary" and that this government "of mediocrities" should be replaced by "capable men," Costa Méndez recalled.[94] His memory matches what Amadeo wrote to Sánchez Bella at the time: "I believe that the Ateneo can fulfill a considerable role of nucleation and civil orientation in the uncertain times ahead," he told his Francoist ally.[95] Indeed, when designing his regime, Onganía sought out the expertise of the Ateneo's Hispanistas, as well as of devout MCC and Opus Dei Catholics, while flouting the neofascist Nacionalistas.[96] By then, his ideological references were also explicit. "Onganía's ideal was Franco, but he realized quite well that Argentina was not Spain and that Franco was anachronistic," remembered Costa Méndez.[97] That is to say, to his men, Onganía was candid about his Francoist inspiration but also purported to transcend the Spanish model toward a somewhat different authoritarian format – one that would overcome Peronism by spurring swift economic growth, without bloodshed, in "peace and liberty."[98]

3.3 THE ARGENTINE REVOLUTION: HISPANIC TECHNOCRACY, FROM THEORY TO PRACTICE

On June 28, 1966, Generals Pascual Pistarini, Adolfo Álvarez, and Benigno Varela overthrew Illia in a bloodless coup d'état. The following day, they handed complete extra-constitutional powers to Onganía. Therefore, technically, Onganía did not seize power militarily, allowing him to present himself as a civil leader who answered neither to a military Junta nor to any political group. Still, Onganía's so-called Argentine

Revolution was, by all standards, a dictatorship. Little did this bother the mainstream Argentine press, which could barely hide its enthusiasm in expectation of economic stagnation being replaced with decisive action. The conservative daily *La Nación*, for instance, launched a series of editorials justifying the dictatorship on the premise that technology "revolutionized collective habits," thus rendering democracy an anachronism.[99] Montemayor, too, praised the new regime, saying that it was not the result of a "classic conspiracy" but the outcome of a civilized debate on "whether or not one should put an end to [Argentina's] constitutional fiction" and "get to the bottom of things."[100] Perhaps the most striking endorsement of the regime was that of the exiled Spanish thinker Salvador de Madariaga, who, on August 5, 1966, published an open letter to Onganía, declaring that democracy did not suit the "Hispanic character." A liberal thinker (but no great democrat, apparently), he mused about a new post-ideological society wherein "both the employers' and the workers' anarchy will give place to a regime of authority."[101]

Regardless of this wave of support, or perhaps because of it, Onganía had few scruples about linking himself with the Francoist regime. On July 13, 1966, he published his regime's first foundational text, pledging to "strengthen Argentina's traditional relations with Spain and the other European nations."[102] Titled "Políticas del Gobierno Nacional," it aroused immediate interest in Spain. Thus, in August 1966, López Rodó added Buenos Aires to his Development Plan tour destinations. He did not arrive unprepared. Sánchez Bella had briefed him on Onganía's declarations beforehand:

> Such an explicit declaration in favor of the Mother Nation had never been uttered since the times of independence. We must take [Onganía] at his word, thanking him and telling him: "President, we are at your service, willing to study and subscribe to concrete and effective formulas" ... We must make him see that autarchy is crazy today; that no country can be enough for itself ... The person who can be most helpful in explaining the Argentine political panorama to you is, without a doubt, Mario Amadeo ... the most unconditional friend that Spain has in that country.[103]

Yet nothing prepared López Rodó for how "affectionate with Spain" his host turned out to be.[104] Onganía and his staff, he wrote, were sincerely enthusiastic about Spain's new role in Argentina's history. "Nations need more than just material progress. They require the spirit to inspire them. Here, they need *Argentinidad*. Spain must give this spirit its form," Onganía told him.[105] Then, he expressed his "interest in the Spanish formula of the Economic and Social Development Plan," not before suggesting sending officials to Spain to "study the Argentine problems with Spanish experts." On this occasion, Onganía also had no problem professing his belief that future "participation of the community" in politics was hazardous, given that Argentina's political parties are "divorced from reality."[106]

In this somewhat sycophantic setting, López Rodó felt liberated to promote Hispanic technocracy in the most gregarious way possible. To an audience of industrialists, he first bestowed an evolutionary process comprising "stabilization, liberalization, foreign investments, and economic flexibility." This progression, he preached, depended on adopting the external convertibility of the currency and the elimination of trade deficits, but even more so, on a "disciplined public sector" devoid of "shortsighted and partisan views."[107] Only thus, he further told Neustadt in an interview, could an industrial sub-peripheral nation modernize its production lines and avoid becoming a "junk museum."[108] According to a local Opus Dei intellectual named Roberto Bosca, these words left a "great impact" in Argentina.[109]

Assuredly, that both guest and host felt a special sense of fraternity did not mean for a moment they did not have other, ad hoc motivations for this celebratory performance. As the correspondence between López Rodó and Onganía's ministers lays bare, the Spaniards sought to reduce their trade deficit and establish a Pegaso assembly center in Argentina. López Rodó even made its installation conditional on impeding competition from Italian companies.[110] Onganía likewise had his motives to expand Argentina's bilateral economic collaboration with Spain, as we shall observe shortly. Still, linking with Francoism clearly meant more to him than economic interests. Perhaps the best example of this was the unusual personal letter he delivered via his Education Minister, the Hispanisa Carlos María Gelly y Obes, to Franco himself, in October 1966. "The Argentine Revolution has emphasized in its founding documents the singular value it attributes to the spiritual community with Spain, and its willingness to translate this appreciation into concrete lines of its foreign policy," it read. Further, the letter heralded Argentina's "adhesion" to the OEI – a measure Onganía believed would "orientate" Argentina's youth "according to the spiritual tradition that has guided Argentina's creation." Lastly, it claimed that to constitute a "richer plot" in Spanish–Argentine relations, "the Spiritual requires the support of the Economic and the Political," and that the two nations' "intimate position" in the international arena should translate into "a closer collaboration in these fields." In his four years in power, Onganía approached no other foreign leader in this manner. Interestingly, Onganía asked Franco for nothing in particular but sought to spell out who he was to his addressee and, in turn, to his *own* followers. This can be gathered from another suggestive line in his letter: "I am convinced that Your Excellency will interpret the meaning of this message, dictated by the desire ... that the substantive values that have given meaning to our national movements will translate into our governments' effective action."[111] Based on his previous statements in Spain, there is no other way to interpret these remarks than that this was Onganía's way of telling Franco that he was a wholehearted Hispanista who should, therefore, receive special economic and political treatment if a Hispanic international of any kind should arise in Latin America.

That being said, there is no indication that Onganía publicly pledged to follow in Franco's footsteps or that the Argentine press seriously considered this eventuality.[112] As a matter of fact, the dictators' styles and temperaments could not be more different. Unlike Franco, Onganía did not institute a cult of personality around himself. And despite relying on sporadic police brutality – most famously during the purging of the University of Buenos Aires – he refrained from terrorizing his opponents, much less assassinating them.[113] On the one hand, Onganía dismissed the supreme court, outlawed political parties, and ousted the provinces' governors. On the other hand, he did not declare a state of emergency, ban the labor unions, or purge the free press – at least during his first year in power. This was part of a calculated strategy to give the public the impression that the regime targeted political "elites" but protected civil liberties.[114] Certainly, he *could* have used violence had he wanted to, he said, but this "was not our way."[115] For Grondona, the fact that the Argentines' "fundamental human rights" remained in place was enough to proclaim that the regime was categorically "not despotic."[116]

Despotic or not, the regime's true colors started becoming manifest when Onganía appointed Costa Méndez as his Foreign Minister and Díaz Colodrero as Secretary of Government. Reverberating López Rodó's title, the latter – a Hispanista and Opus Dei member, as we saw – was to be the dictatorship's chief administrator, bringing together all branches of government toward rapid economic development.[117] "Now they have appointed ... a disciple of mine – Mario Díaz Colodrero," wrote Amadeo to Sánchez Bella in excitement. "On the other hand, poor Goyeneche has not received a piece of the action," he noted.[118] The reason for this was simple: Onganía categorically denied executive power to neofascist Nacionalistas – the "old conflicting Nacionalismo," in

Grondona's words.[119] His cabinet was fully stabilized in January 1967 with the appointment of Adalbert Krieger Vasena as Minister of the Economy, Astigueta as Minister of Education, and Ateneo member Guillermo Borda as Minister of the Interior. For Amadeo, this confirmed that Onganía had made the Ateneo his regime's ideological core. His letters to Sánchez Bella acquired, now, a particularly boastful tone:

> The revolutionary government, because of its political, social, and spiritual orientation, could not have found a more suitable and coherent team in the civil sphere than ours. Argentina suffers from a spiritual – almost psychic – crisis that manifests itself in a collective spirit of discontent, frustration, and destructiveness towards every established thing. This government has the conditions to fulfill its Organizing Mission, which … might take years to accomplish.[120]

Indeed, Amadeo believed nothing could stop him and his followers from fundamentally altering Argentine society.

While the Ateneo was not his only source of functionaries, Onganía undoubtedly handpicked his men according to their spiritual credentials – mainly from Opus Dei, MCC, and ICH.[121] The exception was Krieger Vasena. Hardly a devout Catholic, he was a student of ultra-conservative Argentine ideologue Carlos Moyano Llerena, and therefore, according to Amadeo, an Ateneo associate. Be that as it may, with his team of economic "technicians," Krieger Vasena was tasked with administering an economic shock treatment similar to Spain's 1959 Stabilization Plan. Through a currency devaluation to a national salary freeze, he first sought to curb Argentina's chronic inflation, paving the way for a rapid increase in foreign investment.[122] Then, he eliminated most subsidized economic activities – most famously, the sugar industry in Tucumán province.[123] For some reason, Krieger Vasena believed that the working classes would readily endure this temporary "state of mind of austerity" in return for better-paying jobs and modernized manufacturing in the distant future.[124] Certainly, Onganía's ministers shared the penchant to publicly portray this supposed process – wherein Argentina was to rid itself of "all that is expired," become a "highly technological and complex society," and thus transfer from the "underdeveloped" to the "developed" world – as a collective action supported, if not stipulated, *by the workers*.[125]

Another aspect of this reform was a supposed "decentralization" process, which commonly appeared as the long-awaited "authentic exercise of federalism."[126] As in López Rodó's plan, in practice, "decentralization" meant setting up an administrative center charged with removing state regulations and services.[127] Likewise, tax-free "development poles" and a Territorial Integration Fund were to channel foreign investments to deprived peripheral areas, thereby "correcting the concentrated growth distortion in the metropolitan area."[128] That Díaz Colodrero's formulas resembled the Spanish development plans was quite obvious, so much so that, in an interview with Spanish journalists, he confessed that he had "taken into account the modules used by the Spanish development plan, especially the system of industrial promotion and development poles."[129]

Throughout this process, more discreetly, the Ateneo began to plan the authoritarian state model that would replace Argentina's bygone democracy. "We are in an extremely critical moment for the implementation of a democratic and representative system," Amadeo wrote to Sánchez Bella, "based, not on political parties ... but on natural institutions."[130] Franco's ideologue, as expected, threw his weight behind this process and even outlined the Ateneo's specific role. "It is important that the Ateneo does not dissolve now that it is in power ... but succeeds in creating a new mentality in Argentina, more appropriate than the present one for the technological society in which we live," he replied.[131] As can readily be seen, for these two, the Ateneo was the leading intermediary society through which civil participation was to be practiced, in reality, in Argentina's post-ideological order.

At first, the regime kept its political plans undisclosed. True, Onganía's speeches were full of anti-liberal slogans. On July 4, 1966, commemorating 150 years of independence, he more than insinuated that Argentina's liberal "cycle" had now "reached its conclusion."[132] Even so, during his first months in power, Argentina's political future was not addressed in public. And when it did, this happened somewhat haphazardly – for instance, when Pedro Ancarola, Secretary-General of the Ministry of Welfare, privately published his theory of Argentina's new state model, which he named "Hierarchic Democracy of Total Representation." Whereas "Anglo-Saxon" parliamentarism had enabled a deceitful "collective psychological behavior," he stressed, his model of democracy would produce a culture of collaboration based on "intermediary bodies" such as the family, municipality, and distinctive "development societies."[133] Ancarola was soon joined by Díaz Colodrero, who, early in 1967, went public with several glaringly authoritarian announcements – for instance, that the Argentine Revolution's goal was to "definitively overcome the old electoral groupings"[134] and that Argentina should focus on enjoying the current "rest cure" from its political "anachronisms."[135]

Unfortunately for Onganía, his ministers' chatter meant that, throughout 1967, his authoritarian style came under increasing public criticism.[136]

Subsequently, and with the Peronist labor unions still cooperating with the regime, he published an evolutionary strategy consisting of "economic," "social," and "political" phases.[137] If the first was synonymous with Krieger Vasena's reforms, then the third phase signified the advent of a yet-to-be-defined system of political representation.[138] In July 1967, Onganía elaborated further on his political ideals. Presenting himself as a leader empowered by an "entire citizenry that said enough is enough!" he clarified that democracy should not be confused with the "mechanical act of voting" and that "traditional liberalism" would never be allowed back in Argentina. Thus, he assured his audience that his "political phase" would consist of a new concept of the community, albeit not in any "corporatist" way. "In no way can it be said that I am a corporatist," he declared. Díaz Colodrero likewise rejected any comparison between the political phase and corporatism – a formula that is "a thing of the past."[139]

Still, the more enigmatic of these so-called phases was not the political but the social phase. As Amadeo and Sánchez Bella's correspondence lays bare, it meant changing the Argentines' mentalities and making them obedient and united. Borda – a Peronist in the past and Ateneo member in the present – even said it upfront. "We cannot settle for mere economic prosperity because in its deep essence, the Revolution is spiritual, and its supreme goals are justice and solidarity," he stated.[140] Yet how does one fashion a collective change of mentality? By cultivating a healthy public morality, for one thing. Sure enough, a new patriarchal civic code, followed by restrictions on cultural expression and municipal laws banning miniskirts for women and long hair for men, showcased a regime railing against the alleged damage inflicted by the Western cultural revolution of the 1960s.[141] The education system similarly became a stage for moralist indoctrination. Having abolished academic freedom in April 1967,[142] the regime then vowed to return the entire education system to its "Christian and Hispanic roots."[143] Noteworthy in this respect was Astigueta's 1967 Organic Law of Education – a spiritual manifesto pleading for the restoration of "habits of religious and moral life," thereby undermining Argentina's long-standing secular Law 1420 of Common Education. Assisted by a think tank of Catholic pedagogues of the Consejo Superior de Educación Católica (CONSUDEC), Astigueta wanted more than just mandatory Catholic education, however.[144] Instead, he perceived the education system as the place where youngsters were now to internalize the "value of austerity, of manhood,"[145] and, as a result, be freed from rebelliousness and "return to interiority."[146]

Thereafter, Argentine youngsters would be allowed to choose a vocation within a "human resources policy" – that is, to fulfill their role "according to development plans."[147]

Although not as omnipresent in the Argentine public sphere as in Spain, Opus Dei platforms and intellectuals played a conclusive part in the education reform's theory and promotion. The rapport between García Hoz and Juan Rafael Llerena Amadeo, Astigueta's deputy, may further explain this salient role. Indeed, Llerena Amadeo promoted initiatives that strongly reverberated with Opus Dei's gender ideology, such as to shift Argentina from a mixed school to a gender-separated public school system designed according to gendered social functions.[148] "The complexity of knowledge and self-discipline involved in home management makes the role of the housewife an authentic profession that requires training like any other," he announced elsewhere.[149] In addition, *Cuadernos del Sur* did its utmost to promote Astigueta's reform. Once more, it invited García Hoz to elucidate how one is to counter technological acceleration by stimulating the "spiritual development of man so that he does not become a mere means of production," while imbuing in him the "divine command to work."[150] The notion that there is a deep-seated correlation between humanist education and economic slowdown reached its extreme in the texts of other Opus Dei intellectuals. Delia Brusa – Eugenio Antonio's wife – stated, for instance, that when education emphasizes economic development, "stoical men, even great technicians, are created." By contrast, a pedagogical emphasis on sheer "intelligence" leads to an inability to "cope with the practical sides of life," and thus produces a "caricature of a man."[151] In short, backed by Opus Dei, the reform prioritized the creation of a society of obedient and spiritually trained technicians who would endure the alienating side effects of modern manufacturing without speculating on abstract theoretical questions, such as the causes and meaning of social inequality.

Curiously enough, education was also the arena that saw the first official collaboration between the Argentine Revolution and Franco's Spain. Following the passing of Law 16,981 of October 14, 1966, as Onganía had promised Franco, Argentina began cooperating with the OEI.[152] This invites the question of what Onganía really wanted from this body in the late 1960s – that is, besides a place where Hispanistas such as Gelly y Obes could exclaim that, "reborn from its crises with new vigor and impulse," Spain is "once again our exemplar."[153] Still, this was far from being a purely symbolic adherence. For one thing, this was a prestigious and well-funded apparatus with which Onganía sought to impact the Argentine education system, in the Buenos Aires area in particular. It was also an excellent propaganda tool for the regime. Having replaced Gelly y Obes in office, Astigueta hosted the organization's 1967 Conference of Technical Education – an occasion that featured him and Onganía wedding economic growth to technical education and "respect for order and spiritual and moral values."[154] At one point, Amadeo even promoted Goyeneche as a candidate for OEI secretary-general and even approached Carrero Blanco to influence Marañón to appoint him – in this case, in vain.[155]

These anecdotes cannot be understood divorced from the fundamental presence of Hispanidad in the Argentine Revolution's foreign policy. To put it simply, under Costa Méndez, Onganía's Foreign Ministry and the ICH branch had become one and the same. The fact that it featured Hispanistas such as Mazzinghi, Peltzer, and Etchecopar theorizing Argentina's official "continental mission" as Hispanidad's second pillar was not lost on the press.[156] In truth, Amadeo's letters to Sánchez Bella indicate that the Foreign Ministry became a place of tension for the Hispanistas, who were now infighting over every position. According to Amadeo, the fact that his "disciple since 1945" appointed him only as ambassador to Brazil said a great deal about the "generational rebellion" within the Hispanista camp. To put it mildly, Amadeo was unimpressed with Costa Méndez's diplomacy, accusing him of clumsily turning Argentina into Latin America's "South Africa."[157]

Amadeo was referring to Onganía and Costa Méndez's twofold diplomacy. On the one hand, outwardly, they handled the relationship with the USA and Western Europe with care. This meant that Costa Méndez, who had been antagonistic to the Washington-led Organization of the American States in 1962, tempered his rhetoric considerably. While warning against peripheral countries losing their "national character," Onganía too reassured his fellow Latin American leaders that the continent "is supported by Anglo Saxonian America in a pledge to establish a world of elementary norms of coexistence."[158] And while Costa Méndez's speeches at the UN assembly in 1966 and 1967 were dedicated almost entirely to the Malvinas Islands dispute, this was hardly where the regime's priorities lay.[159] On the other hand, the two presented Latin America, repeatedly and fervently, with political unification schemes enshrouded in Hispanidad mythology.[160] For example, to Bolivian dictator Alfredo Ovando Candía, Onganía pontificated that "Spain's colonial enterprise, the highest spiritual heritage" constitutes the basis for the continent's "politics of integration."[161] Concretely, he and Costa

Méndez proposed to lead the "multinational project of physical integration" of the Plata Basin, based on the hoped-for earnest relationship with the new military dictatorships in Brazil and Peru.[162] Unfortunately for them, Chile, where Frei's government had declared Onganía a persona non grata, would have none of it.[163] It was also averse to Argentina's efforts to institutionalize the Inter-American Defense Board – a defiance that further exacerbated the territorial quarrel between the nations.[164] In August 1966, Onganía contacted Frei proposing to solve the Beagle Straits dispute – to which Frei responded by suggesting the countries turn to international arbitration.[165] Hence, in its short lifespan, the Argentine Revolution's one diplomatic achievement was the Onganía–Frei meeting in 1970 and arbitration process. To Amadeo's mind, this was far too small an accomplishment.

Ultimately, Onganía's relationship with Francoism was the most noteworthy diplomacy his regime undertook, certainly on a symbolic level. This was manifested in the outstanding efforts Spain and Argentina made to festoon one another with honors.[166] Thus, while Argentina honored López Rodó, Spain granted Costa Méndez and Onganía the Spanish Navy Medals of Honor. "You all know how great my love for Spain is," Onganía said on this occasion. "Iberia, a magnificent melting pot of races, upon fertilizing the arrogant American continent, has bequeathed us its glory, the spiritual temple of its greatness," he said emotionally.[167] Symbols then turned into hard currency. Following the closing of the British market to Argentine beef in 1967, Spain came to Onganía's aid by purchasing some 20,000 tons of meat, in what seemed a reverse version of the Franco–Perón Protocols.[168] The Argentine Revolution also attracted the attention of Franco's intellectuals. In 1967, Fernández de la Mora visited the country, presenting his theory on the "twilight of ideologies" to a sympathetic audience.[169] Another visitor from Spain, though not a Spaniard himself, was Fredrick D. Wilhelmsen. An Opus Dei sympathizer, in 1967, he gave a series of lectures in Buenos Aires that drew the vitriol of the liberal newspaper *Inédito*. The "*opusdeísta* Wilhelmsen," it reported, "spoke at the Ateneo de la República, in parishes, and Catholic universities ... all these new promoters of communitarianism, *cursillismo*, corporativism, names behind which clericalism and extreme right-wing fascism are hidden."[170] Thus, somewhat hashed and belated, the Argentine liberal press discovered the Spanish–Argentine special relationship and began to contemplate its meaning for the country's future.

By this time, the Argentine Revolution's nexus with Francoism was anything but hidden. In fact, Onganía's ministers traveled to Spain, issuing telling statements about their mission. In November 1967, as part of an effort to amass foreign credit in Europe, Krieger Vasena arrived in Madrid with a team of experts to explore "Spain's system of administrative decentralization," which, the Spanish dailies explained, had already been applied "as an initial experiment in the Argentine province of Córdoba."[171] Onganía's Minister of Tourism and Press, Federico Frischknecht, also arrived in Madrid in 1967. "I must admit that I feel overwhelmed by the weight of trying to emulate the actions developed by the Spanish Ministry of Information and Tourism," he stated with a deep reverence, not before begging God "to continue enlightening" Franco and Onganía, "who have done so much to lead our nations together in the path of historical destiny."[172] Last, Costa Méndez visited Spain in April 1969. Meeting with Franco, he discussed the similarities between the British occupations of Gibraltar and the Malvinas and the need for "mutual and unyielding diplomatic support" for the recovery of these territories. He, too, could barely rein in the impulse to declare himself and his hosts the guardians of Latin America's "Hispanic truth."[173] In brief, these men purported to want to study the Francoist methods of development, representation, and tourist economy, while voicing enthusiastic expressions on the shared "Hispanic" crusade their regimes were supposedly directing together.

3.4 ONGANÍA'S PENDING "POLITICAL PHASE" AND IGNOMINIOUS DOWNFALL

Whether or not Francoist expertise contributed to the Argentine Revolution's success is difficult to determine. What is beyond doubt, however, is that, between 1967 and 1970, Argentina witnessed Krieger Vasena's reforms ushering in a period of impressive GDP growth, thanks to its stabilized currency and a steady flow of foreign investment. The fact that the working class paid the price for what Krieger Vasena now called the "Argentine miracle" – due to the peso's devaluation, salary freeze, and unemployment – was not an unintended consequence but a calculated risk the regime took in the hope of rapid economic growth.[174] The workers' sacrifice "hurts us and we would have wished it could have been avoided ... But one cannot do distributive justice when there is nothing to distribute," Onganía even said apologetically.[175] All the same, there was hardly any doubt that, in early 1969, Krieger Vasena's economic team was the one division in the regime that showed palpable results and, as importantly, narrated them cohesively to the public.

The same cannot be said about Onganía's team of Ateneo ideologues. As the regime approached its third year, the "political phase" was perhaps tentatively declared but remained largely undefined, leading the press to constant speculation.[176] In the spring of 1968, Borda and Díaz Colodrero were both quoted as confirming the inevitable replacement of parliament with an entirely novel system of representation.[177] But unlike López Rodó and Fernández de la Mora, they were in no hurry to translate these slogans into actions. In effect, despite Amadeo's boasts, the intrigue-ridden Ateneo lacked one authoritative architect to theorize the political phase into an identifiable constitutional text as in the Spanish case in 1967. Thus, even the regime's enthusiasts in *Cuadernos del Sur* appeared perplexed when contemplating Argentina's future "organic" democracy and whether it could be rendered "corporatist." For Edmundo Carbone, the journal's new editor, there was little doubt that Argentina had transcended its ideological past and was ready for an authoritarian model based not on corporatist chambers but on councils consisting of "representatives from different sectors of society extracted from their freely constituted groupings."[178] Unlike him, Bosca spoke of a "democratic corporative system" that would be "neither fascist nor medieval" and thus capable of "alleviating the errors ... of liberalism, neoliberalism, and statism."[179] Amadeo, for his part, muddied the water even more. For the ICH's Congress of the Hispano-Portuguese-American Institute of International Law in Buenos Aires, he invited a list of Francoist ideologues to discuss the applicability of corporatism in Latin America. Then again, he stressed that, of all the models available – communism, fascism, and liberalism – only Frondizi and Onganía had ever proposed a regime model with any "viability."[180] By this, he insinuated that Onganía's regime model had, in fact, already taken its political form.

Onganía did not seem keen to elucidate the intricacies of his political model either. And when he did, his followers later claimed that his ideas were riddled with inconsistencies. "I think the nearest thing to his vision was Franco's Spain," Costa Méndez said in the 1980s.[181] One should take his recollection with a grain of salt. Onganía's actions illustrated one of two things: Either he believed the "political phase" was too distant on the horizon to be defined or, as plausibly, like Amadeo, he thought that his regime was *already* living its political phase. After all, he allowed minor projects that seemingly fostered public participation in governance. The Ministry of Social Welfare, for instance, sponsored the Promoción y Asistencia a la Comunidad (SEPAC) system as a cornerstone of "social participation."[182] In addition, Onganía habitually assembled civil forums such as the Consejo Nacional de Seguridad (CONASE) and Consejo Nacional de Desarrollo (CONADE).[183] Along with the Ateneo and his religious think tanks, these practices of representation may have been, to his mind, all Argentina's new order would ever necessitate. In fact, once more obviously "corporatist" initiatives emerged, they did more harm than good. In one such "pilot" project, in August 1968, Carlos Caballero, the Nacionalista governor of the city of Córdoba, established a "community council."[184] The media immediately labeled it a "preamble for a proper fascist-like corporative chamber," a claim that Onganía was forced to deny. In 1984, he was still arguing that Caballero's initiative had differed markedly from his plans, thus confirming that the "political phase" would have been anything but corporatist.[185]

The problem was that the very prospects of inaugurating a "corporatist" political system proved harmful for Onganía. By late 1968, the Argentine press was taking swipes at this forthcoming authoritarian state model and the ideological groups propagating it and their unmistakable political influence in Onganía's administration and provincial governments. This began as early as 1967 when a damaging report on Opus Dei's position of power in government appeared in the weekly *Análisis*. "One should consider Opus Dei a secret/semi-secret political association and attribute to it an ever-growing, albeit invisible, power," the report stated.[186] In early 1969, *Primera Plana* followed suit in exposing the MCC's political control of Tucumán – a fact that the province's nonelected governor and MCC leader, Roberto Avellaneda, hardly denied.[187] If these reports reflected the political power of these movements, rather than their Francoist linkage, then in 1969, several conspicuous pamphlets circulated in Argentina alleging that the country was headed toward a "communitarian state" that "will rely on bodies similar to those existing in Spain and Portugal, under Opus Dei's influence."[188] In brief, by the spring of 1969, Onganía's political plan, the ideological agencies backing it, and its links to the Iberian Peninsula were subject to critical public scrutiny.

Ultimately, this hostile atmosphere was crucial in spurring the civil resistance that led to Onganía's downfall. On May 29, 1969, a conjuncture of circumstances – including new tax increases, continuous student mobilization, and the intransigence of several labor unions gathered under the name of CGT de los Argentinos – brought this unrest to the surface in Córdoba. Following an alliance between the city's students and the Light and Auto plant unions, demonstrators took over the city for hours, to be overrun by the police later on the same day and suffer up to thirty fatalities.[189] In fact, the "Cordobazo" was just one in a cascade of uprisings between April and October 1969 that rendered manifest that Onganía was neither a consensual "president" nor capable of sustaining "peace and liberty" without lethal brutality.[190] Essentially, they showed that the plan to instigate a Hispanic technocracy reminiscent of Francoism had led Argentines of different ideological hues to conclude that Onganía could only be ousted through civil uprising and, later, urban guerilla activity. This was, at least, what Franco's agents told their superiors. The Córdoba's "effervescence," they reported, did not derive from any "political direction" but from Onganía's austerity plan and reluctance to oppress the public sphere. "Everyone here enjoys the absolute and total freedom of the press," they remarked in surprise.[191]

Interestingly, *Cuadernos del Sur*'s explanation was not entirely dissimilar. Its editorial admitted that the uprising had resulted from Onganía's "economic mistakes" and pleaded that he reveal his entire "political plan." But what was the Opus Dei editors' desired scheme? Certainly not a return to parliamentarism. *Cuadernos del Sur* still insisted that the Argentine Revolution had generated a final "supra-constitutional order," that it relied on a "tacit consensus of the population," and that "one cannot go back to the system concluded on June 28, 1966," since political parties are unable to perform the "colossal" modernizing task facing the nation.[192] In other words, even at this dramatic stage, economic modernization was Opus Dei's principal justification for a new, and indeed infinite, authoritarian order.

Onganía struggled to stay in power for another entire year. While repressing the uprising violently and closing several news outlets, he also sacked the Ateneo ministers, shelved his education reform, and watered down his economic restructurings – actions that indicated that he was attentive to the civil uprising's fundamental causes. Even so, strikingly, he refused to terminate his Francoist nexus. In January 1970, he sent Dardo Pérez Guilhou – his third Education Minister and yet another ICH intellectual – to meet Franco and study Spain's 1970 education reform.[193] Little did this gesture impress the commanders of the armed forces. In May 1970, the Azul high command sent Onganía a memorandum blaming him for "the absence of concrete ideas about the culmination of the revolutionary process and its exit."[194] Ergo, the armed forces surmised that, despite its economic achievements, the Argentine Revolution had reached the limits of its legitimacy and effectiveness. The murder of General Aramburu on May 29, 1970, was another grim signal of the dictatorship's ineptness in the face of left-wing mobilization turning to violence. On June 5, 1970, when the generals demanded that Onganía present the public with a concrete political plan, he returned to them with a statement of "political theory," comprising incoherent technocratic slogans that ignored principles such as the separation of powers.[195] Three days later, led by Lanusse, the generals ousted Onganía.

While it would reach its end only in 1973, following Onganía's ousting the Argentine Revolution was a spent force. This ignominious demise has caused historians to overlook the magnitude of this regime's ideological project. Like Franco's technocrats, Onganía and his men believed they could install an internationally respectable protected society of material abundance and Catholic spirituality at the heart of the Western Hemisphere. Herein, they believed, a new post-ideological Argentine subject who would disdain "irrational" revolutionary movements – be they Peronism or communism – would emerge. The chaotic way the dictatorship behaved after 1970, which we will inspect in Chapter 5, also belies the orderly way its ideology had been in the making since 1962. Arguably, the Argentine Revolution was the most well-designed case study of the three occupying this book. And certainly, Onganía's three "phases" were the most transparent expression of the Hispanic technocracy's deterministic fantasies: An economic shock treatment, followed by a myriad of indoctrination schemes – ranging from changes in the Civic Code to a spiritual educational reform – were to lead the Argentines to willingly accept a new "form of doing politics." Onganía also behaved – and promoted himself to his neighbors – as the second pillar of Hispanidad. There was nothing particularly covert about his discourse or how he sought to link himself to the other pillar in the Iberian Peninsula.

For all his grandiosity, it should be borne in mind that Onganía's regime was the shortest case study in our analysis. Had the regime existed several more years, one might have witnessed Onganía's Hispanic diplomacy and "political phase" come to fruition. While there is nothing in the sources to suggest that political representation was ever meant to take the form of some sort of neo-corporatist system – given that the regime expected the masses to become docile and spiritually elevated consumers and, as such, uninterested in politics – unlike Franco's 1967 Laws, in this case one would never know what the political phase entailed. Still, the question remains: Why did it fail so miserably? The obvious answer is that, unlike Franco, Onganía thought he could transcend the Spanish model by not having to resort to terror or a state of civil war. By believing his dictatorship could seamlessly implement a handful of "techniques" employed in Spain, he thus grossly overlooked the crucial importance of the memory of the Spanish Civil War and Franco's ongoing state-led terror. In brief, Onganía's downfall resulted from his self-perception as a consensual leader and unwillingness to terrorize civil society – the unspoken ingredient of "Franco's peace." A closer look also reveals that, predesigned as it was, the Argentine Revolution's motion from ideology to state ideology occurred somewhat hectically, and relied on deep-seated anti-Peronist sentiments of the middle classes. These sectors could live peacefully with an authoritarian hiatus for the sake of economic modernization but not with the idea of living under a dictatorship ad infinitum. That is to say, Onganía's downfall was not the result of Peronist mobilization but of his misjudgment of Argentina's democratic ethos. Blaming the Peronists for the Cordobazo could not conceal the fact that this was one of Argentina's more consensual and proud moments of collective defiance. This may explain Onganía's lax treatment of the public sphere, his incompetence in overtaking it with his supporting private media corporations, and his unwillingness to empower one ideologue to lead a demonstrable constitutional process – all of which did not bode well for his regime's stability. As we shall see in the next chapter, in Chile, such problems would not reoccur.

4

Augusto Pinochet's Dictatorship

Chile's "Neoliberal" Variant of Hispanic Technocracy (1964–1977)

As mentioned, until 1970, Chile was one of the steadier parliamentary democracies in Latin America. Even Carlos Ibáñez del Campo's first presidency (1927–31) – which saw various forms of dictatorial behavior – did not shake the Chileans' trust in the 1925 constitutional order. Yet, in hindsight, the first signs of this system's disintegration were already there in September 1964, when Christian Democratic candidate Eduardo Frei Montalva won the presidential elections. Defeating the People's National Front candidate Salvador Allende and supported by the conservative polity, he, who had been José Antonio Primo de Rivera's admirer in the 1930s, attained political power by creating a centrist ideology based on the promises of extensive land and educational reforms. Frei's reputed "Revolution in Liberty" was a watershed moment in Chilean politics. Above all, it reflected the disappointment with Jorge Alessandri's presidency and economic model. Since his election in 1958, the conservative president had sought to forge a market-friendly technocracy in Chile. Impacted by Chile's 1960 earthquake, his tenure saw modest economic growth coupled with broadening social inequality. Henceforth, until 1970, the Chilean political sphere was divided evenly between three ideological groups: the conservative right, the Christian Democratic center, and Salvador Allende's Marxist left – the latter two representing programs of profound state intervention in the economy and wealth redistribution.

Having governed Chile since Carlos Ibáñez del Campo's return to the presidency in 1952, the conservatives found their attitudes toward democracy profoundly impacted by these events. To be sure, they were still powerful and well-connected internationally. Indeed, the fact that the CIA took part in the anti-communist scare campaign against Allende illustrated the extent to which their international allies would go to support them.[1] Still, Chile's 1965 parliamentary elections witnessed more than 80 percent of voters electing parties representing redistributionist agendas. In other words, the conservatives faced a reduction in political power in favor of a well-mobilized, and indeed hostile, working class driven by charismatic leaders.[2] Adding insult to injury, Frei was also a Christian Democrat. Building on the guidance of Jacques Maritain and Étienne Gilson and encouraged by the Second Vatican Council, he embodied a new progressive form of Catholic spirituality that went against the conservatives' elitist worldview.

To be sure, the conservatives did not wait until 1964 to render democracy illegitimate. As we have seen, Hispanistas and neofascists of sorts had been voicing anti-democratic sentiments since the 1930s. All the same, Chile's rightists began to mobilize decidedly only in 1963, with the *Estanquero* Hispanistas playing a vital role in this radicalization. As in Spain and Argentina, a younger generation of theorists emerged from within the Hispanistas' cadres of the 1930s. Inspired by Francoist theorists, in the 1960s, they succeeded in distancing themselves from both fascism and traditionalism, thus becoming the heads of a coalition of forces that proposed replacing Chile's democracy with a brand-new format of authoritarianism. Joined and aided by Opus Dei, they thus sought to transcend and perfect the Francoist model, as well as to learn from Onganía's mistakes. Once General Augusto Pinochet had taken power on September 11, 1973, he chose these people to design what ultimately became the third and most cynical version of Hispanic technocracy.[3]

Chile's Hispanic technocracy bore the traces of the ideological project it dethroned: Allende's Unidad Popular (UP). Allende's tragic story is well-known: A Marxist intellectual and politician since 1952, he became Chile's president after winning only 36 percent of the popular vote in the September 1970 presidential elections. Supported by a feeble coalition, he still went ahead with his "Chilean road to socialism" (or "La Via Chilena") – a paradigm by which Chile's mining industries and other private enterprises would be nationalized into areas of "social property" and operate alongside a regulated sphere of private economy. While Allende relied on fanatical popular mobilization and betrayed authoritarian tendencies of his own, his program was hardly a totalitarian "Leninist" regime, as Pinochet's pundits later described it. Even so, it embodied one of the most outstanding plans for governmental economic intervention in Latin America at the time, making him the most prominent symbol of defiance of the USA's economic order since the Cuban Revolution. As such, he represented the materialization of the Chilean conservatives' deepest anxieties and the USA's final disillusionment with the Alliance for Progress. President Richard Nixon, we now know, pledged to unseat Allende by making the Chilean economy "scream." Supported by the CIA, Chile's conservatives thus launched a well-organized campaign of economic destabilization, street mobilization, and moral panic.[4] By doing so, they aimed to prompt either Allende's resignation or impeachment. The unspoken premise behind this campaign was that Allende could not stay in office until the 1976 elections, as by then he might have altered Chilean society beyond recognition. When the armed forces overthrew Allende, Hispanic technocracy was already a well-defined ideological brand. The symbiotic relationship between its theoreticians and Pinochet decided his regime's ideological character.

4.1 CHILE IN THE 1960S: RIGHT-WING MOBILIZATION AND THE RISE OF GREMIALISMO

The division between distinctive neofascist and post-fascist schools also occurred in 1960s Chile, although the two were not as antagonistic as in Argentina. Like in Argentina, though, the neofascist renaissance was initially more noticeable.[5] The Chilean right's effort to pose an anti-communist and anti-capitalist "new order" based on "national syndicalism" dates back to the early 1950s, with the demise of *Estanquero*. Jorge Prat, who was born on the same day as José Antonio Primo de Rivera, identified as the Spanish fascist's reincarnation even before that and began to display ever more national syndicalist theories as the 1950s unfolded. He was joined by ideologues such as Sergio Miranda Carrington and Mario Arnello Romo. The former was Hübner Gallo's student, while the latter completed his PhD at the ICH in Madrid in 1953.[6] Both considered themselves "national syndicalists" and even specialized in José Antonio's ideology. By far, the most anti-capitalist group was the Movimiento Revolucionario Nacional Sindicalista (MRNS), however. Founded in 1952 by Ramón Callís and Gastón Acuña, its publications railed against the "economic tyranny of demo-capitalism."[7] Parliamentary democracy, Callís wrote elsewhere, is "the son of Protestantism. To defend Christianity we must destroy Capitalism."[8] Amid the mobilization around Allende ahead of the 1964 presidential elections, Prat, Miranda Carrington, Arnello, and members of MRNS joined forces and, in November 1963, established a political party named Acción Nacional. The foray of such blatantly neofascist people into mainstream electoral politics did not result in success, however. Having fared poorly in the 1965 congressional elections, its leaders joined Alessandri's electoral conglomerate named the Partido Nacional, in May 1966, but would remain, for the most part, an insignificant ideological movement.

Some of the Hispanistas discussed above did indeed rub shoulders with Prat and his men. Still, emblems such as Oswaldo Lira and Jaime Eyzaguirre remained within the parameters of Chile's Catholic University, while *Estanquero* intellectuals Arturo Fontaine, Hübner Gallo, and Raul Bazán, perhaps identified as "nacionalistas" but were still far more economically liberal than Prat's followers and less inclined to join politics. Nevertheless, they remained ideologically active and, in the mid 1960s, still deplored Sánchez Bella for ever more financial assistance – or "ideological cation" in Bazán's words. Sánchez Bella, now having turned into a technocrat, replied by explaining soft power to his companion. "The institute in Madrid should stay behind curtains, promoting action, suggesting it, in some cases if necessary, financing it, but without appearing as its leader, because once it appears as such, 80 or 90 percent of its effect would be lost," he cautioned Bazán.[9] Still, publicly aligning with Franco, and even convening with him in Madrid – as Hübner Gallo did in 1964 – remained a requisite ritual for the Hispanistas in their pursuit of prestige.[10]

That is not to say that Franco's technocrats lost interest in Chile. On the contrary, the visits of Pérez-Embid in 1965, López Rodó in 1966, and Fernández de la Mora in 1967 indicate just how eager they were to promote their development model to the Chilean conservatives. This did not prove difficult. Spain's Development Plan, announced *El Mercurio*, was synonymous with modernization in "maximum speed, economic stability, and exaltation of the dignity and freedom of man."[11] *El Diario Ilustrado*, for its part, quoted López Rodó for saying that the Spanish miracle was "the fruit of a collective effort of a nation determined to reach a better destination."[12] And when Fernández de la Mora visited Chile, *El Mercurio* hailed him as a man of "scientific rigor and pure rational effort." The daily also quoted him as saying that Spain had gone "from 200 dollars per capita to 700" and that all Spaniards "commute on motorcycles and have televisions." That, from an underdeveloped nation, Spain had become a consumerist society at an astonishing speed and had consequently been liberated from those "ideologies" plaguing "the most underdeveloped areas of the world," was, in short, the narrative that appeared in Chile's conservative media.[13] But were the Chilean conservatives persuaded? For the person who brought Fernández de la Mora to Chile, the answer was no doubt affirmative. In a somewhat sycophantic letter, Fernández Larraín told his guest the following: "You can hardly imagine the profound imprint you left in Chile … with all due justice, I cannot help myself affirming that you are one of the few who have succeeded grasping the very core of our spiritual concerns, with nobility, without hurting, but still with the utmost frankness, without disfiguring your thinking."[14] Seldom can one isolate a moment when ideologies "leap" from one continent to the other. To judge by Fernández Larraín, Fernández de la Mora's visit was one of them.

Shortly after these spectacles, and amid the dissolution of Prat's political project, a new movement began making a name for itself at Chile's Catholic University. Named the Movimiento Gremial de la Universidad Católica (or simply "Gremialismo"), its leader was Jaime Guzmán (Figure 4.1) – the teenager we encountered in this book's introduction "bursting with Hispanismo." As Lira and Eyzaguirre's student, young and impressionable, he arrived in Spain in 1962 to witness its "economic progress."[15] If Spain's economic miracle loomed large in his letter, so did

FIGURE 4.1 Jaime Guzmán, mid 1980s.
Juan Carlos Caceres / Getty Images

José Antonio's myth of "national syndicalism" based on the "Family, Municipality, and Syndicates – intermediary bodies with authentic natural right, between society and the State."[16] To put it simply, Guzmán began his career sounding like a Falangist. By 1967, however, any "national syndicalist" catchwords had disappeared from his texts. As a member of *Fiducia* – TFP's journal in Chile – he aligned with Corrêa de Oliveira's fierce anti-statism, thus depicting private property as "natural law."[17] As such, Guzmán derided fascism's "third path" ethos. "Behind the slogan 'neither capitalism nor communism' ... hides socialism," he stated.[18] Tellingly, he also stopped identifying as a Hispanista. Following Eyzaguirre's death in 1968, Guzmán published an account of his relationship with his "master, example, and friend," where he praised the "unparalleled historical adventure that is the Hispanic."[19] Still, despite being willing to appear as Eyzaguirre's successor, he also sought to be acknowledged as an idiosyncratic ideologue who, like Opus Dei in Spain, had transcended the traditionalist–fascist duality.[20]

A way to begin discussing the Gremialistas' ideology would be to address their name. While Gremialismo means "unionism" in Spanish, trade unions were not at all on their agenda. In their case, *gremial* alluded to the pre-modern guilds that had allegedly guided Chilean society until the arrival of mid nineteenth-century liberalism. The Gremialistas were, in actuality, an elitist student organization devoid of a publishing apparatus and noticeable only in the Catholic University of Chile. Contrary to common wisdom, Guzmán never belonged to Opus Dei. However, he was certainly a spiritual person and consciously cultivated a public persona of chastity. Like Opus Dei, he and his fellow students promoted seemingly urbane notions of Catholic science. "All science ... must be in accordance with the revelation's principles; otherwise, it will be pseudoscience," they declared.[21] Like López Rodó and Ibáñez Langlois before him, he theorized economic performance as a means for spiritual revival. "It is not enough to be technical professionals," he declared, as "life is worthless unless it is utilized in the service of a larger cause."[22] As with Opus Dei in the 1960s, there was little Catholic theology but a fair amount of performance of spirituality in these pledges to ethical superiority.

Guzmán and his followers gradually displayed their own theory of humanity, society, and state. At its core was theorizing private property as society's sacred ethical ground. Any form of wealth redistribution by the state was, for Guzmán, a "socialist and totalitarian" act.[23] Next, the Gremialistas' founding documents acquired a technocratic tenor by advocating a societal "depoliticization" and distinguishing between "social" and "political" power. In this authoritarian model, the regime, after purging society of its internal enemies, invites "intermediary" associations to operate society as they see fit.[24] By 1969, Guzmán was thus speaking of three defined state models: the "liberal/ individualist," the "socialist/statist," and the coveted Catholic "subsidiary state" – the only one conscious "of the transcendent purpose of man." He also exclaimed that in his model, the state would play a "secondary" role compared to the "family, the municipalities, and the unions," thus creating a "truly organic society."[25] It is not difficult to detect how Guzmán's formulations resembled those of Sánchez Agesta. Simply put, his "subsidiary state" was *Quadragesimo Anno* filtered through Francoist lenses. Guzmán never admitted to being inspired by these sources. Like Díaz Colodrero and Ancarola, he presented this ideology as his original creation.

How a lawyer in his mid twenties became Pinochet's most prominent ideologue did not emanate only from the uniqueness of his ideology but from the apparatus promoting him. It is here that Opus Dei reenters our story once more. Even before the closing of *Cuadernos del Sur*, Ibáñez Langlois and his circle had made their way into the Chilean intellectual sphere. First, they collaborated in Eyzaguirre's journal *Finis Terrae*. There, he and intellectuals such as Carlos Vial Correa and Juan de Dios Vial Correa touched on public morality and spirituality in everyday life. Economic development must serve to "Christianize society" and lead to "spiritual salvation," they wrote.[26] Next, they became household names in *El Mercurio*, with Ibáñez Langlois serving as the daily's literary critic. A poet in his own right, he now held a public "debate" with Marxist thought. Better put, in his books *Marxismo y cristianismo, El Marxismo: visión critica*, and countless op-eds, he refuted Marxism by stressing that it is "a secularized and atheist version of the Judeo-Christian hope, of mysticism, of theology, and of the Catholic apocalypse."[27] In turn, Opus Dei was given control over Zig-Zag's prestigious women's magazine *Eva*, which meant that, between 1967 and the mid 1970s, the magazine became strikingly similar to *Telva*. With María Elena Aguirre as its editor, it railed against divorce, Western youth culture, and birth control.[28] It also published a series of articles titled "Eva's Sex Education Encyclopedia," where it stressed that only within wedlock can one "take sexuality to a higher level, that which is human."[29] Indeed, the editors also claimed to be leading an alternative feminist movement. The twentieth century had presented women with two immoral positions, Aguirre alleged: Hitler's chauvinistic "Church, Kitchen, Children" ideal and

Western feminism, which demanded women "be like men." Against these two extremes, she proposed Opus Dei's pseudoscience:

> Women suffer from emotional instability due to the vulnerability of their glandular and neuro-sympathetic systems. Therefore, they aspire to balance and harmony. In contrast, men seek adventure. They are never content with stable situations. They are revolutionary, dissatisfied. Women, as general elections have shown, are much more conservative ... they are less talented in abstract speculation but have a much richer sentimental life than men ... A woman subordinates her work and intellectual activity to her home, her husband, her children. She will never be able to fully focus on her career.[30]

When elucidating the emotional impediments of womanhood, *Eva* frequently evoked other "psychological" features, for instance, by accusing women of having a "Diana complex."[31] Men also received their share of schooling, as *Eva* presented them with an ideal type, who does not "even smoke," does "not like hippies," and who is a leader "without looking for it."[32] Even homosexuality was admitted into the discussion at this point, only to be deemed an "evil spreading in giant steps."[33]

Opus Dei's self-confidence became evident in 1969 when Ibáñez Langlois publicly disparaged TFP for its fundamentalist attitudes. Jesus Christ, he said, should not be brought into political "quarrels."[34] Indeed, while TFP attracted constant public criticism, Opus Dei's moralism suited right-wing politics in Chile better. The first to notice this fact was Guzmán, who disengaged from TFP and began a long and fruitful collaboration with Opus Dei. If Ibáñez Langlois was Opus Dei's spiritual leader, then its ideologue and savvy publisher was Gonzalo Vial Correa. Born in 1930, in the 1960s, this disciple of Eyzaguirre, too, abandoned Hispanidad for more technocratic ideological waters.[35] In fact, the entire Vial Correa family was engulfed in the Opus Dei operation: His sister, Elena Vial Correa (numerary) was a columnist in *El Mercurio* while his wife María Luisa (supernumerary) headed the Barnechea Foundation for Education.[36] A self-professed "Opus Dei syndicate,"[37] Vial Correa founded the journal *Portada*, which, from 1969, published texts explaining "Opus Dei and politics" to the public.[38] More important, *Portada* assembled three generations of rightists: Philippi's Hispanistas, Arturo Fontaine's "nacionalistas," and Guzmán's Gremialistas. Still, its board of editors consisted of Cristián Zegers – a Gremialista and Ibáñez Langlois's close friend – and historian Javier González Echenique, brother of Opus Dei member Eduardo González, and yet another of Guzmán's followers.[39] With *Cuadernos de Sur* members Francisco Orrego Vicuña, Fernando Orrego (supernumerary), and Bernadino Bravo Lira (numerary) on board, *Portada* was dedicated to promoting the Gremialistas' theories in public.[40]

By the 1969 congressional elections – which saw the Partido Nacional coalition winning a scarce 20 percent of the votes – *Portada* featured Guzmán as one of its topmost ideologues. "The great challenge of development is not to seek it at the cost of freedom. And 'state subsidiarity' seems to be the contemporary expression of that freedom . . . This is a dilemma that, going back to the most unfathomable principles of metaphysics, finally reverts to each human being, in their daily life and even in their own dignity," he wrote in what seemed to be his first manifestation of technocratic holism.[41] Against the background of Onganía's failures, he and his companions now underscored that locating a "strong man" should be merely the first step towards society's new organization – a process Onganía failed to enact, to their mind. Indeed, *Portada* spoke of a "new representativity" that would break parliament's monopoly on political representation: "Other forces are as important as political parties, or perhaps more important: unions, guilds, associations, cultural institutions, neighborhood and settler associations, professional organizations, and mothers' centers. All these nuclei lack political influence. Nowadays, they can only obtain it by becoming branches of the parties – which is equivalent to prostituting their true ends."[42] Then again, economic and technological acceleration appeared in *Portada* as impossible challenges for parliamentary politics. "Since 1920, everything has changed continuously, rapidly, profoundly, except for the political parties. Like all anachronisms, this one, under its nineteenth-century facade, hides very modern corruptions and degenerations," wrote its editors. While rejecting the notion of "suppression," they thus demanded that political parties be reduced to the "exclusively political field," while "natural organizations or intermediary groups" be allowed immediate participation in collective action.[43] In this way, *Portada* made authoritarianism appear like *more* democratic and uncorrupted a model than normative Western parliamentarism.

4.2 THE STRUGGLE AGAINST ALLENDE AND THE CONCEPTION OF PINOCHET'S REGIME

Frei's presidency, which began with high hopes, was soon engulfed in a series of economic and political setbacks. Despite his successful agrarian and education reforms, Chile's economic growth rates slowed, foreign debt mounted, and the news was dominated by land occupations and worker strikes. Hence, Chile arrived at the 1970 presidential elections bitterly polarized between its three political groupings: Radomiro Tomic's Christian Democrats, Jorge Alessandri's right-wing alliance (PN-DR), and Salvador Allende's UP coalition. As mentioned, Allende won the elections with a slight majority and, with the Christian Democrats' initial backing, went ahead with the "Chilean road to socialism."[44] While Allende's democratic socialism might seem reminiscent of economies such as that of Norway, in 1970, its symbolism went far beyond the European welfare state. His anti-imperialist oratory and stark defiance of the market-based development model echoed the Cuban Revolution's rhetoric. And despite its claim to be an alternative to Castro's dictatorship, Allende's political project, with its ties to Cuba that led to significant Cuban military assistance, swiftly emerged as the epicenter of Latin America's Cold War. Given Chile's dependency on imports and credits from the USA, this was a colossal gamble that, with hindsight, was hopeless from the start.

Still, there was no way one could have predicted Allende's cataclysmic downfall in September 1970. As we saw, even Franco was more than content to collaborate with the new president as long as Spain could serve as an alternative to Western creditors and auto companies. Allende's fall was thus the result of a conjunction of circumstances and miscalculations. The first was the misfortune of having Richard Nixon as US president and his determination to destabilize Allende's government. The second was Allende's inability to control his own coalition, which splintered between revolutionary communists and pragmatic socialists and which exhibited a fundamental confusion regarding how the "revolutionary" process should be carried out with a minority in the parliament. However, Allende's most significant misunderstanding was of the nature of the Chilean conservatives and their ability to destabilize his government through political delegitimization. Although Allende's program was hardly communist in the Soviet sense of the word, the Chilean conservatives feared that, in a six-year tenure, the socialist leader could potentially redistribute wealth and mobilize the Chilean working class to such a degree that they would never return to power electorally. Perón's ongoing grip on Argentine politics showed just how dangerous such a mobilization could become.[45]

In 1970, Allende was perhaps correct in disregarding the conservatives' influence. Regrouped once more behind the seventy-four-year-old Alessandri, they won only 35.27 percent of the popular vote in the September elections. Why he proved to be a meager candidate resided in his age, but also in his unimaginative "non-ideological" rhetoric. In *Portada*, Vial Correa promoted him as a man who "stands for the end of ideologies" and against anything "disconnected from real life."[46] Once the Christian Democrats gave their support to Allende, Alessandri retired from politics, along with many of his right-wing coalition members. Prat's death in 1971 was yet another sign that this generation of right-wing ideologues was not an agent that could halt Allende's democratic revolution.[47]

The question of who would lead Chile's conservative polity began being answered even before the elections when the public became privy to the activity of a group named Frente Nacionalista Patria y Libertad (FNPL). A brainchild of a young lawyer named Pablo Rodríguez Grez, this group exhibited a neofascist state ideology that was openly "national syndicalist" and even anti-capitalist. In fact, Rodríguez presented himself as the reincarnation of José Antonio Primo de Rivera,[48] and even published his hero's manifesto from May 1936 named "A letter to the soldiers of Spain" – where the Spanish fascist demanded the military overthrow the Second Republic.[49] The FNPL was just one of several neofascist groups mushrooming in Chile in 1970. Sergio Miranda Carrington's Tacna group and Juan Antonio Widow's journal *Tizona* were two other noteworthy examples of "José Antonian" platforms, which, revealingly, also collaborated with Piñar.[50] With the CIA secretly funding their activity, these groups were crucial for generating a political climate necessary for justifying the armed forces' coup d'état.[51]

Still, the FNPL's importance did not stem from its intellectual work but its operations as a paramilitary brute squad, or an instrument of "political provocation," in the words of one of its leaders.[52] This outrageous violence – which soon led to its outlawing – provided a smokescreen for a more sophisticated ideological mobilization within other conservative sectors. While Guzmán initially collaborated with FNPL, he also quickly reached the conclusion that he must play a different role in the preparation for the advent of an unprecedented military dictatorship. Thus, if the FNPL were agents of chaos, the Gremialistas were, in a way, the exact opposite: They served as the respectable association laboring to provide the armed forces with state models and justifications and, as importantly, preparing the public for its collaborative role in the future order. Like the Ateneo de la República, the Gremialistas presented themselves as a think tank of intellectuals, jurists, and economists who assembled voluntarily from within society, thereby embodying a willing transition from democracy to authoritarianism.

Portada was, by then, rife with visible Hispanista slogans – for example, when vowing to defend the ideals of the "Greco-Roman world, Christianity, and Spain."[53] As such, it did not reach a broad audience. Aware of this fact, the *Portada* group launched an ambitious magazine named *Qué Pasa*, where it catered to the centrist middle classes.[54] With Vial Correa as chief editor, Elena Vial Correa as editorial secretary, and Diego Ibáñez Langlois (supernumerary, José Miguel's brother, and a UNAV alumnus) on the editorial board, the journal had nonetheless an unmistakably Opus Dei imprint.[55] In fact, the mystery over the journal's nature was a theme the editors cultivated. "What are we? ... For some *Qué Pasa* is a mummy; for others, Christian Democratic; for some, we belong to Opus Dei; for others, we represent international and national fascism," they wrote sarcastically.[56] In truth, *Qué Pasa* could be best defined as the platform where the Gremialistas led Chile's conservative opposition.

When Allende began implementing his program (the "Vuskovic plan") in 1971, it became apparent that his methods of wealth redistribution were sizable but not entirely uncommon for the Western domain. In fact, most of them were a continuation of Frei's initiatives and included the expansion of land redistribution, the nationalization of the Chilean copper industry (for which a constitutional amendment was issued), and a host of social programs and wage increases. This expansive monetary policy initially positively affected Chile's GDP (over 8 percent) and real wages (rose by 22.3 percent in 1971). Luckily for the conservatives, however, the plummeting of international copper prices began to impact Chile by late 1971. Even more luckily, Allende unwittingly linked himself to Cuba. Not only was Chile the first South American state to restore diplomatic relations with Castro, but his arrival in Chile in November 1971 became the watershed moment of Allende's presidency.

True, the visit revealed the immense differences between the two countries' paths to socialism, leading Castro to depart somewhat disappointed.[57] For the Chilean conservatives, it was an unexpected blessing. Amid the first signs of inflation and shortages, they performed a public spectacle that would later become the dictatorship's foundational political myth. On December 1, 1971, the streets of Santiago were filled with thousands of supposed housewives in what became known as the "March of the empty pots" (or "cacerolas"). This event, orchestrated by Nina Donoso, the head of the conservative group Unión Nacional Femenina (UNAFE), was notably guarded by FNPL's paramilitaries and most effectively narrated in *Qué Pasa*.[58] In what would become its staple self-victimized tone, it stated that "tens of thousands of women willing to face unjust violence" were attacked by Allende's men "with stones, sticks, and even potatoes covered in razors."[59] The "political symbol of the cacerola" had been born, it surmised authoritatively a week later.[60] The march, Donoso would allege in 1974, marked the "beginning of the end" for Allende.[61] That was clearly a self-congratulatory overstatement. If this insular event had any importance, it was in how it served the myth – which the Gremialistas disseminated avidly – by which Pinochet's regime answered the Chileans' collective plea to save them from financial ruin, even from starvation.

In 1972, the conservatives set their sights on the March 1973 congressional elections, hoping that the opposition – which now included the Christian Democrats – would win at least two-thirds of the seats, thereby paving the way for Allende's impeachment. This legalist approach did not deter the Gremialistas in *Qué Pasa* from forcefully promoting a "subsidiary state" as a viable alternative for democracy. To avoid being identified as authoritarian, they emphasized two points. For one, they said that Chile was a society of the "bourgeoisie or middle classes" that, as such, disliked "politics and parties."[62] For another, Guzmán underscored that his state model was neither dictatorial nor fascist. Quite the opposite:

> I think that Gremialismo is the antithesis of fascism. We must not forget that fascism is a totalitarian and statist doctrine … Gremialismo is a modern manifestation of a social democracy of authentic participation. Perhaps its "doctrinal backbone" can be sought in the old philosophical principle of subsidiarity – the key to every libertarian regime by which the State should not directly coordinate civic activities that can be undertaken by intermediate or grassroots organizations.[63]

His texts were not merely public theoretical discussions but a signal to the armed forces whose generals benefited from the FNPL's destabilization acts but at the same time sought to locate a respectable, young, and unidentifiable ideology to legitimize their new order.

A sign of just how rapidly the prestige of the Gremialista–Opus Dei fellowship grew was their presence in various civil forums assembled in 1972 to discuss the eventuality of a coup against Allende. The more famous meeting took place at Chiñigüe on March 4, 1972, and focused on economic destabilization planned for September 1972.[64] Besides several prominent industrialists, it comprised Hispanistas such as Philippi, Fernández Larraín, and Fontaine, and, tellingly, of Vial Correa, Guzmán, and Ibáñez Langlois – the latter two being only twenty-five years old. Another forum was headed by *El Mercurio* editor and one of *Qué Pasa*'s founders, Hernán Cubillos. Gathered weekly in the offices of the Lord Cochrane Publishing House, it saw the presence of Fontaine, Bazán, and Guzmán, who advocated the government's destabilization "in the hope of a coup d'état."[65] Strikingly, the Gremialistas were not mere spectators in these encounters but presented a host of propositions regarding a new constitutional phase and the overhauling of the Chilean economic model. Even if these encounters did not yield a concrete political plan for a post-democratic order, as had been the case in the Argentine Revolution, they still sent an unequivocal message to the armed forces about whom they could realistically mobilize in the near future.

As the conservatives were consolidating their power, the UP found itself torn between its revolutionary factions (the MIR/Communist Party) and the legalists who upheld the constitutional order. Despite a high-profile tour in Europe and a speech at the UN, and notwithstanding a bilateral dialogue with the USA, Allende's popularity waned in the face of an inflation rate of 140 percent and a soaring fiscal deficit. When a truckers' strike in October 1972 paralyzed Chile for three weeks, it was crushed by the UP's mobilized workers rather than the state. This event signaled Allende's decisive alignment with the legalist camp – a process which began with appointing Carlos Prats, his chief of staff, as Interior Minister and ended with the oppression of the copper miners' strike at El Teniente mines in June 1973. Still, the Chilean workers were not to abandon their leader right away. The March 1973 parliamentary elections saw Allende receive a significant 43 percent of the votes. The combination of this relative victory, Allende's commitment to the constitutional order, and his bond with the armed forces meant one thing: His prospects of remaining in office until the 1976 elections drastically increased. Thus, the conservatives had no option but to make a pact with parts of the armed forces and prepare the country for a military solution.

As in 1966 Argentina, the Gremialistas identified a unique opportunity to utilize a moment of political turmoil to restructure the Chilean political landscape entirely. Indeed, publicly and unapologetically, they pledged to serve as an axis that would bring together the armed forces, the "legitimate parties," and the "gremial forces" into a coalition based on a "minimal consensus" regarding a post-political "reconstruction" period.[66] In their view, the question was not whether Allende should be overthrown but how it should be done and what legitimacy would underpin the new order. *Portada*'s answer was explicit: Given that the UP was on an "irreversible path" towards totalitarianism, the "rules of the game" had already been broken. Thus, neither "electoral mechanisms" nor military force would suffice against Marxism but only a new order based on "Catholic social philosophy."[67] To eliminate any doubt, *Portada* also published Álvaro d'Ors's aforementioned "Silent leges inter arma," which rewrote Carl Schmitt's theory of suspending "the validity of the laws" for a martial "law of security."[68] As a last resort, the editors also baselessly warned that, unless they staged a coup d'état, by 1976 the armed forces would become the "Party's armed forces."[69]

Three letters sent by Guzmán to his mother in 1973 offer a glimpse into whether or not these men believed their public rhetoric. On May 15, he wrote to her that "Marxism has decided to take the final leap" and that the armed forces would have to "play the role of referees" in politics.[70] These words aside, less than two weeks before the coup, he assured her that Allende's government lacked sufficient power to "impose a dictatorship" and that left-wing terrorism would "not suffice to configure a civil war."[71] He also bragged about demanding Allende's resignation on live TV, for bringing about the armed forces' "division."[72] These letters illustrate that Guzmán perhaps believed that the Marxists *wanted* to take over the country but that he never assumed that they actually *could* and that his rhetoric regarding the armed forces' polarization was instrumental at best.

In June 1973, General Robert Souper launched a failed coup attempt against Allende. Aided by FNPL members but overpowered by UP activists, it served as a preemptive trial that taught the armed forces about Allende's capacity to mobilize supporters.[73] It also forced Allende to incorporate Pinochet, his new chief of staff, into his cabinet and subdue the workers' resistance even more. In addition, it meant that most of the FNPL members were in exile and conveniently absent from the public sphere in the coup's aftermath. But before that, on August 22, 1973, the Christian Democrats and the Partido Nacional members of the Chamber of Deputies passed a resolution to end Allende's alleged constitutional violations. It declared without proof that Allende was seeking to "acquire absolute power" and inaugurate a "totalitarian system" in Chile. This motion – which nobody expected Allende to acknowledge – aimed to convey one simple truth: that the 1925 Constitution had already been shattered and that, therefore, a new "institutionality" was legitimate. The members of the armed forces in the cabinet did not react immediately. Indeed, Pinochet would remain loyal to Allende until hours before the coup – so he claimed. True or false, this detail was important in and of itself. It meant that, like Onganía before him, Pinochet could present himself as a legalist – if not reluctant – leader who, as the only strongman left, agreed to take Chile's salvation upon himself.

On September 11, 1973, the Chilean armed forces, headed by Pinochet (army), Gustavo Leigh (air force), José Toribio Merino (navy), and César Mendoza (head of police) overthrew Allende in a notoriously violent coup d'état. What do we know about the ideology driving these men? Far less than what we know about Onganía. In Chile, the armed forces were far less politicized than in Argentina, where the military had been meddling in politics since 1930.[74] Still, unlike the Brazilian or Uruguayan military regimes, the Chilean Junta's power grab was achieved by physically annihilating its political rivals. This included assassinating generals standing in its way, thereby terminating the legalist Schneider Doctrine that had licensed Allende's ascendance to power in the first place.[75] Indeed, the dictatorship murdered 1,823 Chilean citizens during its first year alone, thereby going far beyond oppressive measures such as the outlawing of political parties, labor unions, and the free press – the normative "state of emergency" toolkit until then.[76] Yet the Junta said little of the motivation underpinning this dramatic paradigmatic shift. Its first Law Decree vowed to protect Chile's authentic "concepts and values" against "Marxism–Leninism" but, significantly, also pledged to "respect the Constitution and the Laws of the Republic."[77]

Still, the death of Allende (allegedly by "suicide") and the assassination of his followers *en masse* was anything but legal or constitutional and, as such, bore dire consequences for this new military regime. Despite enjoying the USA's backing, it faced a wave of demonstrations and denunciations worldwide. This circumstance called for an extraordinary propaganda effort by the conservative media in what seemed, at first, like a damage control operation – against the "outrageous propaganda machine mounted by communism throughout the world," in Guzmán's words.[78] That the Junta justified its actions in ways that were reminiscent of Franco – that is, as being guided by Divine Providence – did not suffice in this case.[79] While it perhaps prompted Osvaldo Lira to affirm, a week after the uprising, that Pinochet enjoyed the legitimacy of "origin and exercise," since "as St. Paul says, whoever resists authority, resists God," scholastic reasonings were definitely not the leitmotif of *El Mercurio*, *Qué Pasa*, and *Portada* – now serving as the regime's semi-official mouthpieces.[80]

Within this apparatus, the Gremialistas' star shone as the Junta's greatest "propaganda force" in Latin America and Europe, where, according to *El Mercurio*, they successfully elucidated how Chile's "citizens welcomed the military junta."[81] As to why the Chileans would collectively feel this way, *Qué Pasa* was the first to pose the cunning argument that a "bloody civil war"[82] between Chile's ideological fringes was imminent and that this called for the intervention of an arbiter "from outside."[83] Indeed, the themes of preventing a civil war, or suggesting that Chile had *already* been "objectively in a state of civil war," were to be canonized in the Junta's official texts several months later.[84] Alternatively, these platforms suggested that the coup was synonymous with the restoration of human rights, and indeed, as *Eva* alleged, of women's rights.[85] In an effort to solidify Pinochet's leadership, they held several extensive interviews with the general at his home, focusing more on what he *was not* than on his beliefs. Chile's de facto leader was a "man of no ambitions" and definitely not a "corporatist," *Qué Pasa* reported on September 27, but a simple man of honor who was in the throes of devising an "apolitical" team of jurists to undo the "outdated" Constitution of 1925.[86]

Amid its flurry of violence, the regime also recourse to a salient spectacle of legalism in the shape of a commission set in place to design a constitutional reform. It is fair to say that, at this point, the Junta had not the slightest idea what its new constitution would entail. However, it had an entirely defined idea of who did. Only two days after pledging allegiance to the Constitution of 1925, they published an act stating that "the promulgation of a new Political Constitution of the State is under study, work that is directed by the university professor Dr. Jaime Guzmán."[87] Was this appointment pre-planned? After all, the Gremialistas insisted that there were no "civil participants in the planning of the coup."[88] On hearing of the coup, Guzmán also told his mother he knew nothing of its planning.[89] Still, this narrative should be taken with caution. That Guzmán – a lawyer in his twenties – was to lead the constitutional reform process and, later, direct the creation of General Secretariat of Government's propaganda apparatus, indicates that this was no improvisation on behalf of the Junta.[90] Then again, the constitutional commission was, at this point, not more than a device aimed to persuade the international community of the dictatorship's legalistic approach.

Of all the legitimation tactics deployed by the Gremialista network, none was as sinister as *The White Book of the Change of Government in Chile*. This book, which Vial Correa edited and peddled earnestly in his magazines, posed the baseless allegation that Allende had planned a "self-coup." Supported by fictitious evidence supplied to him by the armed forces, its high point was Allende's supposed plan ("Plan Z") to assassinate his political opponents and the heads of the armed forces.[91] An array of books by *El Mercurio* and Zig-Zag publishing houses espoused these assertions further, making them the conservatives' official historical narrative.[92] This regurgitated evidence sufficed Guzmán when briefing the foreign press that Chile was "not a democracy" on September 11, 1973, given that Allende planned to assassinate the armed forces' high command with the help of "13,000 foreigners who entered the country illegally."[93]

All in all, the self-coup falsehood became yet another underpinning for the truism by which Chile's break from the Constitution of 1925 occurred not on September 11 but in the years leading up to it. "It is impossible to go back to yesterday. The outcome of September 11 must be a foundational act of institutionality and – even more so – a new conception of Chile," *Qué Pasa* affirmed.[94] *Portada* concurred: Allende's government was hardly a "minor accident after which political power would almost automatically return to the hands of civilians." The 1925 Constitution, and "inorganic voting" as such, should vanish, it thus demanded, not before suggesting that "the principle of subsidiarity be put into practice, as the only means of establishing orderly and clear relationships between the rulers and the ruled."[95] In late November, *Qué Pasa* published the government's "major lines of action," asserting that Chile was in store for "creative and restorational act of civic–military character." On this occasion, it presented Guzmán as the principal author of the constitutional "puzzle" and the indoctrinating mechanism supporting this transition. "The break of the institutionality under the Allende government has led to the formation, still embryonic, of new institutions that can carry out the Junta's mission," it clarified. [96] The point not to be missed is that at no point can we infer that these platforms parroted the armed forces' propaganda. In fact, the corpus of texts they left behind them suggests it was the other way around: The Gremialistas supplied the regime with the metanarrative they had developed for five odd years and presented themselves as a key civil agent in the midst of it all. This symbiotic relationship was to deepen as the 1970s unfolded.

During these eventful months, one group was peculiarly absent from this propagandistic effort, as well as from the public sphere entirely: Rodríguez's FNPL. Understanding that his fascist militia had served its purpose, in October 1973, he dismembered the group. Still, the FNPL members were the first to be censored by the dictatorship. That is to say, the Junta had no intention of being identified with these neofascist provocateurs once in power.[97] Having fulfilled their historical role as destabilizers, they were now to watch in vain as someone else stabilized the regime in his image. And this person was Jaime Guzmán. Yet Rodríguez would not remain tight-lipped for long. With not one iota of his "program" incorporated into the new regime's texts, in November 1973, he started criticizing the dictatorship in Franco's Spain of all places. Following his demand that the dictatorship hand power back to civil groups instead of "relying on oppression," he was even summoned to the Chilean Embassy for explanations.[98] Still, in the mid 1970s, Chile's neofascists slowly returned to the public sphere – in Miranda Carrington's journals *Orden Nuevo* and *Avanzada*, for instance. There, far from positions of power, they would attack the Gremialistas and demand a national syndicalist revolution in vain, as we shall inspect in Chapter 5.

4.3 PINOCHET'S HISPANIC TECHNOCRACY: NEOLIBERALISM, MORALISM, AND THE SPECTERS OF FRANCOISM

That Pinochet's regime was substantially different from the Second Francoist era and the Argentine Revolution goes without saying. When explaining this dictatorship's longevity, historians have underscored its usage of political violence and the centralization of power in the hands of one decision-maker. As historian Carlos Huneeus has memorably suggested, a combination of three identities – namely, the "coercive identity," "personal identity," and "economic identity" – secured the regime's survival.[99] Assuredly, Pinochet's regime was deadlier to its citizens than previous Cold War dictatorships. With its secret police (DINA) assassinating and torturing opposition members well into the 1980s, it would take more time for the democratic opposition to effectively arise in Chile as it did in 1960s Argentina and Spain. And, as both the head of the armed forces and "head of state," by 1978 Pinochet had constructed a personality cult around him, which meant his regime was more resilient in the face of economic and social crises than, say, Onganía's civil–military arrangement.

Still, these identities did not quite exist simultaneously but, in many respects, replaced one another over the course of a decade. Once in power, unlike Onganía, Pinochet faced an economic crisis of a magnitude that Latin American military dictators had rarely encountered before. Indeed, the destabilization of Allende's government meant that Chile faced financial ruin. In addition, despite being recognized by the

Western Bloc and even by the People's Republic of China, the regime remained under unrelenting international pressure.[100] With the November 1974 UN resolution titled "Protection of human rights in Chile," it ran the risk of becoming a liability for foreign investors.[101] Finally, Pinochet was perhaps the official head of state after July 1974, but faced constant opposition from the other Junta members – particularly Leigh – on economic matters, and was thus hardly a dictator in the simple sense of the word. These interlinked dire circumstances were mirrored in the regime's intensive indoctrination methods.

Ultimately, what made the regime's identities "click" was its cohesive ideology, which further consolidated under the strategical pact between the Gremialistas and their affiliated group of economists later to be known as the "Chicago Boys." As revealed in his initial interviews, Pinochet, like most military generals, was not a skilled orator or thinker in his own right. His talent lay in identifying those who could effectively narrate his new order, thereby mobilizing the conservative polity behind him. True, the Junta was initially in no rush to ceremoniously hand administrative power to civilians as Onganía had done before. In fact, Pinochet alleged that the coup had left "a total civic vacuum" and that the armed forces must, therefore, rule the country single-handedly.[102] Despite this, he acted swiftly, deploying two teams of civil specialists: a squad of economic experts, to stabilize the economy, and a group of "legal experts" to design his state ideology and indoctrination methods. The Gremialistas and ICH ideologues occupied the latter position from the start. Being Pinochet's speechwriter, Guzmán was the author of the Junta's foundational texts and, by 1974, appeared in public as the regime's quasi-official public intellectual.[103] The influential Oficina de Planificación Nacional (ODEPLAN) also came under the Gremialistas' control with the appointment of Miguel Kast as its director. As an insider to this process, Arturo Fontaine would later opine that Pinochet was suspicious of Chile's right-wing political establishment and opted for Allende's "most intransigent" opposition. Besides evoking "authoritarian Portalian formulas" and "Hispanic and monarchical roots," the Gremialistas attracted Pinochet due to their function as a "commando battalion," whose "innovative capacity ran parallel with its capacity to deconstruct routines and consecrated norms," explained the Hispanista.[104]

At first, it seemed that if the regime had learned anything from Onganía's experience, it was that the "political phase" cannot be left for last. When, in October 1973, the Comisión de Estudios de la Nueva

Constitución Política de la República de Chile (CENC, or "Ortúzar Commission") opened its sessions, it did indeed appear as though Chile's "institutionality" was to meet its fate in a matter of months.[105] Headed by Enrique Ortúzar Escobar, but under the unmistakable control of Guzmán, the commission, however, was to remain markedly idle for the next three years. Instead of a political phase, in whatever remained of Chile's bustling public sphere, the public was to be blitzed with the Gremialistas' message regarding the onset of the "subsidiary state" based on "intermediary societies," for which they evoked Álvaro d'Ors's "Autoridad y potestad."[106] The constitutional process, *Portada* even stated in a moment of candor, could and should not be untangled quite yet. After all, a constitution should be tailored to fit a society's social and ethical standards, and so one must wait – many years if needed – for the Chileans to undergo a change of mentality for a healthy political mechanism to take shape.[107]

Thus, in 1974, the regime communicated itself mainly in evasive terms of "realism," speckled with Hispanic mythologies. The March 1974 Declaration of Principles was a case in point. Arguably the hallmark of the Pinochet–Guzmán nexus, it stressed that what was in store for Chile was a "subsidiarity" society where "the word of specialists prevails over slogans."[108] Rather than decoding what this state model meant, it merely pledged to abide by Chile's "Christian and Hispanic" tradition.[109] Enrique Campos Menéndez, an ICH member and now Pinochet's cultural advisor, praised the declaration as the definitive recognition of "Hispanism."[110] In 1974, he mustered Chile's Hispanistas and neofascists in an imposing anthology titled *Pensamiento nacionalista* to articulate the spiritual essence propelling the "magical phenomenon of September 11."[111] In his introduction, he made a surprising remark: "A successful Spanish essayist, years ago, spoke of 'the twilight of ideologies.' He was absolutely right. In the bastion of anxieties and political experiments that the Chilean nation had become after all the ideological disguises had been tried, the programmatic doctrines and labels had lost their meaning and only shreds of hopes and failed experiences remained."[112] Whether or not he truly understood Fernández de la Mora's theory of depoliticization through leisure is perhaps irrelevant. The point is that this was Campos Menéndez's way to convey to his readership what type of theoretical work was expected from Chile's "nacionalistas" – namely, one akin to the Francoist theorist's technocratic worldview.

Indeed, until 1975, the regime betrayed several noteworthy attempts to present itself as yet another chapter of Francoism. In this telling, Chile's struggle against communism and international isolation was tantamount to that of Franco's Spain between 1936 and 1945. In fact, those most targeted by this narrative were the Spaniards. How the new regime approached its supposed exemplar could be seen on September 12, 1973, a mere twenty-four hours after the coup, when Pinochet wrote a personal letter to Franco. "My great and good friend," it opened, only then to announce the substitution of Chile's Ambassador, Óscar Agüero Corvalán. "Please accept my sincere good wishes for the welfare of your excellence and the greatness of Spain. Your loyal and good friend, Augusto Pinochet, the Moneda Palace," it read.[113] Pinochet was neither Franco's friend nor did his laconic message resemble Onganía's flattering letter from 1966. The letter was, in truth, somewhat redundant, as Franco – then eighty years old – had already passed the function of Prime Minister to Carrero Blanco in June that year. Why Pinochet decided to address Franco had everything to do with him wanting to present himself to his idol and confirm their supposed linkage.

Spain, at first, needed some convincing. Under the mono-color government, its reaction to the events in Santiago was hesitant. Unlike Onganía, Pinochet was neither well-known nor respected in Spain, and the news of human rights violations was a tint with which Spain could not afford to be identified amid its efforts to join the European Community. Worse yet, Spain had fostered a friendly relationship with Allende's administration. Fernández de la Mora even represented Franco personally at Allende's inauguration.[114] As he recalled later, Franco told him he wanted to dispel any "doubts about our conception of the [Chilean] State."[115] Pressured by the exit of US companies from Chile in 1971, Allende had motivations of his own to invite Spanish companies such as Pegaso to manufacture vehicles in Chile.[116] In turn, this unlikely partnership resulted in a trade deal (Acuerdo de Cooperación Financiera Hispano-Chileno) in December 1972. To complicate matters, by 1974, Spain witnessed the rise of well-defined anti-Pinochet and pro-Pinochet camps. On the one hand, Spanish reformists such as Joaquín Ruiz-Giménez's journal *Cuadernos para el Diálogo* and Juan Fernández Figueroa's *Índice* fiercely denounced the Chilean dictatorship. Of all places, Spain also became where Chilean exiles disclosed Pinochet's brutalities, backed by a network of Spanish journalists.[117] On the other hand, *Fuerza Nueva*'s neofascists extolled Pinochet.[118] Opus Dei gradually leaned towards the latter camp too, once Álvaro d'Ors had appeared in *Fuerza Nueva* claiming that revolutionary violence could only be answered by the "legitimate violence of the armed forces." Snidely, he then attributed the reformists' rebukes to a "resentment of the vanquished of 1939."[119] His public evocation of the Spanish Civil War left Pinochet's Ambassador in Madrid – retired General Francisco Goigoitía – profoundly moved.[120]

Carrero Blanco ultimately had little choice but to align with the latter camp, too. Besides ordering a symbolic dispatch of military equipment to Chile, he also acted upon Goigoitía's appeals and censored the anti-Pinochet camp.[121] Nevertheless, Pinochet's adherents were left bewildered by Spain's lukewarm support. *Qué Pasa* went so far as to suggest that the tension between the regimes was rooted in the Spanish ambassador's covert action of smuggling Catalan socialist Joan Garcés (the alleged architect of Plan Z) out of Chile, thereby preventing the exposure of the full extent of the Franco–Allende relationship. The article then lauded Carrero Blanco's decision to replace Spain's seemingly moderate Foreign Minister López Bravo with López Rodó, interpreting it as an indication of how Pinochet had successfully propelled Spain to "return to its ideological mindset."[122] Be that as it may, Spain would not come to Chile's aid any further, and, more specifically, refrained from investing in its banking system. Thus, the Chilean pressure continued, as a tense correspondence between Sánchez Bella and Hispanista Óscar Herrera Palacios discloses. Employed at Pinochet's National Press Association, the latter first adduced Plan Z as the proof that Pinochet had saved "tens of thousands" of lives.[123] Then, he demanded Spain's financial backing and support of Chile at the UN by evoking the memory of meeting Franco in 1954, where the dictator allegedly spoke of the international blockade against Spain as being a "Marxist–Masonic conspiracy."[124] His message was clear: 1945 Spain and 1973 Chile were one and the same. It was hardly well-received, and to no avail.

Although Pinochet collaborated with dictatorships around him – most notably with Brazil – the sheer number of official delegations he sent to Spain between 1974 and 1976 is indicative of how important establishing a relationship with Francoism was for him. This traffic began as early as December 1973, when a large-scale mission of jurists led by Silva Bascuñán – now, a distinguished member of the Ortúzar Commission – arrived in Madrid to explain the "illegitimacy for which the previous government had fallen" to Franco's ministers.[125] It was followed by the visits of Hernán Isla Rios (a high-ranking head of police who came to study the Spanish Guardia Civil's operational methods),[126] Education Minister Arturo Troncoso (who visited the OEI in October 1975),[127] and Rubén Díaz Neira (Secretario Nacional de los Gremios), who headed a delegation to study "Spanish syndicalism").[128] Another paradigmatic visit was that of Chile's Women Secretariat director Carmen Grez. Accompanied by the organization's political adviser, ICH member Gisela Silva Encina, the two were Pilar Primo de Rivera's guests in November 1975. "The Falange's Women's Section and Chile's Women's Secretariat," reported Goigoitía, agreed on "sharing experiences that could be used in the plans of the National Secretary of Women in Chile."[129] Another important visit was, in this regard, that of Admiral Merino.[130] In January 1975, the Junta leader signed an economic and cultural agreement between the counties, and shored up Spain's support in the upcoming UN resolutions of 1975.[131] The "approximation" to Spain meant "opening friendly doors in Western Europe," the ambassador hoped.[132] Still, by far the most paradigmatic moment of identification with Franco occurred upon the latter's death. Besides declaring three days of national mourning, it prompted Pinochet to attend Franco's funeral in person.[133] In his singular official visit to Europe, he was greeted cordially by Prince Juan Carlos, and even more enthusiastically by mobs of neofascists.[134] Pinochet was the only world leader at Franco's funeral and the only dictator at the king's coronation three days later.[135] In case any Chilean failed to identify the symbolic meaning of his presence in Spain, *Qué Pasa* was there to explicate it in the most simplistic of terms:

> Franco's figure and achievements are of exceptional importance for Chile today ... as our President has reminded us during his visit to the Mother Nation, it was possible to defeat Soviet communism ... not just once, but twice: the first, on the battlefields; the second, in the offensive of isolation and economic boycott ... That offensive, so similar to the one suffered by Chile today, was defeated by Franco's Spain.[136]

Regardless of whether they sympathized with Pinochet, Spanish officials hesitated to acknowledge this historical parallel publicly. Strikingly, they also refrained from traveling to Chile as they had done in 1966 Argentina, apart from two notable cases. In 1975, Fernández de la Mora returned to Chile. As I will explain shortly, he was stripped from any official role by then and thus liberated enough to state that 1973 Chile resembled "the Spanish situation in 1939." On this occasion, he also exclaimed that Spain's "organic representation" is more democratic than parliamentarism,[137] deemed Western democracy "closer to taboo and superstition than to science and reason," and demanded "replacing ideologies with rigorous ideas."[138] Another visitor was Escrivá de Balaguer. His arrival in July 1974, which had been planned before September 1973, was far less ideological. While avoiding expressing his opinion about the dictatorship, he seized the opportunity to attack progressive Catholic movements as the Church's "disloyal children" and condemn family planning. "The earth is too small? Lies!" he attacked Malthusianism as he understood it.[139] But besides these two, the dialogue between the two dictatorships was hardly reciprocal as Pinochet had hoped.

If anything, Pinochet's identification with Franco betrayed desperation in the face of international isolation and economic depression. Being professional military men, the Junta generals had mixed views on how to orchestrate Chile's economic reforms. The first civilian the Junta appointed was Minister of Economy Fernando Léniz, a businessman and the owner of *El Mercurio*. His reign was marked by a "gradualist" approach, which included basic anti-inflation measures such as currency devaluation and salary freeze but that mirrored the Junta's initial reluctance to liberalize the economy too drastically. The regime also designated a body named the Junta's Advisory Committee to keep Léniz and the ODEPLAN economists from being carried away with their capitalist pipe dreams.[140] Simultaneously, in December 1973, the Junta founded the Comisión Nacional de la Reforma Administrativa (CONARA), designed to reform the public sector and commence a "regionalization" around "development poles" in peripheral towns such as Iquique, Copiapó, and Puerto Montt.[141] "Little by little, Santiago ceased being Chile," reflected Joaquin Lavín, one of the plan's authors.[142] In brief, between 1973 and 1975, the regime opted for an economic reform that was strikingly analogous to the Francoist stabilization and development plans of 1959–64.

Not only did the Gremialistas and their affiliated economists perceive this as too hesitant a makeover, but they overtly posited their alternative, which poured from the mouth and pen of a conspicuous new spokesperson: Sergio de Castro. A University of Chicago alumnus, and famously Milton Friedman's student, this economist was the quintessential "Chicago Boy" and, not coincidentally, the editor of *Qué Pasa*'s economic section. There, he flaunted "the Chilean model" based on drastic economic liberalization based on the "sophisticated recipe of technicians." Having spurred "economic miracles" elsewhere, this model must now acquire its most updated version in Chile, he established.[143] If the Report on the Reorganization of the Central State Administration was López Rodó's ideological roadmap, then the "Chicago Boys" had the Bases of the Economic Policy of the Military Government of Chile, also known as *El Ladrillo* ("The Brick"). In the making since May 1973, mostly by de Castro and Emilio Sanfuentes – an economist and one of *Portada*'s founders – this book was both a narrative deploring Chile's excessive interventionism and a sizable toolkit of reforms, many of which had rarely been tried in the Western hemisphere. Notably, it avoided using the term "subsidiarity," possibly so as not to be associated with Guzmán's discourse. Instead, it focuses on "economic democratization," "decentralization," and "rationalization of the public sector," as well as on pledges to follow the examples of "Germany, Japan, Denmark, Spain, and Brazil." What truly set the text apart was its intriguing interpretation of "intermediary" organizations. "The development of intermediate organizations not only relieves the State of a heavily bureaucratic system, but increases the efficiency of services ... expands the social participation in areas of public interest, and transfers important control mechanisms to the community," it stated.[144] But who exactly were these mysterious organizations? Could they be compared to think tanks or NGOs? The answer to this question remained open-ended. My interpretation is this: *El Ladrillo* never explicitly states that these would not be for-profit organizations. In practice, they often were. In other words, in essence, the book represented a motion from societal corporatism as *representation* to direct *economic control* wherein the state hands all public services to private corporations it deems ethically trustworthy. As such, the book showcased an inversion of Western economic common sense as the public sector appeared in it not as collective property but as an alien domain, whereas the private sector symbolized "the community."

The plummeting of copper prices in the wake of the October 1973 global economic crisis led Chile's economy to nose-dive in early 1974. This calamity sparked Pinochet's interest in de Castro's plan, not solely because of its innovative approach but because of his nexus with the Gremialistas and their proven ability to propagate such a plan. Paradoxically, the economic crisis – which led to a staggering 394 percent inflation rate – helped Pinochet, who had been appointed Chile's president by decree in June 1974, to justify a totalizing revolution of the Chilean way of life based on the fusion of de Castro's neo-feudal economic common sense and the Gremialistas' "subsidiary state."[145] The arrival of the IMF's representative Elieu Kreiss to audit Chile's financial system in late 1974 and Milton Friedman to meet with Pinochet in April 1975 were likewise significant in the plan's public legitimation process. Later in the month, Pinochet appointed de Castro as Minister of the Economy to orchestrate Chile's transition from "gradualism" to shock treatment.

In 1992, Friedman wrote to Hernán Cubillos that the Chileans "were among the best foreign students" and that he was proud that he had "a good influence on them."[146] This self-praising notwithstanding, Friedman's importance for the regime resided not in any specific economic theory but in how Pinochet and his men utilized his international prestige. Even before most reforms were in place, the Chilean public was inundated with a pot-au-feu of peculiar names and slogans. By May 1975, the terms "Chicago Boys" and "El Ladrillo" were already household names after being popularized intensively in *El Mercurio* and *Qué Pasa*.[147] In fact, Friedman spoke directly to the Chilean public in a celebrative *Qué Pasa* interview in April 1975.[148] He, Friedrich Hayek, and Michael Novak all appeared in Chile in these years, willingly lending their reputation to whitewash a ruthless dictatorship that was, otherwise, hardly inviting to Western investors.[149]

Still, in 1975, this was still not neoliberalism as we understand it today. As Pinochet and the Gremialistas were not powerful enough, only a handful of *El Ladrillo*'s components were included in de Castro's 1975 Program of National Recuperation, its essential goal being the reduction of government debt and the elimination of all obstructions to the flow of foreign investment into the country.[150] Once again, with the workforce "depoliticized" through terror, the ability to lay off thousands of public sector employees and conduct steep salary freezes was crucial for the success of this shock treatment. As a result, by 1975, real wages fell by 40 percent from their levels in 1970. The other aspect of this plan was the IMF, which granted Chile more than $150,000,000 in 1975 and 1976.[151] In this regard, there was hardly anything in de Castro's plan that had not been tried in Spain and Argentina. Still, the Chilean case also differed in some respects. Firstly, the link between the economic and ideological teams in Chile was more substantial than in Argentina.[152] Secondly, the extent of Chile's privatization exceeded its counterparts from the start. Between 1975 and 1978, the government restored most of the companies nationalized by Allende's apparatus (CORFO) to their previous owners. Assuredly, anything that could hinder this economic race to the bottom was eliminated, including Chile's membership in the Andean Trade Pact, which was terminated in 1976. Even so, the regime's privatization of CORFO companies was more of an undoing of the Allende years than an economic principle. That the state-owned copper mining company remained in government hands (renamed CODELCO) showcased Pinochet's hypocritical approach to laissez-faire principles as his regime's revenues relied on Allende's chief achievement. Thus, Chile's quintessential "neoliberal" moment arrived only in 1979 with the Siete Modernizaciones reform plan, as I will consider in the next chapter.

Neoliberal or not, the reform's immediate outcome was expectedly devastating for most Chileans. With public expenditure cut by some 80 percent, unemployment reached 20 percent, prompting a surge in immigration, adding to the exile wave of September 1973. How the regime's state ideology developed between 1973 and 1977 was related directly to this social crisis. It meant the Junta not only resorted to oppression but held firmly to most ministerial positions and relied on aggressive indoctrination. And it was for this reason that the spectacle of "subsidiarity" and civil cooperation became so vital. The epicenter of this effort was the Directorate of Civil Organizations, which operated the Women, Youth, Culture, and Trade Unions National Secretariats. Being Guzmán's brainchild, this apparatus was, in fact, proposed to General Leigh in August 1973, as the regime's nucleus of civil "participation."[153] By 1974, it was heralded as the channel wherein the Chilean "new mentality" was to be cultivated.[154] Indeed, Pinochet actively sought to decipher this notion in 1975. For him, to "change the Chileans' mentality" was not akin to "the absurd pretense of making a new Chilean, as postulated by Marxism" but a "realistic and not utopian goal"[155] – one that acted on behalf of the homeland's "permanent spiritual values."[156]

How these ostensibly voluntary apparatuses ("voluntariado" was their nickname) functioned could be best seen in the Women's National Secretariat. Operating side by side with the Mothers' Centers (CEMA-Chile) – which had been taken over by Pinochet's wife Lucía Hiriart – the two exhibited the regime's alternative vision of volunteer-based welfare services.[157] Still, with its publications and lavish happenings, the Women's Secretariat was primarily a propaganda machine wherein Chile's women could display their "gratitude" to Pinochet. With the Silva Encina at its helm, the Secretariat also openly propagated Hispanidad and reiterated the mythological origins of Chilean womanhood. The Chilean race, claimed its publications, was forged in the sixteenth-century Arauco War against the Indigenous Mapuche tribes – when the Spanish conquerors were on the battlefield and the women "led civil life, family, homes, and cities" in the rear.[158] Building on the myth of "cacerolas" – when "each home was a bastion of rebellion" – the Secretariat also underscored women's central role in the depoliticization of Chilean society.[159] According to Carla Scassi, the Secretariat's director, ideologies generate a "deep repulsion" in women, thereby making them the most suitable agents of "unity, service, and pacification."[160] At the same time, together with the Opus Dei-led press, the Secretariat peddled its alternative "feminism." After all, Western feminism aims to "change all traditions" and therefore does not signify liberation but a fraudulent "liberationalism."[161] María Elena Aguirre and Rosario Guzmán, Jaime's sister and a *Qué Pasa* columnist, thus presented the Chilean alternative: Women should possess social agency due to their "sexual presences," but even more so as respectable housewives;[162] they should aspire to higher education, but not replace men in positions of leadership; they should be able to choose whether or not to marry but may have no reproductive or economic rights.[163] Well into the 1980s, the Secretariat was affirming that "men and women are physically, psychically, and spiritually different," and that "ideological" attempts to "desegregate the two sexes" constitute an "error against nature."[164] Once the regime had actually restricted women's labor rights – in its infamous 1974 Work Code, which banned women from performing certain production jobs – some in the Chilean press even expressed episodic discomfort.[165] The Secretariat, however, forcefully backed these measures, insisting that women *can* work in any professions but *should* opt for "artisan" activity in their homes, "in a way that enriches the spirit."[166]

The youth was likewise to play a substantial role in the nation's depoliticization, or in the words of the Gremialista Cristián Zegers, the National Youth Secretariat's director, to be the "vanguard of Chile's spiritual rebirth."[167] As could be expected, the Secretariat's journals *Juventud*, *Revista Araucania*, *Diario Loco*, along with the Opus Dei journal *La Pandilla*, promoted strict norms of behavior as the precondition for a "juvenile mystique" and the remedy for juvenile "restlessness."[168] The Secretariat also collaborated closely with the Gremialistas' youth organization, Frente Juvenil de Unidad Nacional. The head of this body, Javier Leturia, stated that he and his peers "denounce the suicidal weakness of the so-called great contemporary democracies" and swore to establish a new society upon the "Christian, Hispanic, and republican tradition."[169] Together, the two movements were tremendously visible in public life, organizing a host of activities ranging from summer camps to their annual summit at the Santiago Cerro Chacarillas (or "Acto de Chacarillas") – a ceremonious event orchestrated by Guzmán and Campos Menéndez.[170] Truly, in 1975, these "intermediary societies" were more reminiscent of the Hitler Youth than of voluntary elite societies.

In late 1975, as the economy stabilized, the Gremialistas retook their place as Chile's chief "intermediary society," publicly theorizing the regime's political outlook. A special *Qué Pasa* issue named "Chile in

1985" witnessed Guzmán confirming that Chile's future political model would "exclude from civic life" anybody who does not abide by the "common principles" of anti-Marxism, Catholicism, and a "territorially decentralized state." He also assessed that this final state model would be a "presidential regime" that would reduce the "legislative powers of parliament" and elevate the "autonomy of intermediate societies between man and the state" according to the "subsidiarity principle." In fact, he went beyond this: Parliament members would be appointed rather than elected, free speech would not be allowed, and strikes would be "unacceptable," he stated.[171] Ricardo Cox, a *Portada* columnist, offered his perspective on the composition of the unique Chilean parliament. He suggested that to overcome the "crisis of Western democracy," Chile should allow political participation only from men who are free from ideologies (or "demagoguery"), and who demonstrate "internal and voluntary" subordination to a supreme executive authority, all in the name of the "national common good."[172] Briefly put, Chile could expect a final authoritarian model devoid of the separation of powers, but with a parliamentary theater that, in essence, resembled the one put forth in 1967 Spain.

Unlike Franco, however, Pinochet did not bother founding a sham chamber of representatives. Thus, only one group purported to epitomize the autonomous intermediary societies – namely, the Gremialistas themselves. One of the more peculiar aspects of Guzmán's public persona was that, unlike López Rodó or Díaz Colodero, he never held an official governmental position. In effect, he consciously rendered himself and his followers as agents of truth who are above and beyond politics, thereby guaranteeing society's perfection. "We represent an ideal far beyond political power. We are fighting for something that we believe is the very source of a free society: The defense of the autonomy of the Intermediate Societies, one that does not postulate a simply blind or dogmatic path but one based on a doctrine of man and society," Guzmán said forthrightly.[173] These declarations were misleading, to put it mildly. Like Opus Dei in Spain and the Ateneo de la República in Argentina, the Gremialistas' relationship with the regime deepened and evolved over time. Eventually, they also manned ministerial positions. The appointment of Sergio Fernández Fernández as Minister of Labor in March 1976 and his promotion to Interior Minister the following year was a striking example. Robert Moss, *The Economist*'s correspondent and a fierce anticommunist, had this to say:

> The presumptuous influence of a small circle of civil advisers with Francoist tendencies, sometimes bordering on theocratic, is unsettling – and yet, in the current climate, it has almost no competition. People like Jaime Guzmán now represent . . . a kind of total dedication to the system, and an equally total rejection of "foreign" ideas, which is fundamentally at odds with the Chilean society's tradition of *laissez passer*. If they could, they would likely turn Chile into an absolutist, introverted society, in which morality and education would be determined by the state and its church councils.

Disapprovingly, he also stated that it is "most likely" that Pinochet would resemble a "Chilean Franco" and fashion a "personal dictatorship" justified based on its ability to foster "economic prosperity and political stability."[174] That a translated version of the article appeared in *Portada* implies that its editors perceived Moss's views as a source of pride.

Why Gremialismo had "no competition" is a question Moss did not delve into. While this was somewhat of an exaggeration, it is true that, at least until 1980, Pinochet relied almost entirely on the intellectual work of a monolithic circle of thinkers whose publishing apparatus happened to dominate the public sphere. These included not only the Gremialistas but people such as Ibáñez Langlois. In fact, in the late 1970s, Opus Dei's leader had become the regime's semi-official spiritual guide, lecturing the generals on the nature of Marxism.[175] In 1976, he stated that Marxism is "a religious phenomenon, exactly reversed to Christianity." When asked whether he thought Marxism is being effectively expunged in Chile, Ibáñez Langlois displayed a sudden shift of tone: "I do not want to be against anything. I want to be pro. But [Marxism] is intrinsically perverse ... there is something terrible in its basis, it is superhuman, diabolical. But my task stays in the intellectual order ... priests should not make judgments of a political nature."[176] This, indeed, was an Opus Dei answer *by the book*. In 1976 Chile, there was no doubt to whom "Marxism" applied. Ibáñez Langlois chose to name these individuals "diabolical," only then to state that he does not make political judgments.

Returning to Moss's claims, by late 1976, Chile indeed showcased what seemed like a Francoist-oriented team of ideologues, empowered by a military Junta, bound towards what appeared to be a refurbished version of technocratic Spain's legality. In January, Chile's State Council was established, in preparation for this authoritarian setup to progress.[177] In a defiant interview with Swiss filmmakers, Guzmán reaffirmed that Chile's return to parliamentary democracy "is impossible" and heralded the advent of a "technophile democracy" based on "effective social participation" and headed by an authoritarian ruler acting above "the judiciary and the law."[178] Pinochet's address of September 11, 1976, likewise spoke of a "new institutionality capable of shaping a new democracy" but did not utter the word parliament.[179] Thus, at this point, the regime was headed towards a distinctive institutionalization wherein parliament was to function as a selected body of participation at minimum, or as an elected body among several nonelected bodies at best, operating under an authoritarian nonelected executive branch. And yet, Moss erred in assuming that Pinochet wanted to replicate the Francoist model. He and his men clearly sought to "transcend and succeed" Francoism, to borrow historian Kirsten Weld's terms.[180] Another way to approach it is that they formed a third, violent, and gradually neoliberal version of the Francoist modernity that they had witnessed firsthand as youngsters; one that addressed the political and economic contexts of the 1970s but still corresponded to the Chileans' "physiognomy." Fernández de la Mora's repeated appearances in Chile during the late 1970s illustrated that he too identified Chile as the last bastion of the regime model he had hoped Spain would forever maintain. Then, in June 1977, in Chacarillas, Pinochet gave a speech that supposedly ended this trajectory, as we will now observe.

5

Democracies of the Third Wave

Hispanic Technocracy's Decline as a State Model (1973–1988)

The late 1970s saw Southern European and Latin American dictatorships thrust into an era of democratic transitions. Famously labeled by political scientist Samuel Huntington "democracies of the third wave," they resulted from various dynamics. Some dictatorships imploded under the weight of economic and political crises (Portugal and Greece). Others set about reform mechanisms that gave birth to normative democratic regimes (Spain, Brazil). Either way, these transitions were neither imminent nor entirely foreseeable. In fact, the onset of Pinochet's regime only went to show how brazenly the Western powers would collaborate with a ruthless military dictatorship – a behavior they continued to demonstrate in 1976 in Argentina and 1982 in Guatemala. Nevertheless, during the 1970s, a conjunction of historical conditions destabilized the regimes and ideologies that have preoccupied us thus far. In Spain, the so-called democratic opposition – which comprised workers, students, intellectuals, and former regime members – grew significantly in the 1960s, challenging Hispanic technocracy's claim to represent the popular will. It was soon joined by neofascist revolutionaries in a rebuke of the technocratic economic model and spirituality. International circumstances had also impacted this mobilization by now. Following the Second Vatican Council, during Paul VI's papacy, the Catholic Church's support of human rights became definite, making the justification of authoritarianism even more difficult by the 1970s. More than this: By then, the Western Bloc was seeing the uptick of a new sensitivity to human rights violations – what historian Samuel Moyn has branded the "new utopia."[1] This movement corroded the anti-communist legitimation buttressing military dictatorships worldwide. Henceforth, human rights violations would be met with damning UN resolutions, human rights commissions, international shaming campaigns, and hostile diplomacy, especially in Western Europe. Democratization, on the other hand, would be greeted in the West with political and economic rewards.

Still, ironically, what destabilized the Hispanic technocratic system of meaning were its exaggerated narratives, paradoxes, and falsehoods. As an economic model, it relied on low governmental expenditures, foreign loans, and public debt through consumption and was thus prone to overheating and economic crises. Endemic corruption and protectionism further stained the international image of authoritarian development, as did its inability to sustain living standards comparable to those in the "developed" world. The moment when the supposedly newly minted middle classes – those in whom the technocrats took so much pride – joined the opposition in demand for the civil liberties enjoyed in Western societies was when the technocrats learned how swiftly the deterministic narratives underpinning their ideology could be turned against them. For if the nation had been modernized into a society of ideology-free middle-class consumers, why not let parliamentary democracy reign?

For all their efforts to herald authoritarianism as a final condition, once the conservative sectors surmised that they could exert control over electoral politics to their liking or gathered that the dictatorship inhibited rather than promoted their wealth-making, they, too, moved from supporting authoritarianism to backing a return to a democracy that would enshrine their privileges and gains. This last tipping moment signaled a peculiar but fundamental narrative amendment: From being a final state of perfection, Hispanic technocracy reappeared as a transient phase and a *stepping stone to democracy*. Hereafter, conservatives would even take pride in authoritarianism as the embryo where the economic and sociological preconditions for democracy had emerged.

Almost without exception, this book's protagonists did not participate in this democratic makeover. On the contrary: They sabotaged the process by promoting various formats of "protected" parliamentary systems that would be nominally democratic but Hispanic technocratic in essence. Thus, ironically, the technocrats did not believe in their own narratives of modernization and would not allow the masses – "modernized" as they were – back into the political arena. Accordingly, they stymied any effort to fashion a political consensus with the democratic opposition. As we delve into the Hispanic technocrats' ejection from politics, the reader might experience a sense of disintegration in the book's narrative. Indeed, it is commensurate with how our protagonists felt in the 1980s when, wallowing in irrelevance on the fringes of conservative politics, they uttered fragments of their bygone ideology in unpredictable circumstances – in Argentina, amid the rise of an entirely new military dictatorship, and in Spain and Chile, within electoral political parties.

5.1 FROM TECHNOCRACY TO NEOFASCISM: THE UNINTENDED CONSEQUENCES OF ONGANÍA'S AUTHORITARIAN EXPERIMENT

The man who took over the Argentine Revolution, General Lanusse, perhaps disliked Onganía's "semi-feudal traditionalism and fascism" but abhorred democracy and Peronism just like his predecessor.[2] However, by now, he was also painfully aware of the failure of the armed forces to depoliticize the masses.[3] What did he seek to achieve, then? For one, he aimed to finalize Argentina's economic transformation. For another, he sought to stave off the return to democracy in the hope that Perón would age beyond governance capabilities. To this end, he began scheming a constitutional reform that would inhibit Perón's return.[4] In order to camouflage his intentions, and not to appear as Argentina's de facto president, in 1971, he appointed General Roberto Levingston as Onganía's replacement. Levingston, it seemed at first, betrayed Nacionalista and economic protectionism that went against Onganía's ideology. But, in reality, the Argentine Revolution had not changed much. The economic policies of his Minister of Economy, Carlos Moyano Llerena, were identical to those of his disciple, Krieger Vasena, and included yet another devaluation of the Peso in late 1970.[5] Levingston's Education and Interior Ministries were likewise handed to traditionalist and Catholic figures. Argentina's 1970–1974 Development Plan – a realization of Onganía's 1966 Development and Planning Directive which spoke of a nation "integrated spiritually, economically, and physically" – was also indicative of the regime's ideological continuation.[6]

Still, there is no question that the Argentine Revolution had lost its plot. While the platforms supporting it – *Cuadernos del Sur* and Ateneo de la República, to name the obvious culprits – closed in 1970, the mainstream press turned decidedly against the regime and the societies that had fostered it. Hit hardest was Opus Dei, which saw intellectuals such as Gregorio Selser disparaging it for seeking "power conquest" through its Pomaiere editorials and *Cuadernos del Sur*.[7] *Confirmado* and *La Opinion* followed suit by underscoring Opus Dei's connections to Spain and methods of financial collusion.[8] Simultaneously, Spain's ambassador reported to Sánchez Bella that Levingston was "distancing himself from Hispanismo, half disavowing [Onganía's] message addressed to Spain, the only one of its kind."[9] Indeed, Nacionalista in his economic beliefs or not, Levingston did not in the slightest want to be identified with Hispanic spirituality, or with Franco's Spain for that matter.

To secure the special ties between the regimes, López Rodó traveled to Buenos Aires to meet the new president.[10] Before his arrival, though, he sat with Bernardo Neustadt for an eye-opening televised interview, which appeared also in Opus Dei's *Actualidad Española* and Neustadt's magazine *Extra*. It opened with the Argentine publicist raising the question of why Onganía failed where Franco had succeeded. Unlike the Spanish "development plans," which are marked by "authenticity," Onganía's equivalent consisted of "easy slogans," was Neustadt's opinion.[11] As he did not receive a satisfactory answer, he addressed the clichés for which his interviewee had been known in a dialogue that went as follows:

NEUSTADT: Do you believe that ideologies have died?
LÓPEZ RODÓ: I do not believe in the end of the ideologies, although one must ask what we mean by ideologies ... In politics, there are no dogmas, but there are ideals. I do not understand politics as pure management; I do not think that politics can be done without attaining the people's support towards a great national project ...
NEUSTADT: But you do not believe in parliamentary institutions?
LÓPEZ RODÓ: I believe in a legislative chamber ... However, parliamentarism is a degeneration of democracy because the fundamental activity taking place in it is the initiative to overthrow governments.

Brazenly, López Rodó thus reaffirmed the ethical supremacy of authoritarianism with public "support" over democracy.[12] All in all, the two men agreed that it was a botched implementation – not Hispanic technocracy's principles – that brought Onganía's experiment to its end.

Removed from power, Amadeo did not take the Argentine Revolution's ideological turn lightly.[13] Levingston's cabinet suffered from "almost total absence of authentic political thought," he told Sánchez Bella.[14] Amadeo also revealed that he had been in touch with "leading Peronist figures" and was optimistic about the prospects of reaching "understandings with them."[15] Indeed, he now thought that a right-wing Peronist government was better than the generals' ad-libbing. Reactionary military regimes cannot "last long," he surmised.[16] This change of heart derived no doubt from Perón's latest triumph. In November 1970, he and Ricardo Balbín, the leader of the Radical party, put aside their differences and, together with other center-left parties, signed a pact named La Hora del Pueblo, which stipulated an immediate return to democracy without preconditions. The alliance between the Peronists and their political antagonists was yet another definite sign of the Argentine Revolution's dismal popularity.

Impelling Argentina's return to democracy was a combination of continued public mobilization and urban guerrilla. The Cordobazo and Aramburu's murder were watershed moments insofar as they exemplified how simple the tactics for destabilizing a military regime can be. Argentina's urban guerilla movements – the most important of which were the Ejército Revolucionario del Pueblo (ERP) and Peronist Montoneros underground – targeted mostly armed forces personnel and businessmen. In 1971 alone, the ERP slew more than fifty servicemen, thereby becoming the focus of attention of Argentine politics.[17] In conjunction with these attacks, the demonstration movement expanded in 1971 (the "second Cordobazo"), which led Lanusse to appoint himself as president in July that year. Reaping the whirlwind of the wind he himself had helped sow, he introduced oppression methods Onganía had been reluctant to use, such as torture, capital punishment, and even instances of extrajudicial assassinations.[18] Indeed, the armed forces' doctrine of "operation against urban subversion" was founded in the wake of the Cordobazo.[19]

By this time, the regime had lost whatever remained of the Nacionalistas' support. People like Sánchez Sorondo and Leonardo Castellani had been railing against Onganía's "good-for-nothing Catholics" and their economic policies as early as 1967.[20] By the early 1970s, they were joined by a sordid wave of Nacionalista publications that went far beyond the economic critique. On the one hand, they took a swipe at the Argentine Revolution's objective to depoliticize the population through consumption rather than totalitarian indoctrination. Bruno Genta's book *Seguridad y Desarrollo*, for example, held Onganía's pluralism responsible for turning Argentina into a society where one could be anything from a "technocrat, existentialist, psychoanalyst . . . a hippie."[21] On the other hand, people such as Alberto Boixadós, the director of the Córdoba ICH, attacked the technocrats' spiritual project, arguing that those who had tried "to Christianize" society actually "quickly de-Christianized it."[22] More fundamentally, the Nacionalistas agreed on two truths: that the "subversion" against Onganía was not the result of a plausible resistance to authoritarianism but the effect of moral decay, and that this phenomenon should be eradicated through a violent purge and a swift return to political corporatism. While the more anti-capitalist of them – Antonio Mille's Movimiento Nacional Sindicalista, for example – promoted a national syndicalist totalitarianism, Ricardo Curutchet, the editor of the magazine *Cabildo*, perhaps revered José Antonio's "synthesis of tradition and revolution," but his platform ultimately showcased a milder interpretation of this supposed state model.[23]

Still, the most heinous neofascist alternative to Hispanic technocracy emerged within Peronism. Although it is beyond the scope of this book to expand on the Peronist political universe, let us grant the following: The 1960s saw this movement torn between two "revolutionary" projects. On one side was the "Peronist Left" (or "La tendencia revolucionaria"). Theoretically Marxist, it was identified with the Montoneros underground and newspapers such as *El Descamisado* and the Peronist Youth movement. On the other side, was the far smaller "Peronist Right" (or "Orthodox Peronism") – the neofascist clique that was to rule Argentina between 1973 and 1976 and extrajudicially murder short of a thousand left-wing Peronists.[24] If Juan Perón ever "turned right," this correlated with his marriage to María Estela Martínez (or "Isabel" – her stage name) and his choosing Madrid as his residence in January 1960. It was there that Perón's entourage – former MNT members Raúl Jassén and Felipe Romeo, for example – linked with the Falange's neofascist circles and even began referring to themselves as "Joseantonians."[25] And while Perón and Franco remained distant, Pilar, Franco's sister, became Isabel's intimate friend.

Of course, throughout the 1960s, Perón's Puerta de Hierro residence accommodated Peronists of all ideological hues.[26] Still, in their dismay at the trade unionist Augusto Vandor's political power, and the disappearance of electoral politics in 1966, the Madrid Peronists turned from relying on union power to new mobilizing tactics. Thus, they spoke in two voices. On the one hand, in 1968, Perón published a manifesto called *La hora de los pueblos* that catered to the Peronist Left (the "new Justicialista generation") by attacking the USA's "imperialism" (and depicting Onganía's "technocrats" as "satellites of imperialism") while praising Marxism ("peaceful penetration") and communism ("works for the people"). On the other hand, surreptitiously, the Madrid Peronists sought to convey – to the armed forces and the anti-Peronist polity, no doubt – that Peronism had changed since 1955. Articulating the movement's refurbished "truths" was commissioned to Isabel and Perón's personal secretary, José López Rega.[27] In their bulletin, *Las Bases*, the two provocatively evoked José Antonio's national syndicalism as a substitute for Marxism, along with a handful of references to Hispanic and Catholic spirituality.[28] López Rega, the famously self-identified "sorcerer," also used this platform to elaborate on his endeavor to generate a "new man" in Argentina.[29] In short, the Peronist Right proposed to replace the Argentine Revolution with a conspicuous, if bizarre, spiritual project.

Most Argentines were oblivious to this tectonic shift. Under the leadership of Perón's official candidate, Héctor José Cámpora, Peronism even appeared as a rational center-left political party. This is at least what Amadeo thought in 1971 when he published *El camino de la recuperación* – a manifesto that heralded the Argentine Revolution's ending and the return to democracy under a responsible Peronist leadership. Cámpora, Amadeo told Sánchez Bella, was a "decent Christian" and an "anti-Marxist."[30] Thus, together with none other than Sánchez Sorondo, in 1972, Amadeo founded the Movimiento de Acción Nacional (MAN) as a conduit for Nacionalistas to join Perón's political alliance FREJULI.[31] In May 1973, Amadeo revealed to Sánchez Bella that he aimed to "participate actively in defining and organizing" this coalition.[32] Regardless of who joined this coalition, Lanusse would not surrender power without a constitutional reform that would prevent Perón from becoming president. Against La Hora del Pueblo, in July 1971, he announced an initiative named "el Gran Acuerdo Nacional," by which the armed forces could categorically veto any candidate.[33] But his efforts to control the democratic transition were to no avail. On November 17, 1972, Perón returned to Argentina briefly, met with key political leaders, and received their endorsement. Outmaneuvered, Lanusse capitulated, and a general election was called for March 1973. Even though Perón's candidacy was not permitted, FREJULI won 49.11 percent of the popular vote. With Balbín's backing, Cámpora was consequently inaugurated as president on May 25, 1973. Thus, the Argentine Revolution reached its anticlimactic end.

For a fleeting moment, Argentines were gripped with optimism in the expectation for national reconciliation, as Cámpora brought the unions and industrialists to sign a "social pact" and granted amnesty to political prisoners (this was known as "Cámpora's spring"). Alas, ultimately, Cámpora had little choice but to authorize Perón's return and declare yet another general election for November that year. When Perón landed in Argentina on June 20, 1973, the ideological rift in his movement revealed itself in the most ghastly of ways as the Peronist rightists opened fire on a crowd of Peronist leftists awaiting Perón's arrival at the airport.

Known as the "Ezeiza Massacre," this was the first evidence of the murderous violence that would replace the Argentine Revolution's legalist oppression hereafter. When Perón won the November 1973 election with a whopping 62 percent of votes, many believed he would swiftly put an end to the civil war within his party. Instead, he outlawed the Peronist Left and, in due course, ordered its members' extrajudicial murder. These events occurred in tandem with the appearance of Romeo's weekly *El Caudillo* – the official mouthpiece of López Rega's assassination squad, the Argentine Anticommunist Alliance.[34] Rarely had Argentina witnessed a semi-official discourse steeped in such political violence and fascist hallmarks. *El Caudillo* not only identified the nation's enemy as the Jewish-led "sinarquía" but demanded its physical annihilation.[35] A "good enemy is a dead one," was Romero's slogan.[36]

Amadeo and his circle did not fathom the significance of this ideological turn in real time. On March 14, 1974, he spoke at a FREJULI convention, saying that the "tragic Azul episode" had clarified that Marxism must be liquidated. He also rejected the notion that Onganía's "violence from above" caused the "violence from below." On the contrary, Amadeo alleged that the Argentine masses had, by now, lost the capacity for ideological thinking and held only "Christian and national inclinations." In a burst of optimism, he even reminisced about his 1954 Zaragoza speech and announced that the "Spanish-Creole tradition" is the Peronist movement's new ethical ground. Now that Perón is on the "right side of the barricade," the anti-Peronist political camp should cease to exist, he concurred.[37] Writing to Sánchez Bella, he assured his friend that Perón was "physically, mentally, and emotionally" strong and that rumors of his retirement were "wishful thinking" at best.[38]

Yet wishful thinking was what defined Amadeo's interpretation of reality best. Barely eighty years old, Perón died on July 1, 1974, after seven months in office. Isabel, his Vice president, assumed the presidency and, with López Rega at her side, unleashed an all-out war on the Peronist Left. The ensuing twenty months of "Lopezreguismo" thus witnessed the Argentine Revolution's architects disengaged from Peronism. Grondona's new magazine, *Carta Política*, was where some of them gathered to express their repulsion from the Peronist lunacy. Featuring people such as Carlos Alberto Floria (*Cuadernos del Sur*), Costa Méndez, and anti-Peronists such as Félix Luna, the magazine bemoaned Argentina's motion from dignified authoritarianism to a democratic terror regime.[39] On the one hand, these men attacked the neofascist Nacionalistas, stating that the days of "marches and Falanges are over."[40] On the other hand, they revised the Argentine Revolution's history. Onganía's "effort to modernize Argentina" was perhaps "pharaonic" but far superior to that of Isabel, who relied on arbitrary power structures such as the Peronist party and the unions, Grondona argued.[41] As for Amadeo, with FREJULI dissolved, all contacts between him and the Peronist government were cut short by 1975. In January 1976, he wrote to Sánchez Bella of a regime "controlled by events" and of a society on the brink of "falling apart."[42] A month later, the armed forces overthrew Isabel Perón, ushering in the Proceso de Reorganización Nacional (PRN) – a dictatorship in which this book's protagonists attempted to implement their ideology one last time.

5.2 FROM "FRANCOISM WITHOUT FRANCO" TO THE "CONSENSUS": THE HAPHAZARD TRAJECTORY OF THE SPANISH TRANSITION

In 1969, while Franco's deteriorating health was on everyone's mind, the regime seemed as ideologically consistent as ever. With the succession process secured and Carrero Blanco's authority unquestioned, the monocolor government ministers seemingly enjoyed a carte blanche to solidify their state model further in the upcoming years. However, change was in the offing. The MATESA affair brought in its wake a maelstrom of publications – especially by the Paris-based publishing house Ruedo Iberico – disclosing Opus Dei's operational methods and tarnishing its international reputation.[43] Once more, Escrivá did his utmost to rebut these allegations. Another secret memo from the ambassador to the Vatican to Franco described him rudely refusing to meet with Spanish officials. "I want to know nothing of politics ... This had been precisely why I moved my residence from Madrid to Rome," he blasted.[44] His gestures were to no avail. So conspicuous was Opus Dei's involvement in politics that, in 1971, the Falange took Opus Dei to court, accusing it of violating the law prohibiting political associations. By controlling Spain's most important newspapers and Cortes chairs, Opus Dei "participates in national politics and aspires to do so exclusively," the lawsuit stated.[45]

Concurrently, a host of new agents tore into Spain's technocratic model, the loudest being, indeed, the neofascist "bunker." Encompassing newspapers such as *El Alcázar*, *El Imparcial*, and Piñar's *Fuerza Nueva*, they demanded Spain's return to national syndicalism, railed against consumerism and sexual promiscuity, and, more broadly, derided the reduction of politics to questions of science and specialists. As one *Fuerza Nueva* columnist put it:

We do not like this Cold Spain ... where the aroma of a steak is confused with the sweet rhetoric of flexible ideologies of circumstances ... technocratic Spain, the one that tries to educate us in alloys of the spirit, the one that is more attentive to the consumer society than the consummation of society ... this Indirect Spain, we do not like, we do not like it! ... We like the Direct Spain, which attests to the strong Celtiberian courage, which is willing to die for the sake of an ideal.[46]

Indeed, for *Fuerza Nueva*, the "direct Spain" was synonymous with political violence. "Better dead than red," howled Piñar sardonically against what he thought was the technocrats' pacifism.[47] Piñar's critique of the technocrats included a distinctive effort to pair Falangism with Hispanidad traditionalism. By insisting that the two were not "diametrically opposed,"[48] he thus sought to resume the initiative of the "Hispanic community of nations" which, to his mind, the "indirect Spain" had criminally forsaken.[49] Spanish intellectuals, such as Juan Vallet de Goytisolo and Josep Meliá, offered a more sophisticated critique of the technocrats' discourse. For them, the question was not whether the technocrats promoted capitalism but whether they had no "ideology."[50] López Rodó's development plans, they wrote, assume what people want, how to satisfy their needs, and are thus plainly ideological.[51] The Spanish Church, under the influential leadership of Vicente Enrique y Tarancón, also stepped into the fray, expressing concerns about the regime's authoritarian aspirations. From 1972, as the Archbishop of Madrid, Tarancón also displayed a visible hostility towards Opus Dei. The relationship between the Holy See and Spain became "increasingly tense," he remembered, with López Rodó – a priest – "unbelievably" seeking to shield Spain "from the Pope and the Spanish episcopal hierarchy."[52] But perhaps the most striking criticism came from the Western powers that, by 1970, did not shy away from questioning Spain's authoritarian future. During the chancellorship of Willy Brandt, West Germany's Foreign Minister Walter Scheel met opposition leaders in Madrid in broad daylight. The celebrated visit of President Nixon to Madrid in 1970 was not without its tensions either, and saw Secretary of State Henry Kissinger insinuating that Franco "has completed his historical mission."[53] As far as the USA was concerned, Spain would be admitted into NATO only as a democracy.

To judge from López Rodó's finely etched memoirs, the mono-color clique fretted over these pressures regularly and, together with Carrero Blanco, devised strategies to neutralize them. On one occasion, Fernández de la Mora suggested a detailed three-step strategy: "Tactical withdrawal, homogeneous evolution, and sustaining action." By homogeneous evolution, he meant the appointment of a prime minister and enacting municipal representation. By "sustaining action," he championed restricting the press under a new "editorial board."[54] Indeed, the regime ultimately contained the opposition's pressures with an analogous strategy. On the one hand, it intensified its performance of representation. José Luis Villar Palasí's 1970 Education Reform, and the study that antedated it (the "White Book"), was a case in point of a performance of "democratization" of Spain's education system.[55] The 1971 elections for the Cortes's third rank – wherein Spanish heads of family elected a mere 104 out of the 564 parliament members – was an even more blatant bogus democratic spectacle.[56] On the other hand, with Sánchez Bella as Minister of Tourism and Information, the regime suppressed the public sphere more systematically – for instance, by episodically closing down platforms such as *Cuadernos para el Diálogo*. This authoritarian relapse was most noticeable in the 1970 Burgos trials, which sentenced several ETA members to death and drew significant international criticism. Amid this process, the mono-color ministers expressed confidence in the "perfection" of their state model. Strikingly, López Rodó even began presenting himself publicly as a "politician" operating within an entirely normative constitutional system.[57] The publication of the third Development Plan was an opportunity for him to demonstrate that he had taken to heart the criticism against his previous plans. Besides the repetition of words such as "humanism" and "social justice," his propaganda upheld an even more blatant determination to pair development with spirituality. Speaking of the "spiritual values that development should serve," he posited that many modern societies undergo "disappointments sown by simple material progress," not least because this mutation is not "subordinated to the supreme ideals of the Homeland and of man."[58] Spain, he believed, would not succumb to such disappointment.

Still, behind closed doors, and with the disintegration of the Argentine Revolution on everyone's mind, the Spanish technocrats' confidence was, in fact, at its lowest. In 1973, López Rodó and Fernández de la Mora warned Franco that, if the regime was to survive after his death, two "extremes" must be circumvented – namely, "political parties" and a "political vacuum." Besides admitting that the Organic Laws had led to the participation of "bodies on the path of extinction," they were at a loss to explain how public disapproval should be resolved, however.[59] Against the backdrop of this anxiety, and amid a dramatic deterioration in Franco's health, in June 1973, the Council of the Kingdom willingly appointed Carrero Blanco as prime minister, thereby granting him almost limitless executive power. In his inaugural speech, the admiral reiterated that the Spaniards would participate in the state's "tasks" but never decide the identity of its executive branch, lawmakers, or judges.[60] Communism "remains the same" as in 1936, he said on December 19, 1973 – a day before his own death.[61] In a nutshell, it was not Hispanic technocracy's perfection or popularity that was to secure its future but a ruthless tyrant. Sixty-nine years old in 1973, Carrero Blanco's appointment was supposed to prolong the "State of July 18, institutionalized and affirmed as ever," was how Fernández de la Mora summarized it.[62]

Thus, once the ETA underground had assassinated Carrero Blanco in the center of Madrid, Spain's history pivoted in the most haphazard of ways. In later years, López Rodó alleged, as did many others, that the CIA was involved in the act.[63] While no declassified documents have ever verified this myth, it is instructive that he sensed the USA wanted Carrero Blanco gone. These conspiratorial intuitions may have emanated from the dramatic events that ensued. No sooner had the admiral been buried than the Falange overtook the political void he left behind by persuading Franco to replace the mono-color cabinet with Falange ministers. On February 12, 1974, the new prime minister, Carlos Arias Navarro, announced the advent of a new era of political "opening."[64] Being the mayor of Madrid in the 1960s, this Falangist was to represent the "spirit of February 12," which, in actuality, meant a progression from Hispanic technocracy to a more inclusive, yet hardly defined, political culture.[65] López Rodó, who was relegated to being Spain's ambassador in Vienna, attacked these reforms by saying to the Opus Dei press that his mono-color group was the last "legitimate" government to rule Spain.[66] His complaints did not change the fact that Opus Dei was unceremoniously pushed out of politics in a way that, in Tarancón's words, resolved "many ambiguities that in no way favored the Church."[67] Thus, the Francoist political landscape was neatly divided between the Falange's moderate reformists ("aperturistas") and Piñar's neofascist hard-liners ("inmovilistas").[68]

This was just the onset of an overwhelming leadership crisis within Opus Dei. In December 1974, Pérez-Embid died, aged seventy-four. In June 1975, Escrivá de Balaguer also passed away after a period of declining mental and physical health, sending shockwaves throughout this international organization. How Ibáñez Langlois chose to commemorate his master was instructive: Escrivá was a man who "always abhorred personalist governments," said the Chilean spiritual leader.[69] This is not to say that Opus Dei's ideology changed. Álvaro d'Ors and an intellectual named José Zafra Valverde, for example, continued to promote Spain's authoritarian monarchy enthusiastically upon its platforms.[70] Still, that Escrivá's followers began to revise their leader's history in this way spoke to the fact that they too began to rearrange their narratives ahead of a possible democratization process, in Spain as well as in Chile.

While Opus Dei was in disarray, the Falange was likewise hopelessly splintered and far too ale to either change Spain's existing regime model or impact Franco's succession process. Devoid of international backing, its "opening" was destined to fail from the start. All its leaders could do was sit in wait for Franco to die. When this happened, on November 20, 1975, even the most loyal Francoist sounded indefinite about what was to come. Fernández de la Mora, for example, stated that "there was nothing authoritarian" about Franco and that he was responsible for transforming Spain from an "impoverished country" into "a middle-class society."[71] Others, such as Opus Dei's *Mundo Cristiano*, asserted that "all the architecture of the State rested on Franco's personality," and even alleged that Franco had "said that Francoism would end with his death."[72] These texts' objectives were clear: to vindicate those who had served the regime and pave their way into the future political system. In turn, "personalism" – as in "Franco was the dictatorship" – rapidly became the conservatives' watchword when addressing their rapport with Francoism.[73] Paradoxically, by doing so, they admitted that the "model" they had promoted until recently was a castle made of sand.

Of course, Franco never said his regime would end with his death but that he had left Spain "bound and tied" for its authoritarian future.[74] It was his successor, now renamed King Juan Carlos I, who, on being crowned as Spain's sovereign on November 23, 1975, disobeyed Franco's will and – in an unquestionably heroic feat – initiated a shift in Spain's course, from an authoritarian to a constitutional monarchy. Using the Organic Law as his legal anchor, this was, by no means, a simple gambit. In fact, so frail was the king at first that he appointed Arias Navarro to devise this reform.[75] Yet the elderly Falangist was clearly not up to the task. Thus, in July 1976, Juan Carlos exploited López Rodó's creation – namely, the Council of the Kingdom – to appoint the relatively anonymous Adolfo Suárez as Spain's prime minister. An Opus Dei member in the past, and more recently the Movimiento's general secretary, Suárez maneuvered between the Francoist hard-liners and the democratic opposition – which demanded a definite political "rupture" – by prompting a cunning discursive compromise called the "pacted rupture." After capably bringing the armed forces around to cooperate, he managed to get the Cortes to vote for its own dismantling in November 1976. Henceforward, the transitional process was to follow a relatively clear trajectory: Following a yes/no national referendum on the Reform Law, a free general election would be declared. Next, an assembly representing the elected parliament's makeup will draft a new constitution, to be approved in yet another referendum.

In December 1976, the Spanish public approved the reforms overwhelmingly (97.36 percent) and, in June 1977, attended their first general elections in forty years, officially marking the end of one of Europe's longest-surviving dictatorships.[76] Naturally, from an institutional standpoint, Spain did not change overnight. The courts, banking system, education system, and municipalities – not to mention the armed forces – remained manned by Franco's appointees. Still, with the Organic Law eliminated, juridically Francoism faded into history. Nothing exemplified this more than the legalization of the Spanish Communist Party (PCE) in 1977. The fact that, as in Western Europe, Spain allowed "Eurocommunism" into its political system demonstrably negated Francoism's *raison d'être*.[77] How the king and Suárez persuaded the armed forces to agree to this bargain relied on a powerful, if deliberately vague, rhetoric of "consensus." It signified a commitment among all "democratic forces" to avoid a relapse into bloodshed and make the "reconciliation of the two Spains" a reality. This was, at least, how Ruiz-Giménez – one of the chief designers of the "consensus" – described it in 1980, in a UNESCO convention suggestively titled "Consensus and Peace."[78] He was a member of Suárez's political alliance, the Unión de Centro Democrático (UCD) – a hastily assembled conglomerate of parties consisting of former opposition members alongside Francoist functionaries such as Pío Cabanillas.[79] This being the case, the party's members presented themselves not only as the embodiment of the "consensus" but as Spain's "last hope" against a relapse into violence.[80] As the "third Spain," they had nothing to do with the nation's "extremist minorities" responsible for the Civil War to begin with, they even alleged.[81] Anti-ideological to the core, the "extreme center" echoed the technocrats' discourse of the 1960s.[82]

The Opus Dei technocrats were markedly barred from the UCD, with the exception of Antonio Fontán, who, despite his authoritarian rhetoric of the 1950s, proved himself worthy of being labeled a true democrat with *Madrid*.[83] Still, the technocrats' path into parliamentary politics was primarily hampered by their inability to support democratization after

Franco's death. To be sure, taking pride in Franco's achievements was an inclination all conservatives shared well until the 1990s. While *ABC* deemed Franco the "Europeanizer of modern Spain,"[84] the daily *Ya* declared he had made Spain "much better prepared for the new system of national coexistence," for instance.[85] Yet the technocrats belittled the very return to parliamentary democracy. In January 1976, Fernández de la Mora still promoted the Organic Law as an "autochthonous" Spanish model that was "more effective and more susceptible to perfective development" and, therefore, should not be replaced with recipes that "had led Spain to chaos."[86] His 1976 book *La partitocracia* further discredited universal suffrage as an inefficient form of social organization. "The classical theory of democracy is an unsustainable fiction," he argued there.[87] Navarro Rubio, too, juxtaposed Franco's "real democracy" with Western parliamentarism's "clumsy compromises."[88] For him, the Francoist "authority of arbitration" presented the best system of perfection, based on "councils, academies, and specialized associations."[89] López Rodó followed suit with an even more cynical approach: The Organic Law "is not even ten years old" and replacing it would be a "symptom of political immaturity," he opined.[90]

Only with the June 1977 elections' fait accompli did the technocrats shift from resisting democracy to partaking in the electoral game. On October 21, 1976, Fraga, Fernández de la Mora, López Rodó united under the banner of a party named Alianza Popular (AP).[91] "We take responsibility for the past, we know we have made mistakes," Fraga stated apologetically during the party's first press conference.[92] Fernández de la Mora, for his part, made what he thought was a necessary clarification: He had never claimed that "organic democracy or inorganic democracy are bad in themselves," but that they ought to be valued "according to results in specific circumstances." This was the closest he would ever get to supporting democracy. Expectedly, the AP candidates presented themselves as the visionaries of the constitutional monarchy who worked within the limits of a personalist regime.[93] They also relied heavily on moral panic, blaming the transition for turning Spain into a cesspit of "pornography" and "permissiveness."[94] These strategies amounted to little. Excluded from the "consensus" discourse, which benefited the Spanish "center," the AP fared poorly in the 1977 elections (8.3 percent). As opposition members, the technocrats would never hold executive power again.

Even if Spain's 1977 elections were a cause for celebration, the Spanish transition was anything but a peaceful period of reconciliation. In truth, it was one of the most violent and turbulent periods in Spanish history. The symbolic power and plasticity of the "consensus" would need to withstand a relentless barrage of challenges, from continuous ETA attacks to yet another economic crisis.[95] These burdens were the backdrop for Suárez's October 1977 Amnesty Law and Moncloa Pacts. The former pardoned political prisoners and granted impunity for crimes committed by the armed forces during the dictatorship; the latter legalized the labor unions, enshrined liberties of expression, and elevated minimum wages.[96] These events had tremendous symbolic importance, as they showed that the "consensus" was more than just rhetoric. The compromise was manifest: The Spanish working class received a pluralistic parliamentary system and living wages closer to that of their European counterparts in return for the institutional continuation of the Francoist political system and the impunity of its members for any human rights violations committed since 1936. For better or worse, this was the onset of Spain's "pact of silence."[97]

5.3 CHILE'S TRANSITION FROM HISPANIC TECHNOCRACY TO PARLIAMENTARY DICTATORSHIP

The year 1976 started on a positive note for Pinochet's dictatorship. The economy was recovering, and a united team was steering the regime. However, this confidence led to a significant misstep: the assassination of former diplomat Orlando Letelier on September 21, 1976, in the center of Washington, DC. This was not just a routine hit job, but a brazen act that publicly humiliated Chile's key hemispheric ally. While the threats of cutting military aid to Chile never materialized, Pinochet's relationship with the USA was forever damaged. The situation worsened when Jimmy Carter, a staunch anti-Pinochet candidate, won the USA's presidential elections shortly afterward. His presidency immediately posed a threat to the regime, primarily due to its chilling effect on investors. Finally, the onset of Spain's democratization likewise proved that the Chilean dictatorship could soon be an ideological anachronism. Whether in the Chilean press or the Gremialista circles, nobody expected the Spanish transition. Fernández Larraín, for example, was convinced Spain was bound to "perfect the existing system."[98] Chile's ambassador in Madrid, too, refused to accept that democracy was feasible in Spain. "The conception of democracy, as Europe sees it, is very confusing for the average Spaniard," he reported.[99] Francoism was "convincing in 1973," but became "irreparably discredited in 1975 when in less than a year this political construct collapsed," Vial Correa summed it up.[100] The first to respond to these changes were the Gremialistas. Provided that Chile would be pressured to undergo a similar transition, unlike their Argentine and Spanish counterparts, they would not repudiate this process but define it.

In the wake of the Letelier scandal, Pinochet publicly dissolved the DINA (he merely replaced it with another secret police service named El Central Nacional de Informaciones) and discharged Manuel Contreras, the person responsible for the murder. Less visible but still significant was the change he made in the Ortúzar Commission. Riven between its two foremost theoreticians – Guzmán and Silva Bascuñán – the commission had been idle for three years. In 1977, the Christian Democratic leader was replaced by people such as Luz Bulnes Aldunate and Raúl Bertelsen Repetto – an Opus Dei jurist who studied at UNAV and specialized in Francoist law – making the commission more ideologically cohesive.[101] Next, on July 9, 1977, in front of a crowd of Gremialistas at Chacarillas, Pinochet told his citizens that, like the Spaniards, they too would soon be living under a "democracy." Meticulously crafted by Guzmán, the "Chacarillas speech" outlined a democracy never before seen in the Western domain – "authoritarian, protected, integrating, technified, and of authentic social participation."[102] Now, it was up to the Ortúzar Commission to decipher this enigmatic sequence of words. The term "protected" the commission explained as "an ideologically neutral state" devoid of any redistributionist parties. The word "integrating" they elucidated as a society governed according to Catholic and Hispanic ethics. And "technified and of authentic social participation," they interpreted as a state model where the administration and the economy are beyond the masses' reach. Finally, they explained "authoritarian" as the unquestionable supremacy of the executive branch and the armed forces over parliament and the judiciary.[103] In brief, this was a Hispanic technocracy cloaked in parliamentary attire.

Following the speech, the regime turned to conduct its own version of democratic theater, heavily laced with propaganda. In 1978, it held a national referendum (or "consulta") where the Chilean public "reaffirmed" the legitimacy of the regime's "institutionalization process." Against the background of the December 1977 UN resolution against Chile, on this occasion, the voters were also asked to side with their leader against this "international aggression."[104] Simultaneously, to foster the notion that civilians are guiding the reform, Pinochet appointed Gremialistas to positions of leadership. With Sergio Fernández

Fernández as Minister of Interior, Hernán Cubillos as Foreign Minister, and Vial Correa as Education Minister, one could say that Guzmán's "technocrats" – as some now openly called them – presided over the constitutional process.[105] Pinochet understood that they were the most "firm, determined, and effective" group for that purpose, Vial Correa believed.[106] As a part of this process, Pinochet dismissed General Leigh – still his main rival – while Fernández initiated an Amnesty Law for political prisoners.[107] Of course, any temptation to equate Chile's referendum and amnesty process to that of Spain should be ignored. If anything, Pinochet's "transition" resembled Franco's 1966 spectacle more than Suárez's political reform, as the new Spanish daily *El País* indeed noted.[108]

For some rightists, even this performance was an unnecessary risk, though. Like Spain and Argentina, Chile had its own neofascist "hard-liners," consisting of national syndicalists such as Rodríguez and Miranda Carrington, Hispanistas such as Hübner Gallo, and, perhaps most importantly, Pinochet's daughter, Inés Lucía Pinochet.[109] The center she directed, the Corporación de Estudios Nacionales, was the hard-liners' base of operations. Like in Spain, the neofascist "hard-liners," who, to their minds, possessed a valid alternative to Western democracy, were a force to be reckoned with. Writing in *La Tercera*, Rodríguez insisted that national syndicalism was the only viable defense against the masses' enslavement by international oligarchies.[110] Carlos Cruz-Coke equally proposed a state model wherein the legislative authority consists of elected ("political") and corporatist ("functional") chambers.[111] Expectedly, the Spanish neofascists enthusiastically backed the hard-liners. In April 1979, Piñar arrived in Chile, met with Rodríguez and Pinochet, and granted the Chilean president a copy of José Antonio's writings. His message was clear: A parliamentary system is not the only path forward; one can still opt for national syndicalism.[112] Somewhat less expectedly, in November 1979, Fernández de la Mora arrived in Chile as Lucía Pinochet's guest to criticize the constitutional process with Rodríguez and Cruz-Coke.[113] His appearances on TV, Fernández Larraín wrote to him, left a "deep and solid" impression on his audience.[114]

Still, the hard-liners stood little chance vis-à-vis the Gremialistas (the "soft-liners"), whose alliance consisted of the *Portada* publishing group, most Chicago Boys economists, and *El Mercurio* media executives such as Hernán Cubillos, and whose control of *El Mercurio*, *Ercilla* (under Opus Dei control since 1978), *La Segunda*, and *Qué Pasa*, translated into an almost hegemonic narration of the institutionalization process.[115] On top of this, in 1979, Guzmán launched the journal *Realidad*, designed entirely to promote the constitutional reform. Besides featuring a young generation of Gremialistas such as Hernán Larraín Fernández and Joaquín Lavín – along with Ibáñez Langlois's teachings on Marxism – it openly addressed the holistic vision of Chile's modernization. Given that Chile's "valuable heritage" is the "antithesis" of Western "consumer society," much less a "permissive society," an "updated and effective" intermediary agency should see to it that society members perceive life as "a mission of service and duty," it stated.[116] Doubling down on this message was none other than Mariano Grondona, who was invited to preach that democracy is not akin to "periodic elections" but to "effective governance" and that a military regime can be "pre-democratic."[117] There has never been "a wiser, more humane and Christian, than [colonial Spain's] legislation of the Indies," touted the Argentine elsewhere.[118] His evocation of Hispanic mythologies in *Realidad* illustrated how the Argentine and Chilean Hispanic technocrats collaborated in designing a "democratic" process that would perhaps include a performance of universal suffrage to some extent but that would replace Western ideological and cultural pluralism for a Hispanic morality.

By this time, Chile's democratic opposition was finally allowed to mobilize openly. Censored rather than murdered, the editors of magazines such as *APSI* – the Christian Democrats' mouthpiece – even dared mock the "hard-liners/soft-liners" enmity.[119] Neither of them "postulates a return to democracy as we knew it," observed *APSI* columnist Marcelo Contreras.[120] While the former wanted a "dicta-dura" with no voting mechanism the latter promoted a "dicta-blanda" showcasing an ideologically limited parliament, chimed in *Las Últimas Noticias*.[121] Gradually, the opposition also began postulating an alternative to Guzmán's constitutional process by advocating the creation of a representative constituent assembly that would draft a genuinely democratic constitution.[122]

For Guzmán, the presence of three defined ideological camps helped to outline his "minimal basic consensus," which, for him, represented a "compromise" between the "two antagonistic fronts against the constitution."[123] On the one hand, he attacked the hard-liners' fascist legacies, arguing that "corporatism" was perhaps valuable for "medieval monarchs" but signified dated totalitarianism "identical to Italian fascism."[124] On the other hand, he clarified that democracy is not an end in itself but should secure "liberty, security, and progress." Thus, he suggested that universal suffrage be limited to "legitimate options," along with a "vigorization" of the presidential authorities. Guzmán added two other fixings to this basic setup. A successful democratic transition, he wrote, depended on Chile cultivating a "new generation" that would embody the institutionalization's "inspiring principles." Likewise, he insisted that in the modern world, where problems are "increasingly technical, complex, and interdependent," administrations must rely on a "homogeneous vision," which can only be developed "within a Government."[125] As can readily be seen, Guzmán did not forsake his fantasies of a profound mentality change on the one hand and a society operated entirely by specialists beyond the reach of working-class "demagoguery" on the other hand.[126]

Smug as ever, Guzmán juxtaposed his so-called consensus with the Spanish one, igniting a strange confrontation between the countries. In August 1979, Suárez traveled to Quito, where he and other Latin American leaders signed a declaration supporting Latin America's democratization. Guzmán overreacted to this event by saying that Suárez's behavior was "interventionist" and "typical of the *nouveaux riches* of democracy."[127] A month later, when Cubillos arrived in Madrid – the first of Pinochet's officials to visit democratic Spain – tensions were thus high.[128] They obliged Cubillos to state that Guzmán "did not attack the Spanish PM."[129] Amid the aggravating dispute with Argentina over the Beagle Straits, Chile could not afford to lose Spain's support.[130] Suárez, somewhat apologetically, confirmed that Spain's transition can "neither be copied nor transferred."[131] Seeking to encapsulate Spain's conservative polity, he, too, had nothing to gain from clashing with Guzmán over the meaning of democracy.

In October 1978, the Ortúzar Commission submitted its first draft to be ratified by the State Council – the honorary body that included ex-President Jorge Alessandri and was supposed to enhance the text's legitimacy. Unfortunately for the Gremialistas, the council took the liberty to revise the draft profoundly, nullifying many of its authoritarian passages – most importantly, the armed forces' power of veto. As such, the text it submitted to the Junta in July 1980 was closer to the Constitution of 1925 than that devised by the Ortúzar Commission. In turn, Pinochet hastily assembled a new commission comprising of Guzmán, Fernández, Miguel Kast, and even Sergio de Castro, who retrieved the text closer to its authoritarian origin.[132] Years later, Alessandri would allege that Guzmán – who he believed had come under his influence – "betrayed him."[133] But Guzmán deceived nobody. Far from it: He remained loyal to his principles.

Meanwhile, on September 11, 1979, Pinochet announced the Siete Modernizaciones (Seven Modernizations) initiative – a second phase of reforms that Edwards regards as the moment when the "Chilean neoliberal model" was truly "born."[134] That is to say, Chile's fundamental "neoliberal" mannerisms – namely, the elimination of labor unions' power, the disastrous privatization of the national pension system, and the privatization of the education, healthcare, and public transport systems – were decided then. Therefore, when, on September 11, 1980, the Chileans were summoned once again to ratify their so-called democratic constitution in a second referendum, they voted for much more than merely a legal text but a de facto state model that was taking shape before their eyes. In this package deal, for a vague promise of a future parliamentary democracy, their essential public services were handed over to for-profit corporations, where they have remained until today.

Despite the opposition's call to vote "no," 67.04 percent of the voters ratified what became known as the Constitution of 1980. The rampant reports of fraud aside, there is no denying that most Chileans did, in fact, vote "yes." Why? To start with, in contrast to Spain in 1978 or Brazil in 1988, Chile in 1980 was a full-fledged dictatorship with strict censorship and a menacing secret police. Offered to a terrorized citizenry as the only path forward, the referendum was, therefore, a form of political blackmail. With hundreds of thousands of exiles categorically denied from participating in the process, it did not represent the entire Chilean nation to begin with.[135] For another, the referendum ran parallel to the birth of Chile's "economic miracle" narrative, i.e., after four consecutive years of GDP growth. For Chile's conservatives, the referendum was therefore a triumphant event and they rallied behind it faithfully, which resulted in above average turnout rates.[136]

But what did the Chileans actually endorse? In short: an array of mechanisms warranting an exclusive right-wing parliamentary life. For one, the text granted the armed forces a superior position over all branches of government through a National Security Council. For another, retired generals would also be among the nine nonelected senators for life (out of 35), which meant that left-wing presidential candidates would need to obtain a three-quarter electoral victory to theoretically pass legislation. That is, of course, if left-wing parties would be allowed to run for office. After all, the constitution's infamous Article 8 banned any ideology not pertaining to the regime's "concept of society." Additionally, it included clauses making it impossible for elected Presidents to touch on issues such as wealth redistribution, enshrined

Catholic education, banned divorce and abortion, and stipulated a two-thirds quorum seal for its future amendments. And as if this was not authoritarian enough, the text then underscored that "the state recognizes and protects the intermediate societies through which society is organized and guarantees them adequate autonomy to fulfill their specific purposes."[137] Rather than a dull residue from a bygone Hispanic technocratic era, this sentence should be read as an invitation for future presidents to restrict parliament's power even further by deeming most any social activity "autonomous" from politicians' intervention.

It is also crucial to remember that, despite the referendum, the constitution needed to be put into legislation and enforced. As historian Robert Barros has noted, that a living dictator would decide to become bound by a constitution of his own making was not a common sight in Cold War history.[138] This logic is correct only insofar as one believes that the constitution restricted Pinochet. In reality, Chile was led by a man who, unlike the Spanish monarch, was hardly keen to see his constitution materializing. Luckily, if Alessandri's State Council had any impact on the constitutional process, it was its insistence on a fixed schedule for its implementation. Originally a five-year period, Pinochet and Gremialistas extended it to sixteen years, with a referendum set in 1988 to authorize the regime's continuation. Even so, this timeframe defined no concrete transitional mechanisms. Worse yet, Pinochet began distancing himself from the constitution and its designers, believing, somewhat correctly, that the Gremialistas had attained too much political power.

There are several explanations for why Pinochet "shifted to the right" in 1981. One was his international prestige, or, better, lack of it. Much to his surprise, the referendum did not establish him as an acclaimed reformer, as his denied access to the Philippines in 1980 verified. Returning home to a fanatic wave of support, Pinochet sacked Cubillos in what soon became an extensive ministerial reshuffle.[139] Then, at the worst possible moment for the constitutional process, Chile spiraled into the second biggest recession in its history, dwarfed only by Pinochet's own 1975 recession. Overheated and relying heavily on debt, in 1982, the economy saw an 11 percent GDP contraction and unemployment level reaching 30 percent, proving how tenuous Pinochet's "miracle" really was. Only that unlike in 1975, this crisis spurred immediate public mobilization in "national protest days." Now it was the turn of Fernández and de Castro to be held responsible and sacked. Thus, by 1983, the regime was schizophrenically wavering between two opposing positions. On the one hand, Pinochet was appointing hard-liners like

Interior Minister Sergio Onofre Jarpa to steer the nation towards a more protectionist economic path. On the other hand, he attempted to alleviate public unrest through political liberalization. This resulted in the so-called "Jarpa spring", where political parties were allowed to operate openly, and exiles could return to the country.[140] In the midst of these extraordinary developments, the Gremialistas were entering the final phase of their history: the transition from being the quintessential "intermediary society" to being an ordinary conservative political party.

5.4 AFTERMATH: THE TECHNOCRATS BETWEEN DICTATORSHIP AND DEMOCRACY IN THE 1980S

By 1977, with Portugal, Spain, Brazil, Greece, and Chile thrusting towards democratization, a global democratic zeitgeist appeared to be taking shape. Argentina's Proceso de Reorganización Nacional was an exception to the rule that cannot be divorced from the authoritarian experiments that preceded it. Indeed, the dictatorship's leaders presented their regime as the antithesis of both Onganía's legalist authoritarianism and Perón's democratic terror.[141] To be sure, as in June 1966, there was hardly a crisis immense enough to justify a coup in March 1976. Even if Argentina underwent a mild economic crisis in 1975, it happened after enjoying an impressive 5 percent GDP hike in 1974. More importantly, throughout 1975, the armed forces successfully eradicated any guerilla pockets that had appeared in the Argentine countryside in 1974. So why the coup? To put it simply: because they could. Sensing Isabel Perón's dismal popularity, the armed forces seized the opportunity to achieve what the Azules had not dared to imagine. In other words, if Onganía envisioned a spiritual modernization from above, and the Peronists spoke of a plebeian "revolution" from below, General Jorge Rafael Videla, Argentina's de facto president between 1976 and 1981, portrayed the PRN as a regime of "gentlemen" whose mission was simply to purge the country of subversion in "all social fields" and, in turn, restore a "representative, republican, and federal" democracy.[142]

And purge they did. In its seven years of existence, the PRN came to notoriety for claiming the lives of more than fifteen thousand Argentine citizens in a calculated campaign of state-led terror. Given that the PRN's conception of its "subversive" enemy dovetailed with worldviews of men like Genta, as did its pledge to protect the "Christian conception of man," one may infer that this was a Nacionalista regime.[143] Unquestionably, the dictatorship treated the Nacionalistas with solemnity – for example, when authorizing *Cabildo* to return to the public sphere by decree after it had been closed by López Rega in 1975.[144] Still, this was not 1930 or 1943, and the PRN – with the infamous Finance Minister José Alfredo Martínez de Hoz at its helm – opted for a neoliberal reform, not a Nacionalista revolution. As such, it came under the Nacionalistas' rancorous criticism. Videla, stated Ricardo Curutchet, rather than instating a corporatist revolution, "replaced politicians with technocrats, producers with financiers and corporations with lobbyists."[145]

While the PRN's liaison with the Nacionalistas merits a book in and of itself, suffice it to say that Videla, while devoid of any ideological finesse, wanted nothing less than to be identified as a neofascist. His reaction to two Spanish visitors was paradigmatic, in this regard. In 1979, Piñar visited Buenos Aires, where he derided the "tragic" Spanish transition and joined Curutchet and Goyeneche in a spectacle of fascist salutes.[146] Videla avoided meeting with the Spanish neofascist delegation, but bent over backwards to enthrall another Spanish guest, King Juan Carlos, who arrived in Argentina in December 1978 to an extraordinarily royal reception.[147] While Videla sought to be identified as a democratic reformer like his guest, *Cabildo* insulted the democratic monarch by calling him a "strange man" whose "foolish vocation to Europeanize Spain" has destroyed the spiritual harmony inaugurated "by the 20th century's greatest Spaniard."[148] In Argentina too, Hispanidad had become by then the neofascists' exclusive patrimony. Videla could not care less. The PRN, he believed, was a regime of "gentlemen" – not Nacionalista revolutionaries.

Despite *Cabildo*'s harangues, the PRN was hardly "technocratic" either though, at least not in the civil sense of the word. Neither Onganía's men nor any other noteworthy civil group partook in the regime's planning. In fact, Amadeo, who seemed puzzled by Videla's "combat methods," complained to Sánchez Bella that the PNR did not seem to want to establish a wide-ranging civil movement. "Having failed to do so, Onganía had fallen," he remarked.[149] Sure enough, the PRN was a full-fledged military dictatorship and would remain so until its downfall in 1983.[150] Yet in the few instances that it employed civilians, they turned out to be Onganía's spiritual technocrats. This was the case of Education Minister Juan Rafael Llerena Amadeo, one-time Onganía's deputy Minister of Education. Replacing Juan José Catalán (also one of Onganía's officials and an MCC member) his appointment signified the renewal of the collaboration with García Hoz. One can say that the latter's theories of "personalized education" enjoyed a certain renaissance under the PRN, within this regime's own peculiar education reform.[151] Still, the PRN did not betray a technocratic modernization theory remotely as sophisticated or presumptuous as the Argentine Revolution. And that it reused Onganía's functionaries did not mean for a split second that it sought to resume his ideological project.

That is not to say that the Hispanic technocrats of the 1960s did not pursue this goal. Having come to terms with the PRN's militarization of society, they returned to their public platforms where they now justified the new order and suggested ways for it to retrieve power to society's intermediary bodies. Bernardo Neustadt's magazine *Extra*, for example, championed a "clean up" period after which a "distinct new democracy, with authority built-in," would arise. After all, "Videla is not Pinochet," he asserted.[152] Mariano Montemayor chose to work for Admiral Emilio Massera in his bid to replace Videla as supreme commander, upon the tabloid *Convicción*, where he peddled similar ideas.[153] Still, the regime's most prominent public supporter and narrator was Grondona's *Carta Política*, which demanded the PRN complete the unfinished "rationalization" of 1966.[154] It featured Costa Méndez stating that "the revolutionary vanity of the theorists" must be met with a "policy of concretions, of facts."[155] Revealingly, on this occasion, *Carta Política* reflected on the meanings of the Argentine Revolution. "Nobody has done more in this country than Onganía, and nobody has smeared more posters on the walls than Perón," Grondona said.[156] Like Amadeo, the lesson he learned from the Argentine Revolution was that the PRN must enact a "political" phase from the start and eradicate the "heritage of populism," all the while avoiding Nacionalista "corporatist theories."[157]

A more definite articulation of this model developed around 1979, as people such as Amadeo and Grondona began pinning their hopes on General Roberto Viola – Videla's partner and the man designated to replace him as de facto president. Advising Viola on matters of foreign affairs, Amadeo was convinced that the general had full control over the "hotheads" inside the military and, therefore, was "the most qualified" to carry out the regime's "logical institutional evolution."[158] Grondona's collaboration with Viola in 1978 was even more noteworthy. Together, they crafted a document titled "Political bases of the Armed Forces for the PRN" as a blueprint for Argentina's "politico-institutional normalization."[159] After reiterating the "prevalence of spirit over matter," the document proposed a "state with authority" that regulated the "relationship between individuals, the family, intermediate groups, and the state" based on the principles of "subsidiarity and totality."[160] More so than

Pinochet's constitution, this was a plan for an alternative non-parliamentary system of representation.

To promote the new civil phase to their liking, and in preparation for Viola's presidency, in 1980, Grondona launched a magazine named *A Fondo* where he, Costa Méndez, and Hispanistas such as Enrique Pelzer theorized the motion from Videla's "economic phase" to Viola's "political phase."[161] Tellingly, they did not suggest a return to parliamentary democracy. "Our Carter is Peronism, radicalism. Our Reagan is the military. As long as our Reagan is not a man or a party, we will live under the lure of instability," Grondona wrote, suggesting that a dictatorship would reign in Argentina until the masses independently elected a trusted neoliberal leader.[162] On the other hand, they shrewdly advocate a "municipalization" of Argentine politics as an alternative way of "communitarian participation."[163] By the same token, *A Fondo* featured Díaz Colodrero, who had recently given a series of notable lectures to the Escuela de Defensa Nacional. There, he postulated his all-too-familiar principles for Argentina's future:

a. A reform of the state according to the principle of subsidiarity, which demands that the state does not do what municipalities and provinces can do and that the public sector does not do what the private sector can do ...
b. Solidarity rather than the struggle between internal interests, so that each sector acquires a perspective by which the pursuit of its own good would be illusory if done in dissonance ...
c. The 'why' of it all: the transcendental moral values that Argentina has still managed to preserve. For example, family life.[164]

Speaking to active members of a murderous military regime, which "disappeared" thousands of its citizens extrajudicially, Onganía's Opus Dei technocrat promoted a society operating according to spiritual ideals untouched by the state apparatus. Some Opus Dei members were even blunter. In 1982, Roberto Bosca insisted that democracy had led Argentina "to anarchy" and that democracy is "impossible in modern mass society."[165]

Amadeo, for his part, was less convinced of this scheme, and instead promoted his faint vision for an authoritarian democracy. Under Viola, between 1981 and 1984, a political "apertura" would take place based on two premises: that Peronism would "categorically" not be included in the process,[166] and that the generals would not be "subject to judgments of responsibility for the emerging facts of subversion and the repression that was its consequence," he wrote to Sánchez Bella.[167] In other words, unlike Grondona and Díaz Colodrero, he maintained that restoring a parliamentary system was inevitable, although, to his mind, it was not to be identical to the Spanish transition but rather to the Chilean one. When faced with Sánchez Bella's caveats of a democratic transition akin to that of Spain, Amadeo assured him that "authentic Spain will once again impose itself on its internal and external enemies" but warned that this triumph cannot be "identified with a return to anachronistic forms and style."[168] Strikingly, it was these watered-down democratic slogans that led UNESCO to invite Amadeo to Oslo, where he represented his country at the aforementioned 1980 symposium alongside Ruiz-Jiménez, his bygone friend from early ICH days. Here, Amadeo implored the international community to treat the PRN with "generosity" so it could achieve an "authentic" consensus towards what was, in essence, an authoritarian and protected democracy of sorts.[169]

The Hispanic technocrats' gamble on Viola was abortive. In March 1981, he indeed replaced Videla as de facto president. Still, following an economic crisis and social unrest, he was quickly overthrown by General Leopoldo Galteiri, who had a different political project in mind: reclaiming the Malvinas Islands via military invasion. As his main civil collaborator, he chose none other than Costa Méndez. He, who demanded the Malvinas' liberation in 1969 with Franco at his side, was now to lead the PRN's international campaign against Great Britain as Foreign Minister. This, Costa Méndez did willfully, believing that his contacts in Washington could persuade President Ronald Reagan to side with Argentina. Although he could not deny that liberating the islands had been his calling for decades, in later years, he would nonetheless insist that he was a voice of reason in a regime of warmongers.[170]

When the war broke, *A Fondo* had little choice but to join the choir and propagate it as a moment when Argentina recovered "not only its territory but its spirit."[171] Grondona and Amadeo also published an almost illegible "open letter" in English, explaining why Argentina, a "nation of warriors," would undoubtedly defeat the "decaying and absent-minded UK."[172] As we know, this did not happen. Argentina suffered a humiliating defeat in what became known as the Falklands War. The mass protests that engulfed Argentina in its wake signified the dictatorship's loss of legitimacy and shattered any prospect for an "institutionalization" process. With neither a constitution in the making nor a defined state ideology as a base for such a process, the Junta merely granted itself an Amnesty Law before disintegrating entirely.[173]

Delusional as it was, *A Fondo* presented a fourteen-point "social pact" for a democratic transition, where it promoted "mechanisms of oppression" against subversion and pardoning of the "grievances that could remain from a past of which no one is entirely innocent." More bizarrely, it spoke of the "value pyramid," which positions "spirit above matter, man before structures" only to demand that "rationality and efficiency" be the basis for the state's operation.[174] This cryptic hotchpotch of slogans was what remained of Argentina's Hispanic technocracy.

In short, we can confidently say that Amadeo, Grondona, Díaz Colodrero, and Costa Méndez had a limited impact on the PRN's ideological identity. Having learned from the Argentine Revolution, this regime did not believe in "intermediary societies" operating society. Somewhat randomly, it deployed some of Onganía's men and, once again, held neofascist Nacionalistas away from executive power. Even so, the PRN never became what the Hispanic technocrats had wanted it to be. In essence, this regime showcased a military institution overreacting after its legalist and "nonviolent" authoritarian experiment had turned sour, thus replacing a "mentality change" with an all-out "dirty war." This unique character also determined the judicial process that came in its wake. In December 1983, elected president Raúl Alfonsín annulled the PRN's Amnesty Law. This marked the beginning of a unique transitional model, which included the establishment of a national Truth Commission and the subsequent public trials of top-ranking generals. The courtroom, was the theory, would serve as a spectacle to instill confidence in Argentina's democratic institutions. Notably, this process did not lead to the trial of the leaders of the Argentine Revolution or the members of the last Peronist government, despite their roles in the destruction of Argentina's democracy, their blatant corruption, and their human rights violations.[175] Nevertheless, none of these figures would continue to the democratic system in the late 1980s.

Other self-labeled Nacionalistas did, however, continue to operate in the Argentine public sphere unabated. Besides supporting the four military uprisings between 1987 and 1990 (the Carapintadas uprisings), they, too, established political parties and ran for parliament. Alberto Asseff's Partido Nacionalista Constitucional ran in the 1989 general election, gathering some 245 votes. More successful was Aldo Rico's Movimiento por la Dignidad y la Independencia (Modín). This party, which gained an impressive 9.2 percent of the votes in the 1994 Argentine Constitutional Assembly election, splintered ahead of the 1995 presidential elections. One of its remainders, the Frente para la Coincidencia

Patriótica, persuaded the eighty-one-year-old Juan Carlos Onganía to serve as its presidential candidate. Onganía ultimately resigned from the party's leadership just before the elections, though, which saw his party receiving a meager 3,147 votes. He died of a stroke three weeks later. Pitiful as this anecdote was, it was a poignant reminder of the Argentine Revolution's respectability in the memory of Argentine rightists – not to mention a testimony to the Argentine democracy's friability when allowing a former dictator to run for office.

In Spain, while certainly not trialed, the technocrats were nonetheless distanced from political influence, particularly from the drafting of the 1978 Constitution. The AP, which was supposed to be the political home of "the great right," was gradually taken over by Fraga, who ultimately became the party's representative to the Constitutional Commission. In 1979, he tersely removed López Rodó from his party.[176] Publishing in *ABC*, the Opus Dei technocrat would continue to attack the constitution from there. Fernández de la Mora, too, remained high and dry. To Fernández Larraín he complained that:

> Spain's situation is slowly getting worse ... there is hardly any way out of the path on which they have placed us. The so-called transition is carried out with rancor, and ... intellectual and moral mediocrity. My forced immobility has freed me from intervening, as the deputy that I am, in Congress ... The Constitution project is technically bad and politically contradictory and ambiguous. The communists have declared that they could perfectly well govern with it.[177]

Sánchez Bella, for his part, upheld a more amenable public image. Over the passing decade, Francoism had sought an "opening in the economic and political field," he professed. Rather than a "Chief Executive," Franco behaved as an "arbiter," maintaining only "a limited control to prevent the waters from overflowing," he further argued. And besides, life in Madrid is "no different than in Paris, Rome, London – neither in life quality nor in issues of morality," was his summary.[178] Still, backstage, Sánchez Bella wrote Amadeo that the new constitution would generate "unstable governments and unviable situations" and that the situation is "quite analogous to that of 1931–1934."[179] And to Arturo Fontaine, he wrote that Spain is undergoing a "doubtful period of transition that, with God's will, we will be able to overcome."[180] Luckily, Sánchez Bella retired from politics and hardly impacted the transition. This was also the case of Calvo Serer, who, despite having promoted democratization for years, remained aloof. Perhaps the only Opus Dei intellectual who positively influenced the transition was Antonio Fontán. This man, who had been a Francoist diehard in 1956 only to become the moderate editor of *Madrid*, had a significant role in endorsing the constitution as Head of the Senate. If there was ever an Opus Dei intellectual who could be credited as a true democrat, Fontán was him.

The Constitution of 1978 brought Francoism to its definitive end as an ideological system. Endorsed on December 27 that year, it sanctified unionization rights, granted autonomy to Catalonia, enshrined Spain as a welfare state, and was ambiguous enough on issues such as divorce and abortion rights, thus paving the way for their decriminalization. Still, even the constitution's landslide approval by referendum hardly influenced how the technocrats perceived it. López Rodó described the lifting of the Francoist ban on divorce as the result of a "Freudo-Marxist" theory of sexual liberation and a doing that deprives married couples of the freedom "to agree that their marriage will unite them until death separates them."[181] Fernández de la Mora went further than that by insisting that Franco's "organic democracy" was a superior democracy to that of the new "inorganic democracy." After all, in the former, congress members are "professionals, not simply politicians" and are not bound by "redundant taxes demanded by the partitocracy," he wrote in *ABC*.[182] Now, he also became the spokesman of neoliberalism. "As Friedman has shown in economics and Hayek in politics," it is imperative to protect Spain from "bureaucratic elephantiasis," he flagged.[183] Thus, paradoxically, Fernández de la Mora extolled Franco's Europeanization but rejected the notion that Spain could become a European welfare state. This model "applies to West Germany, but not to a country like Spain," he ranted.[184] Along the way, he also returned to Hispanidad. "The Spaniard is de-Hispanicized by anemia due to political prostration," while Latin America is "de-Hispanicized by vassalage to imperialism," he wrote in 1981 in what was, yet again, a faint relic of the 1950s pathos.[185]

Criticizing the democratic order in Spain became almost unthinkable following two major events, however. Amid a steep political crisis, on February 23, 1981, Spaniards watched aghast as a group of Guardia Civil men headed by Antonio Tejero Molina overtook the parliament building in a failed coup d'état attempt. In turn, Spain's 1982 general election saw a landslide victory of PSOE candidate Felipe González. With 48.1 percent of the votes, it was the most significant electoral victory in Spanish history. These events eliminated any ambiguity over what democracy meant. Not by coincidence, *ABC* ceased publishing Fernández de la Mora's columns then. He and other Opus Dei technocrats would brazenly criticize democracy elsewhere – in his journal *Razón Española*, for instance.[186] In 1986, Fernández de la Mora published his most anti-democratic diatribe to date. Titled *Los errores del cambio*, it argued that, since 1975, Spanish society had undergone downright moral decay, including the rise of drug use and the "trivialization of sex." More pointedly, it contended that democracy had brought Spain to a state of "infantilization."[187] This was the flip side of the same coin of the technocrats' paternalism, which had once demanded from the Spaniards to "be a child" and let the elites rule them. In the late 1980s, Fernández de la Mora wrote to López Rodó, criticizing Spain's "unfortunate partitocracy." He also asserted that his book offered the "best-argued defense" of the "Organic Law, of which you were the co-author." The architects of Franco's Hispanic technocracy believed in the superiority of their state model to their last day.[188]

Thus, by the mid 1980s, they had become pariahs. Of the institutions supporting their scholarship, even Opus Dei stopped publishing their new texts after 1977. The ICH barely had time to make similar changes. As a governmental body, it was renamed the Instituto de Cooperación Iberoamericana (ICI) and was redesigned to espouse economic cooperation with Latin America.[189] This deed sent shockwaves throughout the Hispanistas' network. Amadeo would have none of it, and would "continue calling it the Institute for Hispanic Culture," he told Sánchez Bella.[190] Like many others, he understood all too well that, by disowning Hispanidad, Suárez sought to disengage from Latin America's right-wing dictatorships and, in particular, from Pinochet. Spain's vote in favor of the 1978 "Protection of Human Rights in Chile" UN resolution further clarified this point. It led Fernández Larraín to resign from the ICH in ire and Sánchez Bella to write Fontaine that he felt "ashamed as a Spaniard."[191] Fontaine's response was instructive: "We are the true supporters of liberty, unlike Felipe González, the Mitterrands, or the American 'liberals,'" he wrote to Sánchez Bella.[192]

Adding insult to injury, by 1979, Spain had made democratization its new "universal mission," in the king's words.[193] In fact, the ICI was where Spain promoted its transition model to Latin America. In 1983, the institute coordinated extensive conferences in Spain, Chile, and Argentina, where Spain's deputy prime minister, Alfonso Guerra, declared that Spain "undertakes the task to propel the creation of an Ibero-American community of democratic nations."[194] These words went beyond irony; they were the conscious evocation of the Hispanic Community of Nations in the name of a new democratic crusade. If there was a political consensus in Spain now, it was that the Spanish transition should be the blueprint for Latin America. Or, as the prominent *ABC* columnist Manuel Blanco Tobío put it: When "getting off the tiger," Latin Americans have a "model of transition to look up to – the Spanish model."[195] In due course, the ICI conference at the University of Belgrano, Argentina, saw PSOE member José María Benegas stating that Franco was the dictatorship's "only source of power" and that, therefore, the opposition agreed to an "amnesty that would seal the past."[196] In the same spirit, in 1983, the Spanish Christian Democrat Fernando Álvarez de Miranda traveled to Chile, where he promoted the "magic word of 'consensus'" and advised his counterparts to accept any "sincere offer" from Pinochet as long as elections were called.[197]

Chile's democratic opposition took this advice to heart. Even before "Jarpa's spring," the opposition was already well in the process of reconfiguring its tactics. Why this happened had much to do with Frei's death in January 1982. Poisoned to death – probably by the dictatorship – he was replaced by Patricio Aylwin as head of the Christian Democratic Party. With this shift came the opposition's turn to pragmatism and acceptance of the 1980 Constitution as the basis for Chile's democratization process. Indeed, Aylwin and his partners in the "Democratic Alliance" initiative used the Spanish consensus as a central justification for this strategy. "This so-called 'pacted rupture' allowed a peaceful and continuous transition from Francoist authoritarianism to democracy. Why should not our country follow such an example?" was Aylwin's rhetorical question.[198]

The problem was that, under Pinochet's eagle eye, there was hardly any official with whom Aylwin could commence a dialogue reminiscent of the Spanish consensus. The Gremialistas, in particular, rejected any such interchange. Instead, in September 1983, Guzmán and Fernández announced the creation of Unión Demócrata Independiente (UDI). Comprising the Gremialista inner circle, it promoted itself as an ideologically consistent party loyal to the 1980 Constitution's precise wording.[199] Concretely, its mission was securing the regime's continuation until 1996 by jettisoning a democratic consensus with the moderate opposition by deeming it "not valid for a peaceful transition."[200] The UDI's rhetoric was indeed paradoxical. On the one hand, it supported the supremacy of the armed forces, or in Guzmán's words, "not to pit the citizenry against the armed forces."[201] On the other hand, as its name suggests, this was a self-proclaimed "independent" party that – like the "intermediary" society from which it sprouted – was loyal to scientific and spiritual truths rather than to Pinochet. Guzmán even promoted it as a "generational" party that had discovered a "new way of doing politics" and disregarded "any caudillismo or personalist ambition."[202] The UDI, he also clarified, was inclusive to all knowledge, given that it was merely "a doctrine regarding intermediary bodies and not a political ideology."[203]

Still, the UDI was entirely ideological and Hispanic technocratic to the core. Its success rested on its capacity to persuade the public – again, through its substantial publication apparatus – that the Gremialistas had been the architects of Chile's two "great transformations," namely its "modern socioeconomic organization" and "political institutionalization."[204] Once more, "mysticism" appeared as the party's celebrated ethical core and the basis of its ontological claim for infallibility. "There is an objective moral order," stated the party's declaration of principles, that, being the "foundation of Western and Christian civilization," should guide the "organization of society." This "spiritual meaning of life" is "contrary to all forms of doctrinal or practical materialism," they further totalized their state ideology, not before warning of "rigid or totalizing ideological modes." As such, the UDI rejected any "pact or alliance" with Marxism, socialism, or others who agreed to a dialogue with the two. Only thus could it continue to "de-mass" the Chilean populace and rescue it "from slogans and demagogy," its texts clarified.[205]

In 1984, one question remained: If the masses had been "de-massed" since 1973, why are they now demonstrating in the street in such fury? Grasping the magnitude of the Chileans' anti-neoliberal sentiments, the UDI members thus distanced themselves from the Chicago Boys. Now, their language sounded akin to that of a Scandinavian welfare state when assuring that the State should ensure "child nutrition, health, education, a healthy environment, and other areas of similar social importance."[206] Briefly put, the UDI sought to take credit for the regime's economic transformation, while blaming the Chicago Boys for the ills of neoliberalism. Perhaps the person representing this hypocrisy best was Joaquín Lavín. A Gremialista, ODEPLAN economist, and Opus Dei's most famous public figure to date, he was the author of the political myth regarding Chile's "silent revolution."[207] Besides highlighting the Chileans' consumption capabilities, his publications focused on the social engineering in the periphery, i.e., on how his "development poles" had liberated Chile from Santiago's grip.[208] On the other hand, any negative cultural trend associated with consumerism the UDI pinned on Marxism. "Marxism's new face" is synonymous with the "weakening of the family, the legalization of abortion, and the permissiveness towards pornography and drugs," their declarations of principles alleged.[209] The UDI was as paradoxical when outlining which civil liberties one could expect in their future democracy. It demanded not to infringe "personal liberties" while at the same time urging to "respect the natural hierarchies in the various spheres of national affairs."[210] As such, the party stipulated to limit the freedom of expression, to enact strict cultural censorship, and, of course, to control the Chileans' reproductive rights. That is to say, the UDI perceived "liberties" as something that pertains strictly to the economic sphere. Their pledge to "permit" women to "reconcile their activities in society with their other functions, especially those related to motherhood" was, in the 1980s, a patriarchal anachronism that did not sit well with notions of personal liberties in the West.[211]

As an ideological vanguard in its own eyes, the UDI refrained from a dialogue with the hard-liners, who now assembled under political parties named Avanzada Nacional (AN) and Movimiento de Acción Nacional (MAN).[212] This is not surprising also given that the hard-liners were in the midst of vocally criticizing the 1980 Constitution. In 1983, Rodríguez, Federico Willoughby, and Gastón Acuña published a manifesto named *Qué es el nacionalismo hoy?* railing against neoliberalism. "The purpose of September 11 was not importing televisions," Willoughby said. Concomitantly, they demanded replacing the 1980 Constitution with a political system where parliament would be merely one in several bodies operating under a nonelected "authoritarian democratic government."[213] And while Lavín spoke of "silent revolution," they mused over a return to national syndicalism. Or as one AN member asserted: "Here there will be no 'silent revolution'; our mission is to originate and realize a pending revolution."[214] By now, the hard-liners also had an unexpected supporter: Fernández de la Mora. Visiting Chile in September 1985, in a "series of workshops" which saw the attendance of Chile's "most prominent intellectuals and four ministers," he advocated Franco's "corporative" and "organic" democracy, reported the Spanish ambassador.[215] In lengthy interviews with the Chilean press, his aphorisms reached new levels of crudeness. "Ideologies are no longer useful," he said in *Ercilla*.[216] "I evaluate regimes by results and not dogmatisms," he told *La Segunda*.[217] Incredibly, he even suggested that Spain's transition "was not the exigency of the masses but the decision of Spain's political class."[218] This message was particularly well received by his hard-liner friend, Hübner Gallo, who restated his work as the singular analysis of the failures of democracy.[219] Fernández de la Mora's usage of the word "corporatism" (which had never been used in the 1960s) was not accidental but countered Guzmán's effort to dispose of it. In other words, he sought to reestablish the distinction between Franco's regime model and the Gremialistas' protected democracy.

As it happened, this was the last time Hispanic technocracy was espoused in public as a legitimate state model. It did little to change the course of the constitutional process, or the Gremialistas' minds, for that matter. In two confrontational op-eds, Guzmán showed what *he* had learned from the Spanish transition. First, he reminded the Spaniards that it was Francoism that "succeeded in modernizing Spain." While admitting that Franco did not wish for a democracy, he underscored that it *could not have been achieved without him.*[220] Extrapolating the meanings of Francoism to Pinochet's case was, indeed, the point of his essay. Franco's "mistake," he wrote, was not claiming democracy for himself, although he was "its father." Unlike in Spain – where King Juan Carlos had deconstructed a "corporatist state" in favor of democracy – in Chile, the armed forces had never aimed for corporatism but for a "rectifying" democracy, he also insisted. Thus, he urged Pinochet to own Chile's "efficient and stable" democracy.[221] By this time, Guzmán also demonstrated how this owning should be practiced. As a member of a new body named the Comisión de Estudio de las Leyes Orgánicas, he availed himself of Article 8 to disqualified left-wing parties such as Movimiento Democrático Popular.[222] Thus, unlike in Spain, where the socialists partook in the "consensus," and the communists operated legally along with it, in Chile, both were downright outlawed.

In time, the UDI's airtight rejection of "Marxism" became a problem for the center-right coalition as it stood at the heart of the UDI's disagreement with parties such as Onofre Jarpa's Frente Nacional del Trabajo (FNT) and Andrés Allamand's Movimiento de Unión Nacional (MUN). While loyal to Pinochet's regime, the two had a more pragmatic approach to consensus building and pursued a dialogue with the Christian Democracy. This disagreement became more acute in 1985 when Cardinal Juan Francisco Fresno gave his patronage to the Acuerdo Nacional para la Transición a la Plena Democracia initiative. Supported by almost all centrist elements in Chile, it was also backed by Allemand's MUN. The Gremialistas rejected the initiative, illustrating that, like Opus Dei, their spirituality ran counter to the will of the church hierarchy. Their intransigence weakened once Pinochet had appointed the Gremialista Hernán Büchi as Finance Minister in 1985. Hereafter, Chile witnessed a gradual economic recovery and the return of the "miracle" narrative, a process in which the three center-right parties ultimately managed to unify into a party named Renovación Nacional (RN). That its founding documents displayed a lingo identical to that of UDI – including an emphasis on "intermediate bodies" and "objective moral order" – was a testament to how Guzmán controlled this party's platform. Still, pretending to be a position that is neither "left" nor "right," the RN members could hardly agree on anything else, least of all on who should be the party's leader.[223] In essence, though, they could not decide on the meanings of Article 8 – that is, on who should be considered a "Marxist." In July 1987, when Sergio Fernández became Minister of the Interior again with the explicit mission of organizing the referendum and the regime's electoral campaign, the party disintegrated.

Pinochet, for his part, continuously sided with the hard-liners and, in July 1986, even cast doubt on whether the referendum would be held. A failed attack on his life that year did not make him any more democratic, naturally. Still, he reluctantly complied with his constitution's provisions to conduct a referendum in 1988. Surely, he did so assuming that his victory was secure. After all, he was to be "reelected" with no alternative candidate to overshadow him and the public sphere under his control. But to his surprise, the 1988 referendum proved to be different from that of 1980. This time, it was internationally monitored, with none other than Adolfo Suárez chairing the oversite commission. And while the democratic opposition united effectively under the Concertación de Partidos por el No, the conservatives were hopelessly fragmented and operated disjoined campaigns. This did not seem to bother Guzmán, who, in May 1988, upon resuscitating the UDI, published an arrogant text portraying Gremialismo as the regime's ideological cement. He spoke nostalgically of a movement that, born amid the struggle against Frei's "statism," had discovered the "principle of subsidiarity" – a magic component "unknown in our civic life." Along with "the women," Gremialismo thereby became the "main axis in the civil resistance that made possible the September 1973 liberation." What he had to say next about the dictatorship was even more revealing:

> With the rise of the military government, those of us who had formed Gremialismo became one of the most important sources of civil collaboration with the regime. Thus, emerged the mystique of a young generation that – symbolized in Chacarillas – delivered the best of itself to a government that made us participants in the deepest, most creative and fruitful transformation that Chile has experienced in this century.[224]

Evidently, Guzmán was promoting the UDI to the conservative polity, but even more so, to Pinochet himself in the honest belief that – once having won the referendum – he would return to relying on the Gremialistas as his most loyal intermediary society.

Unluckily for Guzmán, the referendum cut Pinochet's political career short. With the "No" campaign winning 55.9 percent of the votes, he stepped down from the presidency but remained the head of the armed forces.[225] On a deeper level, the referendum revealed that the Chileans had not changed their political mentality, despite years of terror, indoctrination, and neoliberal consumption. Indeed, the symbolic impact of the public's opinion being disclosed, along with the extensive international coverage it attracted, facilitated the rise of a political consensus between the DC and RN.[226] At long last, the moderate Chilean center was in dialogue, this time with an undertaking that had been unimaginable up until lately: amending the 1980 Constitution before the upcoming general election. In January 1989, a commission headed by Onofre Jarpa, Allamand, and Aylwin began its work, which resulted in reforms such as the definitive repeal of Article 8 and the increase in the number of elected senators. On July 30, in another referendum, 91.25 % of the voters ratified some fifty-four constitutional amendments – an approval rate higher than that of the September 1980 referendum. Patently, the Chilean public overwhelmingly rejected the constitutional order devised in 1980.

The Gremialistas were conspicuously absent from this reform process. While they shied away from delegitimizing it, they continued to incite anti-communist panic, even when, with the fall of the Berlin Wall, the Cold War was visibly drawing to a close. Ahead of the December 1989 general election, Guzmán accused the Concertación of hosting "Marxist and even Marxist–Leninist formulations."[227] He also belittled its rainbow symbol by arguing it "betrays its unconscious." After all, the "rainbow is an optical illusion that is perhaps beautiful but never lasts."[228] What this jibe revealed, in truth, was Guzmán's own political unconscious. For him, there was only one cosmologic and scientific "truth." A monochrome mindset, it perceived any other opinion of the state's function in modern society as illegitimate by definition. Aside from vowing to stymie further constitutional amendments – for that would cause "institutional instability"[229] – Guzmán adduced democratic Spain as a case in point of a society overwhelmed by social and moral crises. Whereas the international community praised the Spanish transition and even proposed it "as an example for Chile," he would not allow such "disturbance of criteria," he said.[230] These statements echoed Fernández de la Mora's talking points and were divorced from reality. Over the past decade, under González's government, Spain underwent an economic, social, and cultural revival that, in many ways, dwarfed the Francoist "miracle." A European Community member since 1986, Spain saw steady GDP growth coupled with a dramatic increase in public expenditure (from 21.88 percent in 1982 to 37.08 percent in 1992) and the elevation of most life quality indexes (Figures 5.1 and 5.2).

In April 1989, Guzmán retired from the UDI's presidency under the pretext that the party should not be "personalized" by his figure.[231] His departure was symptomatic of a leadership crisis that engulfed the Chilean conservative polity as a whole. With Pinochet's candidacy ruled out, there was no natural successor to fill the void left by his personalist cult. Hence, in July 1989, Büchi reluctantly stepped in as the conservatives' presidential candidate. Embodying the dictatorship's latest economic achievements, he was arguably the best candidate they had. Still, the entrance of independent candidate Francisco Javier Errázuriz into the race, and the constant bickering between the RN and the UDI, meant that the conservatives were, yet again, divided vis-à-vis an ever more confident center-left coalition.

On December 14, 1989, as Chileans exercised their democratic rights for the first time since 1970, Aylwin's decision to accept the 1980 Constitution was revealed as a stroke of astuteness. With a significant 55% of the popular vote, he emerged as Chile's powerful symbol of reconciliation. His exceptional popularity not only facilitated the establishment of the National Commission for Truth and Reconciliation Report but also instilled a sense of hope and unity in the nation. However, Aylwin's lack of majority in the Senate meant that further amendments to the constitution were a complex and challenging task. Worse yet, the Gremialistas stood in his way. Indeed, as a member of the Democracy and Progress electoral alliance, Guzmán was elected a Senate member.[232] From there, he continued to object to any constitutional reform with an increasingly demagogical tone. For instance, against a proposed tax reform, he said that "even Sweden … did not spend more than 5 percent of production in its Government's consumption at the end of the nineteenth century, when it enjoyed a GDP similar to our country today."[233] That is to say, like Fernández de la Mora, he claimed to have modernized Chile, but not enough to allow its citizens to enjoy a welfare state. As to why GDP rates should impact the *proportion* of a government's expenditure, Guzmán had no explanation. With 20.12 percent public expenditure in 1991, Chile lagged behind most all OECD members

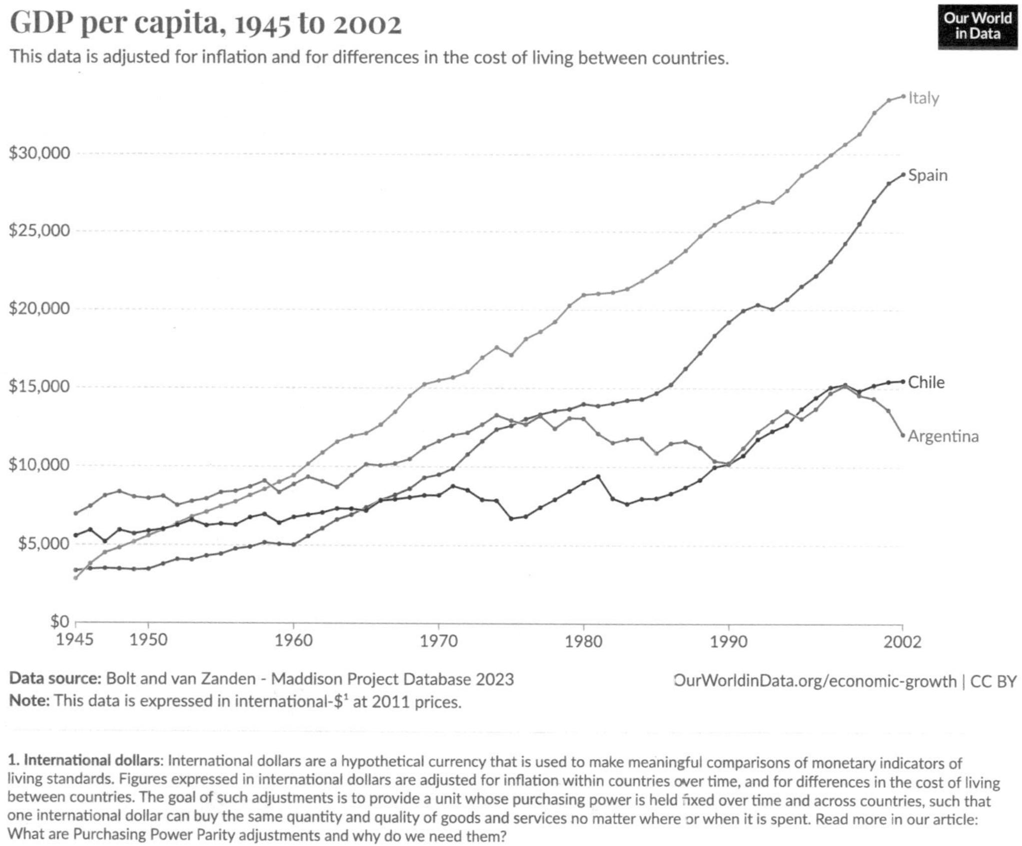

FIGURE 5.1 GDP per capita in Spain, Argentina, and Chile, 1945–2002.
Data source: Bolt and van Zanden, Maddison Project Database 2023. This data is expressed in international dollars at 2011 prices

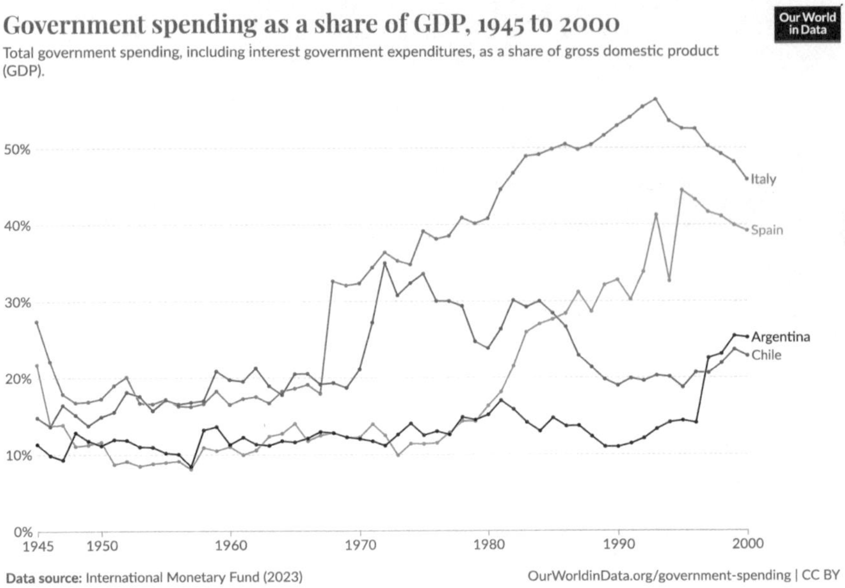

FIGURE 5.2 Government spending as a share of GDP in Spain, Argentina, Chile, and Italy, 1945–2000.
Data source: International Monetary Fund (2023); Bolt and van Zanden, Maddison Project Database 2023. This data is expressed in international dollars at 2011 prices

at the time, as well as recently authoritarian states such as Spain (33.34 percent), Portugal (49.43 percent), and Greece (50.74 percent).[234] For Guzmán, even this was too much. Even more amazingly, by still promoting the "subsidiarity" principle, he questioned the very political system within which he operated unabated.[235] Sinister of all was his opposition to the pardoning of Chileans accused of "terrorist acts" (Article 9) and to the abolishment of capital punishment.[236] "Death is not the destruction of human existence, but a transition to a higher and different form," he said.[237] In a society traumatized by a dictatorship that had slayed more than three thousand of its citizens without trial, these words were as insensible as they were nonsensical.

A few months later, it was Guzmán who transitioned to a higher and different form after being assassinated by members of the left-wing movement Frente Patriótico Manuel Rodríguez. This was a violent removal of the heart and soul of Chile's anti-democratic movement since 1967. Regardless of the illegitimate way of his passing – which had parallels with that of Carrero Blanco – there is no doubt that, with Guzmán as its leader, the UDI was a burden on Chile's democratization. His death spelled the end of Gremialismo as we knew it and, in a sense, of Hispanic technocracy, too. Although the UDI would remain a predominant right-wing party to this day, Guzmán's concepts of "intermediary societies" and "subsidiary state" died with him. By then, in Spain and Argentina, his counterparts had all but disappeared from the public eye. As the Soviet Union dissolved in 1991, their networks and ideology were a thing of the past.

There were significant differences between the Spanish, Argentine, and Chilean democratization processes, certainly regarding their mechanisms of institutional continuation and transitional justice. Even so, several similarities are worth highlighting. In all cases, the conservative political sphere saw a division between pragmatic reformists and neofascist camps. Positioned between them, the Hispanic technocrats sought to forestall the democratic process and sustain the state model they had worked so hard to establish. Unlike the neofascists, their reputation as modernizers allowed them to partake in the democratic system, though. Therefore, for all their notions of authoritarian democracy (Guzmán), ambiguity towards accepting the democratic order (Amadeo, López Rodó), or outright rejection of democracy (Fernández de la Mora, Bosca, Fernández Larraín), these men remained an integral feature of the conservative political panorama in the 1980s. By then, moral panic, rather than anti-communism, had become their main staple. The point not to be missed is that the Hispanic technocrats remained anti-democratic and culturally reactionary for years after their military patron died or retired. As such, people such as Guzmán, Díaz Colodrero, and Fernández de la Mora were as detrimental to their countries' nascent democratic culture as neofascists such as Blas Piñar, Ricardo Curutchet, and Pablo Rodríguez.

Epilogue

Towards a Theory of Hispanic Technocracy

When writing this book, I was reminded of a peculiar conversation I once had in Madrid. Arriving in town late one night, I was invited by a friend to stay at her parents' house on the city's outskirts. Her mother, an anti-Franco activist in the 1970s, had nothing positive to say about the dictatorship. That is until I asked her about Franco's economic miracle. "The miracle was real!" she said, to my surprise. "In the 1950s, my parents could barely buy themselves an automobile, while by the late 1960s, we university students drove to campus in our private cars," was her proof. I vividly remember my reply: My mother's life experience did not differ much from hers. Growing up in the 1950s in Denmark, she also saw her buying power rise significantly throughout the 1960s. Only, she did not perceive this as the trappings of success of an authoritarianism-induced miracle or that she was undergoing a change of psyche. Unfortunately, since then, I have had the "luxury" of listening to many people – in Argentina, Chile, and Brazil – reiterating their dictatorships' narratives of modernity. Thus, this book has been written with the present in mind. It follows the rise, apex, and decline of the Hispanic technocratic ideology, not only out of intellectual curiosity but to question narratives that are still prevalent among self-identified leftists and rightists alike.

To clarify what I mean, and by way of conclusion, let us recap three features: (1) how the Hispanic technocrats narrated their ideology; (2) what came to pass once they reached positions of power; and (3) which of the two people remember today. Historians normally refrain from producing social theories. Instead, we tend to historicize, underline contingent circumstances, expose the exception to any historical determinism and, as such, deconstruct "big theories." I am no different. The following "theory" of Hispanic technocracy is put into *emic* terms. In *their* words. In fact, let us imagine we could gather Sánchez Bella, Fernández de la Mora, López Rodó, Amadeo, Etchecopar, Díaz Colodrero, Vial Correa, Larraín Fernández, and Guzmán in one room in 1969. Indeed, many of them *had been* together in one room multiple times. How would they define their "doctrine" vis-à-vis the totalitarian fascist ideology to which they sought to pose an alternative? How would they "*represent themselves to themselves*," as anthropologist Clifford Geertz once wrote?[1] My suggestion is as follows. For one, they would concur that their doctrine and the fascist project of the 1930s belonged to one theoretical continuum and dovetailed in their requisite objectives: to generate a technically modernized society, purged of the Enlightenment's ideologies, hierarchical, fundamentally patriarchal, and, most important of all, living in a state of spiritual sublimity. All the same, they would claim that fascism had been perhaps a noble experiment but also emphasize that they are painfully cognizant of its destructive perspective. Within a constantly stabilizing Cold War world system, totalitarian nationalism should thus give place to a sophisticated anti-Enlightenment revolution, which would benefit from the Western Bloc's financial systems ("European in the means") while rejecting its ethical order ("Hispanic in the ends"), they would all concur.

As for the role of the state, those who had grown up admiring Mussolini or passionately reading the *Complete Works* of José Antonio Primo de Rivera, would approve of the necessity to shift from "statism" and "corporatism" to an intermediary-bodies-based "subsidiary state"; from political corporatism to an elusive form of societal corporatism. They would also have no qualms in admitting that it is up to the armed forces to eradicate the preexisting parliamentary order – violently, if needed. Still, they would argue that they had replaced the fascist cult of violence with a cult of "peace." In this telling, political violence was no longer an end in and of itself, spiritually or for imperial reasons. In fact, in this story, the nation had *voluntarily* and *collectively* chosen to substitute the "tyranny of the masses" with a realist regime that better served the common good. As such, the brutality of the armed forces was, for the men in the room, a moment of concrete physical salvation, an epistemic break from the era of Enlightenment and, strikingly, the instant when the nation's collective will had been revealed for all to see.

Unlike the fascists of the 1930s, for whom an unchosen leader intuitively channels the nation's will, the men in the room would generally refrain from reiterating the fascist *Führerprinzip*. To their mind, the armed forces and their leader were peacekeepers in principle and in practice. Thus, the men in the room served their dictator loyally and bolstered his cult of personality, all the while insisting that he functioned as an arbiter in a new "supra-constitutional" order and had relinquished power to "civil revolutionaries."[2] As previously mentioned, the notion of replacing an "inorganic democracy" with an "organic" one relied on a rich canon, ranging from Charles Maurras and Vázquez de Mella to Pope Pius XI. Conscious of the anti-fascist sentiments in the West, by the 1960s, the men in the room generally refrained from using the term corporatism, replacing it with technocratic jargon. Instead, they would insist that their regimes practice participation in governance via "novel concepts of the community." Perceiving parliamentary politics as a system that begets illusory demagoguery, they might not even blame "Marxism" for eroding democracy. It would be enough for them to say that parliamentarism brings about the "worst parts of society" to legitimize an alternative separation of powers between like-minded civil "bodies."

Once secured, it is up to this regime – they would concur – to embark on its true mission: modernizing a sub-peripheral nation through an economic "leap forward" and consumption-based "change of mentality." The ideologues in the room believed their societies represented the vanguard of the Christian-occidental civilization. Still, they were keenly aware that they belonged neither to the "first world" nor the "third world" but to the metropole's borderlines. Even Argentina, one of the world's five largest economies in 1900, saw a consensus arising in the 1950s by which a drastic modernizing phase was due for the country to reclaim its global position. The men in the room would repeatedly emphasize that parliamentary democracy is flagrantly unsuitable for this colossal undertaking. In this technocratic telling, amid the "vertigo" of technological "complexity," the nation could withstand neither futile discussions in parliament nor irrational party-driven politics. These must give place to a specialist-led "aerodynamic" administration.

At the crux of the "subsidiary state," the men in the room envisioned two teams of specialists. On the one hand, a unit of economists would design a stabilization plan that would integrate the national economy quickly into the Western financial domain. Relying on the knowledge, material support, and symbolic backing of the IMF and World Bank, the men in the room displayed a firm conviction in their reform's ability to spur an "economic liftoff." On the other hand, a second group of specialists would guarantee this process would not merely follow Western

Europe's precedent. Essentially *their team,* this was the regime's actual ideological dynamo. From crafting its fundamental texts and constitution to designing administrative reforms and the social engineering of the periphery to controlling the regime's indoctrination apparatus – people such as López Rodó, Díaz Colodrero, and Guzmán were more than complementary to the economic team. Rather, they both theorized and, in doing so, epitomized the intermediary societies directing society according to scientific and spiritual absolutes.

Enveloped in neoliberal terminologies or not, economic "stabilization" and "rationalization" eventually translated into similar policies in all three regimes. Its main objectives – namely, curbing inflation and minimizing public debt – could only be achieved by a steep currency devaluation, salary freeze, slashing of subsidized economic activity, and annulment of tariffs. The men in the room would agree that a docile workforce and low taxation were the rudiments of this process. In turn, with three years of consecutive GDP growth behind them, they would maintain that their countries are experiencing an "economic miracle" and that the working classes are losing their ideological inclinations. Almost to a man, they would agree on the veracity of the "twilight of ideologies" narrative and that "economic democratization" is more important than political agency. In effect, they would insist that their citizens *prefer the former over the latter.*

In the same breath, the men in the room would see eye to eye on that, unlike Western technocrats, their development strategy serves a transcendental "cause"; that they act on behalf of "*lo espiritual*," in Onganía's words. This ontology of the spirit was indeed the Archimedean point of both the fascist and post-fascist ethical and ideological edifice. Created by God and confirmed in the Evangelical Revelation and Scholasticism, the spiritual often appeared as a metaphysical matter that dwells in the body and should be protected and nurtured. How? For the fascists and neofascists, heroic violence and war were the main channels for this sublime revival. For the technocrats in the room, however, developing a new spiritual technique that encapsulated all aspects of life – starting with one's body and ending in political life – was the preferable route. Indeed, they would agree that, like in the 1930s, they too aspire to conceive a "new man" who would experience modernity in minimal alienation and maximal spiritual elation. Thus, paradoxically, the men in the room claimed to have "rationalized" the state apparatus while at the same time cultivating their citizens' "irrational" mysticism within a protected zone in the Western hemisphere. If pressed, they would admit that deep down they are Hispanistas, for they too sought to bridge between the twentieth and the eighteenth centuries, thereby terminating the "liberal age." While they perhaps used the term Hispanidad (or from 1970, also "Hispanismo") less often, they still used watchwords such as "physiognomy" to convey the same absolutes.

Some of the assembled men were Catholic priests or distinguished members of societies such as Opus Dei, MCC, and TFP. Others – Jaime Guzmán, for example – cultivated an almost solipsistic aura of mysticism. As such, they would agree that Western feminism, sexual conduct, and youth culture violate their hemispheric sovereignty. Yet, on this occasion, they would also underscore that their spiritual crusade is marked by positive behaviors such as altruism and willing obedience. In effect, they would insist that their state model is liberal – even "libertarian." As to the draconian laws and civil codes they enacted – which represented a stark intervention in their citizens' private lives – these would be justified as a calculated intermediation carried out by spiritual guides and "bridge keepers." In short, Hispanic technocracy was, in its own words, a society willingly administered by technicians of the economy and the spirit.

6.1 BETWEEN POLITICAL MYTH, HISTORICAL REALITY, AND COLLECTIVE MEMORY

The gap between how the men in the room narrated their national realities and what actually happened once their ideology was translated into a state ideology was extensive. Let us begin by highlighting that none of the regimes they served ever relied on public support, as they alleged. Even the supposed mobilizations that led to Onganía and Pinochet's power grab rested primarily on conservative media outlets touting the myth that the armed forces were answering the people's call. The "subsidiary state" was likewise political theater at its best. A corporatist chamber existed only in Spain but was not where "politics" took place in any way. Nor were the "family, guild, and municipality" ever given executive or legislative power. The so-called civil councils, which seemingly showcased a dictatorship heeding the expertise of civilians, were used randomly. Then who were the "intermediary societies"? The answer is obvious: *only* elite societies such as Opus Dei, the Ateneo de la República, and the Gremialistas. In a peculiar symbiotic arrangement, dictators allowed these groups to design, privately propagate, and realize their ideology. In return, they could control financial institutions, media outlets, and universities as they pleased. Why Franco, Onganía, and

Pinochet – generals of different ages and temperaments – granted them power stemmed from a combination of factors such as these groups' ability to master public opinion, their programmatic ideology, and their mystical allure. And, there was one more thing: Soft-spoken, with heavy glasses and stylish suits, these men could not be perceived internationally as "fascist." Once in power, some of them denied their political influence. Others used a mixture of elitist and technocratic reasonings to justify it. They were the nation's altruistic "directing minority" and the most skilled group of experts, they claimed. As such, they also believed in the finitude of their state model. After all, why return to the detriments of parliamentary democracy when one could perfect so efficient a model?

Ultimately, the "subsidiary state" relied not on the "tacit agreement of the population" but on state-led terror, police brutality, the exile of political opponents, and oppression of the public sphere. And even these measures could not prevent resistance from resurfacing. Rather than "peaceful," these regimes were constantly marred by student unrest, workers' strikes, and urban guerilla activities, which in turn, led to more oppression. The Hispanic technocrats never took responsibility for this dynamic – or, as Argentine historian Luis Alberto Romero aptly put it, for opening a "Pandora's box" of violence.[3] For even if Marxism and Peronism were crucial features of Argentina's urban guerillas, overall, they were merely one facet within an array of resistance tactics implemented by the vast majority of the nation's citizens as the last recourse against a regime they neither wished for nor believed in.

This popular resistance was also at odds with the technocrats' narratives of economic miracles. For though technocracy certainly delivered periods of GDP growth, this statistic alone was hardly synonymous with a sustained elevation in average life quality. To start with, in the Spanish case, the miracle merely compensated for previous decades of "absurd economic and social policies," in historian Antonio Cazorla Sánchez's words.[4] Moreover, such positive economic performances depended on foreign credit and on Westerners' willingness to funnel investments to these dictatorships while turning a blind eye towards their oppressive practices. As such, the Hispanic technocrats' "miracles" were likely to be bogged down by periods of recession. Worse yet, these GDP hikes benefited mainly the financial elites directing them.[5] Whereas the Western Europeans enjoyed the emergence of the democratic welfare state, their Spanish, Argentine, and Chilean counterparts withstood governments that invested proportionally far little in their welfare. Stripped of their rights to strike, vote, assemble, or express dissent, the workers nonetheless resisted, thereby elevating their life quality *against* the regime's design. The economic "miracles" also carried dire unintended consequences such as immigration and brain drain, which further damaged economic performance in the long run. And a tenuous rule of law meant they were prone to clientelism and corruption. The MATESA case and a slew of corruption cases in Argentina and Chile in the 1970s and 1980s – in which Pinochet and his wife were indeed embroiled – are indicative of this inclination. In short, with low public expenditure, social polarization, high public debt, and chronic corruption caused by a faulty separation of powers, even Spain was still an "underdeveloped society" in the 1980s, as Catalonian sociologist Vicenç Navarro has established.[6]

Similarly, the image of a post-ideological society whose members revel in leisure and are not interested in politics was a myth. Regardless of their consumption capacities, Spaniards, Argentines, and Chileans were increasingly politically active until after democratic transitions. If anything, the "twilight of ideologies" narrative showcased an exceptionally narrow reading of "ideologies" as childish abstractions rather than sober deliberations on wealth redistribution and the sustainment of middle classes in industrial societies. It also exhibited a spectacular unawareness of the Western European welfare state model. Above all, the Hispanic technocrats' post-ideological myth suffered from a lack of self-awareness. After all, what can be more ideological a statement than juxtaposing fictional "ideologies" with an undisputed "doctrine" concerning the state, society and, at the core of it all, the human spirit?

A more intricate question concerns the Hispanic technocrats' spiritual project and the extent to which it materialized as a cultural and social reality. As we saw, strict censorship, penal codes, and public indoctrination – mainly by state organs pretending to be "intermediary" – meant moralism was present in every aspect of Hispanic technocracy's public life. And the select few who participated in Opus Dei assemblies, the Chacarillas ceremonies, or MCC retreats no doubt experienced a spiritual awakening of one kind or another. Fascinating though this mental condition was, however, we must underline three simple facts about Hispanic technocracy's spirituality: In the first place, one must distinguish here between *indoctrination* and *mobilization*. Surely, the technocrats sought to indoctrinate the entire populace with a particular spiritual technique. But, unlike the 1930s fascists, they also used spirituality to demobilize one part of society while intensely activating another. Indeed, ultimately, spirituality was a credential that qualified some for governance while disqualifying others, thus making political agency exclusive to those who held its correct conception. In the second place, "the spiritual" had little to do with religiosity per se and functioned more as an empty signifier. Lest this sounds like the onset of a theological discussion, it is worth restating that irresectable of the Hispanic technocrats' fervor, they were not fundamentalists acting on behalf of a rigid dogma. If anything, they ignored the church hierarchy or, at a minimum, cherry-picked papal encyclicals that fitted their political doctrine. More often than not, like Hispanidad, "spirituality" translated into nothing more than tautologically pledging to defend the nation's "spiritual values." The usage of pseudoscience – for instance, when yoking psychological pathologies to ordinary cultural trends – spoke volumes of the inability to define what a "spiritual crisis" actually meant. In the third place, even if technocrats brooded over various cultural phenomena, their moral panic, coupled with the demand to halt democratization, was entirely utilitarian. On the whole, Hispanic technocracy was a form of "moral technocracy" – to borrow historian Benjamin Cowan's useful terminology – in that it showcased an effectively censored public sphere but a somewhat meager spiritual project of women's lifestyle magazines and television priests.[7] In other words, unlike Italian Fascism and Peronist post-fascism, which mobilized all classes into rituals of mass hysteria, Hispanic technocracy's spirituality, for all its sophistication and soft power techniques, was limited in its scope and modest in its impacts on the collective.

Thus, should Hispanic technocracy be considered a failed project? Judging by its creators' memoirs, the answer is affirmative. For most of them, democratization meant nothing less than their *magnum opus* being obliterated before their eyes. In hindsight, though, Hispanic technocracy was one of the most successful right-wing ideologies of the Cold War. Unlike Nazism and Italian Fascism, this ideology had not been challenged, let alone eradicated, following the democratic restoration.[8] The consensual transitional framework meant that the dismantling of the juridical and economic realities established in the 1960s and 1970s was virtually impossible. Chile's Constitution of 1980 is perhaps the most glaring example of this dynamic. As political scientist Camila Vergara has fittingly posed, even after being amended, this text is still marked by authoritarian legality and ultra-conservative morality.[9] Accusing the left-wing opposition of not undoing the dictatorship's "structures of power" is commonplace in the literature but also somewhat misplaced.[10] The longevity of the Hispanic technocratic ideology should be attributed to the fact that, while our protagonists retired to write their self-congratulatory memoirs, their disciples rehabilitated their ideology within new genres of democratic conservatism. How conservative parties such as the AP (later renamed Partido Popular), UDI, or the Argentine PRO regained political power relied on their considerable aptitude to control public memory. If Spain, Argentina, and Chile suffer from a structural right-wing bias, it is primarily due to their public spheres being dominated by the same media corporations that had supported authoritarianism for decades.[11] That Opus Dei has remained an influential ultra-conservative pressure group in global politics is no secret. And while Franco's legacy has mostly vanished from public life, people such as Álvaro d'Ors and Pérez-Embid are still venerated in Opus Dei's campuses.[12] Many news outlets quoted above – *ABC*, *El Mercurio*, and *La Nación*, for example – are still the most prominent conservative dailies in their countries. As noted, amazingly, some of them allowed anti-democratic opinions to adorn their pages years after their countries had concluded their democratization process.

The Spanish transition is nowadays considered an era of forgetfulness, but this is not be taken literally. In practice, Spain saw a decoding process in which the conservatives became a part of Spain's democratic history. At times, they joined Franco's list of victims; for the most part, they were credited for creating the conditions underlying Spain's democratization. Unfortunately, scholars have reiterated this narrative over the years. For example, in the 1980s, sociologist José Casanova argued that the Opus Dei technocrats had been "adequate carriers of the Spanish modernization process"[13] and, thus, "served indirectly to prepare the state administration for the role it was called to play in a democratic system."[14] Right-wing revisionists such as Luiz Pío Moa have outdone this narrative in the 1990s by claiming that the Spanish democracy "grew from within Francoism and not from anti-Francoism or the Second Republic."[15] Still, there is no evidence that authoritarianism served democratization in any way. The opposite might be true: Polarizing constitutional frameworks, economic crises, tenuous legality, and political enmity were just a few of the liabilities the Hispanic technocrats bequeathed to the democratic reformers of the 1980s.[16]

Alas, Pío Moa's provocative revisionism dwarfs in comparison with the rhetoric of new right-wing populists in Spain and Latin America. By now, full-fledged admiration of the 1970s' tyrants has become routine. For instance, Brazilian former President Jair Bolsonaro and his followers have repeatedly praised Pinochet for his alleged economic triumphs. Chilean presidential candidate José Antonio Kast – a UDI former member and Guzmán's disciple – has betrayed similar sentiments. His Republican

Party's "guiding principles" – which state that the party "believes in the Good and the Truth as objective realities" – could have easily been taken from one of Guzmán's manifestos. Perhaps the most gruesome example of far-right populism going fully authoritarian is Vox – a Spanish far-right party that is currently reclaiming Hispanidad with its neologism "Iberosfera."[17] It has also established a body named the Madrid Forum to coordinate Latin America's "ethical revolution" against the global liberal "cultural supremacy." Signed by Eduardo Bolsonaro and Kast, the forum's "Madrid Charter" states that Latin America has been "kidnapped by communist-inspired totalitarian regimes, supported by drug trafficking."[18] One of its Latin American collaborators, Argentine journalist María Zaldívar, considers Vox a "crusade" against "sustainability, environmentalism, sex education, LGBTQ movements, and illegal migration."[19] Another associate, the Mexican Raúl Tortolero, considers himself a soldier in a new "Battle of Lepanto" against the "anti-values of socialist globalism." Since he is "liberated from all ideology," he cannot "subscribe" to neoliberalism, he also insists.[20] In sum, just as fascism did not disappear in 1945, Hispanidad and its technocratic offshoots did not simply evaporate with the collapse of the Soviet Union.

Hispanic Technocracy ultimately offers three straightforward commentaries. Firstly, I contend that we should broaden our understanding of what "technocracy" means. The standard denotation of pro-market economic specialists does not suffice to explain the cosmology and fantasies guiding our protagonists. Rather than operating on behalf of wealthy oligarchies, these people represented a new understanding of the state's role in modern societies. Thus, whereas people such as political scientist Eduardo Dargent distinguish between proper "technocrats" in democratic regimes and economic experts "associated with authoritarian and semi-authoritarian regimes," I suggest examining the latter as a distinctive subcategory of technocracy.[21] Secondly, the book pledges us to reconsider the timing and meaning of the birth of neoliberalism. The dismantling of the welfare state in Great Britain and the USA in the 1980s – let alone the Washington Consensus of 1991 – was merely the fruition of processes whose laboratories were, in many cases, the Western sub-periphery. Thus, my book asks anybody who considers Chile's 1975 reforms as neoliberalism's starting gun to rethink how these reforms appeared in real time and how much of them was a novelty. Thirdly, and perhaps most important, the book invites a reappraisal of the meaning of anti-communism in Latin America. The right-wing Cold Warriors of the 1960s were nostalgic for European fascism and the Spanish Empire and, as such, out and out anti-American. Even if the fear of communism was ubiquitous among this book's subjects, so were anxieties over being subjugated to Western liberal ethics. The prevalence of post-fascist movements in Latin America – whether it was Peronism or Hispanidad – was therefore symptomatic of a unique cultural, economic, and geopolitical position vis-à-vis the Global North, to which the "Hispanics" wanted to belong but never entirely did. Indeed, Vox's "Iberosfera" fantasy touches a public nerve that still has the power to mobilize voters.

It is a strange time to write a history of authoritarianism. As a Danish citizen who has grown up on the legacies of the Scandinavian welfare state, I am prone to criticize any modernization project that assumes society should "take care of itself." As an Israeli citizen who has served as a combat soldier in the IDF, I am well acquainted with militarism and far-right political forces pledging to replace democracy with dictatorship. Still, my critique of authoritarianism stems not (only) from liberal ideals but primarily from a somewhat technocratic reasoning. Authoritarianism does not work, at least not in the ways its promoters allege it does. In their important book *How Dictatorships Work* Barbara Geddes, Joseph Wright, and Erica Frantz illustrate that dictatorships perhaps "work" (as in "function"), but also, by definition, struggle to survive and, devoid of legitimacy, "collapse."[22] To this, I add that, whether it is Franco's Spain, Pinochet's Chile, or Putin's Russia, authoritarian development always comes at a price. And the ideologies supporting it are patently self-contradictory, divorced from reality, and, for the most part, simply cruel. I would not mind being labeled a leftist historian – as I expect I will be – if this allegation would be accommodated with evidence regarding when in modern Latin American and South European history authoritarianism worked better than the democratic order that followed it, for the economy, modernization of manufacturing, average quality of life indexes, social solidarity, and the political culture at large.

As historian Eric Hobsbawm has famously said, "nations without a past are contradictions in terms," and we historians, like drug traffickers, "supply the essential raw material for the market."[23] Sadly, nowadays, historians must do more than this. In the bipartisan enmity that world politics has become, it is up to us to outline the boundaries for a public debate on the merits of democracy, compromising neither uncomfortable historical truths – for instance, on Latin America's idiosyncratic populism – nor the ability to communicate with conservative audiences, or those who are nostalgic of authoritarian hiatuses or disenchanted by democratic mass politics in the face of the immense challenges in store for humanity in the twenty-first century. Only thereby would we be capable to conclude that finite systems of knowledge do not bode well to innovation and social progress. Whether or not society would be better off directed by specialists is perhaps an important debate that needs to be held with the global warming crisis ahead. But this too can be done only after bearing in mind the historical lessons from more than half a century of neoliberal technocracy – namely, that everything is political – and indeed ideological – that the common good is an ever-fluid construct, and that no political project can succeed in the long run devoid of wide-ranging solidarity and a politics of care.

Notes

INTRODUCTION

1 "El crepúsculo de las ideologías: conferencia de Fernández de la Mora," *El Mercurio* (October 1, 1967): 47.

2 Juan José Linz, *Totalitarian and Authoritarian Regimes* (Boulder, CO: Lynne Rienner Publishers, 2000), 162.

3 Guillermo A. O'Donnell, *Bureaucratic Authoritarianism: Argentina, 1966–1973, in Comparative Perspective* (Berkeley: University of California Press, 1988), 186.

4 Ibid., 1. For more on this model, see Hector E. Schamis, "Reconceptualizing Latin American Authoritarianism in the 1970s: From Bureaucratic-Authoritarianism to Neoconservatism," *Comparative Politics* 23:2 (1991): 201–20.

5 Ernst Nolte, *Die Krise des liberalen Systems und die faschistischen Bewegungen* (Munich: Piper, 1968), 385. For more on the "fascist minimum" debate, see Stanley G. Payne, *Fascism: Comparison and Definition* (Madison: University of Wisconsin Press, 1983).

6 David Ohana, *The Fascist Temptation: Creating a Political Community of Experience* (New York: Routledge, 2021).

7 Zeev Sternhell, *The Birth of Fascist Ideology: From Cultural Rebellion to Political Revolution* (Princeton, NJ: Princeton University Press, 1995), 10.

8 He defines societal corporatism as "a limited number of singular, compulsory, non-competitive, hierarchically-ordered and functionally-differentiated categories, recognized or licensed by the state and granted a deliberate representational monopoly within their respective categories," in *Corporatism and Fascism: The Corporatist Wave in Europe* (New York: Routledge, 2017), 5.

9 Ibid.

10 Chiara Bottici, *A Philosophy of Political Myth* (New York: Cambridge University Press, 2007), 185.

11 Sebastian Edwards, *The Chile Project: The Story of the Chicago Boys and the Downfall of Neoliberalism* (Princeton, NJ: Princeton University Press, 2023).

12 O'Donnell, *Bureaucratic Authoritarianism*, 10–12.

13 On this process of global "harmonization," see Philipp Lepenies, *The Power of a Single Number: A Political History of GDP* (New York: Columbia University Press, 2016).

14 See for instance Jean Meynaud, *Technocracy* (London: Faber, 1968), 13.

15 Tanya Harmer, *Allende's Chile and the Inter-American Cold War* (Chapel Hill: University of North Carolina Press, 2011), 1.

16 This is the overall metanarrative presented in works such as Lesley Gill, *The School of the Americas: Military Training and Political Violence in the Americas* (Durham, NC: Duke University Press, 2004); Greg Grandin, *The Last Colonial Massacre: Latin America in the Cold War* (Chicago, IL: University of Chicago Press, 2011); Stephen G. Rabe, *The Killing Zone: The United States Wages Cold War in Latin America* (New York: Oxford University Press, 2012); Michael E. Latham, *The Right Kind of Revolution: Modernization, Development, and U.S. Foreign Policy from the Cold War to the Present* (Ithaca, NY: Cornell University Press, 2011).

17 Indeed, being neither pro-American nor pro-USSR was a common stance in the early Cold War; see for example Patrick Iber, *Neither Peace nor Freedom: The Cultural Cold War in Latin America* (Cambridge, MA: Harvard University Press, 2015; Vanni Pettinà, *Historia mínima de la Guerra Fría en América Latina* (Mexico City: El Colegio de México, 2018); Ernesto Bohoslavsky, *Historia mínima de las derechas Latinoamericanas* (Mexico City: El Colegio de Mexico, 2023).

18 On Franco's imperial aspirations in Latin America, see for example Lorenzo Delgado Gómez-Escalonilla, *Imperio de papel: acción cultural y política durante el primer Franquismo* (Madrid: CSIC, 1992); Rosa María Pardo Sanz, *Con Franco hacía el imperio!: la política exterior española en América Latina, 1939–1945* (Madrid: Universidad Nacional de Educación a Distancia, 1995).

19 On this "change of skin," see Tatjana Pavlovic, *The Mobile Nation: España Cambia de Piel (1954–1964)* (Chicago, IL: Intellect, 2011).

20 On how the conservatives resisted the new democratic order in the early twentieth century, see Sandra McGee Deutsch, *Las Derechas: The Extreme Right in Argentina, Brazil, and Chile, 1890–1939* (Stanford, CA: Stanford University Press, 1999).

21 For the latest analyses of this movement see Fernando Devoto, *Nacionalismo, Fascismo y Tradicionalismo en la Argentina moderna: una historia* (Buenos Aires: Siglo Veintiuno de Argentina, 2002); Federico Finchelstein, *The Ideological Origins of the Dirty War: Fascism, Populism, and Dictatorship in Twentieth Century Argentina* (New York: Oxford University Press, 2014); Alberto Spektorowski, *The Origins of Argentina's Revolution of the Right* (Notre Dame, IN: University of Notre Dame Press, 2003); David Rock, *Authoritarian Argentina: The Nationalist Movement, Its History, and Its Impact* (Berkeley: University of California Press, 1993); Daniel Lvovich, *El nacionalismo de derecha: desde sus orígenes a Tacuara* (Buenos Aires: Capital Intelectual, 2006).

22 Raymond Aron, *The Opium of the Intellectuals* (New York: W.W. Norton, 1962), 310–11.

23 Daniel Bell, *The End of Ideology: On the Exhaustion of Political Ideas in the Fifties* (Glencoe, IL: Free Press, 1960), 17.

24 Hannah Arendt, "On the Nature of Totalitarianism: An Essay in Understanding," in Hannah Arendt, *Essays in Understanding, 1930–1954* (New York: Harcourt, Brace & Co., 1994), 349.

25 Slavoj Žižek, *The Sublime Object of Ideology* (New York: Verso, 1989), 95; see also "Why do Empty Signifiers Matter to Politics?" in Ernesto Laclau, *Emancipation(s)* (New York: Verso, 1996), 36–47.

26 Max Horkheimer and Theodor W. Adorno, *The Dialectic of Enlightenment* (New York: Herder and Herder, 1972), 21.

27 Jeffrey Herf, *Reactionary Modernism: Technology, Culture, and Politics in Weimar and the Third Reich* (New York: Cambridge University Press, 1984); Corey Robin, *The Reactionary Mind: Conservatism from Edmund Burke to Sarah Palin* (New York: Oxford University Press, 2011).

28 This type of literature dates back to Seymour Martin Lipset's *Elites in Latin America* (New York: Oxford University Press, 1967). For more contemporary examples see Barry Cannon, *The Right in Latin America: Elite Power, Hegemony and the Struggle for the State* (New York: Routledge, 2016); Edgar González Ruiz, *Cruces y sombras: perfiles del conservadurismo en América Latina* (San José, Costa Rica: Asociación Colectiva por el Derecho a Decidir, 2006).

29 On the cultural revolution and secularization in the 1960s, see Jeremi Suri, *Power and Protest: Global Revolution and the Rise of Détente* (Cambridge, MA: Harvard University Press, 2003); Arthur Marwick, *The Sixties: Cultural Revolution in Britain, France, Italy, and the United States, 1958–1974* (New York: Oxford University Press, 1998).

30 Joseph S. Nye, *Soft Power: The Means to Success in World Politics* (New York: Public Affairs, 2004), 5.

31 Erving Goffman, *The Presentation of Self in Everyday Life* (New York: Doubleday, 1959).

CHAPTER 1

1 "El director del ICH al Ministro de Asuntos Exteriores," March 24, 1947, AGA, box 82/13946.

2 From Arturo Fontaine to Alfredo Sánchez Bella, January 17, 1947, AGUN, doc. 15/08/064.

3 Jaime Guzmán to Carmen Errazuriz, March 10, 1962, in Rosario Guzmán, *Mi hermano Jaime* (Santiago, Chile: Editorial VER, 1991), 79–80.

4 On this discourse, see Justin Crumbaugh, *Destination Dictatorship: The Spectacle of Spain's Tourist Boom and the Reinvention of Difference* (Albany: State University of New York Press, 2009), 76–86.

5 See for example Francisco Javier Conde, *Representación política y régimen español* (Madrid: Subsecretaría de Educación Popular, 1945).

6 The historiography of Francoism has, by now, filled entire bibliographic essays. My work builds on the following analyses: Stanley G. Payne,

Franco's Spain (New York: Crowell, 1967); Paul Preston, *The Politics of Revenge: Fascism and the Military in 20th-Century Spain* (London: Unwin Hyman, 1990); Xosé Manoel Núñez-Seixas, *La España de Franco* (Madrid: Información e Historia, 1996); Carme Molinero, *La anatomía del Franquismo: de la supervivencia a la agonía, 1945–1977* (Barcelona: Crítica, 2008); Javier Tusell, *Spain: From Dictatorship to Democracy, 1939 to the Present* (Malden, MA: John Wiley, 2011); Julio Gil Pecharromán, *Con permiso de la autoridad: la España de Franco (1939–1975)* (Madrid: Temas de Hoy, 2008).

7 Ismael Saz Campos, "Fascism, Fascistization, and Developmentalism in Franco's Dictatorship," *Social History* 29:3 (2004): 342–57.

8 Joan Maria Thomàs and John Bates, *José Antonio Primo de Rivera: The Reality and Myth of a Spanish Fascist Leader* (New York: Berghahn Books, 2019), 22.

9 On the Falange's beginnings, see Joan María Thomàs, *La Falange de Franco: fascismo y fascistización en el régimen Franquista, 1937–1945* (Barcelona: Plaza & Janés, 2001); Stanley G. Payne, *Fascism in Spain, 1923–1977* (Madison: University of Wisconsin Press, 1999); Ismael Saz Campos, *Fascismo y Franquismo* (Valencia: Universitat de València, 2004).

10 On the connection between these groups and Franco's ideology see Raúl Morodo, *Los orígenes ideológicos del Franquismo: Acción Española* (Madrid: Alianza Editorial, 1985); Pedro Carlos González Cuevas, *El pensamiento político de la derecha española en el siglo XX: de la crisis de la restauración al estado de partidos (1898–2000)* (Madrid: Tecnos, 2005).

11 For more on these projects see José Luis de Arrese, *Política de vivienda* (Madrid: Ministerio de vivienda, 1959).

12 On Franco's political theology, see William Viestenz, *By the Grace of God: Francoist Spain and the Sacred Roots of Political Imagination* (Toronto, ON: University of Toronto Press, 2014); Javier Tusell, *Franco y los católicos: la política interior española entre 1945 y 1957* (Madrid: Alianza, 1984).

13 Julián Casanova, *The Spanish Republic and Civil War* (New York: Cambridge University Press, 2010), 292.

14 The historiographical debate on the "Spanish holocaust" began in the early 2000s, and includes monographs such as Montse Armengou, *Las fosas del silencio: hay un holocausto español?* (Barcelona: Plaza & Janés, 2004); see also Paul Preston, *The Spanish Holocaust: Inquisition and Extermination in Twentieth-Century Spain* (London: HarperPress, 2012).

15 Federico Finchelstein, *Transatlantic Fascism: Ideology, Violence, and the Sacred in Argentina and Italy, 1919–1945* (Durham, NC: Duke University Press, 2010), 24.

16 José Antonio Primo de Rivera, "Guidelines of the Falange: The 26 Points," in *Selected Writings* (London: Cape, 1972), 132.

17 Ramiro de Maeztu, "La defensa de la Hispanidad," *Acción Española* 5 (February 16, 1932): 449–50; Ramiro de Maeztu, Defensa de la Hispanidad (Buenos Aires: Editorial Poblet, 1941), 158.

18 Víctor Pradera, "Los falsos dogmas: el pacto social," *Acción Española* 8 (April 1, 1932): 1.

19 Ramiro de Maeztu, *Defensa de la Hispanidad* (Buenos Aires: Editorial Poblet, 1941), 211. The discussions on whether Sephardic Jews could be members of Hispanidad captivated many Hispanistas; see for instance José María Lacalle, "La Hispanidad mediterránea," *Mundo Hispánico* 151 (October 1969): 32–3; Blanca de los Ríos, "Hispanidad," *ABC Sevilla* (October 23, 1953).
20 Manuel García Morente, *Idea de la Hispanidad* (Buenos Aires: Espasa-Calpe, 1939), 19.
21 Maeztu, *Defensa de la Hispanidad,* 72.
22 Morente, *Idea de la Hispanidad*, 54.
23 Carlos Lacalle, "Diez años en la política de la hispanidad," *Mundo Hispánico* 103 (September 1956): 3. For more on the meaning of Hispanidad see Ilan Stavans and Iván Jaksic, *What Is La Hispanidad?: A Conversation* (Austin: University of Texas Press, 2011).
24 On this process see Alberto Reig Tapia, *Ideología e historia: sobre la represión Franquista y la Guerra Civil* (Madrid: Akal, 1984); Julián Casanova (ed.), *Morir, matar, sobrevivir: la violencia en la dictadura de Franco* (Barcelona: Crítica, 2002.
25 For the regime's official version of these events, in English for international audiences, see Manuel Fraga, *How Spain is Governed* (Madrid: Diplomatic Information office, 1950), 45.
26 As historian Paul Preston put it, Franco was "casting off the burdens of Falangism while retaining the regime's essential authoritarianism"; see Preston, *The Politics of Revenge*, 115.
27 In the words of Alfredo Sánchez Bella, see "Informe reservado presentado por Alfredo Sánchez Bella tras su viaje por Hispanoamérica," AGUN, doc. 15/102/6; AGA, box 82/11114.
28 Francisco Franco, "España y el nuevo mundo," *Pensamiento político de Franco* (Madrid: Servicio Informativo Español, 1964).
29 On the regime's oficial diplomacy towards Latin America, see Lorenzo Delgado Gómez-Escalonilla, *Diplomacia franquista y política cultural hacia Iberoamérica, 1939–1953* (Madrid: Editorial CSIC, 1988).
30 According to Javier Tusell, the IEP's reputation of being a "breeding-ground of fascism" never "matched up to its reputation," in Tusell, *Spain: From Dictatorship to Democracy,* 38.
31 Operating between 1941 and 1945, the Consejo de la Hispanidad had but a limited effect in Latin America; see María A. Escudero, *El Instituto de Cultura Hispánica* (Madrid: Editorial MAPFRE, 1994), 41–106.
32 Antonio Cañellas Mas, *Alfredo Sánchez Bella: un embajador entre las Américas y Europa: Diplomacia y política informativa en la España de Franco* (Gijón, Asturias: Ediciones Trea, 2015), 79–80.
33 "Informe de actividades del director del instituto de cultura hispánica, Alfredo Sánchez Bella," August 10, 1949, AGA, box 82/10727.
34 Alfredo Sánchez Bella, *Misión de los institutos de cultura hispánica: finalidades, organización y orientación* (Madrid: Ediciones Instituto Caldense de Cultura Hispánica, 1959), 19. Apparently, Spain financed up to 25 percent of these initial costs; see "Informe reservado presentado por Alfredo Sánchez Bella."

35 Sánchez Bella, *Misión de los institutos de cultura hispánica*, 14.
36 "Informe reservado presentado por Alfredo Sánchez Bella."
37 Sánchez Bella, *Balance y perspectiva de una obra*, 26.
38 "Informe reservado presentado por Alfredo Sánchez Bella."
39 In 1947 and 1948, the ICH hosted the following intellectuals: Juan Carlos Goyeneche, Juan Ramón Sepich, Ignacio Anzoategui, Octavio Derisi, Héctor Sáenz Quesada, José María Rosa, César Pico, Salvador Dana Montaño, Carlos Obligado, and Gustavo Franceschi (Argentina), and Sergio Fernández Larraín, Javier Vergara Barros, Oscar Larson, Jaime Eyzaguirre, Roque Esteban Scarpa, and Anibal Carvajal (Chile); see *Instituto de Cultura Hispánica, resumen de actividades desarrolladas durante el curso de 1947–1948*, 10–12.
40 "El congreso Hispanoamericano de historia," *Cuadernos Hispanoamericnos* 13 (January–February 1950): 195–7.
41 "Resoluciones de congreso de cooperación intelectual," *Cuadernos Hispanoamericanos* 20 (March–April 1951): Appendix: ¿Adónde va Hispanoamérica?
42 "La Hispanidad no puede quedar limitada a un vago sentimentalismo, dijo el sr. Fernández Cuesta," *ABC Madrid* (May 15, 1951): 2.
43 José María Doussinague, *España tenía razón (1939–1945)* (Madrid: Espasa-Calpe, 1950), 9.
44 Blanca de los Ríos, "Hispanidad," *ABC Sevilla* (October 23, 1953): 3.
45 "Informe reservado presentado por Alfredo Sánchez Bella."
46 Alberto Martín-Artajo, *Hacia la Comunidad Hispánica de Naciones; discursos de Alberto Martín Artajo desde 1945 a 1955* (Madrid: Ediciones Cultura Hispánica, 1956), 111.
47 "España, nación americana," *Mundo Hispánico* 90 (September 1955): 5; "Hacía una comunidad económica iberoamericana," *Mundo Hispánico* 86 (May 1955): 9.
48 Martín-Artajo, *Hacia la Comunidad Hispánica de Naciones*, 34.
49 "Informe reservado presentado por Alfredo Sánchez Bella."
50 They sought to merge "Acción Francesa and Mussolini," argued the Nacionalista Ernesto Palacios; see "La cuarta frustración," *Primera Plana* 229 (May 16, 1967): 20.
51 Ibid.
52 Given that "federalism and democracy are simply incompatible," Julio Irazusta, *La Nueva República* (April 12, 1928): 1.
53 "Organicemos la contrarrevolución," in Julio Irazusta, *El pensamiento político nacionalista* (Buenos Aires: Editora Obligado, 1975), 11.
54 "Formación de los poderes de la república," *La Nueva República* (March 7, 1931): 3.
55 Federico Finchelstein, *The Ideological Origins of the Dirty War: Fascism, Populism, and Dictatorship in Twentieth Century Argentina* (New York: Oxford University Press, 2014), 123.
56 On this revisionist school, see Tulio Halperín Donghi, *El revisionismo histórico argentino como visión decadentista de la historia nacional* (Buenos Aires: Siglo Veintiuno, 2005); Amelia Galetti, *El revisionismo como historia oficial*, (Paraná: Dictum Ediciones, 2013).

57 The term was indeed coined in Argentina in 1925 by the Spanish-born priest Zacarías de Vizcarra. For more on this collaboration, see Pedro Carlos González Cuevas, *Maeztu: biografía de un nacionalista español* (Madrid: Marcial Pons Historia, 2003), 315–16; Spektorowski, *The Origins of Argentina's Revolution of the Right*, 116–17.

58 The Argentine government secretly collaborated with Franco's regime and maintained a commercial office in Burgos, a collaboration that continued into the 1940s; see Raanan Rein, *La salvación de una dictadura: Alianza Franco-Perón 1946-1955* (Madrid: Editorial CSIC, 1995).

59 Eugenio Montes, "De Granada a Rocroy," *Sol y Luna* 1 (1938): 63.

60 Juan Carlos Goyeneche, "Eugenio Montes," *Sol y Luna* 1 (1938): 57.

61 "Fides interprita," *Sol y Luna* 3 (1939): 9.

62 José María Pemán, *Seis conferencias pronunciadas en Hispano-América* (Madrid: Sucesores de Rivadeneyra, 1941). The Falange and Consejo de la Hispanidad both operated in Buenos Aires in this period; see Marisa González de Oleaga, *El doble juego de la Hispanidad: España y la Argentina durante la Segunda Guerra Mundial* (Madrid: Universidad Nacional de Educación a Distancia, 2001), 43–8.

63 According to the memory of Brigadier Gilberto Oliva, in "Nacionalistas: La cuarta frustración," 20.

64 "Nacionalistas: La cuarta frustración," 22. On the economic significance of the treaty, see "Significación económica del protocolo Franco-Perón," *Mundo Hispánico* 9 (October 1948): 59.

65 *ABC Madrid* (October 14, 1947).

66 Jesús Evaristo Casariego, "Misión Hispánica de la gran Argentina," *Mundo Hispánico* 9 (October 1949): 68; Martín Artajo, *Hacia la comunidad hispánica de naciones*, 29; *Argentina y España* (Buenos Aires: Ministerio de Asuntos Exteriores y Culto, 1948), 12. On Perón being named "the Paladín of Hispanidad," see Raanan Rein, "Hispanidad y oportunismo político: el caso peronista," *EIAL* 2:2 (1991): 51.

67 "Mensaje de despedida al pueblo español," *ABC Sevilla* (June 27, 1947): 8.

68 Rein, *The Franco-Perón Alliance*, 174.

69 "Texto de telegrama al Embajador en Buenos Aires para hacerlo llegar al Presidente," FNFF, doc. 9734.

70 In the words of Sánchez Sorondo, in "Nacionalistas: La cuarta frustración," 20.

71 Ibid., 20–2.

72 Carlos Ibarguren served as the vice president of the Honorary Commission at the 1949 History Congress; see *Revista de Historia de América* 27 (June 1949): 113. Juan Ramón Sepich's visit to Spain correlated with the production of his texts *Misión de los pueblos hispánicos* (Madrid: Seminario de Problemas Hispanoamericanos, 1949) and *La Hispanidad como problema y destino* (Cuyo: Universidad Nacional de Cuyo, 1948).

73 César Pico, "Hacía La Hispanidad," *Revista de Estudios Políticos* 17–18 (1944): 619.

74 Juan Carlos Goyeneche, "Hacía La Hispanidad (nota preliminar)," *Revista de Estudios Políticos* 17–18 (1944): 593.

75 During his visit Sánchez Bella stayed at Goyeneche's home "various times"; see Alfredo Sánchez Bella to Juan Carlos Goyeneche, May 2, 1946, AGUN, doc. 15/11/366.
76 From September 1948 (volumes 5–6) to January 1950 (volume 13); see also Alfredo Sánchez Bella to Juan Carlos Goyeneche, January 29, 1949, AGUN, doc. 15/11/377.
77 "Manifestaciones del ilustre hispanista argentino don César Pico," *La Vanguardia* (May 15, 1947): 5.
78 Pico, "Hacía La Hispanidad," 608.
79 José María de Estrada, "Reflecciones sobre hispanismo y lo nacional," *Cuadernos Hispanoamericanos* 45 (September 1953): Appendix: ¿Adónde va Hispanoamérica?
80 Máximo Etchecopar to Mario Amadeo," January 27, 1948, private collection of Horacio Sánchez de Loria Parodi; also available in Horacio Sánchez de Loria Parodi, *Máximo Etchecopar: un pensador tucumano olvidado* (Buenos Aires: Torre de Hércules, 2015), 284.
81 Máximo Etchecopar to Mario Amadeo," June 2, 1947, Sánchez de Loria Parodi, *Máximo Etchecopar*, 269; Máximo Etchecopar to Mario Amadeo," September 10, 1947, ibid., 275.
82 Máximo Etchecopar to Mario Amadeo," January 27, 1948, ibid., 284.
83 Mario Amadeo, *Por una conviviencia internacional: bases para una comunidad hispánica de naciones* (Madrid: Ediciones Cultura Hispánica, 1956), 218.
84 Juan Carlos Goyeneche, "Hispanoamérica y la unidad de cultura," *Cuadernos Hispanoamericanos* 21 (May–June 1951): Appendix: ¿Adónde va Hispanoamérica?
85 Mario Amadeo, "Bases para una política Hispanoamericana," *Cuadernos Hispanoamericanos* 20 (March–April 1951): Appendix: ¿Adónde va Hispanoamérica?
86 Amadeo, *Por una convivencia internacional*, 215.
87 Alfredo Sánchez Bella to Juan Carlos Goyeneche, October 2, 1953, AGUN, doc. 015/011/397.
88 According to Amadeo, the publication of his speech was prohibited in Argentina and was followed by an "anti-Spanish campaign"; see Mario Amadeo, *Ayer, hoy, mañana* (Buenos Aires: Ediciones Gure, 1956), 32.
89 Amadeo, *Por una convivencia internacional*, 219.
90 Carlo Scorza, "Nuestro Rumbo," *Dinámica Social* 13–14 (September–October 1951): 4–5.
91 "En el tercer año de vida," *Dinámica Social* 25 (September 1952): 1–2.
92 "La revolución," *Quincena* 4 (October 28, 1953): 1.
93 On this dynamic, see Sofía Correa, *Con las riendas del poder: la derecha chilena en el siglo XX* (Santiago, Chile: Editorial Sudamericana, 2005); Brian Loveman, *Struggle in the Countryside; Politics and Rural Labor in Chile, 1919–1973* (Bloomington: Indiana University Press, 1976).
94 See for instance Pedro Laín Entralgo, "Raíz y misión de Europa," *Estudios* 176 (September 1947): 5–12; Pedro Laín Entralgo, "Idea de Europa," *Estudios* 180 (January 1948): 16–23; Rodrigo Fernández Carvajal, "España como orden de amor," *Estudios* 171 (April 1947): 48–54.

95 "Complejo de inferioridad," *Estudios* 231 (July–August 1953): 3.
96 Julio Phillipi, "El orden politico," *Estudios* 206 (June 1950): 29–40.
97 Alejandro Silva Bascuñán, *Una experiencia social cristiana* (Santiago, Chile: Política y Espíritu, 1949), 70. For more on this influence, see José Díaz Nieva, *Chile, de la Falange Nacional a la Democracia Cristiana* (Santiago, Chile: Universidad Nacional de Educación a Distancia, 2000), 98.
98 "Los 24 puntos de la Falange Nacional," *Yungay: Periódico Falangista* 2 (August 15, 1939): 2.
99 *Padre Osvaldo Lira, en torno de su pensamiento: homenaje en sus 90 años* (Santiago, Chile: Zig-Zag, 1994), 27–8.
100 The title for his work "Hispanidad y mestizaje" was suggested to him by Sánchez Bella; see Elena Sánchez Correa and Sara López Escalona, *R.P Osvaldo Lira P. SS.CC y Clarence Finlayson, bibliografía de dos pensadores chilenos* (Santiago, Chile: Anales de la Facultad de Educación, 1985), 43.
101 Osvaldo Lira, *Hispanidad y mestizaje y otros ensayos* (Madrid: Ediciones Cultura Hispánica, 1952), 58.
102 Osvaldo Lira, "Visión de España," *Cuadernos Hispanoamericanos* 3 (May–June 1948): 439.
103 Jaime Eyzaguirre, "Hispanoamérica del dolor," *Revista de Estudios Políticos* 19 (1945): 219.
104 Eyzaguirre, *Hispanoamérica del dolor y otros estudios*, 18–19.
105 Bernardo Larraín, "En lo económico," *Dialogo conservador* 13 (November–December 1960): 50.
106 Jaime Eyzaguirre, *Fisonomía histórica de Chile* (Mexico City: Fondo de Cultura Económica, 1948); "Significado de la reaparición de Portada," *Portada* 46 (September 1975): 2–5.
107 Jaime Eyzaguirre to Pablo Antonio Cuadra, August 10, 1948, AGUN, doc. 15/106/22.
108 Ricardo Krebs was also the head of the Chilean ICH for several years and one of the designers of the 1958 Bogotá Declaration; see FNFF, doc. 9813.
109 In 1958, Souvirón was appointed the sub-director of *Cuadernos Hispanoamericanos* with Perdo Laín and Luis Rosales.
110 Jorge I. Hübner Gallo, *Los católicos en la política* (Santiago, Chile: Zig-Zag, 1959), 6.
111 "Sergio Fernández Larraín: Dios, patria y familia, versus comunismo," *Qué Pasa* 236 (October 30, 1975): 23.
112 Sergio Fernández Larraín, *El comunismo sigue en marcha* (Santiago, Chile: Del Pregon), 9.
113 "After some months in this country," Fernández wrote an "objective impression" of Franco's regime. This was a country of a "freedom of spoken expression" and the "front-line of anti-communist struggle," he stated; see Confidencial, 154/9 26 de marzo de 1960, AMCAE, Embajada en Madrid, oficios confidenciales, 1960, box 5655.
114 Jorge Iván Hübner Gallo, *El nuevo estado español* (Santiago, Chile: Editorial Universitaria, 1952), 11.
115 Arturo Fontaine to Alfredo Sánchez Bella, January 17, 1947, AGUN, doc. 15/08/064.

116 "Editorial," *Estanquero* 10 (March 27, 1947): 1.
117 "Editorial," *Estanquero* 2 (November 30, 1946): 1.
118 "Editorial," *Estanquero* 12 (April 5, 1947): 1.
119 Sánchez Bella, "Informe reservado," 60–1.
120 "Editorial," *Estanquero* 11 (March 29, 1947): 1.
121 Rafael de la Presa, "Informe del proyecto de doble nacionalidad, Sesión 38 ordinaria, 1 Agosto de 1955," *Discursos parlamentarios de exaltación hispánica: 1953–1965* (Santiago, Chile: Instituto Geográfico Militar, 1965).
122 Alfredo Sánchez Bella to Julio Philippi, December 1, 1958, AGUN ASB/024/108. On Alessandri's administration, see Germán Gamonal, *Jorge Alessandri: el hombre, el politico* (Santiago, Chile: Holanda Comunicaciones, 1987); Jody Pavilack, *Mining for the Nation: The Politics of Chile's Coal Communities from the Popular Front to the Cold War* (University Park: Penn State University Press, 2011).
123 "Jorge Alessandri presidente de Chile agradece de Franco el Gran Collar Isabel la Católica," October 14, 1960, FNFF, doc. 1200.
124 "Memorandum sobre Chile," FNFF, doc. 14870.
125 According to Spain's ambassador, his relationship with Chilean Foreign Minister Germán Vergara was particularly amicable; see "Nota confidencial no. 1," January 7, 1961, FNFF, doc. 6141.
126 *Instituto Chileno de Cultura Hispanica, Tercera memoria, Julio 1953–Julio 1955*, 5; *Libro de actas del patronato y asambleas del Instituto Chileno de Cultura Hispánica,* Acta del 22 julio 1948.
127 "Carta del embajador de España en Chile, Tomás Suñer, al ministro de asuntos exteriores, Don Fernando María Castiella," October 15, 1962, FNFF, doc. 10627.
128 "Memorandum sobre Chile."
129 On the Spanish–US treaties of the 1950s and their consequences, see Manuel Espadas Burgos, *Franquismo y política exterior* (Madrid: Rialp, 1988), 186–97; Ángel Viñas, *Los pactos secretos de Franco con Estados Unidos: bases, ayuda económica, recortes de soberanía* (Barcelona: Grijalbo, 1981); Stanley G. Payne, *El Primer franquismo, 1939–1959: los años de la autarquía de España* (Madrid: Temas de Hoy, 1997).
130 "Notas sobre el informe reservado del viaje a América del Señor director del ICH," 1954, AGUN, doc. 15/102/5.
131 *Itinerarios de cultura hispánica: memoria del segundo Congreso de Institutos de Cultura Hispánica, reunido en Bogotá del 6 al 11 de octubre de 1958* (Bogotá: Ximénez de Quesada, 1958), 34.
132 Mario Amadeo, "Hacia la comunidad hispánica de naciones," *El Diario de Nueva York* (February 27, 1959).
133 "Notas sobre el informe reservado del viaje a América del Señor director del ICH."
134 "Doble nacionalidad o supranacionalidad," *Mundo Hispánico* 141 (January 1960): 4. Following Chile, between 1956 and 1963, Spain signed another nine treaties with the following countries: Peru, Paraguay, Bolivia, Nicaragua, Guatemala, Ecuador, Costa Rica, Honduras, and the Dominican Republic.

135 Mario Amadeo, "La transformación de la vida internacional y la comunidad regional hispano-americana," in *Actas del primer congreso Hispano-luso-americano de derecho internacional* (Madrid: Cultura Hispánica, 1950), 57.
136 "OEI, Generalidades," AGA, box 82/13946.
137 "Política de la OEI," AGA, box 82/13946.
138 Carlos Lacalle, "El OEI y su cooperación en el campo educativo," *Plana: Servicio Informativo Aéreo de la OEI* 11 (May 15, 1956): 1. On the treaty with UNESCO, see *Plana: Servicio Informativo Aéreo de la OEI* 10 (April 30, 1956): 1.
139 "La familia y la educación," *Plana: Servicio Informativo Aéreo de la OEI* 58 (January 15, 1959): 4.
140 Juan Sepich, "Destino de la universidad," *Plana: Servicio Informativo Aéreo de la OEI* 3 (December 22, 1955): 5–7.
141 Carlos Lacalle, "La OEI y la cooperación iberoamericana," *Arriba* (October 12, 1958); also in *Plana: Servicio Informativo Aéreo de la OEI* 54 (October 15, 1958): 4.
142 These countries included Colombia, the Dominican Republic, Ecuador, El Salvador, Nicaragua, Paraguay, and Peru; see *OEI, Balance de actividades durante el quinquenio 1964–1968* (February 17, 1969).
143 Alfredo Sánchez Bella to Ramón Sedó, director general de Política Exterior, February 2, 1959, AGA, box 82/13975.

CHAPTER 2

1 This is Opus Dei's official narrative as it has appeared in countless books since the 1940s; see for example José Luis González Gullón, *Historia del Opus Dei* (Madrid: Rialp, 2021); Andrés Vázquez de Prada, *The Founder of Opus Dei, Volume I: The Early Years* (Strongsville, OH: Scepter Publishers, 2001).
2 "Secreto: febrero 1969, carta de nuestro embajador en la santa Sede, Antonio Garrigues: entrevista con Mons. Escrivá," FNFF, doc. 19244.
3 "El primero instituto secular de la iglesia," *ABC Madrid* (March 15, 1947): 3.
4 Some serve as actual priests, others work in their professions, allegedly giving their salaries to the casa; see Julián Herranz, "Sacerdotes del Opus Dei," *Nuestro Tiempo* 16 (October 1955) 3–11.
5 Leaving Opus Dei was perhaps difficult but not uncommon; see Alberto Moncada, *Historia oral del Opus Dei* (Barcelona: Plaza & Janés, 1987), 77.
6 "A crusade of virility and purity" (stanza no. 121), "Caudillos" (stanza nos. 32, 365, 411, 833, 913), the "love of war" (stanza nos. 308, 311), "militia" (stanza nos. 306, 496, 905), "the enemies of God" (stanza nos. 35, 49, 64, 141, 434, 482, 616, 694, 836).
7 "Nuevos caminos de santidad," *Nuestro tiempo* 65 (November 1959): 565.
8 For more examples of this tendency, see also stanza nos. 557, 626, 852–82. For more on Escrivá's discourse, see Antoni Malet, "José María Albareda (1902–1966) and the Formation of the Spanish Consejo Superior de Investigaciones Científicas," *Annals of Science* 66:3 (July 1, 2009): 307–32.

9 According to the testimony of Opus Dei member Miguel Fisac; see Moncada, *Historia oral del Opus Dei*, 92.
10 These banks included Banco Popular Español, Unión Industrial Bancaria, Banco Europeo de Negocios, Banco Atlántico, Banco de Andalucía, La Vasconia, and Banco de Salamanca; see Ynfante, *La prodigiosa aventura del Opus Dei*, 233; Moncada, *Historia oral del Opus Dei*, 42–3.
11 On the actual size of the "banking group Opus," see "Significación religiosa, económica, y política del Opus Dei," *Horizonte Español 1966, tomo I* (Paris: Ediciones Ruedo Ibérico, 1966) 232.
12 Ibáñez Martín was crucial in persuading Franco to trust Escrivá in the first place, see "1945? s/f Curriculum de D. José María Escrivá de Balaguer Albás, P. Silvestre Sancho y D. Alfonso Ródenaz García," FNFF, doc. 26823.
13 "1952, Julio 14: El Opus Dei por mediación del Procurador General D. Alvaro del Portillo," FNFF, doc. 10868.
14 The full constitutions can be found in Ynfante, *La prodigiosa aventura del Opus Dei*, 395–451.
15 *Estructura y normas del CSIC* (Madrid: CSIC, 1947).
16 José María Albareda, *Consideraciones sobre la investigación científica* (Madrid: CSIC, 1951), 21; here he paraphrased his Opus Dei colleague Ruimundo Pániker – see Raimundo Pániker, "Investigación: En torno a un discurso," *Revista de Filosofía* (1942): 390.
17 The CSIC directed funds from the education ministry to the university chairs, based on personal connections and loyalties; see Malet, "José María Albareda", 329–31; José Ibáñez Martín, "Franco y el Consejo Superior de Investigaciones Científicas," *Arbor* 191 (November 1961): 397–403.
18 Ridruejo and Laín Entralgo edited *Escorial*, a surprisingly liberal journal in which they rejected the validity of Franco's discourse of "crusade" and questioned Spain's anti-modern and anti-European purism; see "Historia de la Cruzada," *Escorial* 6 (April 1941): 159. For more on this group, see Jordi García, *La resistencia silenciosa: fascismo y cultura en España* (Barcelona: Anagrama, 2004).
19 Pedro Laín Entralgo, *España como problema* (Madrid: Seminario de Problemas Hispanoamericanos, 1948), 489.
20 Florentino Pérez-Embid, "Ante la nueva actualidad del 'problema de España,'" *Arbor* 45 (September 1, 1949): 150; also in Florentino Pérez-Embid, "Hacía una superación del patriotismo crítico," *Arriba* (May 24, 1949). For more on this polemic, see Carme Molinero and Pere Ysas, *La anatomía del Franquismo: de la supervivencia a la agonía, 1945–1977* (Barcelona: Crítica, 2008), 22–4; Díaz, *Pensamiento español en la era de Franco*, 50–60.
21 Calvo Serer, *España, sin problema* (Madrid: Rialp, 1949), 27.
22 Rafael Calvo Serer, *Teoría de la restauración* (Madrid: Rialp, 1956), 106.
23 Ibid., 18.
24 His text was titled "La politique intérieure dans l'Espagne de Franco"; on this event, see Díaz Hernández, *Rafael Calvo Serer y el grupo Arbor*, 529–35.
25 "Españolización en los fines y europeización en los medios," see Pérez-Embid, *Ambiciones españolas*, 12.

26 Florentino Pérez-Embid, *Nosotros, los cristianos* (Madrid: Ediciones Rialp, 1956), 48.
27 Ibid., 100–4.
28 In the words of Ángel López-Amo, see Ángel López-Amo, *La monarquía de la reforma social* (Madrid: Ediciones Rialp 1952), 297.
29 Álvaro d'Ors, *De la guerra y de la paz* (Madrid: Rialp, 1954).
30 These encounters appeared in Perez Embid's book series O *crece o muere*; see also Alfonso Candau, "Una vuelta por el Ateneo," *Arbor* 134 (February 1, 1957) 229; see also *Cinco años del Ateneo de Madrid* (Madrid: Ateneo, 1960).
31 Florentino Pérez-Embid, "Crónica cultural española: el Ateneo, tribuna abierta de la cultura española," *Arbor* 61 (January 1, 1951): 119.
32 Opus Dei published Schmitt's somewhat forgotten work on the Spanish traditionalist thinker Juan Donoso Cortés; see Carl Schmitt, *Interpretación europea de Donoso Cortes* (Madrid: Rialp, 1952). For an overview of the publication of Schmitt's work in post-war Europe, see Jan-Werner Müller, *A Dangerous Mind: Carl Schmitt in Post-War European Thought* (New Haven, CT: Yale University Press, 2003).
33 *El Estudio General de Navarra: eco de su constitución como universidad de la iglesia, en la prensa española* (Madrid: P.E., 1961).
34 Rialp was the name of the mountains through which Escrivá and his followers fled to France during the Civil War, see Florentino Pérez-Embid, "Biografía de Monseñor José María Escrivá de Balaguer," *Actualidad Española* 460 (October 27, 1960): 12.
35 Antonio Fontán, "Los Españoles y Europa," *Actualidad Española* 1 (January 12, 1952): 5.
36 "La importancia de la prensa," *Actualidad Española* 13 (April 4, 1952): 14.
37 Calvo Serer, *España sin problema*, 65.
38 Pérez-Embid, "Ante la nueva actualidad," 159.
39 "Anteproyecto sobre la acción intelectual y universitaria de España en América," AGUN, doc. 003/115/120.
40 Based on José Miguel Cejas's interview with Ismael Sánchez Bella, "Los comienzos del Opus Dei en Argentina." See https://opusdei.org/es-ar/article/historia/; see also Juan Claudio Sanahuja, *Los comienzos del Opus Dei en la Argentina* (Buenos Aires: Edita S.A., 1988).
41 Alfredo Sánchez Bella to Antero de Ussaía, March 3, 1950, AGA, box 82/10727.
42 Sánchez Bella, "Los comienzos del Opus Dei en Argentina."
43 María Olivia Mönckeberg, *El imperio del Opus Dei en Chile* (Santiago, Chile: Grupo Zeta, 2003), 144; See also "60 años de la llegada del Opus Dei a Chile," at https://opusdei.org/es-cl/article/60-anos-de-la-llegada-del-opus-dei-a-chile-2/.
44 Isabel Larraín, "Entrevista a Monseñor Adolfo Rodríguez, Obispo de Los Ángeles," *El Sur de Concepción* (May 17, 1992).
45 The journals published Opus Dei's propaganda openly and in a coordinated way; see Julián Herranz, "El Opus Dei," *Istmo* 15 (July–August 1961): 67–76; Julián Herranz, "El Opus Dei," *Arco* 16 (September–October 1961): 350–64.
46 José Miguel Ibáñez to Roque Esteban Scarpa, March 6, 1956, Biblioteca Nacional de Chile, Archivo Roque Esteban Scarpa.

47 Ernesto García Alesanco, written testimony, April 20, 2016.
48 Ernesto García Alesanco, "Reacción antimilitar en argentina," *Nuestro Tiempo* 64 (October 1959): 443; see also Ernesto García Alesanco, "El futuro de la Argentina," *Nuestro Tiempo* 71 (May 1960): 608–11.
49 Ernesto García Alesanco, written testimony, April 20, 2016. The two men were ordained to the priesthood at the Moncloa collage in 1960; see Biblioteca Nacional de Chile, Archivo Roque Esteban Scarpa, 1960 file.
50 For example, David Mejía Velilla, "El comunismo en Hispanoamerica," *Nuestro Tiempo* 69 (March 1960) appeared simultaneously in *Istmo* 8 (March–April 1960); José Orlandis, "La mentira política," *Arco* 8–9 (May–August 1960) appeared in *Istmo* 14 (May–June 1961).
51 José Orlandis, "El catolicismo en la España de hoy," *Istmo* 6 (November–December 1959): 61.
52 Álvaro d'Ors, "Autoridad y libertad," *Arco* 16 (September–October 1961): 333–7.
53 Álvaro d'Ors, "Libertad individual y social," *Istmo* 16 (September–October 1961): 19–24.
54 Following the negotiations in Estoril in 1955, Don Juan de Borbón decided to align with the regime, after many years of anti-Francoist rhetoric. Shortly thereafter, he sent his son Juan Carlos to be educated in Spain. For more on Opus Dei's involvement in this process, see José María Toquero, *Franco y Don Juan: la oposición monárquica al franquismo* (Barcelona: Plaza & Janés, 1989); Antonio Cañellas Mas, *Laureano López Rodó: Biografía política de un ministro de Franco (1920–1980)* (Madrid: Biblioteca Nueva, 2011).
55 People such as Laureano López Rodó said the book influenced them profoundly; see Laureano López Rodó, *Memorias I* (Barcelona: Plaza & Janés, 1990), 70.
56 Ángel López-Amo, *La Monarquía de la reforma social* (Madrid: Ediciones Rialp, 1952), 85.
57 Ibid., 96.
58 Ibid., 312.
59 "Cartas Académicas de Ángel López Amo, 1955–56," FNFF, doc. 26440.
60 Laureano López Rodó, *La administración publica y las transformaciones socioeconómicas: discurso de recepción en la Real Academia de Ciencias Morales y Políticas, pronunciado en la sesión de 29 de mayo de 1963*, 46.
61 Vicente Rodríguez Casado, *La política y los políticos en el reinado de Carlos III*, (Madrid: Rialp, 1962), 16; see also Florentino Pérez-Embid, *Libertad, tradición y monarquía* (Madrid: Ateneo, 1960), 44.
62 Florentino Pérez-Embid, *En la brecha* (Madrid: Rialp, 1956), 169–72.
63 Andrés Vázquez de Prada, "Amistad y política," *Nuestro Tiempo* 7 (January 1955): 6–7.
64 Andrés Vázquez de Prada, "Don Quijote caballero político," *Nuestro Tiempo* 15 (September 1955): 4–5.
65 López-Amo, *La Monarquía de la reforma social*, 104.
66 Andrés Vázquez de Prada, "Amistad y política, II," *Nuestro Tiempo* 8 (February 1955): 10.

67 Pérez-Embid served as General Director of Information (1952–57), the highest rank an Opus Dei intellectual had reached up until then.
68 On the 1956 events, see José Álvarez Cobelas, *Envenenados de cuerpo y alma: la oposición universitaria al Franquismo en Madrid (1939–1970)* (Madrid: Siglo XXI, 2004); Miguel Ángel Ruiz Carnicer, *El Sindicato Español Universitario (SEU), 1939–1965: La socialización política de la juventud universitaria en el Franquismo* (Mexico City: Siglo Veintiuno Editores, 1996).
69 For more on this Falangist project, see Álvaro de Diego, *José Luis Arrese o la Falange de Franco* (Madrid: Actas Editorial, 2001).
70 Luis Carrero Blanco, "Consideraciones sobre el momento actual en España," September 1945, AGUN, box 49/1/31; see also Javier Tusell, *Carrero: la eminencia gris del régimen de Franco* (Madrid: Ediciones Temas de Hoy, 1993).
71 Luis Carrero Blanco, *Lepanto* (Estella: Salvat Editores, 1971); see also Luis Carrero Blanco, *Discursos y escritos (1943–1973)* (Madrid: Estudios Políticos, 1974), 387–484.
72 López Rodó was a fellow at the University of Coimbra, where he became acquainted with Marcelo Caetano of the Law Department in Lisbon, who would later become the last prime minister of the Portuguese dictatorship; see Cañellas Mas, *Laureano López Rodó*, 77.
73 López Rodó, *Memorias I,* 66.
74 "Organizacion del poder central 1957," AGUN doc. 003.116.0023.
75 Ibid.
76 López Rodó, *Memorias I*, 89.
77 "Ley de Régimen Jurídico de la Administración," *BOE (España)* 187 (July 22, 1957): 603–7.
78 "Ley de Principios del Movimiento Nacional," *BOE (España)* 119 (May 19, 1958): 4511–12.
79 López Rodó, *Memorias I,* 145.
80 Officially named "Decreto-Ley 10/1959, de 21 de julio, de ordenación económica," *BOE (España)* 174 (July 22, 1959): 10005–7.
81 Daniel C. Hardy, "Stabilizing an Economy: SPAIN," *Finance & Development* 5:1 (March 1, 1968). www.elibrary.imf.org/view/journals/022/0005/001/article-A006-en.xml
82 Of which the IMF financed $75,000,000, the US government $250,000,000, and US private banks $65,000,000; see López Rodó, *Memorias I*, 188.
83 Bernardo Neustadt, "Mi conversación mayor," *Extra* 76 (November 1971).
84 Benjamin Welles, "Franco's posts go to church group," *The New York Times* (March 7, 1957).
85 "1958 mayo 23. Carta de José María Escrivá de Balaguer felicitando a Franco por los Principios de Movimiento Nacional," FNFF, doc. 957.
86 Julián Herranz, "El Opus Dei y la política," *Nuestro Tiempo* 34 (April 1957): 389–91; see also Julián Herranz, "El Opus Dei," *Arco* 16 (September–October 1961): 350–64; Julián Herranz, "El Opus Dei," *Istmo* 15 (July–August 1961): 67–76; Julián Herranz, "Naturaleza del Opus Dei y actividades temporales de sus miembros," *Arco* 25 (September 1962): 522–3.

87 "Carta de Florentino Pérez-Embid a Benjamin Welles, protesta por las inexactitudes sobre él y sobre el Opus Dei que contiene su artículo de *The New York Times* del 04–01–1960," AGUN 3/10/(Enero).

88 "¿Que es el Opus Dei?" *Actualidad Española* 487 (May 4, 1961): 39–40; "¿Que es el Opus Dei?" *Vida Mundial* 13 (April 29, 1961). Strikingly, not all Opus Dei members were pleased with this modest portrayal of their society; see Antonio Garrigues to Florentino Pérez-Embid, June 14, 1961 AGUN 03/11/(June).

89 Josemaría Escrivá de Balaguer, *Conversations with Monsignor Escrivá de Balaguer* (Shannon: Ecclesia, 1972), 23; Perdo Rodríguez, "Entrevista con Mons. Escrivá de Balaguer," *Palabra* 26 (October 1967): 20–30.

90 Escrivá de Balaguer, *Conversations with Monsignor Escrivá de Balaguer*, 48.

91 "Madrid, 17 de Marzo de I960, Nota informativa," FNFF, doc. 3661.

92 Juan Triguero, "La generación de Fraga y su destino," *Cuadernos Ruedo Ibérico* 1 (January 5, 1965): 5.

93 Rodney H. Mills, "The Spanish 'Miracle': Growth and Change in the Spanish Economy, 1959 to mid-1965," *Review of Foreign Developments* 563 (November 1965), Board of Governors of the Federal Reserve System (U.S.): 18, at www.federalreserve.gov/pubs/rfd/1965/563/rfd563.pdf; see also "La lógica económica de la política emigratoria del régimen franquista," in Joseba de la Torre and Gloria Sanz Lafuente (eds.), *Migraciones y coyuntura económica del franquismo a la democracia* (Zaragoza: Universitarias de Zaragoza, 2008), 221–35.

94 "Hipócriticas," *ABC Madrid* (January 19, 1962): 3.

95 As confirmed by the Chilean ambassador and Piñar's friend Sergio Fernández Larraín; see Confidencial 55/7, January 29, 1962, AMCAE, Embajada en Madrid, oficios confidenciales, 1962, box 6.

96 This initiative was led by Joaquín Ruiz-Giménez, Joaquín Satrústegui, and José María Gil Robles; see Julio Crespo McLennan, *Spain and the Process of European Integration, 1957–85* (New York: Palgrave, 2000), 65–9.

97 In the words of linguist Justine Crumbaugh; see Justin Crumbaugh, *Destination Dictatorship: The Spectacle of Spain's Tourist Boom and the Reinvention of Difference* (Albany: State University of New York Press, 2009).

98 *The Economic Development of Spain: Report of a Mission organised by the International Bank for Reconstruction and Development at the request of the Government of Spain* (London: Oxford University Press, 1963).

99 Laureano López Rodó, "Discurso ante el Pleno de las Cortes Espanolas en defensa del proyecto de Ley que aprueba el I Plan de Desarrollo Econömico y Social. 27 de diciembre de 1963," in Laureano López Rodó, *Política y desarrollo* (Madrid: Aguilar, 1970), 215–28.

100 On the Spanish "growth poles" and whether they lived up to expectations, see Pablo Corral Broto, "Sobreviviendo al desarrollismo. Las desigualdades ambientales y la protesta social durante el franquismo (Aragón, 1950–1979)," *Ager: Revista de Estudios sobre Despoblación y Desarrollo Rural* 10 (April 2011): 111–55; María Ángeles Sánchez Domínguez, "Los polos de crecimiento en Andalucía: una visión crítica del polo de Huelva," in

Joseba de la Torre and Mario García-Zúñiga (eds.), *Entre el mercado y el estado: los planes de desarrollo durante el franquismo* (Pamplona: Universidad Pública de Navarra, 2009), 321–46.

101 "Ahorrar y exportar: premisas fundamentales del Plan de Desarrollo," *ABC Madrid* (June 12, 1963): 47; José Casanova, "The Opus Dei Ethic and the Modernization of Spain," *Social Science* 22:27 (1983): 27–50.

102 Waldo de Mier, *España cambia de piel: (Nuevo viaje por la "España del Milagro")* (Madrid: Editora Nacional, 1964), 163.

103 For more on the "change of skin" discourse, see Tatjana Pavlovic, *The Mobile Nation: España Cambia de Piel (1954–1964)* (Chicago, IL: Intellect, 2011); for more on the 25 years of peace campaign, see Carolyn P. Boyd, *Historia Patria: Politics, History, and National Identity in Spain, 1875–1975* (Princeton, NJ: Princeton University Press, 1997), 273–301.

104 See for example *Discurso del ministro y comisario del Plan de Desarrollo en defensa de la Ley que aprueba el II Plan de Desarrollo Económico y Social* (February 7, 1969).

105 López Rodó, *Política y desarrollo,* 53; his reference was Walt Whitman Rostow, *The Stages of Economic Growth: A Non-Communist Manifesto* (Cambridge: Cambridge University Press, 1961).

106 Laureano López Rodó, "Brindis en el almuerzo ofrecido por el señor Ministro de Asuntos Exteriores y Culto," August 22, 1966, AGUN, 005/424/174.

107 López Rodó, "La reforma administrativa del Estado," *Política y desarrollo,* 123–6.

108 Gonzalo Fernández de la Mora, *El crepúsculo de las ideologías* (Madrid: Rialp, 1965), 10, 34–41.

109 Ibid., 117, 54.

110 Gonzalo Fernández de la Mora, "De la libertad a la seguridad," *Nuestro Tiempo* 75–76 (September–October 1960): 354–61.

111 Gonzalo Fernández de la Mora, "La tecnocracia," *ABC Madrid* (July 21, 1965): 3.

112 López Rodó, *Política y desarrollo*, 262.

113 López Rodó, *Memorias II*, 392–3.

114 López Rodó, *Política y desarrollo*, 74.

115 "Entrevista recogida en el libro 'Conversaciones en Madrid,'" in *Política y desarrollo*, 396.

116 "La destrucción de las corporaciones: Discurso en el Congreso, el 27 de febrero de 1908," in Vázquez de Mella, *Textos de doctrina política* (Madrid: 1953), 69.

117 Luis Sánchez Agesta, *Los principios cristianos del orden político* (Madrid: Instituto de Estudios Políticos, 1962), 89–101.

118 Alvaro d'Ors, "Autoridad y potestad," *Portada* 44 (February 1974): 44.

119 Luis Sánchez Agesta, *Principio de teoría política* (Madrid: Editorial Nacional, 1966), 499–503.

120 Some historians have already identified Spain's economic integration with Europe as the sole reason for this new age of reforms. Despite not applying again until July 1977, these moderation measures did grant Spain a

preferential agreement with the European Community in 1970; see Charles Powel, *The Long Road to Europe: Spain and the European Community, 1957–1986* (Working paper: Elcano Royal Institute, 2015).

121 On this strategy, see Oriol Malló, *El cártel español: historia crítica de la reconquista económica de México y América Latina (1898–2008)* (Madrid: Foca, 2011); Benny Pollack, *The Paradox of Spanish Foreign Policy: Spain's International Relations from Franco to Democracy* (New York: St. Martin's Press, 1987).

122 "Confidencial, 1319/177," September 20, 1973, AMCAE, Embajada en Madrid, oficios confidenciales 1973, box 64.

123 https://data.worldbank.org/indicator/NY.GDP.PCAP.CD?locations = ES. For more on the Spanish "economic miracle," see Sima Lieberman, *Growth and Crisis in the Spanish Economy: 1940–1993* (New York: Routledge, 2005); Ángel Viñas, *En las garras del Águila: los pactos con Estados Unidos, de Francisco Franco a Felipe González (1945–1995)* (Barcelona: Crítica, 2003).

124 Mills, "The Spanish 'Miracle'."

125 "Conversación con Don Cézar I. Urien", *ABC Madrid* (November 18, 1966): 10.

126 See for instance Walter Brekner, "The Change in Mentalities during the Late Franco Regime," in Nigel Townson (ed.), *Spain Transformed: The Late Franco Dictatorship, 1959–75* (New York: Palgrave Macmillan, 2007), 67–84; Cristina Palomares, "New Political Mentalities in the Tardofranquismo," in Townson (ed.), *Spain Transformed*, 118–39.

127 Laureano López Rodó, *Nuevo horizonte del desarrollo* (Madrid: Aguilar, 1972), 32–3.

128 Pérez-Embid, *Libertad, tradición y monarquía*, 7.

129 On the relationship between the two movements, see Francisca Colomer Pellicer, "La relación personal entre san Josemaría Escrivá de Balaguer y mons. Juan Hervás a través de sus cartas," *Studia et Documenta: rivista dell'Istituto Storico San Josemaría Escrivá* 4 (2010): 185–213.

130 Juan Hervás, *Leaders' Manual for Cursillos in Chritianity* (Madrid: Euroamerica, 1964), 18–19.

131 Pérez-Embid, *En la Brecha*, 68–72.

132 Ibid., 142.

133 Víctor García Hoz, *Pedagogía de la lucha ascética* (Madrid: Bolafios y Aguilar, 1942).

134 "The more he is a child, the more his life is new," García Hoz promised; see Víctor García Hoz, *La tarea profunda de educar* (Madrid: Rialp, 1965), 22.

135 Víctor García Hoz, "Un problema complejo: el de la libertad," *Telva* 50 (October 15, 1965): 59.

136 Covadonga O'Shea, "López Ibor: en el estudiante actual predomina la indiferencia," *Gaceta Universitaria* 1 (November 1, 1962).

137 Leandro Benavides, "Juventud en rebeldía," *Nuestro Tiempo* 70 (April 1960): 410–11.

138 López Ibor, "Discurso a los universitarios españoles," *Moncloa* 9 (April 1957): 8.

139 Julián Aznar, "Inquietudes," *Moncloa* 18–19 (March–April 1959): 3.
140 On this organization, see Inbal Ofer, *Señoritas in Blue: The Making of a Female Political Elite in Franco's Spain* (Portland, OR: Sussex Academic Press, 2009); Aurora G. Morcillo, *True Catholic Womanhood: Gender Ideology in Franco's Spain* (DeKalb: Northern Illinois University Press, 2000).
141 Pilar Salcedo, Editorial, *Telva* 1 (October 1963): 5.
142 Isabel Celma, "Profesionalización para la mujer," *Telva* 55 (January 1, 1966): 25.
143 In this case, in the words of Socorro de López Ibor, José's wife; see "La mujer en el trabajo: la mujer, colaboradora del marido," *Telva* 38 (April 15, 1965): 16.
144 Celma, "Profesionalización para la mujer," 25.
145 Mercedes Serra, "Saber descansar: Carlota nos abre las puertas," *Mundo Cristiano* 3 (April 1964): 34.
146 See for example Jesús Urteaga, "La mujer al volante," *Mundo Cristiano* 9 (November 10, 1964): 34. For more on women's melancholia, see "Feliz feliz feliz," *Telva* 53 (December 1, 1965): 75; "El test del optimismo," *Telva* 41 (June 1, 1965): 59–60.
147 María Elena Leguina, "Beatlemania," *Telva* 14 (April 1964): 22–6.
148 Engracia A. Jordan, "No a esto," *Telva* 33 (February 1, 1965): 38–9.
149 "Los Beatles," *Telva* 45 (October 1965): 12.
150 The Spanish pop band happened to include graduates of Opus Dei's Instituto Ramiro de Maeztu; see "El disco de Oro Español 1964," *Telva* 33 (February 1965): 8–9.
151 Piñar mocked the American "snobbery of fashion and dances" and made racist remarks about the "melody of the soul and flees from the noisy din of jazz"; see Blas Piñar, *Combate por España* (Madrid: Fuerza Nueva, 1975), 72.
152 The attacks on Margaret Sanger, neo-Malthusianism, and birth control were among Opus Dei's most recognizable staples; see for instance Manuel Fernández Areal, "Limitaciones a la población mundial," *Nuestro Tiempo* 4 (October 1954): 74–83; José y Saranya, "Malthus, José Pla, y España," *Nuestro Tiempo* 148 (October 1966): 365–8; José María García Hoz, "Conferencia mundial de planificación familiar," *Nuestro Tiempo* 157–158 (July–August 1967): 110–16.
153 "Los que no nacen," *Telva* 10 (February 15, 1963): 24.
154 Sebastian V. Sibecas, "Empieza la colonizacion sexo-economica de espana," *Gazeta Universitaria* 114 (December 15, 1968): 12–15.
155 Jesús Urteaga, *Siempre alegres* (Madrid: Rialp, 1967), 50.
156 Jesús Urteaga, *Dios y los hijos* (Madrid: Rialp, 1960), 31.
157 This was based on the Franco–Don Juan agreements of Estoril from 1957, where the Bourbon king agreed to abdicate the throne. For two detailed narratives on Don Juan's relationship with Franco throughout the 1940s and 1950s, see Charles T. Powell, *Juan Carlos of Spain: Self-Made Monarch* (New York: St. Martin's Press, 1996); Paul Preston, *Juan Carlos: A People's King* (London: HarperCollins, 2004).

158 Javeir Tusell, *Juan Carlos I: La restauración de la Monarquía* (Madrid: Temas de Hoy, 1995), 302; Preston, *Juan Carlos: A People's King*, 135–6; see also César de la Lama, *Juan Carlos I: las ideas y los hechos de un reinado* (Astorga, León: CSED, 2012).
159 "Gregorio Marañón Moya, Informe para el señor ministro de asuntos exteriores," February 10, 1964, AGUN, doc. 148/037/003.
160 López Rodó, *Memorias I*, 496.
161 In Crumbaugh's words, the Law "simply substituted the preventive system with a punitive one"; see Crumbaugh, *Destination Dictatorship*, 50.
162 "Brindis en el almuezo oficial en el circulo español, Santiago de Chile," August 13, 1966, AGUN 005/480/16.
163 Neustadt, "Mi conversación mayor."
164 *Ley Orgánica del Estado, número 1/1967, de 10 de enero, BOE* 9 (January 11, 1967): 466–77.
165 "Tarragona votó sí," *La Vanguardia* (July 7, 1967): 6.
166 Rafael Calvo Serer, *Las nuevas democracias* (Madrid: Rialp, 1964), 173–4.
167 López Rodó said in 1971 that "some of the people who are most distant from me politically belong, precisely, to Opus Dei … like Rafael Calvo, whose qualities and good faith I recognize, but whose political ideas I do not share at all," in Neustadt, "Mi conversación mayor," 15.
168 "No al general De Gaulle," *Madrid* (May 30, 1968); see also Rafael Calvo Serer, "La diversidad política es necesaria," *Madrid* (April 4, 1968).
169 Rafael Calvo Serer to Generalisimo Francisco Franco, June 17, 1968, AGUN, doc. 001/051/131.
170 Antonio Fontán, "La reaparición de Madrid," *Madrid* (September 30, 1968); Rafael Calvo Serer, *España ante la libertad, la democracia, y el progreso* (Madrid: Guadiana de Publicaciones, 1968), 10.
171 Rafael Calvo Serer to Francisco Franco, July 17, 1969, AGUN doc. 001/051/326.
172 López Rodó, *Memorias II*, 317.
173 For more on Carrero's oppression, see Juan Ma de Peñaranda, *Los servicios secretos de Carrero Blanco: los orígenes Del CNI* (Barcelona: Espasa, 2015).
174 "Despacho Garrigues; sus noticias sobre el Opus Dei," September 15, 1965, FNFF, doc. 750.
175 Alfredo Sánchez Bella to Laureano López Rodó, June 25, 1969, AGUN, doc. 15/68/365.
176 Alfredo Sánchez Bella to Luis Carrero Blanco, March 12, 1969, AGUN, doc. 15/44/57.
177 "Texto del mensaje pronunciado por S. E. el Jefe del Estado en las Cortes, 22 de julio de 1969," available at www.generalisimofranco.com/HISTORIA/juramento_rey.htm; www.derechos.org/nizkor/espana/doc/franco4.html.
178 MATESA was a textile-machinery corporation that received an estimated 140 million USD in export credits from the government – exports that, in the words of *The New York Times*, "in large part turned out to be imaginary." Some of the stolen money allegedly made its way to the University of Navarra and Opus Dei's University of Piura in Peru; see Richard Eder, "Cabinet in Madrid Periled by Scandal," *The New York Times* (July 16,

1970); Juan Martínez Alier, "España verano 1970: el miedo empieza a desaparecer," *Cuadernos Ruedo Ibérico* 25 (June–July 1970): 9.

179 Federico Silva Muñoz, *Memorias políticas* (Barcelona: Planeta, 1993), 263.

180 "El golpe de los tecnócratas" *Confirmado* (November 5, 1969): 71.

CHAPTER 3

1 On Perón's vexed relationship with the Church, see Lila M. Caimari, *Perón y la iglesia católica: religión, estado y sociedad en la Argentina, 1943–1955* (Buenos Aires: Ariel Historia, 1995).

2 Prebisch's 1955 economic plan was the first of many that aimed to reform Argentina's economy; see Arturo Jauretche, *El Plan Prebisch: retorno al coloniaje* (Buenos Aires: Peña Lillo, 1984); Gastón Parra Luzardo (ed.), *Raúl Prebisch: pensamiento renovador* (Caracas: Banco Central de Venezuela, 2006).

3 Guillermo A. O'Donnell, *Bureaucratic Authoritarianism*: Argentina, 1966–1973, in Comparative Perspective (Berkeley: University of California University Press, 1988), 10.

4 "Mensaje desde la residencia presidencial de Olivos," December 12, 1956, AGN.DAI/PN.SPD.pp, box 87.

5 Opening with the June 1955 Casa Rosada bombing and ending with the 1956 León Suarez massacre, the armed forces killed tens of Peronists in one year; see Marcelo Cavarozzi, *Autoritarismo y democracia (1955–1983)* (Buenos Aires: Centro Editor de América Latina, 1987), 30; María Sáenz Quesada, *La libertadora: de Perón a Frondizi* (Buenos Aires: Editorial Sudamericana, 2011), 221–4. On the ideology and identity of the armed forces, see Robert Potash, *The Army & Politics in Argentina: 1962–1973; From Frondizi*'s *Fall to the Peronist Restoration* (Stanford, CA: Stanford University Press, 1996).

6 "Mario Amadeo ratifica su franquismo," *El mundo* (May 6, 1956): 5.

7 Cosme Beccar Varela, *El nacionalismo* (Buenos Aires: Tradición, Familia y Propiedad, 1970), 208, 9.

8 Mario Amadeo, *Al día siguiente* (Buenos Aires: 1955), 4, located at Biblioteca Nacional Argentina, BNA-ARCH-CEN-ARQué, Carpeta Mario Amadeo; see also "El día siguiente se atrasó Amadeo," *Que* 59 (November 30, 1955): 4.

9 Máximo Etchecopar, *De la democracia política a la democracia social* (Buenos Aires: Ediciones Sigla, 1958), 16, 30.

10 Arturo Frondizi, "Discurso antes la comisión promotora de la libertad de enseñanza," September 15,1958, AGN.DAI/PN.SPD.pp, box 89. For more on Frondizi's ideology, see Roberto Gustavo Pisarello Virasoro, *Cómo y por qué fue derrocado Frondizi* (Buenos Aires: Editorial Biblos, 1996); Celia Szusterman, *Frondizi and the Politics of Developmentalism in Argentina, 1955–62* (London: Macmillan, 1993); Nicolas Babini, *Arturo Frondizi y la Argentina Moderna: la forja de una ilusión* (Barcelona: Gedisa, 2006).

11 Richard J. Walter, "The Right and the Peronists, 1943–1955," in Sandra McGee Deutsch and Ronald H. Dolkart, *The Argentine Right: Its History*

and Intellectual Origins, 1910 to the Present (Wilmington, DE: Rowman & Littlefield, 1993), 121–4.

12 Mario Amadeo to Alfredo Sánchez Bella, March 22, 1959, AGUN, doc. 15/35/207.

13 Mario Amadeo to Alfredo Sánchez Bella, February 9, 1959, AGUN, doc. 15/35/205.

14 Alfredo Sánchez Bella to Mario Amadeo, February 23, 1959, AGUN, doc. 15/35/206.

15 Alfredo Sánchez Bella to Mario Amadeo, April 10, 1959, AGUN, doc. 15/35/208.

16 Mario Amadeo to Alfredo Sánchez Bella, August 10, 1959, AGUN, doc. 15/35/210.

17 Marcelo Sánchez Sorondo, *Libertades prestadas* (Buenos Aires: ATPE, 1956), 6. Sánchez Sorondo claimed that the journal's sales amounted to 140,000 weekly copies; see ibid., 258.

18 José Antonio Primo de Rivera, "Dureza y claridad," *Combate* 92 (December 8, 1960): 2; "José Antonio," *Combate* 103 (December 16, 1961): 1.

19 Jordán Bruno Genta, *Guerra contrarevolucionaria* (Buenos Aires: Nuevo Orden, 1963), 140.

20 Ibid., 91.

21 "Puntos Programáticos," *Mazocra GRN* 12 (August 1967): 7–8.

22 On this ideological influence, see Daniel Lvovich, *El nacionalismo de derecha:* desde sus orígenes a Tacuara (Buenos Aires: Capital Intelectual, 2006), 81–2; Daniel Gutman, *Tacuara: historia de la primera guerrilla urbana argentina* (Buenos Aires: Vergara, 2012), 57–65. On the neacionalista "groups," see "Guevara: ¿Se puede en la Argentina unir a civiles y Fuerzas Armadas?" *Primera Plana* 4 (December 4, 1962): 19–20.

23 "El comunismo de Frondizi," *Azul y Blanco* 161 (July 14, 1959): 3; "Discurso a las fuerzas armadas," *Azul y Blanco* 109 (July 1958); see also Mario Amadeo to Alfredo Sánchez Bella, February 9, 1959, AGUN, doc. 15/35/205.

24 "El presidente argentino en el Instituto de Cultura Hispánica de Madrid," *Mundo Hispánico* 149 (August 1960): 5

25 "Cita de la Argentina con España: las puertas abiertas de par en par," *Mundo Hispánico* 149 (August 1960): 8–11.

26 Alfredo Sánchez Bella to Mario Amadeo, August 5, 1960, AGUN, doc. 15/35/223.

27 "Mensaje del Presidente de la Nación en la ceremonia de clausura del Congreso Mariano Interamericano," November 13, 1960, AGN.DAI/PN.SPD.pp, box 93.

28 "El Gobierno y el comunismo. Mensaje pronunciado hoy por el presidente de la nación Dr. Arturo Frondizi, por Radiofonía y Televisión," November 23, 1960, AGN.DAI/PN.SPD.pp, box 93.

29 "Explicación y motivos del anteproyecto de Ley de Defensa de la Democracia," BNA-ARCH-CEN, box 1681.

30 Even events such as Eisenhower's visit to Buenos Aires could not persuade the insatiable *Azul y Blanco* commentators that Frondizi was not a communist; see "La visita de Eisenhower," *Azul y Blanco* (March 8, 1960); see also

"Entrevista del Che Guevara con el Dr. Frondizi en la residencia de Olivos," August 18, 1961, BNA-ARCH-CEN, box 1381. On Frondizi's petroleum politics, see Szusterman, *Frondizi and the Politics of Developmentalism in Argentina*, 79.

31 According to Alain Rouquié, the Azules "identified with the ruling classes, the oligarchy of the owners of the land and builders of the country"; see Alain Rouquié, *Poder militar y sociedad política en la Argentina* (Buenos Aires: Emecé Editores, 1983), 214.

32 Onganía was the initiator of the Campo de Mayo Communiqué 150 that pledged to prevent Perón's return to power. See Juan Carlos Onganía, oral history with Robert Potash, 1984. Robert Potash Papers; also discussed in Robert Potash, *The Army & Politics in Argentina, 1962–1973: From Frondizi's Fall to the Peronist Restoration* (Stanford, CA: Stanford University Press, 1996), 73.

33 On Onganía's alleged "obsession" with keeping the military out of politics, see Tomás Sánchez de Bustamante, oral history with Robert A. Potash, 1985, Robert Potash Papers, 7.

34 More on this ideological struggle, see Marvin Goldwert, *Democracy, Militarism, and Nationalism in Argentina, 1930–1966: An Interpretation* (Austin: University of Texas Press, 2014), 188–203; Rodolfo Pandolfi, *Azules y Colorados. El conflicto político y militar a comienzos de los sesenta* (Buenos Aires: Editorial Centro de Estudios Unión para la Nueva Mayoría, 1994).

35 "Por una solución nacional. Discurso pronunciado en la comida del Ateneo de la República, el 21 de diciembre 1962," *Cuadernos del Ateneo de la Republica (Buenos Aires)* 2, BNA-ARCH-CEN-ARQué, Mario Amadeo folder. The Ateneo's other leading figures were the Hispanistas Máximo Etchecopar, Santiago de Estrada, Eduardo Roca, and Basilio Serrano. Interview with Enrique Peltzer, March 15, 2016.

36 Mario Amadeo to Alfredo Sánchez Bella, May 2, 1962, AGUN, doc. 15/35/239.

37 Sánchez Bella wrote to the Argentine ambassador on their behalf; see Alfredo Sánchez Bella to Perdo Radío, February 2, 1949, Archivo del Ministerio de Asuntos Exteriores y Culto, Embajada en Madrid II, box 25; interview with Enrique Pelzer, March 15, 2016.

38 Interview with Enrique Pelzer, March 15, 2016.

39 *Instituto argentino de Cultura Hispánica, veinticinco años de labor cultural*, (Buenos Aires: Cultura Hispánica, 1990), 12.

40 Jorge Mazzinghi, *Ni memorias ni olvido* (Buenos Aires: El Autor, 2015), 104.

41 "Sesenta y cuatro naciones han reconocido ya al nuevo gobierno argentino," *ABC Madrid* (July 17, 1966): 73.

42 *Instituto argentino de Cultura Hispánica, veinticinco años de labor cultural*, 12–13.

43 Mario Amadeo to Alfredo Sánchez Bella, December 30, 1965, AGUN, doc. 15/35/260.

44 Mario Amadeo to Alfredo Sánchez Bella, April 4, 1963, AGUN, doc. 15/35/249.

45 "We believe in the value of the elites and in the power of the Truth," stated *Verbo* in 1960; see "Después de nuestra jordana," *Verbo* 9 (January–February 1960): 5.
46 "¿Que es la revolución?" *Verbo* 2 (June 1959): 2; for more on this society, see "Visión religiosa y acción política. El caso de Ciudad Católica – Verbo en la Argentina de los años sesenta," *PROHAL Monográfico, Revista del Programa de Historia de América Latina* 2 (2010): 33–6.
47 Cosme Beccar Varela to El Instituto de Cultura Hispánica Departamento de Intercambio, March 21, 1957, AGUN, doc. 15/40/64; Cosme Beccar Varela senior, a Nacionalista too, had been Sánchez Bella's business partner and promoted the Spanish book publishers AIZA in Argentina; see Cosme Beccar Varela to Alfredo Sánchez Bella, October 30, 1957, AGUN, doc. 15/40/67.
48 "Sarmiento y Azul y Blanco," *Cruzada* 4 (October 1956); see also "Nacionalismo marxista," *Cruzada* 9 (October 1957); "De la confusión no nace el orden," *Cruzada* 5 (March 1957).
49 Alfredo Sánchez Bella to Cosme Beccar Varela, September 10, 1960, AGUN, doc. 15/40/81.
50 Alfredo Sánchez Bella to Cosme Beccar Varela, April 10, 1962, AGUN, doc. 15/40/88.
51 For more on the rise of this movement in Brazil and its role in society, see Benjamin Cowan, *Securing Sex: Morality and Repression in the Making of Cold War Brazil* (Chapel Hill: University of North Carolina Press, 2016), 43–6.
52 He was referring to the nineteenth-century Decadence movement; see José Miguel Ibáñez Langlois to Florentino Pérez-Embid, AGUN, box 003/016.
53 According to Opus Dei's official narrative; see http://opusdei.org.ar/es-ar/article/historia/.
54 "Documentación: declaraciones del fundador del Opus Dei," *Cuadernos del Sur* 27 (October 1966): 865–71; "Documentación: ¿Que es el Opus Dei?," *Cuadernos del Sur* 51 (October 1968): 880–98; Víctor del Reina, "Camino y el Opus Dei," *Cuadernos del Sur* 61–62 (August–September 1969): 655–8.
55 Jorge Mazzinghi and Samuel Medrano published in the journal too. According to Ernesto García Alesanco, these men joined Opus Dei only in the early 1970s. This claim is supported, in the case of Mazzinghi, by his own autobiography. Still, there is reason to suspect these claims – particularly in the case of Díaz Colodrero, who was one of the founders of *Cuadernos del Sur* and who was clearly aligned with Opus Dei's ideological trends during the mid 1960s. Moreover, according to Argentine publications, Medrano and Mazzinghi were Opus Dei members as early as 1967; see "El Opus Dei, aquí y ahóra," *Análisis* 308 (February 2, 1967), also located at AGA, box 42/09060.
56 "Editorial Pomaire, sociedad de responsabilidad limitada," *BOE (Argentina)* 20,811 (November 2, 1965): 36.
57 José Miguel Ibáñez Langlois, "Planificación y libertad," *Cuadernos del Sur* 6–7 (January–February 1965): 7.
58 Ibid., 16.

59 Ernesto García Alesanco, "En defensa de la libertad," *Cuadernos del Sur* 10 (May 1965): 382.
60 José Miguel Ibáñez Langlois, "El futuro de la revolución social," *Cuadernos del Sur* 15 (October 1965): 898.
61 Ibid., 899.
62 Edmundo Carbone, "El divorcio en la Argentina," *Cuadernos del Sur* 12 (July 1965): 600–9; "Editorial: La familia, eximia obra de Dios," *Cuadernos del Sur* 58 (May 1969): 1–2: Armando Roa, "Psicología del matrimonio moderno," *Cuadernos del Sur* 22 (May 1966): 377–88.
63 As historian Isabella Cosse has shown in her groundbreaking research, the 1960s' "discreet" sexual revolution in Argentina was met by various forms of resistance, not only from the Catholic sectors of society; see Isabella Cosse, *Pareja, sexualidad y familia en los años sesenta: una revolución discreta en Buenos Aires* (Buenos Aires: Siglo Veintiuno Editores, 2010); see also Valeria Manzano, *The Age of Youth in Argentina: Politics, Culture, and Sexuality from Perón to Videla* (Chapel Hill: University of North Carolina Press, 2014); Natalia Milanesio, *Workers Go Shopping in Argentina: The Rise of Popular Consumer Culture* (Albuquerque: University of New Mexico, 2013).
64 José Miguel Ibáñez Langlois, "El pronunciamiento católico sobre la natalidad," *Cuadernos del Sur* 50 (September 1968): 786; see also José Miguel Ibáñez Langlois, "Más sobre el control del nacimiento," *Cuadernos del Sur* 9 (April 1965): 315–17; José Miguel Ibáñez Langlois, "Progestágenos," *Cuadernos del Sur* 1 (August 1964): 17–18.
65 Ibáñez Langlois, "El pronunciamiento católico sobre la natalidad," 762, 787–8.
66 Fernando Jacobelli, "Sobre la educación sexual," *Cuadernos del Sur* 24 (July 1966): 584.
67 Víctor García Hoz, "Educación: libertad y dogmatismo," *Cuadernos del Sur* 11 (June 1965): 469–79.
68 On these women's status in Opus Dei, see María Olivia Mönckeberg, *El imperio del Opus Dei en Chile* (Santiago, Chile: Grupo Zeta, 2003), 604, 644.
69 María Elena Aguirre, "La mujer ante el problema de ser mujer," *Cuadernos del Sur* 17 (December 1965): 1089. See also Elena Vial Correa, "Reforma educacional chilena," *Cuadernos del Sur* 21 (April 1966): 270–3; Lilian Calm, "Indira Gandhi," *Cuadernos del Sur* 22 (May 1966): 363–5.
70 María Elena Aguirre, "Funciones sociales de la mujer actual," *Cuadernos del Sur* 28 (November 1966): 969–73.
71 Aguirre, "La mujer ante el problema de ser mujer," 1089.
72 The letter's context was the Spanish–Argentine economic negotiations, regarding the dispute over Spain's alleged debt to Argentina, and carried by Luis Otero, the head of the Argentine Nacional Bank; see "Información," May 24, 1963, AGN.DAI/PN.SPD.pp, box 97.
73 In the words of the Argentine ambassador in Madrid; see "Monumento iconográfica de la República Argentina," March 29, 1965, AMAEC, Embajada en Madrid II, box 108.
74 "Texto de la carta enviada por el presidente de la nación al Dr. José Maríano Astigueta," June 25, 1963, AGN.DAI/ PN.SPD.pp, box 97.

75 Potash, *The Army & Politics in Argentina*, 76–81.
76 His tenure was actually characterized by economic growth and elevation in life quality; see Rodolfo Pandolfi and Emilio Gibaja, *La democracia derrotada: Arturo Illia y su época* (Buenos Aires: Lumiere, 2008), 1–12.
77 His decrees 744/63 – 745/63, issued on November 15, 1963, nullified the contracts with international oil corporations.
78 This process has been well accounted for in César Tcach Abad, *Arturo Illia: un sueño breve: el rol del Peronismo y de los estados unidos en el golpe militar de 1966* (Buenos Aires: Edhasa, 2006).
79 In the words of Onganía's minister Dardo Pérez Guilhou, Illia was perhaps "a good man" but under his rule "the country was a farce"; see Dardo Pérez Guilhou, oral history with Robert A. Potash, 1984, Robert A. Potash Papers, UMass Amherst University Archives, 6–7.
80 Adelbert Krieger Vasena, oral history with Robert A. Potash, 1984, Robert A. Potash Papers, UMass Amherst University Archives, 27.
81 Mario Días Colodrero, *Dos políticas, dos argentinas: palabras pronunciadas por el Secretario de Gobierno de la Nación, Dr. Mario Díaz Colodrero por la red de radio y televisión, el 15 de marzo 1968* (Buenos Aires: Secretaría de Estado de Gobierno, 1968).
82 Krieger Vasena, oral history with Robert A. Potash, 35.
83 Mariano Grondona, "La dictadura," *Primera Plana* (May 31, 1966): 11.
84 Grondona, oral history with Robert Potash, 1986, Robert Potash Papers, 36.
85 Mariano Montemayor, "Al: El señor presidente," *Confirmado (Buenos Aires)* 26 (October 23, 1965): 5.
86 See for example Bernardo Neustadt, "Proceso a la duda," *Todo* 8 (November 19, 1964): 4; "Las armas y los votos," *Todo* 19 (February 11, 1965): 2; Bernardo Neustadt, "Ref.: un hurto al país," *Todo* 19 (February 11, 1965): 3; Bernardo Neustadt, "Ref.: ¿analfabetos políticos?" *Todo* 23 (March 11, 1965): 1.
87 Antonio Brusa, "Onganía: el hombre y su circunstancia," *Cuadernos del Sur* 18 (January 1966): 30–3.
88 Mariano Grondona, "Quién manda," *Primera Plana* (September 7, 1965): 7. A person who wanted to talk about issues of power, Díaz Colodrero reflected, "wasted time not speaking with Onganía," Mario Díaz Colodrero, oral history with Robert Potash, 1986, Robert Potash Papers, 4; for more on this process, see Liliana de Riz, *La política en suspenso, 1966–1976* (Buenos Aires: Paidós, 2000), 30–42.
89 "Sin ninguna fe en el gobierno," *Primera Plana* (June 1965): 12; "Palabras pronunciadas por el comandante en jefe del ejercito el día 6 de agosto en West Point en oportunidad de realizarse la Conferencia de los Ejércitos Americanos," *Boletín Público de la Secretaría de Guerra* (September 10, 1964).
90 "Audiencia presidida por el presidente de la Nación Argentina, General Onganía y el comisario del Plan de Desarrollo Económico y Social, don Laureano López Rodó," August 19, 1966, AGUN, doc. 005/397/22.
91 "Los ejércitos de Argentina y Brasil estarán unidos frente a cualquier acción comunista," *ABC Sevilla* (September 2, 1965): 23; see also "Un nuevo Onganía," *Primera Plana* (September 21, 1965): 10.

92 According to Potash, whereas Illia appointed Brigadier General Eduardo Castro Sánchez – an officer senior to Onganía – as Secretary of the Army, thereby provoking Onganía's resignation, he did not deliberately cause his departure; see Potash, *The Army & Politics in Argentina*, 151.
93 Díaz Colodrero, oral history with Robert A. Potash, 7.
94 Costa Méndez, oral history with Potash, 3–10.
95 Mario Amadeo to Alfredo Sánchez Bella, December 30, 1965, AGUN, doc. 15/35/260.
96 On this journal, see Valeria Galván, *El nacionalismo de derecha en la Argentina posperonista. El semanario Azul y Blanco (1956–1969)* (Rosario: Prohistoria Ediciones, 2013).
97 Costa Méndez, oral history with Potash, 8.
98 Mario Díaz Colodrero, *Dos políticas, dos argentinas. Palabras pronunciadas por el Secretario de Gobierno de la Nación, Dr. Mario Díaz Colodrero por la red de radio y televisión, el 15 de marzo 1968* (Buenos Aires: Secretaría de Estado de Gobierno, 1968), 10.
99 "Exigencias de la vida actual," *La Nación* (July 1, 1966): 2; "Política educativa, para nuestro tiempo," *La Nación* (July 14, 1966): 2; "Los objetivos del Gobierno," *La Nación* (July 16, 1966): 2.
100 Mariano Montemayor, "Que será la Revolución Argentina," *Confirmado* 55 (July 7, 1966): 14–15.
101 Salvador de Madariaga, "Carta abierta al general-presidente," *La Prensa* (August 5, 1966): 1.
102 Políticas del Gobierno Nacional, AGN.DAI/PN.SPD.pp, box 101.
103 Alfredo Sánchez Bella to Laureano López Rodó, AGUN, doc. 005/154/32.
104 Declaraciones del ministro sin cartera del plan de desarrollo económico social de España Dr. Laureano López Rodó luego de su entrevista con el presidente de la nación, August 19, 1966, AGN.DAI/ PN.SPD.pp, box 101.
105 Audiencia presidida por el presidente de la Nación Argentina, August 19, 1966.
106 Audiencia presidida por el presidente de la Nación Argentina, August 19, 1966. See also López Rodó, *Memorias I*, 68–9.
107 "Conferencia pronunciada por el señor ministro y comisario del plan de desarrollo español, don Laureano López Rodó, en la unión industrial argentina, 19.8.66," AGUN doc. 005/154/28.
108 López Rodó, *Memorias II*, 69.
109 www.perfil.com/noticias/elobservador/roberto-bosca-frustrada-mediacion-de-franco-entre-peron-y-lanusse.phtml
110 Laureano López Rodó to Jorge Ernesto Salimei, December 10, 1966, AGUN, doc. 005/358/9.
111 J214: Información, October 21, 1966, Archivo General de la Nación, Presidencia de la Nación, Secretaría de Prensa y Difusión, Partes de Prensa [hereafter AGN.DAI/PN.SPD.pp], box 102.
112 Mariano Grondona did wonder whether Onganía should walk in the footsteps of French, Spanish, and Brazilian personalist regimes but never identified Onganía with Franco; see Grondona, "Los tres modelos," *Primera Plana* (November 1, 1966): 14.

113 In what came to be known as "the night of the long batons," on July 29, 1966, the federal police stormed the University of Buenos Aires, violently repressing protests against the regime's revocation of academic freedom. On these events, see Sergio Morero, *La noche de los bastones largos. 30 años después* (Buenos Aires: Editorial La Página, 1996); on the Argentine right and the "university question," see Beatriz Sarlo, *La batalla de las ideas (1943–1973)* (Buenos Aires: Emecé Editores, 2007), 85–146.

114 The press, Onganía said, could "help the common man understand contemporary processes." See "Discurso pronunciado por el Señor Presidente de la Nación en la XIV comida anual de la asociación de la prensa extranjera, August 18, 1967," AGN.DAI/ PN.SPD.pp, box 104.

115 "Discurso pronunciado por el Señor Presidente de la Nación Teniente General Juan Carlos Onganía en la comida de camaradería de las Fuerzas Armadas realizada el 6 de julio de 1967" (Buenos Aires: Presidencia de la Nación, 1967), 10–11.

116 Mariano Grondona, "Definiciones," *Primera Plana* (July 5, 1966): 11.

117 "The State Secretariat was to take over everything that had to do with executive action from the Interior Ministry," he said; see Díaz Colodrero, oral history with Potash, 8.

118 "He knows you, even if you do not remember him, he was a fellow in your time," Amadeo said of Díaz Colodrero, in Mario Amadeo to Alfredo Sánchez Bella, November 1, 1966, AGUN, doc. 15/35/264.

119 Mariano Grondona, *Primera Plana* 217 (February 21, 1967): 11.

120 Mario Amadeo to Alfredo Sánchez Bella, January 28, 1967, AGUN, doc. 15/35/266.

121 Others included Máximo Etchecopar (Foreign Ministry's Exterior Service Insitute); Raúl Puigbó (Ateneo, head of the Community Promotion and Assistance office); Samuel Medrano (Opus Dei, Director of Social Security); Pedro Real (Ateneo, head of National Bank); Eduardo Señorans (Opus Dei, head of the information agency SIDE); Ernesto Pueyrredón (Ateneo, Deputy Minister of the Interior), Enrique Pearson (Ateneo, Díaz Colodrero's deputy). For more on these men, see Gabriela Gomes, "Las trayectorias políticas de los funcionarios nacional-corporativistas del Onganiato," in Gabriela Gomes and Martín Vicente (eds.), *Trayectorias de intelectuales en el estado. Actas de jornadas de discusión*, (San Fernando: Edición de la autora, 2016), 33–57.

122 As in France and Spain, the plan consisted of "one big devaluation," thereby achieving currency stabilization; see Krieger Vasena, oral history with Robert Potash, 43.

123 Roberto Pucci, *Historia de la destrucción de una provincia: Tucumán, 1966* (Buenos Aires: Ediciones del Pago Chico, 2007); Silvia Nassif, "La lucha obrera en Tucumán. Del ingenio Los Ralos a la fábrica Textil Escalada (1966–1973)," *Coordenadas: Revista de Historia Local y Regional* 3:1 (2016): 30–52.

124 Krieger Vasena, oral history with Potash, 57–8; on Krieger Vasena's notions of "the role of international capital markets" in Latin America, see Adalbert Krieger Vasena and Javier Pazos, *Latin America; A Broader World Role* (Totowa, NJ: Rowman & Littlefield, 1973), 131–47.

125 "Discurso pronunciado por el doctor Guillermo borda el 24 de Abril de 1968, ante la asociación de Prensa extranjera," *Cinco discursos y una revolución* (Buenos Aires: Ediciones Movimiento Humanista de Derecho, 1968).

126 "Discurso pronunciado por el Señor presidente de la Nación Teniente General Juan Carlos Onganía en la comida de camaradería de las Fuerzas Armadas realizada el 6 de julio de 1967" (Buenos Aires: Presidencia de la Nación, 1967).

127 "Discurso pronunciado por el doctor Mario Díaz Colodrero el 16 de Mayo 1968 en la unión industrial Argentina," in *Cinco discursos y una revolución*, 33–34.

128 *Dos políticas, dos argentinas*, 32. For more on these plans, see Wolf Grabendorff, "Perspectivas y polos de desarrollo en América Latina," *Estudios Internacionales* 13:50 (1980): 252–78; Patricio Narodowski, *La Argentina pasiva: desarrollo, subjetividad, instituciones, más allá de la modernidad: el desarrollo visto desde el margen de una periferia, de un país dependiente* (Buenos Aires: Prometeo Libros Editorial, 2007); Martín Fiszbein, "Crecimiento desbalanceado y estructura productiva desequilibrada en Argentina (1945–1976): problemas e ideas del modelo industrial en retrospectiva," *Estudios sobre la industria argentina* 3:3 (2013): 49.

129 "Argentina necesita grandes contingentes de mano de obra latina y especialmente española," *La Vanguardia* (June 14, 1967).

130 Alfredo Sánchez Bella to Mario Amadeo, September 20, 1966, AGUN, doc. 15/35/263.

131 Alfredo Sánchez Bella to Mario Amadeo, February 22, 1967, AGUN, doc. 15/35/268. Italics in the original text.

132 "Discurso pronunciado por el Presidente de la Nación teniente general Juan Carlos Onganía en la comida de la camaradería de las fuerzas armadas, July 6, 1966," AGN, PN.SPD.pp, box 101.

133 Pedro Ancarola, *La acción desde el poder* (Buenos Aires: Ediciones Nueva Política, 1967), 41, 119–130.

134 "Gobierno: Otro pozo al aire," *Primera Plana* (January 24, 1967): 12.

135 "Gobierno: el plan político," *Primera Plana* (May 23, 1967): 12–13.

136 The liberal magazine *Inédito* condemned him for being a "fascist," while the neofascists moved from backing him to attacking Krieger Vasena's economic policies; see "Plagio?" *Inédito* (January 25, 1967): 2.

137 On the Peronist unions and the reasons for collaborating with Onganía, see Darío Dawyd, "El nuevo autoritarismo burocrático y el sindicalismo peronista. Análisis de la 'participación' junto al gobierno militar de Onganía en la Argentina de los años sesenta," *Confluenze* 4:2 (January 2013): 17; Daniel James, *Resistance and Integration: Peronism and the Argentine Working Class, 1946–1976* (New York: Cambridge University Press, 1988), 215–28.

138 "Discurso pronunciado por el Señor presidente de la Nación Teniente General Juan Carlos Onganía en la comida de camaradería de las Fuerzas Armadas realizada el 6 de julio de 1967."

139 "La revolución argentina cumplirá dos etapas," *ABC Madrid* (June 27, 1967): 72; see also "Gobierno: ¿Ha nacido el plan político?" *Primera Plana* 247 (September 19, 1967): 13.

140 "Discurso pronunciado por el señor ministro del Interior borda Dr. Guillermo A. Borda, III Reunión nacional de ministros de educación," *Reunión nacional de ministros de educación*, December 12–14, 1966.

141 Onganía's Civic Code allowed Argentines to divorce but made this conditional on the verdict of special "judicial decree" (Art. 66) and further granted any "relatives of the future spouses within the second degree of consanguinity" the right to oppose new marriages (Art. 21); see *Boletín Oficial del Estado (Buenos Aires)* 21554 (November 4, 1968). For more on Onganía's "Cinema Law," see Ley 17.741, *Boletín Oficial del Estado* 21.550 (October 28, 1968). For more on these public morality campaigns, see Rouquié, *Poder militar y sociedad política en la Argentina*, 259; Mala Htun, *Sex and the State: Abortion, Divorce, and the Family under Latin American Dictatorships and Democracies* (New York: Cambridge University Press, 2003), 67.

142 "Ley Orgánica las Universidades Nacionales," *BOE (Buenos Aires)* 17.345 (April 21, 1967).

143 "Discurso del secretario del estado de cultura y educación, Prof. Carlos María Gelly y Obes," *III Reunión nacional de ministros de educación* (Buenos Aires: Centro Nacional de Educación e Información Educativa), 21–23.

144 "If this Argentine Revolution is not able to banish secularism from the schools and will not facilitate the reunion of the Argentine people with their more authentic tradition, it will have betrayed its reason for being," declared *Consudec* columnist Benicio C. A. Villarreal; see *Consudec* 83 (January 1967): 2–3.

145 "Discurso del Señor presidente del Consejo Nacional de Educación, Dr. Mariano Astigueta," *III Reunión nacional de ministros de educación,* 97.

146 *Mensaje a la Juventud: discurso pronunciado por el Secretario de Estado de Cultura y Educación, Dr. José Mariano Astigueta, durante el homenaje a los congresales de Tucumán. San Miguel de Tucumán, 8 de Julio de 1968* (Buenos Aires: Secretaria de Estado de Cultura y Educación, 1968).

147 Marcos Ronchino, "La democratización de la enseñanza," *Cuadernos del Sur* 34 (May 1967): 367.

148 "La lucha de las clases," *Primera Plana* 219 (March 7, 1967): 46.

149 Juan Rafael Llerena Amadeo, "Fin de la educación, objetivos del sistema y estructura," *III Reunión nacional de ministros de educación*, 51.

150 Víctor García Hoz, "La problemática perspectiva de la educación actual," *Cuadernos del Sur* 42–43 (January–February 1968): 5–11.

151 Delia Brusa, "Los hijos," *Cuadernos del Sur* 57 (April 1969): 287.

152 The OEI financed and directed the Argentine "middle school" reform, implemented in the province of Buenos Aires and in place until 1971; see OEI, balance de actividades 1964–68, Biblioteca del Ministerio de Educación, OEI/SG/IMF.15.

153 "Incorporación de la Argentina en la OEI," *Plana,* 110 (October–November 1966): 3.

154 *II seminario iberoamericano de enseñanzas técnicas* (Buenos Aires: Oficina de Educación Iberoamericana, September 14, 1967), 10–15.

155 Mario Amadeo to Alfredo Sánchez Bella, November 19, 1970, AGUN, doc. 15/35/298

156 Jorge Pérez Rocco, "Facturas se pagan a preconciliares," *Inédito* 35 (January 10, 1968): 19; interview with Enrique Pelzer, March 15, 2016.

157 Mario Amadeo to Alfredo Sánchez Bella, March 31, 1969, AGUN, doc. 15/35/279.

158 "Discurso del presidente de la nacion Argentina al declarar inaugurada la tercera conferencia interamericana extraordinaria de cancilleres," February 15, 1967, AGN.DAI/PN.SPD.pp, box 103.

159 *Discurso del Ministro de Relaciones Exteriores y Culto de la Republica Argentina, Dr. Nicanor Costa Méndez, en el 22 periodo de las Naciones Unidas, September 27, 1967*; also at www.youtube.com/watch?v = YEGjE1jSKxk.

160 "Palabras de aliento de Onganía a la reunión de cancilleres de la OEA," *ABC Madrid* (February 17, 1967).

161 "Discurso pronunciado por el señor presidente de la nación teniente general Juan Carlos Onganía en la comida realizada en la residencia de Olivos," December 15, 1966. AGN.DAI/ PN.SPD.pp, box 102.

162 "Discurso pronunciado por el doctor Nicanor Costa Méndez, el 9 de Mayo, ante la asociación cristiana de dirigentes de empresa," in *Cinco discursos y una revolución*, 14.

163 "En el extranjero, la Democracia Cristiana de Chile declaró a Onganía persona no grata," *Primera Plana* 150 (September 21, 1965).

164 Onganía sought to change the operation of Latin America's armies by institutionalizing the Inter-American Defense Board (IDB) within the Organization of American States (OAS), a motion that would have given military dictatorships in the continent a bigger say in the institution, as well as a symbolic seal of approval – all the while without having to actually commit to establishing an international task force. For more on the Chilean, Colombian, and Mexican objection to the Argentine "Natoization" of the OAS, see Gregorio Selser, *El Onganiato: La espada y el hisopo, vol II* (Buenos Aires: Carlos Samanta Editor, 1966), 105; Andrew Hurrell, "The Politics of South Atlantic Security: A Survey of Proposals for a South Atlantic Treaty Organization," *International Affairs* 59:2 (1983): 179–93.

165 "Eduardo Frei, Cartas con Juan Carlos Onganía, Fundación Eduardo Frei, Proyecto Digitalización Archivo Historico," doc. 1654, CD ROM 9.

166 In 1967, Franco decorated Onganía and Costa Méndez with the Spanish Navy Medals of Honor. In return, Onganía honored three Spanish ministers, most tellingly López Rodó himself. No German, French, Brazilian, British, Mexican, or US official received any such honors from Onganía. See Decreto 7999/1967, *Boletín Oficial del Estado* 21306 (November 3, 1967); and Decreto 1319/1970, *Boletín Oficial del Estado* 21964 (July 6, 1970).

167 "Palabras del presidente de la Nación, Juan Carlos Onganía, al recibir la medalla de oro de la marina de España," February 5, 1967, AGN.DAI/PN.SPD.pp, box 103.

168 "Firmóse un acuerdo de carnes con España," *La Nación* (August 6, 1967): 1; on this crisis, see Roberto Roth, *Los años de Onganía. Relato de un testigo* (Buenos Aires: Ediciones La Campana, 1981), 240–1.
169 "Conferencia de Fernández de la Mora en Buenos Aires," *ABC Madrid* (September 24, 1967): 93.
170 "La banca del señor Palanca o la palanca del señor Labanca," *Inédito* (September 27, 1967): 3.
171 "El ministro argentino de economía esperado hoy en Madrid," *ABC Sevilla* (November 12, 1967): 66; among them was the Argentine Minister of Social Security, Alfredo Manuel Cousido. For more on the Argentine–Spanish Social Security treaty, see *Boletín Oficial del Estado* 269 (November 10, 1967): 15513–15.
172 (Document without title) AGA, box 42/08973, 4.
173 "La verdad hispana ha de ser divulgada por nosotros dijo el canciller argentino," *ABC Madrid* (April 15, 1969): 29.
174 On the economic transformations Argentina underwent throughout this period, see Juan Carlos de Pablo, *La economía argentina en la segunda mitad del siglo XX* (Buenos Aires: La Ley, 2005); Aldo Ferrer, *La economía argentina: desde sus orígenes hasta principios del siglo XXI* (Buenos Aires: Fondo de Cultura Económica, 2004); Paul H. Lewis, *The Crisis of Argentine Capitalism* (Chapel Hill: University of North Carolina Press, 1990).
175 *Discurso pronunciado por el Presidente de la Nación Teniente General Juan Carlos Onganía, en el acto de clausura de la Primer a Junta de Gobernadores de la Patagonia* (Buenos Aires: Presidencia de la Nación, 1967), 7.
176 "Argentina: ¿Empezó el tiempo político?" *Primera Plana* (January 30, 1968): 32; "Gobierno: la ilusión del consejalismo," *Primera Plana* (August 20, 1968): 20; "Participacionismo: ¿una mala palabra?" *7 Días (Buenos Aires)* (August 12, 1968): 19.
177 "Expuso el doctor Borda la idea política del gobierno," *La Nación* (April 25, 1968): 1; "Declaraciones en Jujuy del Dr. Díaz Colodrero," *La Nación* (May 19, 1968). Since 1967, Díaz Colodrero had denied that his ideology was corporatism, as this "political formula" was "a thing of the past," he said; see "La revolución argentina cumplirá dos etapas," *ABC Madrid* (June 27, 1967): 72.
178 Edmundo J. Carbone, "Una política maniquea," *Cuadernos del Sur* 52 (November 1968): 999.
179 Roberto Bosca, "Un problema explosivo: La representación política," *Cuadernos del Sur* 61–62 (August–September 1969): 680–3.
180 Mario Amadeo to Alfredo Sánchez Bella, August 24, 1969, AGUN, box 15/35/282.
181 Nicanor Costa Méndez, oral history with Robert A. Potash, 42.
182 For more on these initiatives, see Gabriela Gomes, "El Onganiato y los sectores populares. Funcionarios, ideas y políticas de la Secretaría de Estado de Promoción y Asistencia a la Comunidad (1966–1970)," *Anuario del Centro de Estudios Históricos* 11:11 (2011): 279–302; Guido Giorgi, "Refundar la sociedad. El comunitarismo como política de Estado en el Gobierno de Onganía," in Valeria Galván and Florencia Osuna (eds.), *Política y cultura durante el "Onganiato": nuevas perspectivas para la*

investigación de la presidencia de Juan Carlos Onganía (1966–1970) (Rosario: Prohistoria, 2014), 105–18.

183 Onganía, oral history with Potash, 17–18. For more on CONASE and CONADE, see Aníbal Jáuregui, "El CONADE: organización y resultados (1961–1971)," *Anuario IEHS* (2014): 141–58; Aníbal Jáuregui, "La planificación en la Argentina: El CONADE y el PND (1960–1966)," *Anuario del Centro de Estudios Históricos* 13 (2013): 243–66.

184 "Próximas novedades," *Inédito* (August 7, 1968): 5. For more on this episode, see James P. Brennan, *Córdoba rebelde. El Cordobazo, el clasismo y la movilización social* (La Plata: De la Campana, 2008), 88–101.

185 Onganía, oral history with Robert Potash, 1984.

186 The report presented Díaz Colodrero, Jorge Mazzinghi (sub-director of the Foreign Ministry), and Samuel Medrano (Ministry of the Interior) as examples of the group's power; see "El Opus Dei, aquí y ahóra," *Análisis* (Buenos Aires) (February 6, 1967): 16–20. As mentioned, *Inédito* also reported regularly on these organizations. See "Próximas novedades"; "Opus Dei/Ateneo."

187 "Tucumán: reino del cursillismo," *Primera Plana* (February 4, 1969): 1.

188 Similitud de organismos, AGA, box 42/08972.

189 According to historian Daniel James, the regime's determination to control the unions meant a "weakened and divided union movement," torn between pragmatism and calls for aggressive opposition. Once the situation in Córdoba escalated, the Peronist unions joined the mobilization; see James, *Resistance and Integration*, 220–3.

190 Córdoba was only one of several uprisings, which included the Ocampazo (April 1969), Correntinazo (May 1969), First Rosariazo (May 1969), the Salteñazo (May 1969), the first Tucumanazo (May 1969), the Second Rosariazo (September 1969), and the Cipolletazo (September–October 1969). For more on this, see Emilio Ariel Crenzel, *El Tucumanazo* (Tucumán: Universidad Nacional de Tucumán, 1997); Riz, *La política en suspenso*, 67–80; Beba Balvé, *El '69 huelga política de masas. Rosariazo, cordobazo, rosariazo* (Buenos Aires: Editorial Contrapunto, 1989).

191 "La subversión argentina," AGA, box 42/08972.

192 "Balance de tres años," *Cuadernos del Sur* 60 (July 1969): 531–3.

193 Pérez Guilhou stated that this reform, also known as the "White Book," might serve as the basis for educational reforms "in other countries in the Spanish-speaking community"; see Dardo Pérez Guilhou, oral history with Robert Potash, 1984, Robert Potash Papers, 8–9, 29; see also "Llega el ministro argentino de cultura y educación," *ABC Madrid* (January 27, 1970): 27.

194 Onganía, oral history with Potash, 25.

195 Potash, *The Army & Politics in Argentina*, 298–300.

CHAPTER 4

1 Marcelo Casals Araya, *La creación de la amenaza roja: del surgimiento del anticomunismo en Chile a la "campaña del terror" de 1964* (Santiago, Chile: LOM Ediciones, 2016).

2 Chile's acute social inequalities and polarization date back to the end of the nineteenth century. Brian Loveman's seminal work on land distribution in Chile has linked Chile's authoritarian turn with this social crisis; see Brian Loveman, *Struggle in the Countryside: Politics and Rural Labor in Chile, 1919–1973* (Bloomington: Indiana University Press, 1976).
3 This connection was debated openly on opposition platforms in the late 1970s; see for example Miguel Rojas-Mix, "El hispanismo: Ideología de la dictadura en Hispanoamérica," *Araucaria de Chile* 2 (1978): 47. On Pinochet's Francoist inspirations, see Isabel Jara Hinojosa, *De Franco a Pinochet: el proyecto cultural franquista en Chile 1936–1980* (Santiago, Chile: Universidad de Chile, 2006); Isabel Jara Hinojosa, "La ideología franquista en la legitimación de la dictadura militar chilena," *Revista Complutense de Historia de* América 34 (2008): 233–53; Kirsten Weld, "The Spanish Civil War and the Construction of a Reactionary Historical Consciousness in Augusto Pinochet's Chile," *Hispanic American Historical Review* 98:1 (2018): 77–115.
4 "Meeting with President of Chile at 15:25, September 15, 1970. Present: John Mitchell and Henry Kissinger," National Archives, RG 59, Chile–ITT–CIA 1963–1977, Lot 81D121, Chile ITT.
5 For an overview of the Chilean right in a broad perspective, see Sofía Correa, *Con las riendas del pode: la derecha chilena en el siglo XX* (Santiago, Chile: Editorial Sudamericana, 2005); Luis Roniger and Mario Sznajder. *The Legacy of Human-Rights Violations in the Southern Cone: Argentina, Chile, and Uruguay* (New York: Oxford University Press, 1999).
6 Arnello Romo's thesis was tellingly titled "El sindicato español."
7 Ramón Callís, *La revolución del hombre* (Santiago, Chile: Publicaciones Bandera Negra, 1955): 5.
8 Editorial, *Bandera Negra* (September 14, 1954): 1.
9 From Alfredo Sánchez Bella to José María Alavares Romero, June 17, 1966, AGUN, doc. 15/35/174.
10 Speaking at the Ateneo de Madrid he stressed that "there is no need to worry about population explosion," because of the "law of natural self-regulation"; see Jorge Iván Hübner, "El falso catastrofismo," *El Mercurio* (March 3, 1967); see also "Visita del jefe del estado una comisión del arma de artillería," *ABC Madrid* (October 22, 1964); "Hübner Gallo en el Ateneo," *ABC Madrid* (October 26, 1966).
11 "El plan de desarrollo español da primacía a la empresa privada: declaraciones exclusivas para El Mercurio del ministro español Laureano López Rodó," *El Mercurio* (August 14, 1966).
12 *El Diario Ilustrado* (August 12, 1966); see also "Reseña de la rueda de prensa celebrada en la embajada de España," August 11, 1966, AGUN, box 005/480.
13 "El crepúsculo de las ideologías."
14 Sergio Fernández Larraín to Gonzalo Fernández de la Mora, January 22, 1968, Epistolario Fernández de la Mora, Correspondencias con Sergio Fernández Larraín, *Razón Española* 142 (2007): 129.
15 Jaime Guzmán to Carmen Errazuriz, March 10, 1962, in Rosario Guzmán, *Mi hermano Jaime,* (Santiago, Chile: Editorial VER, 1991), 79–80.

16 "Viva Franco, Arriba España!" *La Revista Escolar: Colegio de los Sagrados Corazones* 436 (I trimester, 1962): 17.

17 "El derecho de propiedad y el proyecto de reforma constitucional," *Fiducia* 13 (November 1964): 12; see also "Relaciones diplomáticas con los países comunistas," *Fiducia* 13 (November 1964): 9.

18 "El capitalismo y los católicos de tercera posición," *Fiducia* 20 (October 1965): 9.

19 Jaime Guzmán Errázuriz. "Don Jaime Eyzaguirre: Maestro, ejemplo y amigo," *Política, Economía, Cultura* 297 (September 6, 1968): 26.

20 For more on this early stage of Guzmán's carree, see José Manuel Castro, *Jaime Guzmán. Ideas y politica 1946–1973* (Santiago, Chile: Ediciones Centro de Estudios Bicentenario, 2016); Belén Moncada Durruti, *Jaime Guzmán: una democracia contrarevolucionaria: el político de 1964 a 1980* (Santiago, Chile: RiL editores); Cristián Gazmuri, *Quién era Jaime Guzmán?* (Santiago, Chile: RiL editores, 2013); Renato Cristi, *El pensamiento político de Jaime Guzmán: autoridad y libertad* (Santiago, Chile: LOM Ediciones, 2000).

21 "A la escuela de derecho: declaration de principios del movimiento gremial," Fundación Jaime Guzmán, GRE.00.01.08.

22 "Discurso a nombre de alumnos nuevos Facultad de Derecho, ceremonia de inauguración del año académico de 1969, la Facultad de Derecho," Fundación Jaime Guzmán. As Castro has noticed, the sentence "la vida no vale la pena si no es para quemarla al servicio de una empresa grande" is a direct quotation from Primo de Rivera's speech on February 25, 1934, in Carpio de Tajo; see Castro, *Jaime Guzmán: ideas y política*, 105; see also José Antonio Primo de Rivera, *Textos de doctrina política* (Madrid: Sección Femenina de la FET, 1971), 176.

23 Jaime Guzmán, "El derecho de propiedad y el proyecto de reforma constitucional," *Fiducia* 13 (November 1964): 9; see also Jaime Guzmán, *Escritos personales* (Santiago, Chile: Zig-Zag, 1992), 153.

24 "Discurso a nombre de alumnos nuevos Facultad de Derecho," Fundación Jaime Guzmán.

25 Jaime Guzmán, "El miedo, síntoma de la realidad político-social chilena," *Portada* 2 (1969): 5–7, 14.

26 "Subdesarrollo espiritual," *Finis Terrae* 49 (May–June 1965): 2–5; see also "Universidad y profesión," *Finis Terrae* 45 (September–October 1964): 3–4; "Iglesia y divorcio," *Finis Terrae* 44 (July–August, 1964): 5–7.

27 "El demonio es una verdad incómoda," *Qué Pasa* 153 (March 29, 1974): 18–19; see also "El marxismo ateísmo en forma de religión," *El Mercurio* (April 7, 1974); "Utopía del tercer milenio," *Ercilla* (July 16, 1980); "Teología de la liberación traiciona la causa de pobre," *La Tercera* (July 30, 1985). Some of Ibáñez Langlois's texts were published in Spain, in Jesus Urteaga's *Mundo Cristiano* booklet series; see José Miguel Ibáñez Langlois, *Marxismo y cristianismo* (Madrid: Mundo Cristiano, 1974).

28 "La píldora de la discordia," *Eva* 1250 (April, 11, 1969): 30–5; "¿Qué es lo que cambia con la píldora?" *Eva* 1383 (November 26, 1971): 30–3; "Hasta que la muerte nos separa?" *Eva* 1278 (October 24, 1969): 96–7; "La fidelidad," *Eva* 1239 (January 24, 1969): 76–9; María Elena Aguirre, "A propósito

de fidelidad," *Eva* 1243 (February 21, 1969): 18; "Eva opina: la juventud y sus dioses," *Eva* 1227 (November 7, 1968): 9–11.

29 "Educación sexual," *Eva* (April 17, 1970): 31.

30 "1968, la mujer busca su destino," *Eva* 1234 (December 20, 1968): 55–7.

31 "Es usted una mujer acomplejada?" *Eva* 1223 (September 19, 1968): 26–32. See also "Soy sentimental?" *Eva* 1269 (August 22, 1969): 16; "1969: doce meses para ser feliz," *Eva* 1235 (December 27, 1968): 56–62.

32 "Por qué soy líder," *Eva* 1236 (January 3, 1969): 84–96; see also Ignacio Vicuña, "Honorosa Hippilancia?" *Eva* 1296 (February 27, 1970); "Londres: furibunda rebelión anti-hippie," *Eva* 1300 (March 27, 1970): 24–7.

33 Gloria Urgelles, "Lesbianismo: un mal solo para discretas," *Eva* 1380 (November 5, 1971): 33.

34 "Respuesta al R. P. José Miguel Ibáñez Langlois," *Fiducia* 22 (February–March 1966): 9–11; see also "Fiducia y los pecados del mundo," *Portada* 7 (1969): 27.

35 Gonzalo Vial Correa, "Actualidad de Jaime Eyzaguirre," *Portada* 7 (1969): 33–5.

36 For more on the Vial Correa family, see Mönckeberg, *El imperio del Opus Dei en Chile*, 215.

37 Gonzalo Vial Correa, *Pinochet: la biografía* (Santiago, Chile: Aguilar, 2002), 394.

38 Fernando Orrego, "El Opus Dei y la política," *Portada* 9 (1970): 30.

39 "Falleció destacado historiador Javier González Echenique," *La Segunda* (August 18, 2004): 4.

40 "Nacionalismo y estatismo," *Portada* 6 (1969): 7.

41 "El miedo. Síntoma de la realidad político-social chilena," *Portada* 2 (1969): 14.

42 "Crisis de autoridad," *Portada* 5 (1969).

43 "Desorden social y crisis politica," *Portada* 9 (1970): 6.

44 On Allende's program, see Harmer, *Allende's Chile and the Inter-American Cold War*, 107–49; Angela Vergara, *Copper Workers, International Business, and Domestic Politics in Cold War Chile* (University Park, PA: Penn State University Press, 2010), 155–78; Víctor Farías, *La izquierda chilena (1969–1973): documentos para el estudio de su línea estratégica* (Berlin: Wissenschaftlicher Verlag, 2000).

45 "Argentina en busca de una salida" *Que Pasa* 2 (April 29, 1971): 9.

46 Gonzalo Vial Correa, "Alessandri y alessandrismo," *Portada* 10 (1970): 2.

47 Prat, to whom Vial Correa served as a personal secretary, died in 1971, while Allesandri would return to serve Pinochet's regime in the late 1970s. For more on the Alessandri decline, see Patricia Arancibia, Alvaro Góngora, and Gonzalo Vial, *Jorge Alessandri 1896–1986. Una biografía* (Santiago, Chile: Zig-Zag, 1996).

48 J. Servando Balaguer, "La Falange y hispanoamerica," *Fuerza Nueva* 419 (January 18, 1975): 29.

49 "Carta a los militares de España," *Patria y Libertad* 28 (1971): 9; see also "Datos biográficos de don Sergio Miranda Carrington," *Avanzada* 52 (1988): 7.

50 "El peso de la purpura"; "Hipócriticas"; "Como cayo Portugal," in *Tizona* 53 (April 1974). Blas Piñar also had Widow in his journal *Fuerza Nueva*; see Juan Antonio Widow, "El comunismo y los católicos," *Fuerza Nueva* 17 (May 6, 1967): 26.
51 *Covert Action in Chile 1963–1973: Senate Select Committee on Intelligence Activities*, www.archives.gov/files/declassification/iscap/pdf/2010-009-doc17.pdf.
52 Manuel Fuentes Wendling, *Memorias secretas de Patria y Libertad: y algunas confesiones sobre la guerra fría en Chile* (Santiago, Chile: Grijalbo SA, 1999), 9.
53 "Ideas nacionalistas chilenas," *Portada* 29 (March 1971): 12.
54 "La oposición: temperaturas distintas y armas a elegir," *Qué Pasa* 36 (December 23, 1971): 1; "El futuro de la oposición," *Qué Pasa* 54 (April 27, 1972): 5.
55 On this person, see Mönckeberg, *El imperio del Opus Dei en Chile*, 264; see also Diego Ibáñez Langlois, *Sentido común y educación en la familia* (Santiago, Chile: Universidad Católica de Chile, 1989).
56 "¿Que somos?" *Qué Pasa* 100 (March 15, 1973): 5.
57 CIA Intelligence Information Special Report, enclosure, Memorandum, Thomas Karamessines, Deputy Director of Plans to DCI Helms, "Cuban Disappointment with the Chilean Experiment," May 31, 1972, CREST/NARA; see also Harmer, *Allende's Chile*, 109.
58 Margaret Power, *Right-Wing Women in Chile: Feminine Power and the Struggle Against Allende, 1964–1973*. (University Park, PA: Penn State University Press, 2002), 153.
59 "Poder y violencia al límite," *Qué Pasa* 34 (December 9, 1971): 7–8.
60 "Como nació el símbolo de la cacerola," *Qué Pasa* 33 (December 2, 1971): 8.
61 Teresa Donoso Loero, *La epopeya de las ollas vacías* (Santiago, Chile: Gabriela Mistral, 1974).
62 "El fenómeno gremialista," *Portada* 22 (June 1971): 17–18.
63 "Jaime Guzmán y el desafío gremial," *Qué Pasa* 80 (October 26, 1972): 38.
64 Sergio Silva Bascuñán to Jaime Guzmán, February 10, 1972, Fundación Jaime Guzmán; see also "Conclave golpista!" *Puro Chile* (March 5, 1972); "Gobierno: 'Reunion de Chinigue es sediciosa,'" *El Siglo* (March 7, 1972).
65 Patricia Arancibia, *Conversando con Roberto Kelly* (Santiago, Chile: Biblioteca Americana, 2005), 128–9.
66 "La vía chilena al archivo," *Qué Pasa* 99 (March 1973): 7.
67 Editorial, "El irreversible camino a la Sociedad socialista," *Portada* 38 (April 1973): 7.
68 Editorial, *Portada* 41 (June 1973): 32–6.
69 "Parálisis Suicida," *Portada* 40 (June 1973): 5.
70 Jaime Guzmán to his mother, May 15, 1973, in Guzmán, *Escritos personales*, 72.
71 Jaime Guzmán to his mother, August 29, 1973, ibid., 81–4.
72 Jaime Guzmán to his mother, October 15, 1973, ibid., 86–9.
73 *Covert Action in Chile 1963–1973: Senate Select Committee on Intelligence Activities*, www.archives.gov/files/declassification/iscap/pdf/2010-009-doc17.pdf.

74 Historians Thomas Davis and Brian Loveman have already laid the initial foundations for the debate over the "antipolitics" legacies of Latin America's militaries wherein the case of Chile looms large; see Thomas Davies and Brian Loveman, *The Politics of Antipolitics: The Military in Latin America* (Lincoln: University of Nebraska Press, 1978).
75 James R. Whelan, *Desde las cenizas: vida, muerte y transfiguración de la democracia en Chile, 1833–1988* (Santiago, Chile: Zig-Zag, 1993), 450.
76 *Informe sobre calificación de victimas de derechos humanos y de violencia política* (Santiago, Chile: Corporación Nacional de Reperación y reconciliación, 1996), Table 20. These included *El Siglo, La Nación, Puro Chile, Ultima Hora, El Rebelde, Chile Hoy, Clarín, De Frente, Ramona, Punto Final, La Quinta Rueda,* and *Paloma.*
77 Law Decree No. 1, Santiago, Chile, September 11, 1973.
78 Jaime Guzmán to his mother, October 15, 1973, in Guzmán, *Escritos personales*, 86.
79 *Actas oficiales de la comisión constituyente,* Sesión 68, 23.
80 "El R.P. Osvaldo Lira declaró: 'el Gobierno tiene legitimidad de origen y de ejercicio," *El Mercurio* (September 23, 1973).
81 "Gremialistas explicarán al mundo la realidad de lo sucedido en Chile," *El Mercurio* (September 17, 1973): 1.
82 "11 de septiembre," *Qué Pasa* 126 (November 20, 1973), edición especial.
83 "No hay vuelta atrás," *Qué Pasa* 128 (October 4, 1973): 5.
84 *La junta de gobierno frente a la juridicidad de los derechos humanos: discurso pronunciado por el General Leigh, el 29 de abril de 1974, en la universidad católica de Chile* (Santiago, Chile: Gabriela Mistral, 1974).
85 The regime even recognized *Eva* for the "courageous attitude it showed during the three years of Marxist government"; see "A próposito de restauración," *Eva* (December 5, 1973): 4.
86 "El General Pinochet recibe a Qué Pasa," *Qué Pasa* 127 (September 27, 1973): 7; see also "En la familia Pinochet, el mando esta compartido," *Eva* 1484 (September 2, 1974): 86–7.
87 Acta Secreta no. 1, Junta Militar, September, 13 1973. Biblioteca del Congreso Nacional de Chile. https://obtienearchivo.bcn.cl/obtienearchivo?id=recursoslegales/10221.3/34263/1/acta1_1973.pdf.
88 "El viejo gobierno: 24 horas finales," *Qué Pasa* 126 (November 20, 1973) edición especial.
89 Jaime Guzmán to his mother, October 15, 1973, in Guzmán, *Escritos personales*, 88.
90 Ibid., 91.
91 *The White Book of the Change of Government in Chile* (Santiago, Chile: Secretariat-General of the Government, 1973), 71.
92 These included, for instance, Hernán Millás and Emilio Filippi, *Chile 70–73: crónica da una experiencia* (Santiago, Chile: Zig-Zag, 1974); Hernán Millás and Emilio Filippi, *Anatomía de un fracaso: la experiencia socialista chilena* (Santiago, Chile: Zig-Zag, 1974); Teresa Donoso Loero, *Breve historia de la Unidad Popular: documento de El Mercurio* (Santiago, Chile: El Mercurio, 1974).

93 *Documental Chile: Orden, Trabajo, Obediencia* (1977), directors: André Gazut and Claude Smadja, at https://vimeo.com/40748738; www.youtube.com/watch?v = VgwQ_kKGNWs.
94 "11 de septiembre," *Qué Pasa* 126 (November 20, 1973), special edition.
95 "La búsqueda de una nueva institucionalidad," *Portada* 42 (September–October 1973), 3–5.
96 "El Comite Asosor de la Junta," *Qué Pasa* 136 (November 30, 1973).
97 Manuel Fuentes Wendling, *Memorias secretas de Patria y Libertad: y algunas confesiones sobre la guerra fría en Chile* (Santiago, Chile: Editorial Grijalbo SA, 1999), 29.
98 "Documento 5304," November 28, 1973, AMCAE, Embajada en Madrid, oficios confidenciales, 1973, box 64.
99 Carlos Huneeus, *The Pinochet Regime* (Boulder, CO: Lynne Rienner Publishers, 2007), 1–30.
100 Samuel Moyn, *The Last Utopia: Human Rights in History* (Cambridge, MA: Harvard University Press, 2010), 140–4.
101 Patrick Kelly, *Sovereign Emergencies: Latin America and the Making of Global Human Rights Politics* (Cambridge: Cambridge University Press, 2018), 134–66; see also Klaas Dykmann, *Philanthropic Endeavors or the Exploitation of an Ideal? The Human Rights Policy of the Organization of American States in Latin America (1970–1991)* (Frankfurt am Main: Vervuert, 2004), 197ff.
102 *A seis meses de la liberación nacional: mensaje al país del presidente de la justa de gobierno General Don Augusto Pinochet Ugarte pronunciado al día 11 de marzo 1974* (Santiago, Chile: Gabriela Mistral, 1974), 25.
103 In a letter to his mother, Guzmán wrote: "I collaborate in a commission destined to write a new Constitution, and also in the organization of propaganda and of youth, in the General Secretariat of Government"; see Jaime Guzmán to his mother, October 15, 1973, in Guzmán, *Escritos personales*, 91.
104 Arturo Fontaine Aldunate, *Los economistas y el presidente Pinochet* (Santiago, Chile: Zig-Zag, 1988), 103–4.
105 *Declaration of Principles of the Chilean Government* (Santiago, Chile: Government of Chile, 1974), 30.
106 Álvaro d'Ors, "Autoridad y potestad," *Portada* 44 (February 1974): 44–8.
107 "La búsqueda de una nueva institucionalidad," *Portada* 42 (September–October, 1973): 3–5.
108 *Declaration of Principles of the Chilean Government*, 33.
109 Rojas-Mix, "El hispanismo: ideología de la dictadura en Hispanoamérica," 47.
110 *Departamento Cultural de la Secretaría General de Gobierno* (Santiago, Chile: Gabriela Mistral, 1974), 39.
111 Enrique Campos Menéndez (ed.), *Pensamiento nacionalista* (Santiago, Chile: Gabriela Mistral, 1974), 9.
112 Ibid., 8–10.
113 "Septiembre 12, carta del presidente de Chile, Augusto Pinochet," FNFF, doc. 21953.

114 See for instance Pedro Carlos González Cuevas, "La hispanidad tecnocrática: Gonzalo Fernández de la Mora en Iberoamérica," in Cañellas Mas, *La tecnocracia hispánica*, 105–34.

115 Gonzalo Fernández de la Mora, *Rio arriba* (Barcelona: Planeta, 1995), 232.

116 By inviting Pegaso to produce trucks in Chile, Allende wanted to assuage the damage caused by the exit of Ford from the country in 1971. Moreover, in March 1971, Spain's Foreign Minister Gregorio López Bravo met with Allende and signed a treaty on "touristic cooperation" between the countries; see "Convenio de cooperación en la esfera turística entre Chile y España," March 26, 1971, AGA, box 42/08982.

117 Two examples were Ignacio Gayango's book *Chile: el largo camino al golpe* (Barcelona: Editoral Dirosa, 1974) and Hernán Antonio Valdés's *Tejas Verde: diario de un campo de concentración en Chile* (Esplugues de Llobregat: Editorial Ariel, 1974). On how the Chilean embassy reacted to these publications see "Estrictamente confidencial, 1129/92," AMCAE, Embajada en Madrid, oficios confidenciales, 1974, box 70; "Reservado, 1378/5," September 17 1974, AMCAE, Embajada en Madrid, oficios confidenciales, 1974, box 70.

118 "Da asco!" *Fuerza Nueva* (November 3, 1973).

119 Álvaro d'Ors, "Tres breves reflexiones sobre la crisis chilena," *Fuerza Nueva* 372 (February 23, 1974): 6–7.

120 "Confidencial 363/11," March 12, 1974, AMCAE, Embajada en Madrid, oficios confidenciales, 1974, box 71.

121 In November 1973, the ambassador reported that his operation in Madrid had "silenced numerous attacks"; see "Oficio confidencial no. 1764/212 del embajador chileno Francisco Goigoitía al Ministro de Asuntos Exteriores," November 27, 1973, AMCAE, Embajada en Madrid, oficios confidenciales, 1973, box 63.

122 "Espana cambia politica latinoamericana," *Que Pasa* 128 (October 4, 1973): 47.

123 From Óscar Herrera Palacios to Alfredo Sánchez Bella, 19/12/1973, AGUN, doc. 15/61/495.

124 From Óscar Herrera Palacios to Alfredo Sánchez Bella, October 10, 1975, AGUN, doc. 15/61/497.

125 "Confidencial 1690/207," December 10, 1973, AMCAE, Embajada en Madrid, oficios confidenciales, 1973, box 65.

126 "Confidencial, 981/81, visita a Madrid de oficial relacionado púbico de carabineros de Chile," July 1, 1974, AMCAE, Embajada en Madrid, oficios confidenciales, box 70.

127 "Reservado, no. 14/3," January 2, 1976, AMCAE, Embajada en Madrid, oficios confidenciales, 1976, box 1.

128 "Reservado, no. 1458/179, Informe sobre viaje a España del secretario nacional de los Gremios de Chile," November 19, 1976, AMCAE, Embajada en Madrid, oficios confidenciales, 1976, box 1.

129 "Reservado, 1944/170, Informe sobre la visita a España de la Sra. Carmen Grez, secretaria nacional de la mujer," December 12 1975, AMCAE, Embajada en Madrid, oficios confidenciales, 1975, box 76.

130 Ascanio Cavallo, *La historia oculta del régimen militar* (Santiago, Chile: La Epoca, 1988), 94.

131 Allegedly, it was the USA and Ford Company that pressed Pinochet to decline the deal, which he initially did, later to return to the negotiating table with Spain in 1975; see José Manuel Azcona Pastor, *Emigración y relaciones bilaterales España-Chile. 1810–2015* (Madrid: Dykinson, 2016), 190. See also "La junta militar chilena cancela el acuerdo con Pegaso: la decisión está motivada por presiones de las grandes companias norteamericanos," *Ya* (May 22, 1974); "Éxito diplomático fue gira de Merino," *Qué Pasa* 197 (January 30, 1975): 10–11.

132 "Secreto, no. 7," December 18, 1975, AMCAE, Embajada en Madrid, oficios confidenciales, 1975, box 76.

133 "Duelo oficial en Chile por tres días," *El Mercurio* (November 21, 1975): 3.

134 A scene that has recently been portrayed fully by historian Kirsten Weld; see Weld, "The Spanish Civil War and the Construction of a Reactionary Historical Consciousness in Augusto Pinochet's Chile," 106.

135 Prince Juan Carlos I was not eager to be identified with the Chilean dictator and rejected the Chilean ambassador's invitation to visit Chile, arguing that "his international tours are regulated by the Ministry of Foreign Affairs and ultimately by General Franco"; see "Secreto, no. 3, Visita príncipe de España a Chile," July 2, 1975, AMCAE, Embajada en Madrid, oficios confidenciales, 1975, box 76.

136 "Franco: sus lecciones para Chile," *Qué Pasa* 240 (November 27, 1975): 5.

137 "Situación Española en 1939 era similar a chilena de hoy," *El Mercurio* (August 12, 1975).

138 "Gonzalo Fernández de la Mora: un apasionado de la razón," *Qué Pasa* 226 (August 21, 1975): 16–19.

139 "Del autor de Camino a los chilenos," *Qué Pasa* 168 (July 12, 1974): 13.

140 "El Comite Asosor de la Junta," *Que Pasa* 136 (November 30, 1973): 8–9.

141 For years ODEPLAN was under the direction of the Gremialista Miguel Kast. Its "regionalization" plans were already designed in the 1960s and returned to become the center of Pinochet's policies; see El Federico Arenas, "El Chile de las regiones: una historia inconclusa," *Estudios Geográficos* 70:266 (January–June, 2009): 11–39; see also Verónica Valdivia, *La alcaldización de la política: los municipios en la dictadura pinochetista* (Santiago, Chile: LOM Ediciones, 2012).

142 Joaquín Lavín, *Chile: revolución silenciosa* (Santiago, Chile: Zig-Zag, 1987), 61.

143 "El modelo chileno," *Qué Pasa* 129 (October 11, 1973): 20–1.

144 *"El Ladrillo": bases de la política económica del gobierno militar chileno* (Santiago, Chile: Centro de Estudios Públicos, 1992), 70.

145 Marcus Taylor, *From Pinochet to the 'Third Way': Neoliberalism and Social Transformation in Chile* (Ann Arbor, MI: Pluto Press, 2006), 1.

146 Milton Friedman to Hernán Cubillos, June 2, 1992, Hernán Cubillos Sallato Papers, Hoover Institution Archives, box 1.

147 "Los Chicago Boys: De Castro enfrenta la criticas," *Qué Pasa* 214 (May 29, 1975): 10–12.

148 Milton Friedman, "Medidas graves para una grave enfermedad," *Qué Pasa* 206 (April 3, 1975): 52.

149 Guzmán hosted Hayek during his visit to Chile in 1975; see Bruce Caldwell and Leonidas Montes, "Friedrich Hayek and his visits to Chile," *The Review of Austrian Economics* 28:3 (2015): 261–309; see also "Crisis in Chile," *Crisis Magazine* (June 1, 1983), at www.crisismagazine.com/1983/crisis-in-chile.
150 *"El Ladrillo,"* 52–4; for more on the Chilean capitalist turn and its ramifications, see Manuel Gárate Chateau, *La Revolución capitalista de Chile: (1973–2003)* (Santiago, Chile: Ediciones Universidad Alberto Hurtado, 2012).
151 IMF, "Chile: History of Lending Commitments as of January 31, 2019," www.imf.org/external/np/fin/tad/extarr2.aspx?memberkey1 = 170& date1Key = 2019-01-31
152 They worked "without friction," stated Sergio Fernández; see Sergio Fernández Fernández, *Mi lucha por la democracia* (Santiago, Chile: Editorial los Andes, 1994), 136.
153 Fontaine Aldunate, *Los economistas y el presidente Pinochet*, 84.
154 "Coronel Orlando Jerez: hacía un chileno con nueva mentalidad," *Qué Pasa* 202 (March 6, 1975): 18–19.
155 "El general Pinochet y el futuro de Chile," *Qué Pasa* 193 (January 2, 1975): 55–8.
156 *El General Pinochet se reúne con la juventud: textos de los discursos pronunciados en el primer aniversario de la Secretaria Nacional de la Juventud* (Santiago, Chile: Gabriela Mistral), 8.
157 This apparatus was also at the heart of recent revelations regarding Pinochet's fraud; see "La Justicia arrincona a la viuda de Pinochet," *El País* (December 10, 2016); "Pinochet's widow under investigation on suspicion of swindling millions," *The Guardian* (August 19, 2016).
158 *Sí a Chile* (Santiago, Chile: Secretaria Nacional de la Mujer, 1975), 5.
159 *Mensaje a la mujer chilena: texto del discurso pronunciado por el presidente de la Junta de Gobierno, General Augusto Pinochet, en al acto organizado por la Secretaria Nacional de la mujer, April 24, 1974* (Santiago, Chile: Gabriela Mistral, 1974), 6–7.
160 "Y ahora qué?: responde Carla Scassi de Lehmann, presidenta de la Secretaria de la Mujer," *Eva* (I quincena de Enero, 1975): 80.
161 Nuestras femenistas," *Qué Pasa* 208 (April 17, 1975): 34.
162 "Profesión: simple dueña de casa," *Qué Pasa* 149 (December 4, 1974): 8–13.
163 Or in Aguirre's words, "one has to be very little a woman, not to have an instinct to save the life of a child," in "Nuestras femenistas," 35.
164 *Valores patrios y valores familiares* (Santiago, Chile: Secretaria de la mujer, 1982), 22; see also "La participación de la mujer," *Amiga* 17 (June 1977): 3.
165 See for example "Trabajos prohibidos a las mujeres," *Eva* (April 24, 1974): 5.
166 "Y ahora qué?" 80. Tellingly, some of these publications promoted "household education," with its publications issuing guidelines for house cleaning; see for instance "Vital para toda la familia: normas básicas para una dueña de casa," *Amiga* 10 (November 1976): 39–40; "Su trabajo es trabajo," *Amiga* (June 1976): 33–4.
167 "Vanguardia de un nuevo renacer," *Juventud* 12 (April 1976).
168 "La juventud trabaja por Chile," *Juventud* 5 (August 16, 1977): 16–17; "Sorprendente: un loco escribe a un diario loco," *Diario Loco: diario*

quincenal de la juventud 1 (1980): 1; "La mística juvenil nace del trabajo responsable," *Revista Araucania* 1 (1982). According to Mönckeberg, Opus Dei was influential within the Women and Youth Secretariats; see Mönckeberg, *El imperio del Opus Dei en Chile*, 210. For more on *La Pandilla*, see Francisco Soto, *Fascismo y Opus Dei en Chile: estudios de literatura e ideología* (Barcelona: Avance, 1976), 157–260.

169 "Proclama de la juventud," *Secretaria Nacional de la Juventud: Boletín Informativo* 6 (August 1, 1975). Zegers was an ICH member; see *El Instituto Chileno de Cultura Hispánica, Memoria de actividades 1967*, 1. See also "Cristián Valdés Zegers: la juventud, principios valores y estilo," *Qué Pasa* 202 (March 6, 1975): 36–9.

Jaime Guzmán, "Chile en 1985: la vida politica," *Qué Pasa* 193 (January 2, 1975): 41–3.

170 On the history of this spectacle, see Felipe Reyes and Guido Arroyo, *Chacarillas: los elegidos de Pinochet.* (Santiago, Chile: Editorial Alquimia, 2019); see also Yanko González, *Los más ordenaditos: fascismo y juventud en la dictadura de Pinochet* (Santiago, Chile: Hueders, 2020).

171 Jaime Guzmán, "Chile en 1985: la vida politica," *Qué Pasa* 193 (January 2, 1975): 41–3.

172 Ricardo Cox, "Chile ante la crisis democrática de occidente," *Portada* 47 (November 1975): 31.

173 "Jaime Guzmán habla del frente juvenil," *Qué Pasa* 281 (September 9, 1976): 9; on the Gremialistas' activities in these years, see Huneeus, *The Pinochet Regime*, 225–70.

174 Robert Moss, "La tribulacion de Chile," *Portada* 46 (March 1976): 12–15.

175 This series of eight lectures before the military authorities even made it to an edited volume; see José Miguel Ibáñez Langlois, *Marxismo: religión al revés, síntesis de las ocho conferencias desarrolladas por el sacerdote José Miguel Ibáñez Langlois ante las autoridades de Gobierno* (Santiago, Chile: División de Comunicación Social, 1982).

176 "P. José Miguel Ibáñez, vocación: Opus Dei," *Qué Pasa* 286 (October 14, 1976): 22.

177 "Decreto Ley N.° 1.319," January 9, 1976.

178 *Documental Chile: Orden, Trabajo, Obediencia.*

179 *Mensaje Presidencial: 11 septiembre 1975 – 11 septiembre 1976 – S.E. el Presidente de la República General de Ejército Augusto Pinochet Ugarte informa al país* (Santiago, Chile: Presidencia de la Nación,) 29.

180 Weld, "The Spanish Civil War and the Construction of a Reactionary Historical Consciousness in Augusto Pinochet's Chile," 81.

CHAPTER 5

1 Samuel Moyn, *The Last Utopia* (Cambridge, MA: Harvard University Press, 2010).

2 Alejandro A Lanusse, *Confesiones de un general* (Buenos Aires: Planeta, 1994), 258.

3 Dardo Pérez Guilhou, oral history with Robert A. Potash, 1984, Robert A. Potash Papers, Special Collections, University Archives Umass Amherst, 25.
4 Alejandro A. Lanusse, oral history with Robert A. Potash, December 15, 1983, Robert A. Potash Papers, Special Collections, University Archives Umass Amherst.
5 For more on the differences between the economic policies of Onganía and Levingston, see Rubén M. Perina, *Onganía, Levingston, Lanusse: los militares en la política Argentina* (Buenos Aires: Editorial de Belgrano, 1983), 121–31.
6 *Plan de desarrollo de la Republica Argentina, 1970–1974* (Buenos Aires: Presidencia de la Nación), 6–7.
7 Jorge Pérez Rocco, "Opus Dei: ¿Santa mafia o masonería tecnócrata?" *Inédito* 80 (October 1970): 18–19; "Opus Dei: ¿Santa mafia o masonería tecnócrata?" *Inédito* 81 (November 1970): 22–6; Gregorio Selser, "Adela: un pulpo con nombre de mujer," *Inédito* 74 (April 1970): 19–21.
8 "El Opus Dei sobre la educación argentina," *Inédito* 82 (December 1970): 28; "Opus Dei, el poder invisible," *Confirmado* (November 26, 1969): 76; "Los secretos del Opus Dei," *Confirmado* (January 21, 1971): 54–7; Silvia Rundi, "La trayectoria del Opus Dei, I–IV," *La Opinion* (December 14–17, 1971).
9 José María Alfaro to Alfredo Sánchez Bella, June 17, 1970, AGUN, doc. 15/35/33.
10 "The President told me," López Rodó recalled, that Frondizi had advised him to emulate the Peruvian revolution's protectionist model, but that he was skeptical whether Peru's model, with its "six million Indians," could serve Argentina. After all, "Argentines are European," Levingston remarked; see Laureano López Rodó, *Memorias III* (Barcelona: Plaza & Janés, 1990), 168.
11 Bernardo Neustadt, "Mi conversación mayor," *Extra* 76 (November 1971): 10.
12 Ibid., 11.
13 For more on the gradual deterioration of the regime during the "Levingston interlude," see Perina, *Onganía, Levingston, Lanusse*, 204–11; Robert A. Potash, *The Army & Politics in Argentina*: From Frondizi's Fall to the Peronist Restoration (Stanford, CA: Stanford University Press, 1996), 289–359.
14 Mario Amadeo to Alfredo Sánchez Bella, August 17, 1970, AGUN, doc. 15/35/296.
15 Mario Amadeo to Alfredo Sánchez Bella, November 19, 1970, AGUN, doc. 15/35/298.
16 Mario Amadeo to Alfredo Sánchez Bella, June 5, 1972, AGUN, doc. 15/35/309.
17 For more on these movements, see Richard Gillespie, *Soldiers of Perón: Argentina's Montoneros* (New York: Oxford University Press, 1982).
18 See for instance Natalio Botana, Rafael Braun, and Carlos A. Floria's editorials in *Criterio*, in *El régimen militar (1966–1973)* (Buenos Aires: Ediciones La Bastilla, 1973).
19 *Operaciones contra la subversión urbana: 0293* (Buenos Aires: Instituto Geográfico Militar, 1969).
20 "La cuarta frustración," *Primera Plana* 229 (May 16, 1967): 20.

21 Jordán B Genta, *Seguridad y desarrollo: reflexiones sobre el terror en la Argentina* (Buenos Aires: Editorial Cultura Argentina, 1970), 25.
22 Alberto Boixadós, *España entre Europa e Hispanoamérica* (Buenos Aires: Areté, 1973), 92.
23 "Destino y legado de José Antonio," *Cabildo* 7 (November 1, 1973): 16.
24 On this murder campaign, see Patricia Marchak and William Marchak, *God's Assassins: State Terrorism in Argentina in the 1970s* (Montreal, QC: McGill-Queen's University Press, 1999).
25 Raúl Jassén even became a *Fuerza Nueva* contributer; see "Fuerza Nueva e Hispanoamérica," *Fuerza Nueva* 419 (January 18, 1975): 29. Romeo stated that, having studied in Madrid, he had become a "Joseantoniano" and even alleged that Perón's ideology stemmed from the Falange; see "La importancia de contar con una prensa nacional," *El Caudillo*, 37 (August 2, 1974): 8–9.
26 From leftists such as Envar El Kadri and Rodolfo Galimberti, to right-wingers José Ignacio Rucci and Norma Kennedy, there was hardly any type of Peronist who did not arrive at Perón's mansion at Puerta de Hierro.
27 López Rega joined Perón in Madrid in July 1965 and was his personal secretary ever afterwards. For more on this person, see Marcelo Larraquy, *López Rega: el peronismo y la Triple A* (Buenos Aires: Punto de Lectura, 2007); Marcelo Larraquy, Katherine Cortés Guerrieri, Guido Bilbao, María José Grillo, and Daniel Guebel, *López Rega: la biografía* (Buenos Aires: Sudamericana, 2004).
28 Isabel de Perón, "Como doctrina económica el Justicialismo realiza la economía social, poniendo el capital al servicio de la economía y está al servicio del bienestar social," *Las Bases* 19 (August 17, 1972): 13–14; Isabel de Perón, "La verdad no. 11: el peronismo anhela la unidad nacional y no la lucha; desea heroes pero no mártires," *Las Bases* 14 (June 6, 1972): 9.
29 José López Rega. "Para la juventud: filosofía del hombre nuevo," *Las Bases* 10 (April 4, 1972): 30–5; José López Rega, "Filosofía del hombre nuevo," *Las Bases* 6 (February 1, 1972): 32–3.
30 Mario Amadeo to Alfredo Sánchez Bella, May 8, 1973, AGUN, doc. 15/35/313.
31 "El nacionalismo argentino: Un futuro sin Falanges," *Carta Política* 16 (2nd week of February 1975): 21.
32 Mario Amadeo to Alfredo Sánchez Bella, May 8, 1973, AGUN, doc. 15/35/313.
33 For more on Lanusse's initiatives, see Perina, *Onganía, Levingston, Lanusse,* 212–14.
34 On the nexus between the two movements, see Federico Finchelstein, *The Ideological Origins of the Dirty War*: Fascism, Populism, and Dictatorship in Twentieth Century Argentina (New York: Oxford University Press, 2014), 116–18.
35 "Oime Barbudo!" *El Caudillo* 2 (November 23, 1973); "Guerra a la oligarquía," *El Caudillo* 30 (June 7, 1974).
36 Felipe Romeo, "Hay que dar la cara," *El Caudillo* 43 (September 13, 1974). This statement has been frequently quoted in the Argentine press ever since; see "Murió Felipe Romeo, vocero de la banda de ultraderecha Triple A,"

Clarín (May 5, 2009); "El órgano oficial de la Triple A y del Brujo," *Pagina 12* (January 7, 2007).

37 Mario Amadeo, *La opción argentina: conferencia pronunciada en el Círculo del Plata el 14 de marzo de* 1974 (Buenos Aires: Ediciones Ateneo de la República, 1974), 6.

38 Mario Amadeo to Alfredo Sánchez Bella, April 1 1974, AGUN, doc. 15/35/318.

39 Mariano Grondona, "Del Peronismo al Lóperreguismo," *Carta Política* 24 (5th week of May 1975): 16.

40 "El nacionalismo argentino: un futuro sin Falanges," *Carta Política* 16 (2nd week of February 1975): 14.

41 "La estructura del poder," *Carta Política* 11 (November 1974): 11.

42 Mario Amadeo to Alfredo Sánchez Bella, January 14, 1976, AGUN, doc. 15/35/322.

43 "Significación religiosa, económica y política del Opus Dei," *Horizonte español* 1 (1966): 225–52; Jesús Ynfante, *La prodigiosa aventura del Opus Dei*: génesis y desarollo de la santa mafia (Paris: Ruedo Ibérico, 1970); Daniel Artigues, *El Opus Dei en España* (Paris: Ruedo Iberico, 1971).

44 "Secreto: febrero 1969, carta de nuestro embajador en la santa Sede, Antonio Garrigues: entrevista con Mons. Escrivá," FNFF, doc. 19244.

45 Alberto Royuela Fernández, "Al juzgado de instrucción," July 30, 1971, AGUN, box 001.021.

46 Ricardo Horcajada, "España Directa y España tecnócrata," *Fuerza Nueva* 228 (May 22, 1971): 26.

47 Blas Piñar, *Combate por España* (Madrid: Fuerza Nueva, 1975), 134.

48 "Blas Piñar, en el eje de una idea," *Fuerza Nueva* 200 (November, 1970): 12.

49 "Una tarea de nuestro tiempo: Comunidad hispánica de naciones," *Fuerza Nueva* 208 (January 2, 1971): 34–7.

50 Juan Vallet de Goytisolo, *Ideología "praxis" y mito de la tecnocracia* (Madrid: Montecorvo, 1971), 63–4; Josep Meliá, *Carta abierta a los tecnócratas* (Madrid: Ediciones 99 SA, 1973).

51 Vallet de Goytisolo, *Ideología "praxis" y mito de la tecnocracia*, 92. Another critique of the technocratic development came from political scientist Manuel García-Pelayo, who asked: "An optimal path invites the question: For what? For whom? In the name of which values?" in Manuel García-Pelayo, *Burocracia y tecnocracia y otros* escritos (Madrid: Alianza Editorial, 1974), 94.

52 Vicente Enrique y Tarancón, *Confeciones* (Madrid: PPC, 1996), 276.

53 López Rodó, *Memorias III*, 85.

54 Ibid., 35–6.

55 The law was the brainchild of CSIC's pedagogues Díez-Hochleitner and Joaquín Tena Artigas. In later years this reform would be presented as key for the democratization of the Spanish population; see "La reforma educativa española y la educación permanente," *Experiencias e inovaciones en educación* 31 (Paris: Unesco, 1977).

56 Some argue that these elections served as an "escape valve" for political pressure; see Cazorla Sánchez, *Fear and Progress*, 5. Others argue that they had a positive

effect on the Spanish democratic culture; see Pamela Beth Radcliff, *Making Democratic Citizens in Spain: Civil Society and the Popular Origins of the Transition, 1960–78* (New York: Palgrave Macmillan, 2011).

57 Negrin, "Un político," *Pueblo* (September 28, 1971); "Todo un político," *Nuevo Diario* (September 29, 1971). The appearance of his books *Politica y desarrollo* and *Nuevo horizonte del desarrollo* led Pérez-Embid to contend that López Rodó "had always, fundamentally, done politics"; see López Rodó, *Memorias III*, 172.

58 "Intervención ante la Comisión de Leyes Fundamentales y Presidencia del Gobierno, de las Cortes Españolas, al iniciarse los debates del III Plan de Desarrollo, Madrid, 14 de marzo de 1972," *Nuevo horizonte del desarrollo*, 10.

59 "Despacho con Franco (desde las 7 hasta las 8 y 10 minutos), Participación, Asociaciones políticas," Epistolario Fernandez de la Mora, Correspondencias con Laureano López Rodó, *Razon Española* 122 (2003): 261; see also López Rodó, *Memorias III*, 367.

60 "Designación del Presidente del Gobierno, Discurso en el Pleno de las Cortes españolas, celebrado el día 20 de julio de 1973," Carrero Blanco, *Discursos y escritos*, 332; for more on this phase in Carrero's political career, see Javier Tusell, *Carrero: la eminencia gris del régimen de Franco* (Madrid: Ediciones Temas de Hoy, 1993); Fernando Vizcaíno Casas, *1973, el año en que volaron a Carrero Blanco* (Barcelona: Planeta, 1993).

61 López Rodó, *Memorias III*, 516–18.

62 Gonzalo Fernández de la Mora, "Carrero," *ABC Madrid* (December 21, 1974): 3.

63 López Rodó, *Memorias III*, 524.

64 "En el futuro, el consenso nacional entorno al régimen habrá de expresarse en forma de participación," *La Vanguardia* (February 13, 1974).

65 For more on this process, see Cristina Palomares, *The Quest for Survival after Franco: Moderate Francoism and the Slow Journey to the Polls, 1964–1977* (Portland, OR: Sussex Academic Press, 2004).

66 "Siempre he sido falangista: entrevista en Viena con López Rodó," *Actualidad Económica* 867 (October 26, 1974): 31–4.

67 Tarancón, *Confeciones*, 696–7.

68 The repercussions of the 1975 military tribunals and executions were considerable, as the international press, the pope, and even the Spanish press condemned the killings; see Walter Schwarz, "Spain Erupts into Fury," *The Guardian* (September 29, 1975); "Mañana, primer aniversario de las últimas penas de muerte ejecutadas en España," *El País* (September 26, 1976); "Las presiones internacionales no pudieron frenar los cinco fusilamientos del 27 de septiembre de 1975," *El País* (September 27, 1985).

69 "Monseñor Escrivá de Balaguer," *El Mercurio* (July 13, 1975), 8.

70 José Zafra Valverde, *Alma y cuerpo del movimiento nacional* (Pamplona: Ediciones Universidad de Navarra, 1975), 111–46; José Zafra Valverde, *Régimen político de España* (Pamplona: Ediciones Universidad de Navarra, 1973); Álvaro d'Ors, "Tres breves reflexiones sobre la crisis chilena," *Fuerza Nueva* 372 (February 23, 1974).

71 Gonzalo Fernández de la Mora, "Franco," *ABC Madrid* (November 21, 1975): 3.
72 Gonzalo Lobo Méndez, "Una llamada a la responsabilidad social," *Mundo Cristiano* 155 (December 1975): 13.
73 Pedro Sáinz Rodrígues, *Testimonios y recuerdos* (Barcelona: Planeta, 1978), 10–11. According to Falangist intellectual Antonio Tovar, "a dictator and a handful of retired generals" had robbed Spain of its identity; see Antonio Tovar, "José Antonio Primo de Rivera y el 18 de Julio," *El País* (July 23, 1980).
74 At least not in his "last message" to the Spanish nation; see "Ultimo mensaje de Franco," *Actualidad Española* 258 (December 1975): 7–8.
75 The agency of the king during the Spanish transition was crucial and has become the topic of numerous historical analyses; see for instance Javier Tusell, *Tiempo de incertidumbre: Carlos Arias Navarro entre el Franquismo y la transición (1973–1976)* (Barcelona: Crítica, 2003); Paul Preston, *The Triumph of Democracy in Spain* (New York: Methuen, 1986); Preston, *Juan Carlos: A People's King* (London: HarperCollins, 2004); Tusell, *Juan Carlos I: La Restauración de la Monarquía* (Madrid: Ediciones Temas de Hoy, 1995).
76 *Ley para la Reforma Política*, 1/1977.
77 Following the January 1977 Atocha murders, see Javier Tusell, *La transición española a la democracia* (Madrid: Historia 16, 1997), 117.
78 *Consensus and peace, Oslo 1980* (Paris: UNESCO), 179.
79 For more on this party and its politics, see Juan Francisco Fuentes, *Adolfo Suárez: biografía política* (Barcelona: Planeta, 2011); José García Abad, *Adolfo Suárez: una tragedia griega* (Madrid: Esfera de los Libros, 2005); Charles T. Powell, *Adolfo Suárez* (Barcelona: Ediciones B, 2004); Gutmaro Gómez Bravo, *Conflicto y consenso en la transición española* (Madrid: Editorial Pablo Iglesias, 2009); Santos Juliá, *Transición: historia de una política española* (1937–2017) (Barcelona: Galaxia Gutenberg, 2017).
80 Fernando Álvarez de Miranda, *Al servicio de la democracia* (Madrid: S.N. 1979), 81. For similar UCD narratives, see Francisco Fernández Ordoñez, *La España necesaria* (Madrid: Taurus, 1980); Joaquín Garrigues Walker, *Una política para España* (Madrid: Unión Editorial, 1976); José Luis Meilán Gil, *Escritos sobre la transición política española* (Madrid: Mayler, 1979).
81 Carlos Seco Serrano, "Catastrofistas," *ABC Madrid* (January 6, 1978); Carlos Seco Serrano, "Ni 'bunker' ni Ariete," *ABC Madrid* (May 26, 1976); Carlos Seco Serrano, "Razon de ser de centro," *ABC Madrid* (March 3, 1978). *Ya* commentator José Jiménez Blanco also spoke of a "dialectics of minority extreme positions, which nonetheless succeeded in imposing a Civil War on all of us"; see José Jiménez Blanco, "Pequeña historia del centro," *Ya* (June 8, 1977); see also Santiago Araúz de Robles, "La utopia del centro (2)", *Ya* (January 11, 1977).
82 As the Falangist intellectual Tierno Galván later admitted, Suárez "had no political ideology," in Tusell, *La Transición*, 91.
83 Adolfo Suárez would not allow even López Bravo to overshadow him, said López Rodó; see López Rodó, *Memorias IV*, 316.

84 "Franco," *ABC Madrid* (November 20, 1976): 3.
85 "Primer aniversario," *Ya* (November 20, 1976): 5.
86 Gonzalo Fernández de la Mora, "Defensa de la constitución," *ABC Madrid* (December 6, 1975); see also Gonzalo Fernández de la Mora, "La democracia real," *ABC Madrid* (January 21, 1976); for other Opus Dei figures attacking the reform, see Luis Valls Taberner, "El Rey no gobierna," *ABC Madrid* (December 16, 1975).
87 Gonzalo Fernández de la Mora, *La partitocracia* (Madrid: Instituto de Estudios Políticos, 1977).
88 Mariano Navarro Rubio, "Democracia democrática de verdad," *ABC Madrid* (November 27, 1975): 3.
89 Mariano Navarro Rubio, "Postulados," *ABC Madrid* (January 6, 1976): 3.
90 Laureano López Rodó, "Enmiendas de la constitución," *ABC Madrid* (February 27, 1976).
91 "Una rueda de prensa espectacular," *ABC Madrid* (October 22, 1976): 3.
92 "Esperamos serenos y optimistas el veredicto final del pueblo español," *ABC Madrid* (October 22, 1976): 3.
93 López Rodó's self-congratulatory memoirs were quickly mocked in the press for this narrative; see Turcuato Luca de Tena, "La larga marcha hacia la monarquía," *ABC Madrid* (July 6, 1977).
94 "Esperamos serenos y optimistas el veredicto final del pueblo español," *ABC Madrid* (October 22, 1976).
95 Several historians have recently begun depicting the Spanish transition as a period of extreme violence and collective sense of crisis; see Sophie Baby, *Le mythe de la transition pacifique: violence et politique en Espagne, 1975–1982* (Madrid: Casa de Velázquez, 2012); Mariano Sánchez Soler, *La transición sangrienta: una historia violenta del proceso democrático en España, 1975–1983* (Barcelona: Península, 2010); Andrea Davis, "Enforcing the Transition: The Demobilization of Collective Memory in Spain, 1979–1982," *Bulletin of Hispanic Studies* 6, (2015): 667–89.
96 The law pardons "misconduct and crimes that might have been committed by the authorities, functionaries and agents of public order." In turn, Spain's 1978 Constitution included a definite "principle of non-retroactivity" (Article 9.3) which further bans retroactive justice.
97 For more on this trade-off and the Spanish "pact of silence," see Ferran Gallego, *El mito de la transición: la crisis del Franquismo y los orígenes de la democracia (1973–1977)* (Barcelona: Crítica, 2008); Paloma Aguilar Fernández, *Memory and Amnesia: The Role of the Spanish Civil War in the Transition to Democracy* (New York: Berghahn Books, 2002); Gregorio Morán *El Precio de la transición* (Barcelona: Editorial Planeta, 1991).
98 *Francisco Franco! Presente!, Conferencia pronunciada en la Sede del Instituto Chileno de cultura Hispánica por D. Sergio Femández Larraín, ex-Embajador de Chile en España, el 18 de diciembre de 1975, con motivo del solemne homenaje rendido al Jefe del Estado Español* (Santiago, Chile: Instituto Chileno de Cultura Hispánica), 45, 55.
99 "Reservado, 9/2, situación política española," January 2, 1976, AMCAE, Embajada en Madrid, oficios confidenciales, 1976, box 1.

100 Gonzalo Vial Correa, *Pinochet: la biografía* (Santiago, Chile: Aguilar, 2002), 365.
101 See Raúl Bertelsen Repetto, *El Senado en España* (Madrid: Instituto de Estudios Administrativos, 1974); Raúl Bertelsen Repetto, *Control de constitucionalidad de la ley* (Santiago: Ed. Jurídica de Chile, 1969).
102 That Guzmán was the author of the speech had been confirmed multiple times; see for example Carlos Huneeus, *The Pinochet Regime* (Boulder, CO: Lynne Rienner Publishers, 2007), 357; Renato Cristi, *El pensamiento político de Jaime Guzmán: autoridad y libertad* (Santiago, Chile: LOM Ediciones, 2000), 12.
103 *Actas oficiales*, sesión 296, Juny 9, 1977, 1156.
104 See www.bcn.cl/historiapolitica/elecciones/detalle_eleccion?handle = 10221.1/63185&periodo = 1973-1990.
105 They were also being identified as technocrats in the press by then; see Pablo Huneeus, "La tecnocracia triunfal," *Ercilla* (March 21, 1979). On Chacarrillas, see Felipe Reyes and Guido Arroyo, *Chacarillas: Los elegidos de Pinochet* (Santiago, Chile: Editorial Alquimia, 2019).
106 Vial Correa, *Pinochet*, 338.
107 He did so following Leigh's interview with *Corriere della Sera* on July 18, 1978, in which he criticized Pinochet's leadership.
108 "Chile en el corazón," *El País*, January 6, 1978, https://elpais.com/diario/1978/01/06/opinion/252889203_850215.html
109 Vial Correa, *Pinochet*, 422.
110 Pablo Rodríguez Grez, "Envoltorio nuevo para ideas viejas," *La Tercera* (December 12, 1977): 3.
111 Carlos Cruz-Coke Ossa, "Hacia una constitución nacionalista," *Revista de Derecho Público* 18 (July–December 1975): 317–26.
112 "Especial América de Fuerza Nueva," *Fuerza Nueva* 644 (May 12, 1979): 25.
113 In Gonzalo Vial Correa's words, these debates aimed to "reduce, if not eliminate, the political weight of suffrage and parties"; see Vial Correa, *Pinochet*, 370.
114 De F. Larraín, 22-11-79, Epistolario Fernández de la Mora, Correspondencias con Sergio Fernández Larraín, *Razón Española* 142 (2007).
115 "Si!" *Qué Pasa* 349 (December 29, 1977): 1.
116 "¿Consumismo en Chile?" *Realidad* 12 (May 1980): 10; see also "El tema de la crisis moral," *Realidad* 3:35 (April 1982): 3–9.
117 José Miguel Ibáñez Langlois, "Marxismo religión al revés," *Realidad* 27 (August 1981): 35–9; Mariano Grondona, "Terrorismo y democracia," *Realidad* 7 (December 1979): 45–6.
118 Mariano Grondona, "Pragmatismo y principismo," *Realidad* 2:1 (June 1980): 39–43.
119 "Enfrentamiento sesgado," *APSI* 72 (May 1980): 5.
120 Mercelo Contreres, "Los caminos que se abren," *APSI* 68 (January 1, 1980): 3.
121 Filebo, "'Duros' vs. 'blandos'," *Las Últimas Noticias* (April 5, 1980): 5.

122 "Asamblea constituyente requisito democrático," *APSI* 58 (July 1, 1979): 1.
123 "El Camino político," *Realidad* 7 (December 1979): 3–4; "Dos frentes antagónicos contra la Constitución," *Realidad* 24 (May 1981): 3–7.
124 Jaime Guzmán, "El sufragio universal y la nueva institucionalidad," *Realidad* 1 (June 1979): 36; see also Gonzalo Rojas Sánchez, "Estatismo y corporativismo en 1982," *Realidad* 3:38 (July 1982): 29–36.
125 Guzmán, "El sufragio universal y la nueva institucionalidad."
126 Jaime Guzmán, "La definición constitucional," *Realidad* 3 (August 1980): 33.
127 "Una gira eminentemente política," *Qué Pasa* (September 27, 1979): 6–7.
128 "Positiva es considerada gira de Cubillos a España," *La Tercera* (September 9, 1979); "Un viaje esclarecedor," *Realidad* 5 (October 1979): 3.
129 "Poderes Fuertes al presidente y exclusión de doctrinas totalitarias," *Informaciones* (September 7, 1979).
130 "Hernán Cubillos: un diplomático por naturaleza," *Qué Pasa* (May 4, 1978): 24–6; "Cansillería en vías de apertura," *Ercilla* (May 24, 1978).
131 "Experiencia española no es trasmisible, ni copiable," *La Tercera* (September 9, 1979); for more journalistic accounts of this visit, see The Hoover Institution Archive, Hernán Cubillos Sallato papers, Box 10.
132 Rafael Valdivieso Ariztía, *Crónica de un rescate: Chile, 1973–1988* (Santiago, Chile: Editorial Andrés Bello, 1988), 218; Augusto Pinochet, *Camino recorrido: memorias de un soldado* (Santiago, Chile: Instituto Geográfico Militar de Chile, 1990), 237.
133 Eduardo Boetsch, *Recordando con Alessandri* (Santiago, Chile: Universidad Nacional Andrés Bello, 1998), 185.
134 Sebastian Edwards, *The Chile Project: The Story of the Chicago Boys and the Downfall of Neoliberalism*. Princeton, NJ: Princeton University Press, 2023), xv.
135 On the political rights of exiles during these years, see Mario Sznajder and Luis Roniger, *The Politics of Exile in Latin America* (New York: Cambridge University Press, 2009).
136 Jaime Guzmán, "La definición constitucional," *Realidad* 3 (August 1980): 21.
137 *The Constitution of Chile*, at http://hrlibrary.umn.edu/research/chile-constitution.pdf.
138 Robert Barros, *Constitutionalism and Dictatorship: Pinochet, the Junta, and the 1980 Constitution* (New York: Cambridge University Press, 2002), 1–3.
139 Sergio Fernández claimed that the Filipinazo "helped the institutionalization "; see Fernández, *Mi lucha por la democracia*, 130. For more on the "Filipinazo" and its effects, see "Hernán Cubillos rompe su silencio," *Qué Pasa* (November 13, 1986): 32–3; Augusto Varas, "The Crisis of Legitimacy of Military Rule in the 1980s," in Paul W. Drake and Ivan Jaksic (eds.), *The Struggle for Democracy in Chile* (Lincoln: University of Nebraska Press, 1995).
140 Marcelo Pollack, *The New Right in Chile, 1973–1997* (New York: St. Martin's Press, 1999), 86.
141 Selected analyses of this regime's ideology would include Marguerite Feitlowitz, *A Lexicon of Terror: Argentina and the Legacies of Torture*

(New York: Oxford University Press, 1998); Donald C. Hodges, *Argentina's "Dirty War": An Intellectual Biography* (Austin: University of Texas Press, 2014); Gabriela Águila, *Historia de la última dictadura militar: Argentina, 1976–1983* (Buenos Aires: Siglo Veintiuno Editores, 2023); Horacio Verbitsky, *Doble juego: la Argentina católica y militar* (Buenos Aires: Editorial Sudamericana, 2006).

142 "Declaraciones del Señor Presidente de la Nación en la sala de periodistas de la casa de gobierno," April 12, 1976, AGN.DAI/ PN.SPD.pp, box 112.

143 "Palabras Del Excelentísimo Señor Presidente de la nación, Pronunciadas al recibir a los Integrantes del XXV congreso Mundial del la Publicidad," May 19, 1976, AGN.DAI/PN.SPD.pp, box 113.

144 "Fue levantada la prohibición sobre las revistas Cabildo y Fortín," June 17, 1976, AGN.DAI/PN.SPD.pp, box 113.

145 "Editorial," *Cabildo* 2:36 (September 1980): 3.

146 "Blas Piñar hablo de la situación española," *La Nación* (April 29, 1979); see also "Para Blas Piñar el marxismo no es una avalancha faltamente victoriosa," *Convicción* (May 3, 1979): 6.

147 He also successfully repatriated six Spaniards imprisoned by the Junta, see "El rey hizo en Argentina una decidida defensa de los derechos humanos," *ABC Sevilla* (December 1, 1978).

148 "De las vicisitudes de un rey demócrata," *Cabildo* 21 (December 1978): 10–11.

149 Mario Amadeo to Alfredo Sánchez Bella, August 24, 1976, AGUN, doc. 15/35/324.

150 On this regime's deployment of civil groups, see Hugo Quiroga, *El tiempo del proceso: conflictos y coincidencias entre políticos y militares. 1976–1983* (Rosario: Fundación Ross, 1994); Paula Canelo, *El Proceso en su laberinto: la interna militar de Videla a Bignone* (Prometeo, Buenos Aires, 2008); Gabriela Águila, *Historia de la última dictadura militar, Argentina, 1976–1983* (Buenos Aires: Siglo Veintiuno Editores, 2023).

151 The Argentine Centro de Investigacion y Accion Educativa (CINAE) published six of García Hoz's booklets, as well as the Spanish José Rodríguez Diégez and Amparo Martínez Sánchez, both specialists in "Personalized education": *La universidad*; *Una pauta para la evaluación de centros educativos*; *El Proyecto educativo*; *Predicación y la evaluación personalizada*; and *¿Qué es la educación personalizada?*; see also Víctor García Hoz, *La universidad: su misión, su poder* (Buenos Aires: Docencia, 1980). García Hoz did not hold any important public position in Spain in the late 1970s, but did remain the director of CSIC's Institute of Pedagogy until 1980.

152 Bernardo Neustadt, "La Situación," *Extra* 138 (December 1976): 9.

153 Claudio Uriarte, *Almirante Cero: biografía no autorizada de Emilio Eduardo Massera* (Buenos Aires: Edición Editorial Planeta Argentina S.A., 1992), 213; see also Marcelo Borrelli and Jorge Saborido, "La prensa del 'Proceso.' El diario Convicción durante la dictadura militar argentina (1976–1983)," *Estudios sobre el Mensaje Periodistico* (2008): 49; Daniel Muchnik, "El diario de Massera, el marino cruel que quiso ser presidente," *Perfil* (November 12, 2010).

154 "Subversión y racionalidad," *Carta Política* 31 (May 1976): 6.

155 Nicanor Costa Méndez, "Americanos del sur, a los hechos," *Carta Política* 33 (July 1976): 73.
156 "La idea-fuerza," *Carta Política* 32 (June 1976): 5.
157 "Los 100 días de Videla," *Carta Política* 33 (July 1976): 7.
158 Mario Amadeo to Alfredo Sánchez Bella 15/35/335.
159 For more on this cooperation, see Martín Sivak, *El Doctor: biografía no autorizada de Mariano Grondona* (Buenos Aires: Aguilar, 2005).
160 *Documentos Básicos y bases políticas de las Fuerzas Armadas para el Proceso de Reorganización Nacional* (Buenos Aires: Congreso de la Nación, 1980), 59, available at Biblioteca Nacional de Maestros, www.bnm.me.gov.ar/giga1/documentos/EL000162.pdf.
161 "El capitán, el puerto, y la tormenta," *A Fondo* 6 (March 1981): 18–19.
162 "Nuestro Carter es el Peronismo, el radicalismo. Nuestro Reagan, la institución militar, *A Fondo* 2 (November 1980): 1.
163 Adalberto Zelmar Barbosa, "El municipio y la renovación política," *A Fondo* 3 (December 1980): 66; "El municipio, estructura política vital y completo," *A Fondo* 13 (October 1981): 92.
164 "Cuatro ideas fuerza y entre ellas una novísima: el 'capital moral'," *A Fondo* 4 (January 1981): 14.
165 Roberto Bosca, "Municipio, participación y democracia," *Verbo* 221 (April 1982): 17–22.
166 Mario Amadeo to Alfredo Sánchez Bella, February 7, 1980, AGUN, doc. 15/35/335.
167 Mario Amadeo a Alfredo Sánchez Bella, April 14, 1980, AGUN, doc. 15/35/337.
168 Ibid.
169 *Consensus and peace,* 134.
170 In interviews in later years, this serene Nacionalista defended his deeds during his short and calamitous tenure; see *The Falklands-Malvinas War: An interview with Nicanor Costa Méndez by James S. Sutterlin*, United Nations Oral History Project.
171 Mariano Grondona, "Sea cual fuera …" *A Fondo* 18 (April 1982): 1.
172 "Open letter to those who do not know us," *A Fondo* 19 (May 1982): 28.
173 For more on Bignone's Law 22,924, see Carlos Santiago Nino, *Radical Evil on Trial* (New Haven, CT: Yale University Press, 1996), 64–5.
174 "El pacto social que nuestra democracia reclama," *A Fondo* 25 (December 1982): 34–5.
175 For more on the intricacies of the last Argentine transition, see Horacio Verbitsky, *Civiles y militares: memoria secreta de la transición* (Buenos Aires: Editorial Sudamericana, 2003); J. Patrice McSherry, *Incomplete Transition: Military Power and Democracy in Argentina* (New York: St. Martin's Press, 1997); Marina Franco, *El final del silencio: dictadura, sociedad y derechos humanos en la transición (1979–1983)* (Buenos Aires: Fondo de Cultura Económica, 2018).
176 López Rodó, *Memorias IV*, 443.
177 Fernández de la Mora to Fernández Larraín, July 30, 1978, Epistolario Fernández de la Mora, Correspondencias con Sergio Fernández Larraín, *Razón Española* 142 (2007): 130.

178 Declaraciones de Don Alfredo Sánchez Bella sobre los resultados electorales españoles," AGUN, doc. 15/61/534.
179 Alfredo Sánchez Bella to Mario Amadeo, December 2, 1977, AGUN, doc. 15/35/330.
180 Alfredo Sánchez Bella to Arturo Fontaine, December 19, 1978, AGUN, doc. 15/46/217.
181 Gonzalo Fernández de la Mora, "Divorcio y freudo-marxismo," *ABC Madrid* (January 24, 1981): 7.
182 "La democracia orgánica," *ABC Madrid* (February 4, 1978): 3.
183 "La democracia antiliberal," *ABC Madrid* (April 30, 1982): 3.
184 "El Ahorro, pelanizado," *ABC Madrid* (April 15, 1978): 3.
185 "Sociobiologia de la Hispanidad," *ABC Sevilla* (October 13, 1981): 3.
186 *Razón Española*'s editorial board included Opus Dei ideologues Antonio Millán Puelles, Luis Suárez, and Juan José López Ibor. Alfredo Sánchez Bella and Laureano López Rodó also published there as commentators.
187 Gonzalo Fernández de la Mora, *Los errores del cambio* (Barcelona: Plaza & Janes, 1986), 20–1.
188 Fernández de la Mora to López Rodó, (1989, sin fecha), Epistolario Fernandez de la Mora, Correspondencias con Laureano López Rodó, *Razón Española* 122 (2003): 259.
189 Real Decreto 2305/1977, de 27 de agosto 1977, *BOE (España)* 213, September 6, 1977.
190 Mario Amadeo to Alfredo Sánchez Bella, October 17, 1978, AGUN, doc. 15/035/331.
191 "Sergio Fernández L. Renunció al Instituto De Cultura Hispánica," *El Mercurio* (December 28, 1978); see also Alfredo Sánchez Bella to Arturo Fontaine, December 19, 1978, AGUN, doc. 05/46/217.
192 Arturo Fontaine to Alfredo Sánchez Bella, January 2, 1979, AGUN, doc. 05/46/218.
193 "Discurso de don Juan Carlos I en Cartagena de Indias el 12 de octubre de 1976," in *España en el Mundo. Discursos de S.M. el Rey. 1976–1979* (Madrid: Oficina de Información Diplomática, 1979).
194 Rafael Fraguas, "El Gobierno español se compromete a impulsar la creación de una comunidad iberoamericana de naciones democráticas," *El País* (April 28, 1983); see also Alfonso Guerra, "Discurso del Sr. D. Alfoso Guerra, vicepresidente del gobierno de España," *Iberoamérica encuentro en la democracia* (Madrid: Ediciones Cultura Hispánica, 1983), 30.
195 Manuel Blanco Tobío, "Bajarse del tigre," *ABC Madrid* (July 11, 1983): 3.
196 *La transición a la democracia en España, hoy*, 65.
197 "No se pueden hacer remedos de transición," *Hoy* 335 (1983): 19; "Consenso, palabra mágica," *Hoy* 337 (1983): 28–9.
198 Patricio Aylwin, *Un desafío colectivo* (Santiago, Chile: Planeta, 1988), 127; see also Daniel Gunnar Kressel, "'Getting off the Tiger': The Spanish Transitional Model and Its Influence on the Democratic Transitions in Argentina and Chile, 1977–1990," *Global Society* 33.3 (July 3, 2019): 316–31.
199 Gonzalo Vial Correa, "Como un cáncer," *Qué Pasa* (August 1, 1985): 14–16.

200 "AD no es un factor válido para una transición pacífica," *La Tercera* (March 10, 1984): 13.
201 Jaime Guzmán, "UDI no enfrentará a la ciudadanía con las FFAA," *La Tercera* (January 20, 1984): 6.
202 *UDI Bolitin Informativo* 1 (December 1983): 1.
203 "Gremialismo: patrimonio de los democratas," *UDI Bolitin Informativo* (January 24, 1984): 3.
204 "UDI, generación creadora," *Ercilla* (May 18, 1988); also in Fundación Jaime Guzmán, doc. CJG.88.57.
205 *Declaración de Principios: Partido Unión Demócrata Independiente,* 1983, Fundación Jaime Guzmán, UDI.83.41
206 Ibid.
207 Joaquín Lavín, "Chile y su experiencia de planificación," *Qué Pasa* 305 (February 24, 1977): 6; "Cómo nacieron la extrema izquierda y la ... extrema pobreza," *El Mercurio* (June 15, 1980); "Decibeles de una revolución," *Ercilla* (March 30, 1988): 37–8; Joaquín Lavín Infante, *Chile, Revolución Silenciosa* (Santiago, Chile: Zig-Zag, 1987).
208 "Gradually Santiago stopped being Chile," he said, and even compared the area of Copiapó to the Israeli Negev Desert development experiment (of which he, apparently, knew very little); see Lavín, *Revolución silenciosa*, 61–3.
209 *Declaración de Principios: Partido Unión Demócrata Independiente.*
210 "Gremialismo: patrimonio de los demócratas," *UDI Bolitin Informativo* 2 (January 24, 1984): 3.
211 *Declaración de Principios: Partido Unión Demócrata Independiente.*
212 Díaz Nieva, "Avanzada Nacional: La derecha a la derecha de Pinochet."
213 "El 11 de septiembre no se hizo para importar televisores," *Panorama Literario e Informativo* 65 (October 1983): 12; see also Gastón Acuña, Federico Willoughby, and Pablo Rodríguez Grez, *Qué es el nacionalismo hoy?: síntesis de un ideario* (Santiago, Chile: SP, 1983).
214 Libio Perez, "La increible y caotica historia de la derecha derrotada," *Análisis* 256 (December 5, 1988): 10. For more on the hard-liners in the 1980s, see Pablo Rubio Apiolaza, *Los civiles de Pinochet: la derecha en el régimen militar chileno, 1983–1990* (Santiago, Chile: Centro de Investigaciones Diego Barros Arana), 2013; Daniel Gunnar Kressel, "'Los Duros': The Neo-Fascist Opposition to Chile's 1980 Constitution, and its Francoist Connections," *Interdisciplinarios de América Latina y el Caribe* 33:2 (December 2022): 69–89.
215 "1147, visita a chile del embajador Gonzalo Fernández de la Mora," October 1, 1985, AGA, box 82/07900.
216 "Las ideologías ya no sirven," *Ercilla* (September 25, 1985).
217 "Fernández de la Mora: 'El cambio en España se hizo marginando y persiguiendo a la derecha,'" *La Segunda* (September 27, 1985).
218 Tomas Mac Hale, "Gonzalo Fernández de la Mora: la transición española," *El Mercurio* (September 29, 1985).
219 "El pensamiento de Fernández de la Mora," *La Tercera* (December 4, 1986).
220 "Jaime Guzmán, "España: recordando lo que hoy se calle," *La Segunda* (July 19, 1985).

221 Jaime Guzmán, "Dos casos radicalmente diferentes," *Ercilla* (December 17, 1986): 9.
222 Guzmán would brag about this achievement in his campaigns; see "UDI, generación creadora."
223 "Renovación Nacional. Un partido de la mayoría, para todos los chilenos," *La Tercera* (February 8, 1987).
224 "UDI, generación creadora."
225 https://nsarchive2.gwu.edu/NSAEBB/NSAEBB413/docs/nodiajuntameeting.pdf.
226 For more on the meaning of "gradualism," see Claudio Fuentes, "Chile: Democratization through Constitutional Reforms," in Detlef Nolte and Almut Schilling-Vacaflor (eds.), *New Constitutionalism in Latin America: Promises and Practices* (Burlington, VT: Ashgate Publishing, 2012), 243; Isabel Torres Dujisin, "Memory and the recent past: Chile, from revolution to repression," in Trever Hagen and Anna Lisa Tota (eds.), *Routledge International Handbook of Memory Studies* (New York: Routledge, 2016), 371–81.
227 "Discurso del presidente de Unión Demócrata Independiente, Jaime Guzmán, ante el Consejo Nacional del Partido," April 15, 1989, Fundación Jaime Guzmán, doc. UDI.89.02.04.
228 "Guzmán: la concertación tiene mentalidad estatista," Fundación Jaime Guzmán, doc. CAM.89.04.47.
229 "Con estas reformas es suficiente," *Ercilla* (August 2, 1989): 8.
230 "Guzmán ante el Consejo Nacional de UDI, 1989," Fundación Jaime Guzmán, doc. UDI.89.1.06, 2.
231 Ibid.
232 He came third with a mere 17.19 percent of the votes but, with the binomial system, managed to secure his place.
233 *Diario de sesiones del senado: intervención reforma tributaria*, 1990, Fundación Jaime Guzmán, doc. DJG.90.11, 3.
234 Our World in Data, "History of government spending," https://ourworldindata.org/government-spending#history-of-government-spending.
235 *Diario de sesiones del senado: intervención indefinición del gobierno,* 1990, Fundación Jaime Guzmán, doc. DJG.90.12, 3.
236 *Diario de sesiones del senado: intervención libertad de expresión,* 1990, Fundación Jaime Guzmán, doc. DJG.90.13, 3.
237 *Diario de sesiones del senado: intervención pena de muerte,* 1990, Fundación Jaime Guzmán, doc. DJG.90.14 3.

EPILOGUE

1 Clifford Geertz, *Local Knowledge: Further Essays in Interpretive Anthropology* (New York: Basic Books, 1983), 58.
2 Pedro Ancarola, *La acción desde el poder* (Buenos Aires: Ediciones Nueva Política, 1967), 21.
3 Luis Alberto Romero, "A 40 años del golpe contra Illia: el espejismo de Onganía," *La Nación* (June 25, 2006), www.lanacion.com.ar/opinion/a-40-anos-del-golpe-contra-illia-el-espejismo-de-ongania-nid817585/.

4 Antonio Cazorla Sánchez, *Fear and Progress*: Ordinary Lives in Franco's Spain, 1939–1975 (Hoboken, NJ: John Wiley & Sons, 2009), 94.

5 A partial list of this type of critique, especially in regard to Chile, would include: Cal Clark, *Challenging Neoliberalism: Globalization and the Economic Miracles in Chile and Taiwan* (Northampton, MA: Edward Elgar Publishing, 2016); Marcus Taylor, *From Pinochet to the "Third Way": Neoliberalism and Social Transformation in Chile* (Ann Arbor, MI: Pluto Press, 2006); Larissa Adler de Lomnitz, *Chile's Middle Class: A Struggle for Survival in the Face of Neoliberalism* (Boulder, CO: Lynne Rienner Publishers, 1991); Patricio Silva, *In the Name of Reason: Technocrats and Politics in Chile* (University Park, PA: Penn State University Press, 2008).

6 Vicenç Navarro, *El subdesarrollo social de España: causas y consecuencias* (Barcelona: Editorial Anagrama, 2006).

7 Benjamin A Cowan, *Securing Sex: Morality and Repression in the Making of Cold War Brazil* (Chapel Hill: University of North Carolina Press, 2016).

8 The literature on German memory has recently begun to challenge this alleged "denazification" of German society; see for example Robert G. Moeller, *War Stories: The Search for a Usable Past in the Federal Republic of Germany* (Berkeley: University of California Press, 2001); Norbert Frei, *Vergangenheit spolitik: Die Anfänge der Bundesrepublik unddie NS-Vergangenhei*t (Munich: C. H. Beck, 1996).

9 Camila Vergara, *Systemic Corruption: Constitutional Ideas for an Anti-oligarchic Republic* (Princeton, NJ: Princeton University Press, 2020).

10 Juan Luis Cebrián, "The pre-constitutional experiment," in José Luis Cagigao, John Crispin, and Enrique Pupo-Walker (eds.), *Spain, 1975–1980: The Conflicts and Achievements of Democracy* (Madrid: J. Porrúa Turanzas, 1982), 15.

11 All three countries have allowed the activity of foundations that eulogize authoritarianism, such as the Francisco Franco Foundation (Spain), the Jaime Guzmán and President Pinochet Foundations (Chile), and Instituto Bibliográfico Antonio Zinny (Argentina).

12 "Inaugurado un busto en la UN en recuerdo de Álvaro d'Ors, una gran persona crucial para el centro universitario," *Europapress* (April 25, 2013); "Presentan libro en homenaje a Álvaro d'Ors," *Udep hoy* (April 27, 2012), http://udep.edu.pe/hoy/2012/presentan-libro-en-homenaje-a-alvaro-dors; Ana Barrero, "Homenaje a Ismael Sánchez Bella, Pamplona: Universidad de Navarra, 1992," *Anuario de historia del derecho español* (1993): 1303–11.

13 José V. Casanova, "The Opus Dei Ethic, the Technocrats and the Modernization of Spain," *Social Science Information* 22:1 (1983): 27.

14 José V. Casanova, "Modernization and Democratization: Reflections on Spain's Transition to Democracy," *Social Research* 50:4 (1983): 963. Elsewhere Casanova claimed that the technocrats had "promised that democracy would come automatically when Spain reached the $1000" per capita level, and thereafter "found themselves helpless to bring about democratization"; see José V. Casanova, "The Opus Dei Ethic, the Technocrats and the Modernization of Spain," 41.

15 Pío Moa, *Contra la mentira* (Madrid: Libros libres, 2003), 226.

16 See for example Javier Couso, "Trying Democracy in the Shadow of an Authoritarian Legality: Chile's Transition to Democracy and Pinochet's Constitution of 1980," *Wisconsin International Law Journal* 29:2 (2011): 393–415; Claudia Heiss and Patricio Navia, "You Win Some, You Lose Some: Constitutional Reforms in Chile's Transition to Democracy," *Latin American Politics and Society* 49:3 (2007): 163–90.
17 "Doce de octubre: de la Hispanidad a la Iberospfera," *Efemérides* 11 (October 12, 2021): 1–6.
18 *Carta de Madrid: en defensa de la libertad y la democracia en la Iberosfera*, https://fundaciondisenso.org/wp-content/uploads/2021/09/CARTA-DE-MADRID-1.pdf.
19 María Zaldívar, "Venezuela-Argentina-España, la peligrosa alianza que se materializa a través del Grupo de Puebla," *La Gaceta* (October 31, 2021), https://gaceta.es/actualidad/venezuela-argentina-espana-la-peligrosa-alianza-que-se-materializa-a-traves-del-grupo-de-puebla-20211031-0903/.
20 Raúl Tortolero, "El conservadurismo (explicado a losniños)", *La Gaceta* (October 27, 2021), https://gaceta.es/opinion/el-conservadurismo-explicado-a-los-ninos-20211027-1900/.
21 Eduardo Dargent, *Technocracy and Democracy in Latin America: The Experts Running Government* (New York: Cambridge University Press, 2015); for another example of this use of the term, see Andra B. Chastain and Timothy Lorek (eds.), *Itineraries of Expertise: Science, Technology, and the Environment in Latin America's Long Cold War* (Pittsburgh, PA: University of Pittsburgh Press, 2020).
22 Barbara Geddes, Joseph Wright, and Erica Frantz, *How Dictatorships Work: Power, Personalization, and Collapse* (New York: Cambridge University Press, 2018).
23 Eric Hobsbawm, "Ethnicity and Nationalism in Europe Today," in Gopal Balakrishnan and Benedict Anderson (eds.), *Mapping the Nation* (London: Verso, 2000), 255.

Bibliography

ARCHIVAL COLLECTIONS

Archivo de la Administración, Santiago, Chile.
Archivo Fundación Jaime Guzmán, Santiago, Chile.
Archivo General de la Administración (AGA), Alcalá de Henares, Spain.
Archivo General Histórico del Ministerio de Asuntos Exteriores (AGMAE), Santiago, Chile.
Archivo General de la Nación (AGN), Buenos Aires, Argentina.
Archivo General de la Universidad de Navarra (AGUN), Pamplona, Spain.
Archivo del Ministerio de Asuntos Exteriores y Culto (AMREC), Buenos Aires, Argentina.
Archivo del Ministerio de Educación, Alcalá de Henares, Spain.
Archivo del Ministerio de Educación, Buenos Aires, Argentina.
Archivo National, Santiago, Chile.
Archivo Privado Gonzalo Fernández de la Mora.
Arquivo Nacional do Brazil, Rio de Janeiro, Brazil.
Biblioteca Nacional de Chile, Archivo del Escritor, Santiago, Chile.
Biblioteca Nacional, Fondo Centro de Estudios Nacionales, Buenos Aires, Argentina.
Centro de investigaciones de izquierdas (CEDINCI), Buenos Aires, Argentina.
Fundación Nacional Francisco Franco (FNFF), Madrid, Spain.
The Hoover Institution Archive, Palo Alto CA, USA.
Instituto Científico Judío (IWO), Buenos Aires, Argentina.

DIGITAL ARCHIVES

Archivo Patrimonial, Universidad Alberto Hurtado.
Fundación de Documentacion y Archivo de la Vicaria de la Solidaridad, Arzobispado de Santiago, Chile.
Fundación Jaime Guzmán.

Fundación Patricio Aylwin Azócar.
UMass Amherst, Special Collections and University Archives.

NEWSPAPERS AND PERIODICALS

Argentina

A Fondo
Así
Azul y Blanco
Bandera Popular
Cabildo
Carta Política
Clarín
Combate
Convergencia
Consudec
Criterio
Cruzada
Cuadernos del Sur
Cuyo hispánico
Dinámica Social
El Caudillo
El cronista comercial
El Fortín
El Pampero
Extra
Gente
Inédito
La Gaceta de Tucumán
La Nación
La Nueva República
La Opinión
La Prensa
La Razón
Las Bases
Mazocra
Nosotros
Ofensiva
Palabra Argentina
Panorama
Pregón
Premisa
Primera Plana
Quincena
Restauración

Sol y Luna
Tacuara: Vocero Oficial de UNES
Todo
Tradición, familia, propiedad
Verbo
7 Días

Chile

Amiga
APSI
Araucaria de Chile
Bandera Negra
Cosas
Dialogo conservador
Diario Loco
El Diario Ilustrado
El Mercurio
El Siglo
El Sur
Ercilla
Estanquero
Estudios
Eva
Fiducia
Finis Terrae
Forja
Hoja informativa, Opus Dei
Hola
Juventud
La Pandilla
La Segunda
La Tercera
Las Últimas Noticias
Noticia
Patria y Libertad
Política, Economía, Cultura (PEC)
Portada
Presencia
Puro Chile
Qué Pasa
Realidad
Revista Araucanía
Revista de Educación
Secretaria Nacional de la Juventud: Boletín Informativo
Tacna

Tizona
Yungay: Periódico Falangista

France

Le Monde
Table Ronde

Italy

Corriere della Sera

México

Istmo

Spain (Including Newspapers in Exile)

ABC Madrid/ Sevilla
Acción Española
Actualidad Económica
Actualidad Española
Arbor
Arriba
Atlántida
Blanco y negro
Cambio 16
Clavileño
Cuadernos Hispanoamericanos
Cuadernos para el dialogo
Cuadernos Ruedo Ibérico
El Alcázar
El País
Fuerza Nueva
Gaceta Universitaria
Ibérica
Índice
Ínsula
La Vanguardia
Madrid
Moncloa
Mundo Cristiano
Mundo Hispánico
Nuestro Tiempo

Nuevo Diario
Palabra
Pueblo
Punta Europa
Revista de Administración Publica
Revista de Estudios Políticos
Revista de Historia de América
Telva
Ya

United Kingdom

The Guardian
The Statist

USA

El Diario de Nueva York
The New York Times
Time magazine

Venezuela/Colombia

Arco: Revista de las áreas culturales bolivianas

INTERVIEWS

Roberto Bosca
Ernesto García Alesanco
José Miguel Ibáñez Langlois
Enrique Mario Mayochi
Alberto Moncada
Enrique Peltzer
Alfredo van Gelderen

SELECTED PUBLISHED PRIMARY SOURCES

Aguirre, María Elena (ed.). *La dignidad de la mujer hoy*. Santiago, Chile: Universidad Católica de Chile, 1989.

Albareda, José María. *Consideraciones sobre la investigación científica*. Madrid: Aguilar, 1951.

Amadeo, Mario. *Ayer, hoy, mañana*. Buenos Aires: Ediciones Gure, 1956.

La encrucijada argentina. Madrid: Epesa, 1956.

Por una convivencia internacional: bases para una comunidad hispánica de naciones. Madrid: Ediciones Cultura Hispánica, 1956.
Política internacional: los principios y los hechos. Buenos Aires: Instituto Argentino de Cultura Hispánica, 1970.
Beccar Varela, Cosme. *El nacionalismo: una incógnita en constante evolución*. Buenos Aires: Ediciones Tradiciones, Familia, Propiedad, 1970.
Boixados, Alberto. *España entre Europa e Hispanoamerica*. Buenos Aires: Areté, 1973.
Bravo Lira, Bernadino. *Régimen de gobierno y partidos políticos en Chile, 1924–1973*. Santiago, Chile: Editorial Jurídica de Chile, 1978.
De Portales a Pinochet: gobierno y régimen de gobierno en Chile. Santiago, Chile: Editorial Jurídica de Chile, 1985.
Calvo Serer, Rafael. *España, sin problema*. Madrid: Rialp, 1949.
Política de integración. Madrid: Rialp, 1955.
Teoría de la restauración. Madrid: Rialp, 1956.
La fuerza creadora de la libertad. Madrid: Rialp, 1959.
Las nuevas democracias. Madrid: Rialp, 1964.
Campos Menéndez, Enrique. *España y sus siglos de oro*. Santiago, Chile: Secretaria General del Gobierno, 1974.
Conde, Francisco Javier. *Representación política y régimen español*. Madrid: Subsecretaría de Educación Popular, 1945.
Correa Morandé, María. *La guerra de las mujeres*. Santiago, Chile: Editorial Universidad Técnica del Estado, 1974.
Díez Hochleitner, Ricardo. *La educación permanente y la reforma educativa española*. Santander: Universidad Menéndez Pelayo, 1971.
Donoso Loero, Teresa. *La epopeya de las ollas vacías*. Santiago, Chile: Gabriela Mistral, 1974.
Escrivá de Balaguer, Josemaría. *Camino*. Madrid: Luz, 1945.
4 preguntas sobre el Opus Dei. Madrid: Astygi, 1971.
Estrada, José María de. *El legado del nacionalismo*. Buenos Aires: Ediciones Gure, 1956.
Etchecopar, Máximo. *De la democracia política a la democracia social*. Buenos Aires: Ediciones Sigla, 1958.
Esquema de la Argentina. Buenos Aires: Club de Lectores, 1966.
El fin del nuevo mundo: ensayo sobre la independencia de los pueblos americanos. Buenos Aires: Ediciones Corregidor, 1979.
Eyzaguirre, Jaime. *Fisonomía histórica de Chile*. Mexico City: Fondo de Cultura Económica, 1948.
Hispanoamérica del dolor y otros estudios. Madrid: Ediciones de Cultura Hispánica, 1979.
Fernández Fernández, Sergio. *Mi lucha por la democracia*. Santiago, Chile: Editorial los Andes, 1994.
Fernández Larraín, Sergio. *Y el comunismo sigue su marcha*. Santiago, Chile: Del Pregón, 1963.
Fernández de la Mora, Gonzalo. *La quiebra de la razón de estado*. Madrid: Ateneo, 1956.
El crepúsculo de las ideologías. Madrid: Rialp, 1965.

La partitocracia. Madrid: Instituto de Estudios Políticos, 1977.
Los errores del cambio. Barcelona: Plaza & Janés, 1986.
Fontán, Antonio. *Los tópicos y la opinión*. Madrid: Ateneo, 1956.
Los católicos en la universidad española actual. Madrid: Rialp, 1961.
Fraga Iribarne, Manuel. *How Spain is Governed*. Madrid: Diplomatic Information Office, 1950.
Organización de la convivencia. Madrid: Comercial Española de Ediciones, 1961.
Promoción social y educación. Madrid: Ateneo, 1961.
Fuentes Wendling, Manuel. *Memorias secretas de Patria y Libertad: y algunas confesiones sobre la guerra fría en Chile*. Santiago, Chile: Editorial Grijalbo SA, 1999.
García-Pelayo, Manuel. *Burocracia y tecnocracia y otros escritos*. Madrid: Alianza Editorial, 1974.
García Hoz, Víctor. *Pedagogía de la lucha ascética*. Madrid: CSIC, 1946.
Principios de pedagogía sistemática. Madrid: Rialp, 1960.
La universidad: su misión, su poder. Buenos Aires: Docencia, 1980.
La tarea profunda de educar. Madrid: Rialp, 1965.
García Morente, Manuel. *Idea de la Hispanidad*. Buenos Aires: Espasa-Calpe, 1939.
Genta, Jordán Bruno. *Guerra contrarevolucionaria*. Buenos Aires: Nuevo Orden, 1963.
Principios de la política: la guerra subversiva en nuestra patria. Buenos Aires: Editorial Cultura Argentina, 1970.
Seguridad y desarrollo: reflexiones sobre el terror en la Argentina. Editorial Cultura Argentina, 1970.
Giménez Caballero, Ernesto. *Genio de España*. Madrid: Ediciones Gaceta Literaria, 1932.
Grondona, Mariano. *La Argentina en el tiempo y en el mundo*. Buenos Aires: Editorial Primera Plana, 1967.
Los dos poderes. Buenos Aires: Emecé Editores, 1973.
Guzmán Errázuriz, Jaime. *Teoría sobre la universidad*. Santiago, Chile: Universidad Católica, 1970.
Escritos personales. Santiago, Chile: Zig-Zag, 1992.
Jaime Guzmán, espiritualidad y fe en sus escritos. Santiago, Chile: Fundación Jaime Guzmán, 2003.
Hervás, Juan. *Leaders' Manual for Cursillos in Christianity*. Madrid: Euroamerica, 1964.
Hübner Gallo, Jorge Iván. *El nuevo estado español*. Santiago, Chile: Editorial Universitaria, 1952.
Los católicos en la política. Santiago, Chile: Zig-Zag, 1959.
El mito de la explosión demográfica: la autorregulación natural de las poblaciones. Madrid: Ateneo, 1967.
Panorama de los derechos humanos. Santiago, Chile: Andrés Bello, 1973.
Ibáñez Langlois, José Miguel. *El marxismo: visión crítica*. Santiago, Chile: Ediciones Nueva Universidad, 1973.
Marxismo: religión al revés, síntesis de las ocho conferencias desarrolladas por el sacerdote José Miguel Ibáñez Langlois ante las autoridades de Gobierno. Santiago, Chile: División de Comunicación Social, 1982.

Doctrina social de la iglesia. Santiago, Chile: Ediciones Universidad Católica de Chile, 1986.
Teología de la liberación y libertad cristiana. Santiago, Chile: Ediciones Universidad Católica de Chile, 1989.
Lavín Infante, Joaquín. *Chile, revolución silenciosa*. Santiago, Chile: Zig-Zag, 1987.
Legaz y Lacambra, Luis. *Estudios de doctrina jurídica y social*. Barcelona: Bosch, 1940.
Lira, Osvaldo. *Ortega en su espíritu*. Santiago, Chile: Editorial de la Universidad Católica, 1965.
López-Amo, Ángel. *La monarquía de la reforma social*. Madrid: Rialp, 1952.
Sobre el estudio profundo de las revoluciones. Pamplona: Estudio General de Navarra, 1956.
López Ibor, Juan José. *Rebeldes*. Madrid: Rialp, 1965.
La aventura humana. Madrid: Rialp, 1965.
López Rodó, Laureano. *Política y desarrollo*. Madrid: Aguilar, 1970.
Nuevo horizonte del desarrollo. Madrid: Aguilar, 1972.
Memorias. Barcelona: Plaza & Janés, 1990.
Maeztu, Ramiro de. *Defensa de La Hispanidad*. Buenos Aires: Editorial Poblet, 1941.
Martín-Artajo, Alberto. *Hacia la Comunidad Hispánica de Naciones; Discursos*. Madrid: Ediciones Cultura Hispánica, 1956.
Mayochi, Enrique Mario. *Fundamentos constitucionales del sistema educativo argentino*. Buenos Aires: A. Estrada, 1969.
Meliá, Josep. *Carta abierta a los tecnócratas*. Madrid: Ediciones 99 SA, 1973.
Mier, Waldo de. *España cambia de piel: nuevo viaje por la "España del Milagro."* Madrid: Editora Nacional, 1964.
Millán-Puelles. Antonio. *La síntesis humana de naturaleza y libertad*. Madrid: Ateneo, 1961.
La ideología de la "protesta universitaria." Santander: Universidad Menéndez Pelayo, 1969.
Millás, Hernán and Filippi, Emilio. *Anatomía de un fracaso: la experiencia socialista chilena*. Santiago, Chile: Zig-Zag, 1974.
Chile 70–73: crónica da una experiencia. Santiago, Chile: Zig-Zag, 1974.
Navarro Rubio, Emilio. *El momento de la unión del alma con el cuerpo*. Pamplona: Studium Generale, 1957.
La corriente social. Barcelona: Ateneo Barcelonés, 1966.
La participación social. Madrid: Imprenta Ferreira, 1967.
Ors, Álvaro d'. *Forma de gobierno y legitimidad familiar*. Madrid: Ateneo, 1960.
Sistema de las ciencias. Pamplona: Ediciones Universidad de Navarra, 1970.
Pérez Embid, Florentino. *Ambiciones españolas*. Madrid: Editora Nacional, 1955.
En la brecha. Madrid: Rialp, 1956.
Acción de España en América. Barcelona: AHR, 1958.
Libertad, tradición y monarquía. Madrid: Ateneo, 1960.
Piñar, Blas. *Combate por España*. Madrid: Fuerza Nueva, 1975.
Hacia la III República? Madrid: Fuerza Nueva, 1979.
Pío Moa, Luis. *Contra la mentira*. Madrid: Libros libres, 2003.

Los crímenes de la guerra civil y otras polémicas. Madrid: La esfera de los libros, 2004.

Rodríguez Casado, Vicente. *La política y los políticos en el reinado de Carlos III*. Madrid: Ediciones Rialp, 1962.

Rodríguez Grez, Pablo. *El mito de la democracia en Chile*. Santiago, Chile: Eves Ediciones, 1985.

Una revolución pendiente. Santiago, Chile: Eves Ediciones, 1988.

Sánchez Agesta, Luis. *Historia del constitucionalismo español*. Madrid: Instituto de Estudios Políticos, 1955.

Principio de teoría política. Madrid: Editora Nacional, 1966.

Los principios cristianos del orden político. Madrid: Instituto de Estudios Políticos, 1962.

Sánchez Sorondo, Marcelo. *La revolución que anunciamos*. Buenos Aires: Ediciones Nueva Política, 1945.

Libertades prestadas. Buenos Aires: APLE, 1970.

Schmitt, Carl. *Interpretación europea de Donoso Cortes*. Madrid: Rialp, 1952.

Sepich, Juan Ramón. *Misión de los pueblos hispánicos*. Madrid: Seminario de Problemas Hispanoamericanos, 1949.

Vallet de Goytisolo, Juan. *Ideología "praxis" y mito de la tecnocracia*. Madrid: Montecorvo, 1971.

Valls Taberner, Luis and Formica, Mercedes. *Falsas y verdaderas formas del feminismo*. Madrid: Hauser y Monet, 1975.

Varas, Florencia and Vergara, José Manuel. *Operación Chile*. Buenos Aires: Pomaire, 1973.

Vial Correa, Gonzalo. *Pinochet: la biografía*, Santiago, Chile: Aguilar, 2002.

Villar Palasí, José Luis. *Administración y planificación*. Madrid: Ediciones Cultura Hispánica, 1952.

Experiencias políticas del mundo actual. Madrid: Instituto de Estudios Políticos, 1962.

Urteaga, Jesus. *El valor divino de lo humano*. Madrid: Rialp, 1948.

Dios y los hijos. Madrid: Rialp, 1960.

Siempre alegres. Madrid: Rialp, 1967.

Zafra Valverde, José. *Régimen político de España*. Pamplona: Ediciones Universidad de Navarra, 1973.

Alma y cuerpo del movimiento nacional. Pamplona: Ediciones Universidad de Navarra, 1975.

Zanotti, Luis Jorge. *La misión de la pedagogía*. Buenos Aires: Editorial Columba, 1967.

SELECTED SECONDARY LITERATURE

Águila, Gabriela. *Historia de la última dictadura militar: Argentina, 1976–1983*. Buenos Aires: Siglo Veintiuno Editores, 2023.

Aguilar, Enrique. *Ortega y la Argentina*. Buenos Aires: Fondo de Cultura Económica, 1997.

Aguilar Fernández, Paloma. *Memoria y Olvido de la Guerra Civil Española*. Madrid: Alianza, 1996.

Akin, William E. *Technocracy and the American Dream: The Technocrat Movement, 1900– 1941*. Berkeley: University of California Press, 1977.

Albanese, Matteo. *Transnational Fascism in the Twentieth Century: Spain, Italy and the Global Neo-Fascist Network*. New York: Bloomsbury Academic, 2016.

Altamirano, Carlos. *Bajo el signo de las masas: (1943–1973)*. Buenos Aires: Ariel, 2001.

Álvarez Cobelas, José. *Envenenados de cuerpo y alma: la oposición universitaria al Franquismo en Madrid (1939–1970)*. Madrid: Siglo XXI de España Editores, 2004.

Arancibia, Patricia. *Conversando con Roberto Kelly*. Santiago, Chile: Biblioteca Americana, 2005.

Arceneaux, Craig L. *Bounded Missions: Military Regimes and Democratization in the Southern Cone and Brazil*. University Park: Pennsylvania State University Press, 2001.

Arenal, Celestino del. *Política exterior de España hacía Iberoamérica*. Madrid: Editorial Complutense, 1994.

Arendt, Hannah. *Essays in Understanding, 1930–1954*. New York: Harcourt, Brace & Co., 1994.

Armengou, Montse. *Las fosas del silencio: hay un holocausto español?* Barcelona: Plaza & Janés, 2004.

Aron, Raymond. *The Opium of the Intellectuals*. New York: W.W. Norton, 1962.

Artigues, Daniel. *El Opus Dei en España*. Paris: Ruedo Ibérico, 1971.

Baby, Sophie. *El mito de la transición pacífica: violencia y política en España (1975–1982)*. Madrid: Ediciones Akal, 2018.

Bar-On, Tamir. *Where Have All the Fascists Gone?* London: Routledge, 2016.

Barchino, Matías (ed.). *Chile y la guerra civil española: la voz de los intelectuales*. Madrid: Calambur, 2014.

Barros, Robert. *Constitutionalism and Dictatorship: Pinochet, the Junta, and the 1980 Constitution*. New York: Cambridge University Press, 2002.

Balech, Mercedes (ed.). *El Opus Dei y la restauración católica*. Buenos Aires: Capital Intelectual, 2002.

Bell, Daniel. *The End of Ideology: On the Exhaustion of Political Ideas in the Fifties*. Glencoe, IL: Free Press, 1960.

Beraza, Luis Fernando. *Nacionalistas: la trayectoria política de un grupo polémico, 1927–1983*. Buenos Aires: Cántaro, 2005.

Blee, Kathleen M. and Deutsch, Sandra McGee. *Women of the Right: Comparisons and Interplay Across Borders*. University Park, PA: Penn State University Press, 2012.

Binns, Niall. *Argentina y la guerra civil española: la voz de los intelectuales*. Madrid: Editorial Cumio, 2012.

Bohoslavsky, Ernesto. *Historia mínima de las derechas Latinoamericanas*. Mexico City: El Colegio de Mexico, 2023.

Bottici, Chiara. *A Philosophy of Political Myth*. New York: Cambridge University Press, 2007.

Boyd, Carolyn P. *Historia Patria: Politics, History, and National Identity in Spain, 1875–1975*. Princeton, NJ: Princeton University Press, 1997.

Brands, Hal. *Latin America's Cold War*. Cambridge, MA: Harvard University Press, 2012.
Brennan, James P. *Córdoba rebelde: el Cordobazo, el clasismo y la movilización social*. La Plata: De la Campana, 2008.
The Politics of National Capitalism: Peronism and the Argentine Bourgeoisie, 1946–1976. University Park, PA: Penn State University Press, 2009.
Britt, Christopher. *Quixotism: The Imaginative Denial of Spain's Loss of Empire*. Albany: State University of New York Press, 2005.
Buchrucker, Cristián. *Nacionalismo y Peronismo: la Argentina en la crisis ideológica mundial (1927–1955)*. Buenos Aires: Sudamericana, 1987.
Burdick, Michael A. *For God and Fatherland: Religion and Politics in Argentina*. Albany: State University of New York Press, 1995.
Burns, E. Bradford. *Elites, Masses, and Modernization in Latin America, 1850–1930*. Austin: University of Texas Press, 1979.
Caimari, Lila M. *Perón y la iglesia católica: religión, estado y sociedad en la Argentina, 1943–1955*. Buenos Aires: Ariel Historia, 1995.
Cañellas Mas, Antonio. *Laureano López Rodo: biografía política de un ministro de Franco, 1920–2000*. Madrid: Biblioteca Nueva, 2011.
Alfredo Sánchez Bella: un embajador entre las Américas y Europa: diplomacia y política informativa en la España de Franco. Gijón: Ediciones Trea, 2015.
(ed.). *La tecnocracia Hispánica: ideas y proyecto político en Europa y América*. Gijón: Ediciones Trea, 2016.
Canelo, Paula. *El Proceso en su laberinto: la interna militar de Videla a Bignone*. Buenos Aires: Prometeo, 2008.
Cannon, Barry. *The Right in Latin America: Elite Power, Hegemony, and the Struggle for the State*. New York: Routledge, 2016.
Carassai, Sebastián. *The Argentine Silent Majority: Middle Classes, Politics, Violence, and Memory in the Seventies*. Durham, NC: Duke University Press, 2014.
Carreras, Albert. *Historia económica de la España contemporánea, 1789–2009*. Barcelona: Crítica, 2010.
Casals, Xavier. *Neonazis en España: de las audiciones wagnerianas a los skinheads (1966–1995)*. Barcelona: Grijalbo, 1995.
Casals Araya, Marcelo. *La creación de la amenaza roja: del surgimiento del anticomunismo en Chile a la "campaña del terror" de 1964*. Santiago, Chile: LOM Ediciones, 2016.
Casanova, José V. "The Opus Dei ethic, the technocrats and the modernization of Spain," *Social Science Information* 22 (1983): 27–50.
Casanova, Julián. *La iglesia de Franco*. Madrid: Ediciones Temas de Hoy, 2001.
(ed.). *Morir, matar, sobrevivir: la violencia en la dictadura de Franco*. Barcelona: Crítica, 2002.
Castro, José Manuel. *Jaime Guzmán: ideas y política 1946–1973*. Santiago, Chile: Ediciones Centro de Estudios Bicentenario, 2016.
Cavallo C. Ascanio. *La historia oculta del régimen militar*. Santiago, Chile: La Epoca, 1988.
Cavarozzi, Marcelo. *Autoritarismo y Democracia (1955–1983)*. Buenos Aires: Centro Editor de America Latina, 1987.

Cazorla Sánchez, Antonio. *Fear and Progress: Ordinary Lives in Franco's Spain, 1939–1975*. Hoboken, NJ: John Wiley & Sons, 2009.

Chastain, Andra B. and Lorek, Timothy (eds.). *Itineraries of Expertise: Science, Technology, and the Environment in Latin America's Long Cold War*. Pittsburgh, PA: University of Pittsburgh Press, 2020.

Cierva, Ricardo de la. *El Opus Dei: controversia y camino*. Madrid: Arc Editores, 1997.

Clark, Cal. *Challenging Neoliberalism: Globalization and the Economic Miracles in Chile and Taiwan*. Northampton, MA: Edward Elgar, 2016.

Coatsworth, John H. *Central America and the United States: The Clients and the Colossus*. New York: Twayne Publishers, 1994.

Constable, Pamela. *A Nation of Enemies: Chile under Pinochet*. New York: W.W. Norton, 1991.

Corbière, Emilio J. *Opus Dei: el totalitarismo católico: acerca del integrismo y del progresismo cristiano*. Buenos Aires: Editorial Sudamericana, 2002.

Corral Broto, Pablo. "Sobreviviendo al desarrollismo. Las desigualdades ambientales y la protesta social durante el franquismo (Aragón, 1950–1979)," *Ager: Revista de Estudios sobre Despoblación y Desarrollo Rural* 10 (2011): 111–55.

Correa Sutil, Sofía. *Con las riendas del poder: la derecha chilena en el Siglo XX*. Santiago, Chile: Penguin Random House, 2011.

Cosse, Isabella. *Pareja, sexualidad y familia en los años sesenta: una revolución discreta en Buenos Aires*. Buenos Aires: Siglo Veintiuno, 2010.

Costa Pinto, António. *Corporatism and Fascism: The Corporatist Wave in Europe*. New York: Routledge, 2017.

Costa Pinto, António and Finchelstein, Federico (eds.). *Authoritarianism and Corporatism in Europe and Latin America: Crossing Borders*. New York: Routledge, 2019.

Cowan, Benjamin A. *Securing Sex: Morality and Repression in the Making of Cold War Brazil*. Chapel Hill: University of North Carolina Press, 2016.

Crenzel, Emilio Ariel. *El Tucumanazo*. Tucumán: Universidad Nacional de Tucumán, 1997.

Crespo McLennan, Julio. *Spain and the Process of European Integration, 1957–85*, New York: Palgrave, 2000.

Cristi, Renato. *El pensamiento político de Jaime Guzmán: autoridad y libertad*. Santiago, Chile: LOM Ediciones, 2000.

Cristi, Renato and Ruiz, Carlos. *El pensamiento conservador en Chile*. Santiago, Chile: Editorial Universitaria, 1992.

Crumbaugh, Justin. *Destination Dictatorship: The Spectacle of Spain's Tourist Boom and the Reinvention of Difference*. Albany: State University of New York Press, 2009.

Dandan, Alejandra and Heguy, Silvina. *Joe Baxter: del nazismo a la extrema izquierda: la historia secreta de un guerrillero*. Buenos Aires: Editorial Norma, 2006.

Dargent, Eduardo. *Technocracy and Democracy in Latin America: The Experts Running Government*. New York: Cambridge University Press, 2015.

Dávila, Jerry. *Dictatorship in South America*. Hoboken, NJ: John Wiley & Sons, 2013.

Delgado Gómez-Escalonilla, Lorenzo. *Diplomacia franquista y política cultural hacia Iberoamérica, 1939–1953*. Madrid: CSIC, 1988.

Imperio de papel: acción cultural y política durante el primer Franquismo. Madrid: CSIC, 1992.

Deutsch, Sandra McGee and Dolkart, Ronald H. *The Argentine Right: Its History and Intellectual Origins, 1910 to the Present*. Wilmington, DE: Rowman & Littlefield, 1993.

Las Derechas: The Extreme Right in Argentina, Brazil, and Chile, 1890–1939. Stanford, CA: Stanford University Press, 1999.

Devoto, Fernando. *Nacionalismo, fascismo y tradicionalismo en la Argentina moderna: una historia*. Buenos Aires: Siglo Veintiuno de Argentina, 2002.

Díaz, Elías. *Pensamiento español en la era de Franco: 1939–1975*. Madrid: Tecnos, 1983.

Díaz Hernández, Onésimo. *Rafael Calvo Serer y el grupo Arbor*. Valencia: Universitat de València, 2011.

Díaz Nieva, José. *Chile, de la Falange Nacional a la Democracia Cristiana*. Santiago, Chile: Universidad Nacional de Educación a Distancia, 2000.

Patria y Libertad: el nacionalismo frente a la Unidad Popular. Santiago, Chile: Ediciones Centro de Estudios Bicentenario, 2015.

Breve historia del neofascismo y de la derecha radical. Santiago, Chile: Akhilleus Ediciones, 2017.

Dinges, John. *The Condor Years: How Pinochet and His Allies Brought Terrorism to Three Continents*. New York: New Press, 2004.

Domínguez, Francisco, Lievesley, Geraldine, and Ludlam, Steve (eds.). *Right-Wing Politics in the New Latin America: Reaction and Revolt*. New York: Zed Books, 2011.

Domínguez, Jorge I. (ed.). *Authoritarian and Democratic Regimes in Latin America*. New York: Garland Publishing, 1994.

Drake, Paul W. and Jaksic, Ivan (eds.). *The Struggle for Democracy in Chile*. Lincoln: University of Nebraska Press, 1995.

Durham, Martin and Power, Margaret. *New Perspectives on the Transnational Right*. New York: Palgrave Macmillan, 2011.

Edwards, Sebastian. *The Chile Project: The Story of the Chicago Boys and the Downfall of Neoliberalism*. Princeton, NJ: Princeton University Press, 2023.

Elliott, J. H. *Spain, Europe and the Wider World, 1500–1800*. New Haven, CT: Yale University Press, 2009.

Encarnación, Omar G. *The Myth of Civil Society: Social Capital and Democratic Consolidation in Spain and Brazil*. New York: Palgrave Macmillan, 2003.

Democracy Without Justice in Spain: The Politics of Forgetting Philadelphia: University of Pennsylvania Press, 2014.

Ensalaco, Mark. *Chile under Pinochet: Recovering the Truth*. Philadelphia: University of Pennsylvania Press, 2010.

Escudero, María A. *El Instituto de Cultura Hispánica*. Madrid: Editorial MAPFRE, 1994.

Espadas Burgos, Manuel. *Franquismo y política exterior*. Madrid: Rialp, 1988.

Estruch, Juan. *Saints and Schemers: Opus Dei and Its Paradoxes*. New York: Oxford University Press, 1995.
Feitlowitz, Marguerite. *A Lexicon of Terror: Argentina and the Legacies of Torture*. New York: Oxford University Press, 1998.
Fillipa, Nelly. *Educación personalizada y dictadura militar en Argentina, 1976–1983*. San Juan: Universidad Nacional de San Juan, 1997.
Finchelstein, Federico. *Transatlantic Fascism: Ideology, Violence, and the Sacred in Argentina and Italy, 1919–1945*. Durham, NC: Duke University Press, 2009.
The Ideological Origins of the Dirty War: Fascism, Populism, and Dictatorship in Twentieth Century Argentina. New York: Oxford University Press, 2014.
From Fascism to Populism in History. Oakland: University of California Press, 2017.
Franco, Marina. *El final del silencio: dictadura, sociedad y derechos humanos en la transición (1979–1983)*. Buenos Aires: Fondo de Cultura Económica, 2018.
Galasso, Norberto. *Perón: exilio, resistencia, retorno y muerte, 1955–1974*. Buenos Aires: Ediciones Colihue, 2005.
Galetti, Amelia. *El revisionismo como historia oficial*. Paraná: Dictum Ediciones, 2013.
Gallego Margaleff, Ferran. *El mito de la transición: la crisis del franquismo y los orígenes de la democracia (1973–1977)*. Barcelona: Crítica, 2008.
Galván, Valeria. *El nacionalismo de derecha en la Argentina posperonista: el semanario Azul y Blanco (1956–1969)*. Rosario: Prohistoria Ediciones, 2013.
Gárate Chateau, Manuel. *La revolución capitalista de Chile (1973–2003)*. Santiago, Chile: Ediciones Universidad Alberto Hurtado, 2012.
García, Jordi. *La resistencia silenciosa: fascismo y cultura en España*. Barcelona: Anagrama, 2004.
García, José Fernando (ed.). *El discurso de la derecha chilena*. Santiago, Chile: CESOC, 1992.
García Abad, José. *Adolfo Suárez: una tragedia griega*. Madrid: Esfera de los Libros, 2005.
Garretón Merino, Manuel A. *Incomplete Democracy: Political Democratization in Chile and Latin America*. Chapel Hill: University of North Carolina Press, 2003.
Gazmuri, Cristián. *Quién era Jaime Guzmán?* Santiago, Chile: RiL editores, 2013.
Gil Pecharromán, Julio. *Con permiso de la autoridad: la España de Franco (1939–1975)*. Madrid: Temas de Hoy, 2008.
Gill, Lesley. *The School of the Americas: Military Training and Political Violence in the Americas*. Durham, NC: Duke University Press, 2004.
Gillespie, Richard. *Soldiers of Perón: Argentina's Montoneros*. New York: Oxford University Press, 1982.
Goldwert, Marvin. *Democracy, Militarism, and Nationalism in Argentina, 1930–1966: An Interpretation*. Austin: University of Texas Press, 2014.
Gomes, Gabriela D. "El Onganiato y los sectores populares: funcionarios, ideas y políticas de la Secretaría de Estado de Promoción y Asistencia a la Comunidad (1966–1970)," *Anuario del Centro de Estudios Históricos* 11:11 (2011): 279–302.

González, Julio C. *Isabel Perón: intimidades de un gobierno*. Buenos Aires: Editorial El Ateneo, 2007.

González, Yanko. *Los más ordenaditos: fascismo y juventud en la dictadura de Pinochet*. Santiago, Chile: Hueders, 2020.

González Cuevas, Pedro Carlos. *Maeztu: biografía de un nacionalista español*. Madrid: Marcial Pons Historia, 2003.

El pensamiento político de la derecha española en el siglo XX: de la crisis de la restauración al estado de partidos (1898–2000). Madrid: Tecnos, 2005.

La razón conservadora: Gonzalo Fernández de la Mora, una biografía político-intelectual. Madrid: Biblioteca Nueva, 2015.

González de Oleaga, Marisa. *El doble juego de la Hispanidad: España y la Argentina durante la segunda guerra mundial*. Madrid: Universidad Nacional de Educación, 2001.

González-Rivera, Victoria and Kampwirth, Karen. *Radical Women in Latin America: Left and Right*. University Park, PA: Penn State University Press, 2001.

González Ruiz, Edgar. *Cruces y sombras: perfiles del conservadurismo en América Latina*. San José, Costa Rica: Asociación Colectiva por el Derecho a Decidir, 2006.

Grandin, Greg. *The Last Colonial Massacre: Latin America in the Cold War*. Chicago, IL: University of Chicago Press, 2011.

Grandin, Greg and Joseph, Gilbert M. (eds.). *A Century of Revolution: Insurgent and Counterinsurgent Violence during Latin America's Long Cold War*. Durham, NC: Duke University Press, 2010.

Green, James. *We Cannot Remain Silent: Opposition to the Brazilian Military Dictatorship in the United States* (Durham, NC: Duke University Press, 2010).

Griffin, Roger. *The Nature of Fascism*. New York: St. Martin's Press, 1991.

Griffin, Roger and Feldman, Matthew. *Fascism: Critical Concepts in Political Science: Post-War Fascisms*. New York: Routledge, 2004.

Halperín Donghi, Tulio. *The Peronist Revolution and its Ambiguous Legacy*. London: University of London, Institute of Latin American Studies, 1998.

El revisionismo histórico argentino como visión decadentista de la historia nacional. Buenos Aires: Siglo Veintiuno Editores, 2005.

Harmer, Tanya. *Allende's Chile and the Inter-American Cold War*. Chapel Hill: University of North Carolina Press, 2011.

Heiss, Claudia and Navia, Patricio. "You Win Some, You Lose Some: Constitutional Reforms in Chile's Transition to Democracy," *Latin American Politics and Society* 49:3 (2007): 163–90.

Henríquez Uzal, María José. *¡Viva La Verdadera Amistad!: Franco y Allende, 1970–1973*. Santiago, Chile: Editorial Universitaria, 2014.

Herf, Jeffrey. *Reactionary Modernism: Technology, Culture, and Politics in Weimar and the Third Reich*. New York: Cambridge University Press, 1984.

Herrán Ávila, Luis Alberto. "Las guerrillas blancas: anticomunismo transnacional e imaginarios de derechas en Argentina y México, 1954–1972," *Quinto Sol* 19:1 (June 2015): 1–26.

Hodges, Donald C. *Argentina's "Dirty War": An Intellectual Biography*. Austin: University of Texas Press, 2014.

Horkheimer, Max and Adorno, Theodor W. *The Dialectic of Enlightenment.* New York: Herder and Herder, 1972 [1944].
Htun, Mala. *Sex and the State: Abortion, Divorce, and the Family under Latin American Dictatorships and Democracies.* New York: Cambridge University Press, 2003.
Huneeus, Carlos. *El régimen de Pinochet.* Santiago, Chile: Editorial Sudamericana, 2000.
"Technocrats and Politicians in an Authoritarian Regime. The 'ODEPLAN Boys' and the 'Gremialists' in Pinochet's Chile," *Journal of Latin American Studies* 32:2 (May 2000): 461–501.
Huntington, Samuel P. *The Third Wave: Democratization in the Late Twentieth Century.* Norman: University of Oklahoma Press, 1991.
Iber, Patrick. *Neither Peace nor Freedom: The Cultural Cold War in Latin America.* Cambridge, MA: Harvard University Press, 2015.
Jara Hinojosa, Isabel. *De Franco a Pinochet: el proyecto cultural franquista en Chile 1936– 1980.* Santiago, Chile: Universidad de Chile, 2006.
Jauretche, Arturo. *Política nacional y revisionismo histórico.* Buenos Aires: Peña Lillo, 1970.
El Plan Prebisch: retorno al coloniaje. Buenos Aires: Peña Lillo, 1984.
Joseph, Gilbert M. and Spenser, Daniela. *In from the Cold: Latin America's New Encounter with the Cold War.* Durham, NC: Duke University Press, 2008.
Kornbluh, Peter. *The Pinochet File: A Declassified Dossier on Atrocity and Accountability.* New York: New Press, 2013.
Laclau, Ernesto. *Emancipation(s).* New York: Verso, 1996.
Laqueur, Walter. *Fascism: Past, Present, Future.* New York: Oxford University Press, 1996.
Larraquy, Marcelo (et al.). *López Rega: el peronismo y la Triple A.* Buenos Aires: Punto de Lectura, 2007.
Latham, Michael E. *The Right Kind of Revolution: Modernization, Development, and U.S. Foreign Policy from the Cold War to the Present.* Ithaca, NY: Cornell University Press, 2011.
Latour, Bruno. *We Have Never Been Modern.* Cambridge, MA: Harvard University Press, 1993.
Lemus López, Encarnación. *En Hamelin: la transición española más allá de la frontera.* Oviedo: Septem Ediciones, 2001.
Lepenies, Philipp. *The Power of a Single Number: A Political History of GDP.* New York: Columbia University Press, 2016.
Lewis, Paul H. *The Crisis of Argentine Capitalism.* Chapel Hill: University of North Carolina Press, 1990.
Authoritarian Regimes in Latin America: Dictators, Despots, and Tyrants, Lanham, MD: Rowman & Littlefield, 2006.
Lieberman, Sima. *Growth and Crisis in the Spanish Economy: 1940–1993.* New York: Routledge, 2005.
Linz, Juan José. *Totalitarian and Authoritarian Regimes.* Boulder, CO: Lynne Rienner Publishers, 2000.
Llairó, María Monserrat. *Frondizi: un nuevo modelo de inserción internacional.* Buenos Aires: Eudeba, 2003.

Lipset, Seymour Martin. *Elites in Latin America.* New York: Oxford University Press, 1967.

Lomnitz, Larissa Adler de. *Chile's Middle Class: A Struggle for Survival in the Face of Neoliberalism.* Boulder, CO: Lynne Rienner Publishers, 1991.

López, Fernando. *The Feathers of Condor: Transnational State Terrorism, Exiles and Civilian Anticommunism in South America.* Newcastle: Cambridge Scholars Publishing, 2016.

Loveman, Brian. *Struggle in the Countryside: Politics and Rural Labor in Chile, 1919–1973.* Bloomington: Indiana University Press, 1976.

The Constitution of Tyranny: Regimes of Exception in Spanish America. Pittsburgh, PA: University of Pittsburgh Press, 1993.

Loveman, Brian and Davies, Thomas M. (eds.). *The Politics of Antipolitics: The Military in Latin America*, Wilmington, DE: Scholarly Resources, 1997.

Luna, Juan Pablo and Kaltwasser, Cristóbal Rovira (eds.). *The Resilience of the Latin American Right.* Baltimore, MD: Johns Hopkins University Press, 2014.

Lvovich, Daniel. *Nacionalismo y antisemitismo en la Argentina.* Buenos Aires: Grupo Zeta, 2003.

El nacionalismo de derecha: desde sus orígenes a Tacuara. Buenos Aires: Capital Intelectual, 2006.

Malló, Oriol. *El cártel español: historia crítica de la reconquista económica de México y América Latina (1898–2008).* Madrid: Foca, 2011.

Mangabeira Unger, Roberto. *Democracy Realized: The Progressive Alternative.* New York: Verso, 1998.

Manzano, Valeria. *The Age of Youth in Argentina: Politics, Culture, and Sexuality from Perón to Videla.* Chapel Hill: University of North Carolina Press, 2014.

Marwick, Arthur. *The Sixties: Cultural Revolution in Britain, France, Italy, and the United States, 1958–1974*, New York: Oxford University Press, 1998.

Mayayo, Andreu. *Economía Franquista y corrupción.* Barcelona: Flor del Viento Ediciones, 2010.

McGuire, James W. *Peronism without Perón: Unions, Parties, and Democracy in Argentina.* Stanford, CA: Stanford University Press, 1997.

McLeod, Hugh. *The Religious Crisis of the 1960s.* New York: Oxford University Press, 2007.

McSherry, J. Patrice. *Incomplete Transition: Military Power and Democracy in Argentina.* New York: St. Martin's Press, 1997.

Predatory States: Operation Condor and Covert War in Latin America. Lanham, MD: Rowman & Littlefield, 2005.

Medina, Alberto. *Exorcismos de la memoria: políticas y poéticas de la melancolía en la España de la transición.* Madrid: Ediciones Libertarias, 2001.

Menotti, Emilia Edda. *Arturo Frondizi: biografía.* Buenos Aires: Planeta, 1998.

Meynaud, Jean. *Technocracy.* London: Faber, 1968.

Middlebrook, Kevin J. (ed.). *Conservative Parties, the Right, and Democracy in Latin America.* Baltimore, MD: Johns Hopkins University Press, 2000.

Miguez Macho, Antonio. *Genocidal Genealogy of Francoism: Violence, Memory and Impunity.* Eastbourne: Sussex Academic Press, 2017.

Milanesio, Natalia. *Workers Go Shopping in Argentina: The Rise of Popular Consumer Culture*. Albuquerque: University of New Mexico, 2013.

Molinero, Carme. *Productores disciplinados y minorías subversivas: clase obrera y conflictividad laboral en la España Franquista*. Madrid: Siglo XXI, 1998.

Molinero, Carme and Ysas, Pere. *La anatomía del Franquismo: de la supervivencia a la agonía, 1945–1977*. Barcelona: Crítica, 2008.

Moncada, Alberto. *Historia oral del Opus Dei*. Barcelona: Plaza & Janés, 1987.

Moncada Durruti, Belén. *Jaime Guzmán: una democracia contrarrevolucionaria*. Santiago, Chile: RiL editores, 2006.

Mönckeberg, María Olivia. *El imperio del Opus Dei en Chile*. Santiago, Chile: Ediciones B, Grupo Zeta, 2003.

Morcillo, Aurora G. *True Catholic Womanhood: Gender Ideology in Franco's Spain*. DeKalb: Northern Illinois University Press, 2000.

Morero, Sergio. *La noche de los bastones largos: 30 años después*. Buenos Aires: Editorial La Página, 1996.

Morodo, Raúl. *Los orígenes ideológicos del franquismo: Acción Española*. Madrid: Alianza Editorial, 1985.

Moyn, Samuel. *The Last Utopia*. Cambridge, MA: Belknap Press of Harvard University Press, 2010.

Müller, Jan-Werner. *A Dangerous Mind: Carl Schmitt in Post-War European Thought*. New Haven, CT: Yale University Press, 2003.

Muñoz Tamayo, Víctor. *Historia de la UDI: generaciones y cultura política (1973–2013)*. Santiago, Chile: Ediciones Universidad Alberto Hurtado, 2016.

Narodowski, Patricio. *La Argentina pasiva: desarrollo, subjetividad, instituciones, más allá de la modernidad: el desarrollo visto desde el margen de una periferia, de un país dependiente*. Buenos Aires: Prometeo Libros, 2007.

Navarro, Marysa. *Los nacionalistas*. Buenos Aires: Editorial J. Alvarez, 1968.

Navarro, Vicente. *Bienestar insuficiente, democracia incompleta: sobre lo que no se habla en buestro país*. Barcelona: Editorial Anagrama, 2002.

El subdesarrollo social de España: causas y consecuencias. Barcelona: Editorial Anagrama, 2006.

Negró Acedo, Luis. *El diario El País y la cultura de las élites durante la transición*. Madrid: Foca, 2006.

Nino, Carlos Santiago. *Radical Evil on Trial*. New Haven, CT: Yale University Press, 1998.

Nolte, Ernst. *Die Krise des liberalen Systems und die faschistischen Bewegungen*. Munich: Piper, 1968.

Novaro, Marcos and Palermo, Vicente. *La dictadura militar, 1976–1983: del golpe de estado a la restauración democrática*. Buenos Aires: Paidós, 2003.

Núñez-Seixas, Xosé Manoel. *La España de Franco*. Madrid: Información e Historia, 1996.

Ser españoles: imaginarios nacionalistas en el siglo XX. Barcelona: RBA Libros, 2013.

Nye, Joseph S. *Soft Power: The Means to Success in World Politics*. New York: Public Affairs, 2004.

O'Donnell, Guillermo A. *Bureaucratic Authoritarianism: Argentina, 1966–1973, in Comparative Perspective*. Berkeley: University of California University Press, 1988.
Ofer, Inbal. *Señoritas in Blue: The Making of a Female Political Elite in Franco's Spain*. Portland, OR: Sussex Academic Press, 2009.
Ohana, David. *The Fascist Temptation: Creating a Political Community of Experience*. New York: Routledge, 2021.
Ollier, María Matilde. *Golpe o revolución: la violencia legitimada, Argentina, 1966–1973*. Buenos Aires: EDUNTREF, 2005.
Pablo, Juan Carlos de. *La economía argentina: en la segunda mitad del siglo XX*. Buenos Aires: La Ley, 2005.
Palomares, Cristina. *The Quest for Survival after Franco: Moderate Francoism and the Slow Journey to the Polls, 1964–1977*. Portland, OR: Sussex Academic Press, 2004.
Pandolfi, Rodolfo. *Azules y colorados: el conflicto político y militar a comienzos de los sesenta*. Buenos Aires: Editorial Centro de Estudios Unión para la Nueva Mayoría, 1994.
La democracia derrotada: Arturo Illia y su época. Buenos Aires: Lumiere, 2008.
Pardo Sanz, Rosa María. *Con Franco hacia el Imperio!: la política exterior española en América Latina, 1939–1945*. Madrid: Universidad Nacional de Educación a Distancia, 1995.
Pavilack, Jody. *Mining for the Nation: The Politics of Chile's Coal Communities from the Popular Front to the Cold War*. University Park, PA: Penn State University Press, 2011.
Pavlovic, Tatjana. *The Mobile Nation: España Cambia de Piel (1954–1964)*. Chicago, IL: Intellect, 2011.
Paxton, Robert O. *The Anatomy of Fascism*. New York: Knopf, 2004.
Payne, Stanley G. *Fascism: Comparison and Definition*. Madison: University of Wisconsin Press, 1983.
El primer franquismo, 1939–1959: los años de la autarquía de España. Madrid: Temas de Hoy, 1997.
Fascism in Spain, 1923–1977. Madison: University of Wisconsin Press, 1999.
Peñaranda, Juan María de. *Los servicios secretos de Carrero Blanco: los orígenes del CNI*. Barcelona: Espasa, 2015.
Pérez Montfort, Ricardo. *Hispanismo y Falange: los sueños imperiales de la derecha española y México*. Mexico City: Fondo de Cultura Económica, 1992.
Perina, Rubén M. *Onganía, Levingston, Lanusse: los militares en la política argentina*. Buenos Aires: Editorial de Belgrano, 1983.
Pettinà, Vanni. *Historia mínima de la Guerra Fría en América Latina*. Mexico City: El Colegio de México, 2018.
Pisarello Virasoro, Roberto Gustavo. *Cómo y por qué fue derrocado Frondizi*. Buenos Aires: Editorial Biblos, 1996.
Pollack, Benny and Hunter, Graham. *The Paradox of Spanish Foreign Policy: Spain's International Relations from Franco to Democracy*. New York: Pinter Publishers, 1987.

Potash, Robert A. *The Army & Politics in Argentina, 1962–1973: From Frondizi's Fall to the Peronist Restoration.* Stanford, CA: Stanford University Press, 1996.

Powell, Charles T. *Juan Carlos of Spain: Self-Made Monarch.* New York: St. Martin's Press, 1996.

Del autoritarismo a la democracia: estudios de política exterior española. Madrid: Silex Ediciones, 2007

Power, Margaret. *Right-Wing Women in Chile: Feminine Power and the Struggle Against Allende, 1964–1973.* University Park, PA: Penn State University Press, 2002.

Preston, Paul. *The Politics of Revenge: Fascism and the Military in 20th-Century Spain.* London: Unwin Hyman, 1990.

Juan Carlos: A People's King. London: HarperCollins, 2004.

The Spanish Holocaust: Inquisition and Extermination in Twentieth-Century Spain. London: HarperPress, 2012.

Pucciarelli, Alfredo R. (ed.). *Empresarios, tecnócratas y militares: la trama corporativa de la última dictadura.* Buenos Aires: Siglo Veintiuno Editores Argentina, 2004.

Quiroga, Hugo. *El tiempo del proceso: conflictos y coincidencias entre políticos y militares. 1976–1983.* Rosario: Fundación Ross, 1994.

Rabe, Stephen G. *The Most Dangerous Area in the World: John F. Kennedy Confronts Communist Revolution in Latin America.* Chapel Hill: University of North Carolina Press, 1999.

The Killing Zone: The United States Wages Cold War in Latin America. New York: Oxford University Press, 2012.

Radcliff, Pamela Beth. *Making Democratic Citizens in Spain: Civil Society and the Popular Origins of the Transition, 1960–78.* New York: Palgrave Macmillan, 2011.

Ramond, Allen. *What Is Technocracy?* New York: Whittlesey House, McGraw-Hill, 1933.

Reig Tapia, Alberto. *Ideología e historia: sobre la represión Franquista y la Guerra Civil.* Madrid: Akal, 1984.

Anti-Moa: la subversión neofranquista de la historia de España. Barcelona: Ediciones B, 2006.

Rein, Monica. *Politics and Education in Argentina, 1946–1962.* Armonk, NY: M.E. Sharpe, 1998.

Rein, Raanan. "Hispanidad y oportunismo político: el caso peronista," *Estudios Interdisciplinarios de América Latina y el Caribe* 2:2 (1991): 51–69.

La salvación de una dictadura: alianza Franco-Perón 1946–1955. Madrid: Editorial CSIC, 1995.

Peronismo, populismo y política: Argentina, 1943–1955. Buenos Aires: Editorial de Belgrano, 1998.

Reyes, Felipen and Arroyo, Guido. *Chacarillas: los elegidos de Pinochet.* Santiago, Chile: Editorial Alquimia, 2019.

Riz, Liliana de. *La política en suspenso, 1966–1976.* Buenos Aires: Paidós, 2000.

Robin, Corey. *The Reactionary Mind: Conservatism from Edmund Burke to Sarah Palin.* New York: Oxford University Press, 2011.

Rock, David. *Authoritarian Argentina: The Nationalist Movement, Its History, and Its Impact*. Berkeley: University of California Press, 1993.

Rodríguez, Álvaro. *La legitimación política del franquismo: de la II Republica a la instauración de la democracia en España*. Madrid: Editorial CSED, 2014.

Rodríguez Lamas, Daniel. *La Presidencia de Frondizi*. Buenos Aires: Centro Editor de América Latina, 1984.

La Revolución Libertadora. Buenos Aires: Centro Editor de América Latina, 1985.

Romero, Luis Alberto. *La política en consignas: memoria de los setenta*. Rosario: Homo Sapiens Ediciones, 2002.

Roniger, Luis and Sznajder, Mario. *The Legacy of Human-Rights Violations in the Southern Cone: Argentina, Chile, and Uruguay*. New York: Oxford University Press, 1999.

Rostow, Walt Whitman. *The Stages of Economic Growth: A Non-Communist Manifesto*. Cambridge: Cambridge University Press, 1961.

Royo, Sebastián. *"A New Century of Corporatism?": Corporatism in Southern Europe, Spain and Portugal in Comparative Perspective*. Westport, CT: Praeger, 2002.

Rubio Apiolaza, Pablo. *Los civiles de Pinochet: la derecha en el régimen militar chileno, 1983–1990*, Santiago, Chile: Centro de Investigaciones Diego Barros Arana, 2013.

Ruiz Carnicer, Miguel Ángel. *El Sindicato Español Universitario (SEU), 1939–1965: la socialización política de la juventud universitaria en el Franquismo*. Mexico City: Siglo Veintiuno Editores, 1996.

Sáenz Quesada, María. *Isabel Perón: la Argentina en los años de María Estela Martínez*. Buenos Aires: Grupo Editorial Planeta, 2003.

La libertadora: de Perón a Frondizi (1955–1958): historia pública y secreta. Buenos Aires: Editorial Sudamericana, 2011.

Sánchez de Loria Parodi, Horacio. *Máximo Etchecopar: un pensador tucumano olvidado*. Buenos Aires: Torre de Hércules, 2015.

Sánchez Recio, Glicerio (ed.). *La internacional católica: Pax Romana en la política europea de Posguerra*. Alicante: Universidad de Alicante, 2005.

Sánchez Soler, Mariano. *La transición sangrienta: una historia violenta del proceso democrático en España, 1975–1983*. Barcelona: Península, 2010.

Sanchis Sinisterra, José. *Terror y miseria en el primer Franquismo*. Madrid: Cátedra, 2003.

Sapag, M. Pablo. *Chile, frente de combate de la guerra civil española: propaganda republicana y franquista al otro lado del mundo*. Valencia: Centro Francisco Tomás y Valiente, 2003.

Saz Campos, Ismael. *Fascismo y Franquismo*. Valencia: Universitat de València, 2004.

"Fascism, Fascistization, and Developmentalism in Franco's Dictatorship," *Social History* 29:3 (August 2004): 342–57.

Las caras del franquismo. Granada: Editorial Comares, 2013.

Schamis, Hector E. *From Bureaucratic-Authoritarianism to Neoconservatism: Reassessing the Military Regimes of the Southern Cone*. New York: Columbia University, ILAS, 1988.

Selser, Gregorio. *La espada y el hisopo*. Buenos Aires: Hyspamerica, 1973.
Sheinin, David M. K. *Consent of the Damned: Ordinary Argentinians in the Dirty War*. Gainesville: University Press of Florida, 2013.
Silva, Patricio. "Technocrats and Politics in Chile: From the Chicago Boys to the CIEPLAN Monks," *Journal of Latin American Studies* 23:2 (May 1991): 385–410.
In the Name of Reason: Technocrats and Politics in Chile. University Park, PA: Penn State University Press, 2008.
Sivak, Martín. *El doctor: biografía no autorizada de Mariano Grondona*. Buenos Aires: Aguilar, 2005.
Smith, William C. *Authoritarianism and the Crisis of the Argentine Political Economy*. Stanford, CA: Stanford University Press, 1991.
Soto, Francisco. *Fascismo y Opus Dei en Chile: estudios de literatura e ideología*. Barcelona: Editorial Avance, 1976.
Spektorowski, Alberto. *The Origins of Argentina's Revolution of the Right*. Notre Dame, IN: University of Notre Dame Press, 2003.
Spooner, Mary Helen. *Soldiers in a Narrow Land: The Pinochet Regime in Chile*. Berkeley: University of California Press, 1999.
Stern, Steve J. *Reckoning with Pinochet: The Memory Question in Democratic Chile, 1989–2006*. Durham, NC: Duke University Press, 2010.
Sternhell, Zeev. *The Birth of Fascist Ideology: From Cultural Rebellion to Political Revolution*. Princeton, NJ: Princeton University Press, 1994.
Suárez Fernández, Luis. *Franco y la iglesia: las relaciones con el Vaticano*. Madrid: Homo Legens, 2011.
Suri, Jeremi. *Power and Protest: Global Revolution and the Rise of Détente*. Cambridge, MA: Harvard University Press, 2003.
Sznajder, Mario and Roniger, Luis. *The Politics of Exile in Latin America*. New York: Cambridge University Press, 2009.
Szusterman, Celia. *Frondizi and the Politics of Developmentalism in Argentina: 1955–62*. Oxford: Macmillan, 1993.
Taylor, Marcus. *From Pinochet to the "Third Way": Neoliberalism and Social Transformation in Chile*. Ann Arbor, MI: Pluto Press, 2006.
Thomàs, Joan María. *La Falange de Franco: fascismo y fascistización en el régimen Franquista, 1937–1945*. Barcelona: Plaza & Janés, 2001.
Thomàs, Joan María and Bates, John. *José Antonio Primo de Rivera: The Reality and Myth of a Spanish Fascist Leader*. New York: Berghahn Books, 2019.
Toquero, José María. *Franco y Don Juan: la oposición monárquica al franquismo*. Barcelona: Plaza y Janés, 1989.
Torre, Joseba de la and García-Zúñiga, Mario (eds.). *Entre el mercado y el estado: los planes de desarrollo durante el Franquismo*. Pamplona: Universidad Pública de Navarra, 2009.
Torre, Joseba de la and Lafuente, Gloria Sanz (eds.). *Migraciones y coyuntura económica del Franquismo a la democracia*. Zaragoza: Prensas Universitarias de Zaragoza, 2008.
Townson, Nigel (ed.). *Spain Transformed: The Late Franco Dictatorship, 1959–75*. New York: Palgrave Macmillan, 2007.
Traverso, Enzo. *The European Civil War, 1919–1945*. New York: Verso, 2016.

The New Faces of Fascism: Populism and the Far Right. New York: Verso, 2019.

Tusell, Javier. *Franco y los católicos: la política interior española entre 1945 y 1957*. Madrid: Alianza, 1984.

La España de Franco: el poder, la oposición y la política exterior durante el franquismo. Madrid: Historia 16, 1989.

Carrero: la eminencia gris del régimen de Franco. Madrid: Ediciones Temas de Hoy, 1993.

Juan Carlos I: La restauración de la Monarquía. Madrid: Ediciones Temas de Hoy, 1995.

Valdés, Juan Gabriel. *Pinochet's Economists: The Chicago School in Chile*. Cambridge: Cambridge University Press, 1995.

Valdivia Ortiz de Zárate, Verónica. *Nacionales y Gremialistas: el "parto" de la nueva derecha política chilena, 1964–1973*. Santiago, Chile: LOM Ediciones, 2008.

La alcaldización de la política: los municipios en la dictadura pinochetista. Santiago, Chile: LOM Ediciones, 2012.

Varon, Jeremy. *Bringing the War Home: The Weather Underground, the Red Army Faction, and Revolutionary Violence in the Sixties and Seventies*. Berkeley: University of California Press, 2004.

Veigel, Klaus Friedrich. *Dictatorship, Democracy, and Globalization: Argentina and the Cost of Paralysis, 1973–2001*. University Park: Penn State University Press, 2010.

Verbitsky, Horacio. *Civiles y militares: memoria secreta de la transición*. Buenos Aires: Editorial Sudamericana, 2003.

Doble juego: la Argentina católica y militar. Buenos Aires: Editorial Sudamericana, 2006.

Vergara, Angela. *Copper Workers, International Business, and Domestic Politics in Cold War Chile*. University Park: Penn State University Press, 2010.

Vergara, Camila. *Systemic Corruption: Constitutional Ideas for an Anti-oligarchic Republic*. Princeton, NJ: Princeton University Press, 2020.

Vezzetti, Hugo. *Pasado y presente: guerra, dictadura y sociedad en la Argentina*. Buenos Aires: Siglo XXI, 2002.

Viestenz, William. *By the Grace of God: Francoist Spain and the Sacred Roots of Political Imagination*. Toronto, ON: University of Toronto Press, 2014.

Vilarós, Teresa M. *El mono del desencanto: una crítica cultural de la transición española, 1973– 1993*. Madrid: Siglo Veintiuno Editores, 1998.

Viñas, Ángel. *En las garras del Águila: los pactos con Estados Unidos, de Francisco Franco a Felipe González (1945–1995)*. Barcelona: Crítica, 2003.

Weld, Kirsten. "The Spanish Civil War and the Construction of a Reactionary Historical Consciousness in Augusto Pinochet's Chile," *Hispanic American Historical Review* 98:1 (2018): 77–115.

Westad, Odd Arne. *The Global Cold War: Third World Interventions and the Making of Our Times*. Cambridge: Cambridge University Press, 2005.

Whelan, James R. *Desde las cenizas: vida, muerte y transfiguración de la democracia en Chile, 1833–1988*. Santiago, Chile: Zig-Zag, 1993.

Wiarda, Howard J. *Corporatism and Comparative Politics: The Other Great "Ism"*. Armonk, NY: M.E. Sharpe, 1997.

Winn, Peter (ed.). *Victims of the Chilean Miracle: Workers and Neoliberalism in the Pinochet Era, 1973–2002*. Durham, NC: Duke University Press, 2004.

Ynfante, Jesús. *La prodigiosa aventura del Opus Dei: génesis y desarollo de la santa mafia*. Paris: Ruedo Ibérico, 1970.

El santo fundador del Opus Dei: biografía completa de Josemaría Escrivá de Balaguer. Barcelona: Crítica, 2002.

Zanatta, Loris. *Perón y el mito de la nación católica: iglesia y ejército en los orígenes del Peronismo (1943–1946)*. Buenos Aires: Editorial Sudamericana, 1999.

Zanca, José A. *Los intelectuales católicos y el fin de la cristiandad: 1955–1966*. Buenos Aires: Fondo de Cultura Económica, 2006.

Žižek, Slavoj. *The Sublime Object of Ideology*. New York: Verso, 1989.

Zuleta Álvarez, Enrique. *El nacionalismo argentino*. Buenos Aires: Ediciones La Bastilla, 1975.

España en América: estudios sobre la historia de las ideas en Hispanoamérica. Buenos Aires: Editorial Confluencia, 2000.

Index

Other Books in the Series (continued from page ii)

99 *Black Saint of the Americas: The Life and Afterlife of Martín de Porres*, Celia Cussen
98 *The Economic History of Latin America since Independence, Third Edition*, Victor Bulmer-Thomas
97 *The British Textile Trade in South America in the Nineteenth Century*, Manuel Llorca-Jaña
96 *Warfare and Shamanism in Amazonia*, Carlos Fausto
95 *Rebellion on the Amazon: The Cabanagem, Race, and Popular Culture in the North of Brazil, 1798–1840*, Mark Harris
94 *A History of the Khipu*, Galen Brokaw
93 *Politics, Markets, and Mexico's "London Debt," 1823–1887*, Richard J. Salvucci
92 *The Political Economy of Argentina in the Twentieth Century*, Roberto Cortés Conde
91 *Bankruptcy of Empire: Mexican Silver and the Wars Between Spain, Britain, and France, 1760–1810*, Carlos Marichal
90 *Shadows of Empire: The Indian Nobility of Cusco, 1750–1825*, David T. Garrett
89 *Chile: The Making of a Republic, 1830–1865: Politics and Ideas*, Simon Collier
88 *Deference and Defiance in Monterrey: Workers, Paternalism, and Revolution in Mexico, 1890–1950*, Michael Snodgrass
87 *Andrés Bello: Scholarship and Nation-Building in Nineteenth-Century Latin America*, Ivan Jaksic
86 *Between Revolution and the Ballot Box: The Origins of the Argentine Radical Party in the 1890s*, Paula Alonso
85 *Slavery and the Demographic and Economic History of Minas Gerais, Brazil, 1720–1888*, Laird W. Bergad
84 *The Independence of Spanish America*, Jaime E. Rodríguez
83 *The Rise of Capitalism on the Pampas: The Estancias of Buenos Aires, 1785–1870*, Samuel Amaral
82 *A History of Chile, 1808–2002, Second Edition*, Simon Collier and William F. Sater
81 *The Revolutionary Mission: American Enterprise in Latin America, 1900–1945*, Thomas F. O'Brien
80 *The Kingdom of Quito, 1690–1830: The State and Regional Development*, Kenneth J. Andrien
79 *The Cuban Slave Market, 1790–1880*, Laird W. Bergad, Fe Iglesias García, and María del Carmen Barcia
78 *Business Interest Groups in Nineteenth-Century Brazil*, Eugene Ridings
77 *The Economic History of Latin America since Independence, Second Edition*, Victor Bulmer-Thomas
76 *Power and Violence in the Colonial City: Oruro from the Mining Renaissance to the Rebellion of Tupac Amaru (1740–1782)*, Oscar Cornblit
75 *Colombia before Independence: Economy, Society and Politics under Bourbon Rule*, Anthony McFarlane
74 *Politics and Urban Growth in Buenos Aires, 1910–1942*, Richard J. Walter

73 *The Central Republic in Mexico, 1835–1846, 'Hombres de Bien' in the Age of Santa Anna*, Michael P. Costeloe
72 *Negotiating Democracy: Politicians and Generals in Uruguay*, Charles Guy Gillespie
71 *Native Society and Disease in Colonial Ecuador*, Suzanne Austin Alchon
70 *The Politics of Memory: Native Historical Interpretation in the Colombian Andes*, Joanne Rappaport
69 *Power and the Ruling Classes in Northeast Brazil, Juazeiro and Petrolina in Transition*, Ronald H. Chilcote
68 *House and Street: The Domestic World of Servants and Masters in Nineteenth-Century Rio de Janeiro*, Sandra Lauderdale Graham
67 *The Demography of Inequality in Brazil*, Charles H. Wood and José Alberto Magno de Carvalho
66 *The Politics of Coalition Rule in Colombia*, Jonathan Hartlyn
65 *South America and the First World War: The Impact of the War on Brazil, Argentina, Peru and Chile*, Bill Albert
64 *Resistance and Integration: Peronism and the Argentine Working Class, 1946–1976*, Daniel James
63 *The Political Economy of Central America since 1920*, Victor Bulmer-Thomas
62 *A Tropical Belle Epoque: Elite Culture and Society in Turn-of-the-Century Rio de Janeiro*, Jeffrey D. Needell
61 *Ambivalent Conquests: Maya and Spaniard in Yucatan, 1517–1570*, Second Edition, Inga Clendinnen
60 *Latin America and the Comintern, 1919–1943*, Manuel Caballero
59 *Roots of Insurgency: Mexican Regions, 1750–1824*, Brian R. Hamnett
58 *The Agrarian Question and the Peasant Movement in Colombia: Struggles of the National Peasant Association, 1967–1981*, Leon Zamosc
57 *Catholic Colonialism: A Parish History of Guatemala, 1524–1821*, Adriaan C. van Oss
56 *Pre-Revolutionary Caracas: Politics, Economy, and Society 1777–1811*, P. Michael McKinley
55 *The Mexican Revolution, Volume 2: Counter-Revolution and Reconstruction*, Alan Knight
54 *The Mexican Revolution, Volume 1: Porfirians, Liberals, and Peasants*, Alan Knight
53 *The Province of Buenos Aires and Argentine Politics, 1912–1943*, Richard J. Walter
52 *Sugar Plantations in the Formation of Brazilian Society: Bahia, 1550–1835*, Stuart B. Schwartz
51 *Tobacco on the Periphery: A Case Study in Cuban Labour History, 1860–1958*, Jean Stubbs
50 *Housing, the State, and the Poor: Policy and Practice in Three Latin American Cities*, Alan Gilbert and Peter M. Ward
49 *Unions and Politics in Mexico: The Case of the Automobile Industry*, Ian Roxborough
48 *Miners, Peasants and Entrepreneurs: Regional Development in the Central Highlands of Peru*, Norman Long and Bryan Roberts

47 *Capitalist Development and the Peasant Economy in Peru*, Adolfo Figueroa
46 *Early Latin America: A History of Colonial Spanish America and Brazil*, James Lockhart and Stuart B. Schwartz
45 *Brazil's State-Owned Enterprises: A Case Study of the State as Entrepreneur*, Thomas J. Trebat
44 *Law and Politics in Aztec Texcoco*, Jerome A. Offner
43 *Juan Vicente Gómez and the Oil Companies in Venezuela, 1908–1935*, B. S. McBeth
42 *Revolution from Without: Yucatán, Mexico, and the United States, 1880–1924*, Gilbert M. Joseph
41 *Demographic Collapse: Indian Peru, 1520–1620*, Noble David Cook
40 *Oil and Politics in Latin America: Nationalist Movements and State Companies*, George Philip
39 *The Struggle for Land: A Political Economy of the Pioneer Frontier in Brazil from 1930 to the Present Day*, J. Foweraker
38 *Caudillo and Peasant in the Mexican Revolution*, D. A. Brading, ed.
37 *Odious Commerce: Britain, Spain and the Abolition of the Cuban Slave Trade*, David Murray
36 *Coffee in Colombia, 1850–1970: An Economic, Social and Political History*, Marco Palacios
35 *A Socioeconomic History of Argentina, 1776–1860*, Jonathan C. Brown
34 *From Dessalines to Duvalier: Race, Colour and National Independence in Haiti*, David Nicholls
33 *Modernization in a Mexican ejido: A Study in Economic Adaptation*, Billie R. DeWalt
32 *Haciendas and Ranchos in the Mexican Bajío, Léon, 1700–1860*, D. A. Brading
31 *Foreign Immigrants in Early Bourbon Mexico, 1700–1760*, Charles F. Nunn
30 *The Merchants of Buenos Aires, 1778–1810: Family and Commerce*, Susan Migden Socolow
29 *Drought and Irrigation in North-east Brazil*, Anthony L. Hall
28 *Coronelismo: The Municipality and Representative Government in Brazil*, Victor Nunes Leal
27 *A History of the Bolivian Labour Movement, 1848–1971*, Guillermo Lora
26 *Land and Labour in Latin America: Essays on the Development of Agrarian Capitalism in the Nineteenth and Twentieth Centuries*, Kenneth Duncan and Ian Rutledge, eds.
25 *Allende's Chile: The Political Economy of the Rise and Fall of the Unidad Popular*, Stefan de Vylder
24 *The Cristero Rebellion: The Mexican People Between Church and State, 1926–1929*, Jean A. Meyer
23 *The African Experience in Spanish America, 1502 to the Present Day*, Leslie B. Rout Jr.
22 *Letters and People of the Spanish Indies: Sixteenth Century*, James Lockhart and Enrique Otte, eds.
21 *Chilean Rural Society from the Spanish Conquest to 1930*, Arnold J. Bauer

20 *Studies in the Colonial History of Spanish America*, Mario Góngora
19 *Politics in Argentina, 1890–1930: The Rise and Fall of Radicalism*, David Rock
18 *Politics, Economics and Society in Argentina in the Revolutionary Period*, Tulio Halperín Donghi
17 *Marriage, Class and Colour in Nineteenth-Century Cuba: A Study of Racial Attitudes and Sexual Values in a Slave Society*, Verena Stolcke
16 *Conflicts and Conspiracies: Brazil and Portugal, 1750–1808*, Kenneth Maxwell
15 *Silver Mining and Society in Colonial Mexico: Zacatecas, 1546–1700*, P. J. Bakewell
14 *A Guide to the Historical Geography of New Spain*, Peter Gerhard
13 *Bolivia: Land, Location and Politics Since 1825*, J. Valerie Fifer, Malcolm Deas, Clifford Smith, and John Street
12 *Politics and Trade in Southern Mexico, 1750–1821*, Brian R. Hamnett
11 *Alienation of Church Wealth in Mexico: Social and Economic Aspects of the Liberal Revolution, 1856–1875*, Jan Bazant
10 *Miners and Merchants in Bourbon Mexico, 1763–1810*, D. A. Brading
9 *An Economic History of Colombia, 1845–1930*, W. P. McGreevey
8 *Economic Development of Latin America: Historical Background and Contemporary Problems*, Celso Furtado and Suzette Macedo
7 *Regional Economic Development: The River Basin Approach in Mexico*, David Barkin and Timothy King
6 *The Abolition of the Brazilian Slave Trade: Britain, Brazil and the Slave Trade Question, 1807–1869*, Leslie Bethell
5 *Parties and Political Change in Bolivia, 1880–1952*, Herbert S. Klein
4 *Britain and the Onset of Modernization in Brazil, 1850–1914*, Richard Graham
3 *The Mexican Revolution, 1910–1914: The Diplomacy of Anglo-American Conflict*, P. A. R. Calvert
2 *Church Wealth in Mexico: A Study of the 'Juzgado de Capellanias' in the Archbishopric of Mexico 1800–1856*, Michael P. Costeloe
1 *Ideas and Politics of Chilean Independence, 1808–1833*, Simon Collier

Printed by Integrated Books International,
United States of America